THIS LIFE OF MINE

A true story of a life filled with wealth, defeat, greatness, excitement, false promises, the mob, tragedy, love, and truths.

I have conversations with the deceased, and they talk back for over forty years.

STEVEN M. WALLACH

Copyright © 2025 Steven M. Wallach
All rights reserved
First Edition

Fulton Books
Meadville, PA

Published by Fulton Books 2025

ISBN 979-8-89427-168-2 (paperback)
ISBN 979-8-89427-171-2 (hardcover)
ISBN 979-8-89427-170-5 (digital)

Printed in the United States of America

I am a man of my word. I have taken many years of thought, advice, and determination to make me who I am today. My life consists of numerous health issues that gave me a reason to fight and maintain a position in my life to see things through.

I am a man of compassion, which is noticeable to others. I have had to face medical issues, including bone cancer, kidney cancer, and, unfortunately, a sleuth of other medical situations. But through them all, I continued to fight the fight, and yes, I absolutely believe (to this day) that my prayers to our G-d Almighty got me through the turmoil of possibly facing death due to my illnesses. When you are told that you may only have five months left to live, your mind goes through many changes—changes that will determine what your fate is. I realized that I am a fighter, and I will do my best to continue filling the hearts of others through my guidance, attention, and love.

I dedicate my deepest appreciation to some very special people, for without them, I do not believe I would still be here, breathing and remembering such wonderful times.

Joyce Wallach brought me into this world and taught me right and wrong, taught me how to love others but always to love myself, smile, and believe in family. To share my heart when others may need compassion. To my mother first and then my best friend, I dedicate the writings in the book to you. From reading your own journals after your passing, you have once again taught me to go after my dream: tell the world of your story.

Bernard Wallach was not only my father but, through time, became my mentor, my friend, and my confidant. His teachings took time for me, but it is because of you that I have been able to accomplish everything I set out to. Some with great success and others not so great. You taught me never to look at something as a failure. Learn from it and turn it into something great. I dedicate the smiles and tears in the writings and always know that if it were not for you and your guidance, I would not be the man I am today. Thanks, Pop!

Fanny "Nanny" Bolton was the most wonderful person I ever knew. Even though she passed when I was only nine years old, for anyone to understand the strength between us, you would have to live in my shoes and have my heart and soul. I dedicate everything about me because of this woman. I love you, Nanny, and I know we will see each other again and again and again.

Traci Ann Eells, I thank you for coming into my life when you did. The timing was perfect. I believe and feel that I am here because of you. You have become my perfect angel, and the magic we continue to build only strengthens what we already have. Your persistence in convincing me to write this book has a fantastic ending now. Thank you, Traci, for being you. I love you with my heart and look forward to continuing our lives together.

My G-d and my G-d Almighty, You continue to teach me daily. I found strength and memories because You were my writing partner. You stayed with me and guided me when I asked of You. You allowed me to think through many portions on my own, yet I always felt Your presence. Thank you for giving me the strength to complete something I so very much wanted to do. B'Shalom!

Introduction

Would I title this as my autobiography, or would I title this book simply for its contents and stories? I was leaning toward my autobiography, I would guess. It is all about me. Well, maybe not just me, but it is basically about me. You see, it all comes back to me, so the purpose of my writing is to share with you just who I am and what I went through to be where I am today.

It's funny how one can look at something that then triggers something from within, whether good or bad. There have been many times that without even thinking about something from twenty-five, forty, or even fifty-plus years ago, it becomes clearly visual as if you thought about it yesterday. What causes certain memories and situations to remain deep in our minds? Is it easily accessible? Or…do you really want to reopen that memory? The choice of our thoughts and memories is our own. Or are they?

Why write a book? Why not? What makes other people's stories more interesting than your own? I guess you can say that some people's lives are far more exciting and interesting than, let us say, yours or mine. Or is it? It is not that their lives are far more exciting. It has to do with what each of us brings to this world. We are all unique in our own ways. Now what we do know is that so many truly gifted and educated people among us have created, through their own experiments, medical miracles, inventions, and a sleuth of other avenues, their creations that have made our world a better place to live. Through their medical breakthroughs, more people can live longer lives. Stop for a moment and think, Do I fit into this category? If not, then which one am I? You see now why we each have something to offer?

I write this book as it is important to realize that for our world to stay viable and strong, it is up to each of us to leave something that we think will improve even one person's life. I hope my book does just that. I have been told by some wonderful writers and publishers that I carry with me an excellent gift for writing. "Steve, one publisher said to me, don't let anyone tell you that you need a ghost writer to help with your writing. You have a very rare and wonderful gift. You write like your talk." At first, I did not understand what she was referring to. I thought, *Did I not write properly? Was there an actual method for all writing?* She asked me to read a small part of my writing to her. She chose a small portion, and I began to speak. I heard me reading as if I was just speaking to her. I saw and understood what she meant; therefore, I followed her advice.

My prereaders thought it would be funny if they were given a photograph of me sitting at a table holding my book as if I were going to read it. Grab a photo, and here we go!

The End

Hello,

I have led a very interesting life thus far. I have traveled extensively throughout the world, meeting some of the most beautiful people imaginable, and have met with many others. I found that the memories I have been able to surface over the years have enabled me to see that I have covered miles of ground, and now it is only fitting that I share them with you.

From family issues to friendships to my firsthand experience in death also, including a wide selection of professions, I have conquered almost everything I set out to do. I do not weigh them as a competition within myself, but as a matter of setting a goal, and whether it was financially successful or not, the success of it made me a winner. Because deep down inside each of us, we are all winners.

My experiences have all been real, and I have been fortunate to have lived through them. What I have experienced in the aftermath and what I remember from them only gives me proof that those I imagine are fortunate like me can recall every part of their own flatline. I believe I am extremely fortunate because I had the experience of being in a position to remember what took part. Is there life after death? Who really knows the answer? I hope I have explained it best so you will read further.

As young as I can remember, my life was filled with adventures. I can recall so much of my childhood, both the good and the bad. The house at 37-05 Lenox Drive, Fair Lawn, New Jersey, would remind you of houses all aligned with the same size lots (except for the corner houses). As I look back, my mind is acting like today's drones. I am seeing the houses, the well-kept lawns, two cars on the driveways, and white picket fencing separating the property lots in the backyard, leaving the front yards open so that we all can enjoy our neighbors. But we each knew that this line could be crossed at any time for any reason. You see, this was growing up in the New Jersey suburbs in the fifties. Windows were kept open with that warm East Coast breeze during the warm months. We were either playing stickball or hopscotch in the streets or playing army, maybe even cowboys and Indians. No matter what we were doing, I knew that playing outside was a part of growing up.

One of the biggest thrills of the neighborhood was when the Good Humor Ice Cream truck would show up with their music bells playing a carnival-like sound. All the children (and some adults) would be patiently waiting to hear the musical sounds. We knew the schedule and had it down to a tee. Once a week, on either Saturday or Sunday, was the day of ice cream. The excitement on our faces told the story. The pleasures of our smiles and ice cream mustaches ended our day with a smile. Our day in the neighborhood was complete and another day can be filed in our minds as being a great success.

I can also remember the amusement trucks that would come by during the summer months. I have never seen them since, but oh, how do I remember them? One was called the Whip. It was built on a flatbed truck and had approximately eight shell-style units able to fit just one small child. The center of the truck contained most of the working parts. I remember that there was a well-greased massive chain that, when operating, would pull the shells around, and when you made the corners, the shell would spin you. This, I always thought, was the coolest thing to come into my neighborhood.

The second ride was an actual Ferris wheel. Same style truck except that it contained probably the smallest working Ferris wheel ever made. The wheel contained six single metal seats with a bar that extended over your waist to keep you secured. We would enter from the side, and the ride attendant would gradually bring each set leveled for its rider. It was truly a blast. As much as I remember the rides, I also remember that each child stepping off the truck was able to reach into an open cardboard box and pull out a surprise gift. The gifts were not of any value. They were just a small keepsake of your ride for that day. But no matter what we chose, it came from riding the great Ferris wheel.

Local amusement rides, Fair Lawn, New Jersey

    I knew from a young age that my father worked hard, and so did my mother. My father was in real estate, and my mother worked in this huge department store named J Alexander's. Dad would leave home every morning after your typical 1950s family breakfast and return usually the same time Monday to Friday evening at six o'clock. Dinner would be ready, and we each would take our assigned seat at the dinner table and discuss the day's events. Now granted, my days may not have been as exciting as my parents, but to me, they were always filled with something new. Round table dinners stayed in my family for years to come. While we all lived together, there was always the family dinner. Okay, the older I get, the smaller the table seats. Nonetheless, it is still a tradition in my home.

My mother was the assistant manager of a few departments in this massive store. I remember when they were going to place this bigger-than-life painted mural on the outside. The artist painted this unique sculpture on snowy skies. I can still see him skiing across this plastic mold with a backpack filled with paint, a spray nozzle, and sky poles. I guess someone liked his work. Nonetheless, that is where my mother worked for a short time.

My father was always on the phone or reading newspapers. His work never finished when he came home at the end of a working day. I remember listening to him (even at a young age) say things like "This is the best deal you'll get" or "Don't let this deal pass you by." I knew that my father was in commercial real estate when I saw photographs of shopping centers and building complexes. I also thought that was exciting. Watching his reactions when speaking with my mom, I could not help but allow me to think that they were excited and were going to celebrate whatever my dad just did.

It is funny how you remember things from years ago. Your surroundings may have changed somewhat, but your imagination of memory can be pulled at the drop of a hat. Well, sometimes....

Even though I can recall certain memories as an infant before my story, nothing seems to be as strongly remembered as my yellow bucket. Any recollection, as hard as if I have tried recalling, is absent. I remember years ago asking my mother if she, by chance, had any recollection of this story of the yellow bucket in Atlantic City. Staring back at me with this puzzled look, her reply was, "Steve, how do you remember such things? You were two years old." As I grinned and felt my face tightening up, I thought, Was this a first reaction to this story that has stayed with me for over sixty- five years?

Growing up, we loved as a family going to the beach in Atlantic City, New Jersey, back in the '50s. From the smell of fresh pizza to the scent of burgers and grilled hot dogs being cooked on the famous Atlantic City Boardwalk, you could not help but recognize that you were walking on one of the most famous boardwalks in America, the Atlantic City Boardwalk. From all the walk-up open stores and places for a quick slice to those storefront windows offering the smells of some of the best-made taffy anywhere, displaying

THIS LIFE OF MINE

freshly made water taffy, bathing suits, and T-shirts. The beaches of Atlantic City were where it was to be. At two years old, who knew? All I know is this....

I can picture my brother Chuck and I building this sandcastle right on the water's breakers at the shore's edge. We had enough room where the breakers would not crash over our sand piles but enabled the ocean's water to keep refilling the mote that surrounded our fortress made of sand and mud. It had tunnels and walls, and for some strange reason, I still can see it right in front of me. The area looked as though we were building huge castles and forts. We had shovels, sifters, and cups for piling sand structures on top of each other. Most importantly, I had my yellow bucket. It was with this bucket that we were able to make sand pilings strong enough to hold up the world on its base. This yellow bucket enabled us to dig a mote around our castle to protect all who lived there from the sea's wrath and from outside strangers. The harder I packed the sand, the more detailed it showed after it had been turned upside down to mimic the faces of those wonderful zoo animals.

The Yellow Bucket had four sides to it. Not even squares but more like a pale with angled sides that gradually get larger toward the top. Let me help you picture this. You see, each side had an animal printed inside the mold. Simple to picture in your mind. The elephant with its trunk, the profile of a tiger, the monkey sitting on a branch, and the king of the jungle, lion. Even the handle was yellow. All the other shovels, sifters, and cups we had in our inventory could never match up to the yellow bucket. This bucket was the savior of our sandcastle building.

I recall that I always had this sensational imagination. So here we are. Finished and complete. Yet, as we all can relate to any time spent at any beach, there is always something to patch on your own sandcastle. The work is never through, though, is it?

"Steve, my mother called out, not at screaming level but close enough to grasp my attention. Look!" She was pointing past me to the ocean.

As I turn around from our sand fortress, I see a wave crashing down within the feet of what we believe to be an architectural masterpiece, causing the sea to penetrate our sea wall. As the water began to wash away our sandcastle with a force that made our proud castle look as if it had a hard meltdown, sand peaks were now smooth, and the mote was no more. The ocean decided to surround my yellow bucket as each ripple carried it further out to sea.

I can barely hear myself scream out, "DAD, DAD! My bucket!"

I can picture my dad running into the ocean's wake to save my day. But unfortunately, that never happened. I remember hearing my father's words, "Sorry, son, I could not find it anywhere. Must have been taken out to sea."

For some reason, the loss of this yellow bucket could only be compared to losing a friend, I would guess now. Looking back on this throughout my years never changed this childhood story. I know that the loss created a huge blow to me emotionally, and I now understand it also affected my thoughts on how to calm someone down in a time of need. The words of both my mother and father had to control me like a hypnotist does to his guests. I immediately controlled and suppressed my emotions because I remember my tears stopped, and the frown with the lower lip shakes ended. I felt safe once again in the arms of my parents. This may have been my first entry into emotional trust as I sat there and cried. It was the first time I knew I had no control over everything. Here I was, sitting at the water's edge in the sand, covered with sand particles, showing that I spent hours in the heat as sweat and tears rushed down my sunburned face. My recollection only bears the thought of my mother holding me and my father standing there feeling hopeless. But for it, he who tried to rescue the ill-fated yellow bucket. This I remember, why? I have no idea.

As we started to pack up and leave, I still, to this day, recall hearing my dad say, "Son, don't worry. I'll replace it."

I said, "The exact same with the same animals and designed?"

And his answer was yes. All seemed to be fine now. It was settled.

The image of this memory fades as quickly as it comes. Did we leave the beach? Did a spaceship come hovering over us and beam us up? Did we drive the one and one-half hours back home or maybe we stopped somewhere for dinner or lunch? What time of day was it?

THIS LIFE OF MINE

I would think it was a weekend because as we got older, my parents would take us to the Atlantic City Boardwalk/Beach or the swim club we later joined on weekends. I have no idea. All I realized was that remembering this type of dream enlightened me to know that emotion starts in your earliest years of life. When do we start to remember what the real importance is of who we are and why? All this happened to me, a two-year-old child.

As a family, we used to take Saturday drives to go visit with my grandparents on my father's side. Maybe because it became a ritual, the thought of this is quite clear. Since most of our drives were identical routes, it became easier to know how far we were to our arrival. The closer we came, the more rambunctious my brother and I would get. Like Heinz ketchup that can take forever, our anticipation became routine.

Around the corner, there was an A&P grocery store, and next to them was a bakery. Not just a bakery but a bakery that was always busy. You could smell the fresh-scented breads and pies a city block away. I remember that their cakes had toys, actual toys, that you would keep after your stomach moans of fullness filled the air. There were the army cake decorations with real little plastic army men and a plastic jeep. Another was that ballerina with the girl dressed in her tutu and her leg bent forward in what seemed to be that perfect silhouette spin. But there was this other one. You know, the one that stood out over the others. The one who seemed to be the most sought out. It was none other than the cowboys and Indians decoration.

One cowboy looked like a true cowboy with his cowboy hat, boots, and spurs, chaps, six-shooters, and in the riding position. You know that position when you are already sitting high on the horse, legs spread wide and bowed. That was the only thing about these rubber cake figures you could not bend them. The cake came fully decorated with one cowboy seated on top of this brown stallion horse and what appeared and dressed to be an Indian with full head garb, a shirtless man sitting tall on his brown & white horse. I always thought they were the Sheriff and Indian Chief. Also included were a cowboy kneeling with a rifle on the ready and another Indian in full garb standing in front of this tepee. Sounds like a lot to fit on your typical birthday cake, but it did fit, horses and all.

That evening after dinner, I remember playing on the top floor landing, where I could turn the banister into a scene from whatever game I was playing. My mother said I had a wild imagination, so as I recall, no telling what I would sometimes use as people. But this evening, I had something special. I was the first to have at the top of the stairs in a house located on Lenox Drive, Fair Lawn, New Jersey, a standoff between the cowboys and the Indians. The only problem that really stood out was when my father came around the corner and started climbing the stairs.

Picture a cat that just had its tail stepped on by a giant moose. That is exactly how I felt my face turn within seconds. Not seconds, but more like millimeter seconds! Picture this. You are in a room in complete silence. The only sound you hear is your own breathing. As this sound continues to grow louder and louder and you can feel your heart ready to burst out of your chest, you realize you have been BUSTED! You try to be cool and collective even though you are about to be interrogated by "the man," your father.

Right away, I have changed into my eight-year-old cool style. "What's that you have their son?" my father said as his voice started to get deeper.

Without a thought, I said, "Oh, I got this from the bakery. That was true as I swallowed, and I found that my throat was as dry as desert sand.

"Did you pay for it, or did somebody else because I know I didn't pay for it," came the words that rumbled the ground from my father.

So now what to do? Do I stop and tell the truth, knowing that the price to pay may include some welts on my derriere, or do I continue with my acting skills? One saying that I carry to this day came from my father's words. When this would come out from either of my parents, I knew I had no choice. Raise the white flag and surrender. Any other words that were said or may be said can never match up against these simple yet powerful words.

"Remember, before you even utter one word, before you choose to continue with some ridiculous story, before you even waste another minute thinking of what would be best to say, realize this, I may already know the answer."

Now you have two choices: they already know the answer, and I am thrown to the wolves, or I can stand up and acknowledge that I did do something wrong. The next hardest thing was admitting it to your parents as they stood there looking larger than life in front of you. One thing I was taught as far back as I remember, if you tell one lie, you will need to tell another lie to back up the first lie. But we know that is not all. I would then have to tell another lie to cover for the other lie that covered for that other lie, and this could go on indefinitely. I chose to get it over with. As I looked at my father, I felt my head fall forward in shame as I said, "I didn't pay for it, and no one bought it for me."

Waiting to feel my punishment, it was then, for the first time, I saw my father not say a word but walk away. Normally, there would be some yelling, but this time, nothing, as if there was not a care in the world. Was I just part of a dream, or did this really happen? The silence that ran through the house was the loudest thing I ever heard. It made me go straight to my room and finish out the day there. Why did he not start yelling at me? How was I able to be sitting here and not feeling the wrath of my father's belt?

It was now Sunday morning, and we were all in the kitchen waiting on Mom to cook up one of her great Sunday morning breakfasts. Always a great way to start the day. As I could hear the snapping of the bacon, my father came into the kitchen, looked at me, and said, "You ready? Let's go."

"Go where?" I said, sounding as confused as his question.

He grabbed a piece of buttered toast off the plate, kissed my mother, and calmly said to me, "Come on. I want to get there before they get busy. You know how Sundays are there." As I stood here staring now at my mother for some sign, my father replied to his own comment. "That's right. We're going back to return the stolen toys and ask the owner of the bakery to accept your apology for shoplifting."

It was right then did I first encountered that feeling of an empty stomach followed by the sweats at the same time, realizing that this was not going to be a good Sunday morning.

I will never forget that day. The bakery was packed as if they were giving away free cookies and cakes. I looked around in fear, knowing that I had to talk to the owner and ask for forgiveness. Standing in front of me about two feet away stood this little lady. She had a baker's smock on with stains of dough, sparkles, and glitters, and her hair looked as if she walked through a wind tunnel. As I made my way closer to her, I could hear my father clearing his throat, which immediately caused me to go into emergency protection mode and say, "Can I have everyone's attention, please. Please, will everyone look this way?"

What was going on here? I thought as I could feel the hair on my neck start to stand out. Was I about to hear that my father is the baker for this bakery? Was he going to announce that he decided to buy the bakery and call it Steve's Bakery? As the store became quiet and it looked like a row of eyes glaring back, my father explained to all the following.

With a firm voice, he said, "Folks, my son Steven has something he would like to say to the owner and all of you."

As my father's head turned to me, it was my turn—my turn to either fall and cry and beg for forgiveness from the bakery court or admit that I did, in fact, shoplift these toys yesterday.

I stood there, feeling the eyes of as if millions were upon me. Many looked puzzled as their eyes would squint, and others, well, let's just say that they looked as though they were the jury in a murder case.

So in a quivering voice, I looked first to the floor and said, "Hello, my name is Steve Wallach, and I shoplifted this cowboy and Indian set without paying for it yesterday."

I looked directly at the owner and said I was sincerely sorry and asked her for forgiveness. What seemed to be just seconds but felt like hours. I stared at her with a frozen look and finally heard her say, "Yes. I forgive you and appreciate that you came back to tell me the truth.

At first, it was silent, but then I recall hearing a few people start to clap, then a few more, then a few more until I felt myself smile and realize that standing up, correcting your wrong, and just being truthful pays off. It really made me feel good. My dad and I left the store and got back in the car and headed home. I felt good in that car. I remember hearing my dad say he was proud of me for doing that but made sure to let me know if I did that again, my butt would be red for days. This was the first real time I realized what the consequences were, how they were planned, and the outcomes. To this day, I will always remember that. It was my first and last store heist.

My early years growing up, I do recall times when things were not perfect. I do not believe any family is perfect. Faults, stories, and bad choices reign throughout every family. Now you need to understand that my father spoke in a powerful voice. Well, at least not me. I guess, like all families, there comes a point when your parents can be heard screaming at each other and slamming doors. Thank goodness, my family never experienced any physical abuse, only verbal. To me, it was just the way it was. Never directed to the children, but I recall him and my mom getting into some loud verbal arguments. There was the one time that I was in the den playing with the chips from a Pokeno Game as if they were Army men. Do not ask. Do not even question as to how did I compare a small plastic game chip to that of an Army man. This was the start of my love for imagination, I guess.

My mother came into the den and told me to put the chips away and follow her. We were packing our bags and leaving. It startled me since this was the first time I ever faced this fear I saw in my mother's eyes. That was also the first time I stood to protect my mother. I felt like I was Hercules standing and guarding her from harm. We never left the house. I stayed in the den and dropped chips off the bookshelf as if they had been shot and were falling to their death. I didn't find out from my mom until many years later that my mom didn't like my father flirting with Edith. Edith Aronowitz lived across the street from us. Always dressed in her makeup perfectly, Edith was like the neighbor who gardened in a bright yellow dress with white shoes and a photo finish face. Edith's husband was this skinny little man, and Edith, who always dressed in style, carried herself like a Hollywood celebrity. I guess my father would smile a lot. Maybe a little too much, but he was completely dedicated to my mother and my mother to him. They were a power couple who played off each other with nothing but love and admiration. A marriage that lasted over sixty-five-plus years until my dad's untimely death.

I can remember that family was the most important thing to my parents. The family had to be strong and united and have the same beliefs. These were the things instilled in us as we continued to grow up in Fair Lawn. Family vacations were awesome because I remember loading up the car and heading off to places unknown. There was one time my father took out the map of the East Coast and said, "Let's close our eyes and the first place I point to will be our next vacation." As his finger flew through the air as if it were a plane or rocket, with eyes closed, my father landed on Lake George, New York. I do not remember much about it except we had a cabin right there on the beach where we stayed. The lake was not more than twenty-five feet from our door, and it made for a wonderful spot. Or so I think. I recall going out in the paddleboats and enjoying playing with the other sport items. That was it, though. Nothing else. I do not know why this particular time stayed with me. Was it because it gave me time with my father more than I got from him at home? Or was it being free and not a care in the world? From a child's point of view, I guess it was the thought that counted when reminiscing. You see, that is all I have of Lake George vacation. But I remember it more than other places we vacationed to through the years.

I recall my parents traveling more than my other friends' parents. There would be trips to Miami, Florida, the Bahamas, Cuba, Aruba, and cruises. I remember these places because, for so many years, this was their routine. Now we were never left out. There was always that ten-day trip to Florida's Colonial Hotel, Miami Beach, every year. To this day, I can picture and visually see the entire layout of the lobby area, gift shop, sundry shop, elevators, and the lower-level nightclub. Walking past the elevators were the doors to take you out back to where this huge pool was surrounded by lounge chairs and tabletops, but also, farther out was this fantastic white sandy beach inviting you into the Florida blue sea. Our summer months, we would head to the Catskills, New York, to my uncle's hotel, Zalkin's Birchwood Lodge. There was no better place to grow up the way I did. Having such enjoyment at such an early age but not really understanding its impact at that time. Here, too, I can see every inch of the entry from the circular driveway, bringing you to the center to this massive set of steps that will lead you to their full-length patio and the main entrance. Once inside, the grand stars were directly in front of you. The registration desk was to the left, followed by steps leading down into the Live Showroom. They had top headliners such as Steve Lawrence and Eydie Gorme, Shecky Green, Jackie Mason, Rodney Dangerfield, and a sleuth of others. We would sneak in through the back kitchen doors to watch.

On the other side of the lobby was the entrance into the three dining rooms. For some reason, the one thing I remember from the dining room was their butter. You know, the one pad of butter stuck on a square waxed cardboard with a peel-off waxed paper. The taste was sensational. I can still taste it on a small warm dinner roll. They had, in front of the dining area, this fantastic old-fashioned soda fountain, stocked with five types of ice cream, chocolate syrup, toppings, strawberry sauce, bananas for those banana splits, and those old Hamilton Milk Shake machines lined against the back counter. The countertop had your typical napkin stands, salt and pepper shakers, menus tucked neatly in its section holder, and the old swivel chairs. I think there were either of them. We would go in and try to spin all of them at the same time.

The rooms were nice on the second and third floors. Every door had slats in two square sections. There were no solid doors to any of the sleeping rooms. Granted, you could not see through the slats, but you would know if the lights were on. Never thought anything about this until later in life I noticed all hotels and motels had solid doors. Remember, this was during the 1950s when we lived in a very different society as of today. Me, I would prefer going back to the old days. It was safer, simpler, and healthier.

I think of one place that we frequented as young adolescents. It was a building that stood by itself. On a fairly busy street named Morlot Avenue stood Kinds Dairy—a true old-fashioned ice-cream shop that featured so many ice-cream flavors it was somewhat difficult to have a number one. I did. Every time an adventure would bring me to Kind's Dairy, whether on foot or by car, I knew there was a large black raspberry ice cream in a sugar cone with my name on it. The first lick was always the highlight. Immediately having my taste buds react to something so familiar always sent a rush through my mouth to my stomach. Second, third, and fourth licks did the same, but that initial lick, boy, was magic. Walking back having conquered my desire, another memory was seeing that first drop slide down the side of the cone. Lick quick! Those were the two words that all of us knew. The challenge was licking quick enough to savor every stream of black raspberry. Oh, how I can still taste that final bite of the sugar cone filled with the last of that wonderful desert.

My sister died. Her name was going to be Stephanie. This was a very dark time for me. I remember playing on the top floor landing in the hallway of our home in Fair Lawn, New Jersey. My parents and our neighbor Faye Feuerstein were in their bedroom as was my brother in his. I recall their bedroom door flying open and my father running down the stairs, yelling, "They're on the way! They're on the way!" *Who is on the way?* I thought to myself. What was going on was another flash question that I could not answer at the time. Tensions were building in everyone, which caused me to really feel the pain. I became frightened as the time went by.

Within minutes, I could see red lights flashing outside the front storm door. My father was leading people into the house carrying medical suitcases and other equipment on their gurney. Up the stairs, they came as I was waiting in my bedroom doorway, piercing out as not to be seen or in the way. All I knew was that with the worried look I saw on my father's face; my mom may have been really sick. Within a few minutes, my mother was being carried down the stairs on the same gurney that was used to carry medical supplies in. I will never forget my mother calling out to me that everything was going to be alright.

"They just want to make sure." She called back to me just as she was being taken out the front door. "I love you, my son," she called out as she was being carried out.

Our next-door neighbor's daughter, Marsha, came over to sit with Chuck and me as leaving us alone would not be a wise choice. We still had no idea what was going on. As quick as my panic button went off, I recall Marsha calming me down. That was it. Never recalled anything else about that evening. The next morning, my dad sat us down and explained that Mom was pregnant, but due to some serious medical issues, Mom had lost the baby. I didn't understand the medical side, but I did know that I wouldn't have a sister named Stephanie. Broke my heart even at a young age. The questions filled my childhood head. *She* never hurt anyone. Why would this happen to my mom? Even today, I sometimes find myself reaching back to my mind for answers. None.

I was in the second grade at Milnes School, not far from my house at all. We were not picked up by a school bus. We walked. The walk was along tree-lined sidewalks. I remember we would meet up with all the other kids that lived in the neighborhood as they would come out of their homes and join in what looked as though was a marching group. Morlot Avenue was the only major street we had to cross, so there was a wonderful lady who was there for years as the crossing guard. Her name was Angie with salt-and-pepper-colored hair that she would comb and spray high time. I guess that was one of those hairdos back then. She was dressed in a blue skirt and white blouse that had epaulets on the shoulders where she would have her crossing guard belt meticulously placed. I cannot forget that red octagon Stop sign in one hand and her whistle in the other, which she blew proudly when it was time to cross. The walks allowed us to plan what we were going to do after school. Those plans would get us through the days of schooling, knowing that there would be some form of excitement for us after school.

I was in Mrs. Ball's fifth-grade class at Henry B. Milnes Elementary School, Fair Lawn, New Jersey, during the time my parents were on their first of many luxury cruises to the Caribbean. Do you ever find yourself remembering only a handful of your teacher's names over sixty years ago? Are these the teachers who helped mold you into who you are today, or were they just a part of one's memory? Ms. Nakeeto was my kindergarten teacher. She was from Japan, and I do recall some incidents that happened in her class. Lying quietly on mats when it was nap time was something I can look back on. Getting twelve five-year-olds to lie quietly on a mat was a chore in itself. But as I remember, she had that control. I remembered her voice to be soft and gentle. It was very melodic as if she was singing her words to us. When she needed our full attention, her tone would change, where there was no more melody. This is what I remember about her. I recall her comforting one of the little girls in the class because she had an "accident" in her pants. Why on earth would I remember that, I thought. Guess I felt that this, too, was another part of my puzzle showing concern and understanding from an adult to a child.

My first time seeing a ship was awesome. Not an ordinary ship like a fishing boat, but a ship, a cruise ship in the New York Harbor. It was a Saturday, and my parents were going on their cruise aboard Home Lines' *Homeric*, a cruise to the Caribbean. Driving from New Jersey to New York, we entered the Lincoln Tunnel, which completely blew my mind. My father explained that this tunnel connected the two states of New Jersey and New York and that this tunnel went under the Hudson River. I thought to myself, *Should I go into panic as I sat there, thinking we were all going to drown, or was I to sit back and have that excited look on my face but without the fright glare?*

We had a full load in the car: my father, mother, Chuck, Grandma Nanny (on my mother's side), Fannie and Pop Greenstein (on my dad's side). Followed behind us were Edith and Stanley Aronowitz, and my aunt Faye and Uncle Eddie Feuerstein. Now Faye and Eddie were not really my aunt and uncle, but back in the '50s, friendships were looked upon as being part of the family, and they were a huge part—from weekend barbecues, vacations, dinners, and more, always good times with them.

The pier was full of cars, trucks, and people. An area that was filled with excitement brought on by hundreds of people getting ready to board this luxury liner. Years ago, they never had to concern themselves with security risks at the New York Ports. Passengers and their guests were able to board altogether. So here we are, dressed for the hill. Back then, when you traveled, it was always proper to be dressed accordingly. So here were all the men and boys in suits and ties, and the women and girls in dresses. Some of the women also wore white gloves to keep in style, I would imagine.

I could not get over the size of this luxury cruise ship. The lounges all had bars, and the decor was flashy and decadent, waiters walking around serving little sandwiches on little napkins with a toothpick through the top holding that olive in place. The dining room seemed to go on forever. People standing in a line to meet with the staff over where their dining table was.

My father looked down at me and said, "I already took care of all that," knowing I was just about to ask him.

Returning to their cabin, we were met by an attendant to offered us the same drinks and sandwiches as I saw in the lounges. I thought, wonder why my parents have their own attendant. Then I realized that we were not in an ordinary cabin; it was a suite. Plenty of room for us all to sit and mingle. I recall the only small area was the bathroom, and squeezing past our friends to gain bathroom entry was a bit tight but manageable.

My father decided it was time to explore the ship's public areas. As we walked throughout the ship, gazing at every statue, plant, artwork, Italian marble, and so many other people doing the same, I recall saying to my father repeatedly, "Boy, you and mom are so lucky to be able to travel aboard a cruise ship."

Like it was yesterday, I can still hear my father's remarks, "Son, just remember that anyone can achieve as long as they put their mind to it and focus."

I never forgot those words. Focus was the key. I thought that working on a cruise ship seemed to be exciting. You get to mingle with so many affluent people and travel all over the world. I never thought later in life my direction would be so strong within the cruising industry.

The announcements started from the ship's speakers: "This is the final call for all visitors not sailing on Home Lines' *Homeric* to kindly make your way to the gangway."

Yes, it was time for us to go. The tradition back then was that most of those visiting the ship would line the port behind wooden fences and rails to wave goodbye, colorful streamers in hand, waiting for the traditional toss into the air. As we joined in this celebration, the passengers aboard the *Homeric* had also lined the outside decks following the sea's tradition, waiting for that first toss. Once the first streamer was thrown, you could see a wall of beautiful colors filling the air from both the dock area and from this wonderful ship called *Homeric*. Over the cheers and shouts coming from so many, you were still able to clearly hear some calling out to their parents, "Hey, Mom, we love you!" and "Daddy has a great time!" It was clear that this was the beginning in my path. They say all of us remember things of happiness along with something that also includes some sadness. Human nature? I do not know what to call it professionally, but I do know that it's a phenomenon because it happens all the time—at least with me.

With so many events that I was a part of during my adolescence, some things stand out far more than others. I guess that is because we value our thoughts differently, depending on the seriousness of it. This was the most important and hardest memory for me. My parents were still on their Caribbean cruise, and my mother's mother (Nanny) was staying with us during this time.

Nanny was the most influential person in my life. From as far back as I can remember, our times together (even though not long-lasting) made huge impressions on me from a personal standpoint. Living in the next town over, Nanny lived in a manicured apartment complex. Row buildings side by side, all with the same frontage, sidewalks, and perfectly cut grass. It was a place I used to take walks with her. Best part was that Nanny lived just a few blocks from Petak's Delicatessen. Mountains of freshly made assorted bagels and bialys filled the front large window display. When you walked into Petak's, you knew immediately that you entered an establishment filled with the smells of hot fresh pastrami, corned beef, homemade soups and salads, salamis, and other meats hanging from the ceilings, encased glass display counters showing off all their homemade delicacies. Remember those old-fashioned dried-out apricot and strawberry rolls? Peeling the fruits off from the wrapping was half the fun, but when that first bite touched your tongue, that taste just went through you. So for my Nanny and I to take many walks to Petak's was a ritual. Besides going to Petak's as an outing, my Nanny made some of the best food I've ever had. Even to this day, my cooking habits and her recipes are an active part of my cooking and who I am today. From her sweet-and-sour stuffed cabbage, cabbage soup, noodle kugel, brisket, and more, it started with my Nanny. All my mother's recipes came from her, and for them to be passed down to me meant so much to me. The only meal that no one else (to this day) enjoys or desires was my grandmother's cooked cereal! I get excited just mentioning it, but it really left a mass impression on me. This one meal is great for breakfast, lunch, dinner, or anytime! It is also great when you have stomach pains but know you need something to eat that's settling and easy. It was the famous Malt-O-Meal Farina Original, enriched creamy hot wheat cereal. Cooked with just milk and stirring, to me, this was the best and no. 1 cereal of all time. Oh, and it had to have lumps in it. Without the lumps, it did not mimic my Nanny's. This one recipe was taught to my mother and our live-in maid (no political correctness in the '50s or '60s), and to this day, I am still the only one who loves and eats it.

Another thing my grandmother instilled in me was to have faith in my religion, respect for my parents, love for others, but most importantly, to love myself and show respect to myself, for without these traits, one would lead a very confused and unwanted path in life. Truly a very inspirational lady who showered me with unconditional love.

By the fourth day of my parents' cruise, my Nanny became ill. Our neighbor, Faye, came over to see what she could do about my grandmother's illness. By the fifth day, I recall that Nanny was getting worse, and Aunt Faye decided it was best to take her to the hospital. I remember crying to Aunt Faye to call my parents, but that was not possible as they were in the middle of the ocean on a cruise ship on their way back to New York Port. I do know that Uncle Eddie drove to New York on the day of their arrival to tell them what happened to Nanny and bring them back to the hospital in New Jersey.

That day stands out as I recall being in Mrs. Ball's classroom when I was called to the principal's office over the loudspeaker. My dad was standing there waiting as I came around the corner. I was so happy to see him, but I stopped and noticed that my mother was not with him. After the excitement of seeing my father, I questioned on where my mother was, and he, in a very quiet voice, said that Mom was at the hospital to see Nanny, her mother. I asked if Nanny was going to be okay, and I will never forget his reply, "Son, Nanny is very sick right now. The doctors are doing all they can."

"All they can," I said. "For what? That is my Nanny! She never gets sick! That's my Nanny!" I yelled out.

A few days later, the most important person in my life was gone. I never got to say goodbye. I never got to say I love you. I never got to be with her! I realized at that time what a true heartbreak felt like. The stabs in my heart and the constant flow of tears left me feeling helpless. Seeing my mother's reaction to the loss of her mother felt as though all I wanted to do was take the pain always from her. It did break my heart to see and understand at such a young age the loss of a loved family member.

Following the traditions and beliefs of my Jewish faith, my wonderful Nanny was put to rest two days later next to her husband, Charles Bolton, in New Haven, Connecticut. My father's Jewish traditions and beliefs under Cohan Rule. He would not allow my brother nor I to go into the grounds of the cemetery. I remember I was furious at him. I could not understand why he would act in such a manner as not to allow me to be there with the most amazing woman in my life, my Nanny. Under Cohan Law, Cohan's are not permitted to attend any funeral in a cemetery unless it was immediate family. For years, I never understood then why we were not allowed in. This was our grandmother. This was my mother's mother. For over the next sixteen years, this was always a thorn in my side. It was not until my mother sat me down and told me she was adopted by Nanny and Charles Bolton. Therefore, she was not from the same bloodline. My honest opinion on his reasoning—bullshit! I would have never stopped my child from saying goodbye to their grandmother, blood or not. My father did regret this and, in fact, made his apologies to my brother and me years later.

As we sat in the back seat of my father's Fleetwood Cadillac, I looked up into the sky as if I was sending my Nanny off. It was then that I now believe was my first encounter with a power that I never shared with anyone for many years. As I gazed up into the gray-filled sky, I noticed a small area where the clouds were forming a circle. It was not noticeable, but to me, it was very clear. From within this circle, I could vividly hear my Nanny's voice, telling me that things were going to be okay, that she would always be with me as long as my mother was here as well. A few other words were spoken, but I swore that I would take those words to my grave. Was this just my imagination, or did I just have a conversation with my deceased grandmother? I recall my brother saying in the car, "Steve, who are you talking to? What are you doing?" *Was I to tell him?* I thought to myself. If I did, I knew he would make fun of me, so I have kept this to myself for over sixty years.

Grave-sight of Charles and Fannie Bolton

To this day, I really do not know if I ever knew what the true diagnosis was. I fully recall her funeral. The long list of cars and people, I was so very proud that many came to pay for their final condolences and respect to a wonderful and loving lady, my grandmother, Fannie Bolton. I do not remember much that day except that I knew the cemetery was next to a school, and there was an Esso gas station on the corner. To date, this is still the only way I can remember where their gravesites are. Interesting how certain landmarks are recalled in memories. The memories that I remember from this sad time were all family and friends being at my aunt Irma and uncle Hal Horowitz's home. They had a wraparound porch that welcomed you before you entered their home—a home that I can only remember pieces of. I recall my aunt Irma asking me if I really remember her house some fifty years ago. She was shocked yet had this wonderful smile on her face when I described her living room; there was a couch and end tables, and there was a love seat. You know, the kind that was the length of a small couch but had built-in seats facing opposite of each other, thus, allowing a couple to sit and look at each other. The smile on Irma's face was priceless. She and my mother started reminiscing on their childhood in that home, and that alone left me with these great memories. The one thing that stood out the most in her living was this magnificent sold black grand piano. A Steinway, in fact. I will never forget the stories told to me about this piano. Irma's mother, my great-aunt Dora, was the number one silent film piano player on the East Coast. Silent film piano player! Those stories of when she would travel to all the movie theaters that had silent movies, and she would sit at the piano located in front of the large screen and play just made me want to become a piano player. The rest became history, which will all be explained and outlined.

Raised for my first ten years in a very quiet suburb section of a town named Fair Lawn, New Jersey, life and family were remembered mostly for their happy times. Most of us had your typical white picket fences separating our family properties only from the back of the homes and sides. Very rare to see any fencing or gates in the front of any home in our neighborhood.

I recall that our home, 37-05 Lenox Drive, was second to the last house before the corner at the corner. The memories of neighbors standing out on their front lawns talking to each other on the property line while the fathers and sons were watering and cutting the lawns. I'll always remember the smell of fresh-cut grass. Even to this day, it brings back memories of those days gone by but not forgotten.

The one thing that stood out was that my parents introduced us to a lady named Lulu Bell Gandy, who was going to live with us in the capacity of housekeeper and chef. Lulu Bell was this tall black woman who had two gold teeth in the front of her mouth. Lulu had to have been the darkest black person I had ever seen. So when she smiled, you couldn't help but notice her smile, gold teeth, and pearly whites. No disrespect, but Lulu bathed in a mixture of bleach and water to try to lighten her complexion. She would iron her hair after shampooing with beer, eggs, and water in an effort to make it softer. She would also brush her teeth with baking soda. With all her antics, we loved her, and she grew into our family as a part of us. Could she cook! She was still one of the best cooks around and our evening meals were always prepared by Lulu. Even for breakfast in the mornings, Lulu was there.

Lulu came from the next town over to us called Patterson, New Jersey. Back then, Patterson was a hardworking middle- to lower-class city that had some upscale homes and workable factories but also had some predominantly black communities that were known for high crime, shootings, robberies, etc. Where was Lulu Bell from? Right in the middle of all the bars and crowded streets. Lulu would work for my family Monday through Friday evening. Either she would take a bus, or my parents would bring her back to the home she shared with her son and a sleuth of grandchildren in Patterson. I recall there being at least four small children in the apartment where she lived. Most times, my mother would drive into Patterson every Sunday late afternoon to pick Lulu up. That pickup itself was dangerous. I can recall many times when my innocent mother would pull up to Lulu's apartment building, which was located above a bar establishment, and call out for her.

"Lulu Bell! Lulu Bell Gandy! It's Momma J. Let's go!"

To some who had no idea who my mother was, they would start to surround that car, yelling out words about why she was in "their" neighborhood. All it took was for my mom to yell out through the closed window, "Didn't you hear me? I'm here to pick up Lulu Bell." As if it were yells from Charlton Heston in the Ten Commandments, the crowd would stand down, and there would be a man-made open path from the steps of the building directly to the car as if we were waiting for a diplomat to enter. In a way, Lulu Bell Gandy was a diplomat. She was the queen of this area in Patterson, New Jersey. When she spoke, you would listen. When she yelled, you would stop and cower back. We loved it! Lulu would get into the car and laugh so loud as she would say, "Okay, Ms. Joyce, let's go home!"

I think Lulu played a big part in raising both my brother and me. It was she who fulfilled the role as the house nanny besides the cooking and cleaning. I cannot speak for my brother, so I have no idea what he thought about her or even if he recalls anything about Lulu Bell. I, on the other hand, remember many events that Lulu was a part of. It was she who made sure I followed the rules of right and wrong. Not to mention my manners. I believe she saw what my father offered her, and she realized just what kind of loving and caring person my mother was. On the other hand, could do no wrong in Lulu's eyes. There were times when Lulu would cover for me, and if it was very slight, she'd blame it on my brother. Nothing serious, mind you, just small tales. Lulu was with us for many years. She started with us in Fair Lawn, New Jersey, and was with us when we first moved to Holmdel, New Jersey. Between her and, of course, my mother, I know I was raised properly. Okay, there were times when I pushed the envelope too far, but no matter what I did, I always had Lulu and my mother there to pick me up.

Fair Lawn had its very own amusement/animal park called Kiddie Zoo. To me, it was as exciting to go as if I were being taken down to the Atlantic City Boardwalk. As we entered the parking lot at Kiddie Zoo, you could not help but see the entrance welcoming all! There was a white wooden fence that separated the parking lot from the actual park. The entrance was painted red, white, and blue and had shooting sparkling gold stars with Welcome to Kiddie Zoo high above. The merry-go-round was straight ahead as you entered, and the closer you approached the gate, you could hear the music and see the golden hand carrying that magic gold coin ring. I used to ride the merry-go-round as much as I was allowed. Trying for the gold coin ring was exciting. I was so busy looking left and right, trying to capture every ride and candy stand in sight. I do not know why I knew exactly where everything was. The thrill was seeing if something new had been added.

As you walked further into this wonderful amusement park, past the merry-go-round, you could not help but start to smell those scents that are synopsis to any zoo. The closer you walked, the stronger the odor became until you knew exactly where you were. Writing this, I cannot help but feel an adrenaline rush, knowing that the roars of the lions and tigers made the excitement that much more powerful as my mind would begin to wander with these animals and I leading some magnificent exploration but with an audience.

Our neighborhood was not far from Kiddie Zoo. By car, the drive was easy. Out of our driveway, turn left and follow to the end. Turn right on Morlot Avenue and follow to the end and then turn left on Fair Lawn Avenue and continue until you pass "The Lady in the Woods" on the right-hand side. This statue in color was blue and white and was strategically placed at the forest's edge on the property of a local Catholic Church. At night, I can remember driving by and seeing this statue lit by this one powerful and bright spotlight. She was always referred to as the Lady in the Woods. Less than five minutes later, my father would turn right into this gravel parking lot. We're here!

I drifted for a minute. As I was saying, we lived in proximity to Kiddie Zoo and on an early Sunday morning, if we listened carefully, in the early morning calmness, we could hear the roar of the lions. Even though the sound was faint, it was still powerful enough to hear and exciting knowing that you're (living) near a zoo.

I remember the monkey cages were tall and filled with different types of monkeys. You were able to purchase small brown paper bags of peanuts that the monkeys knew were for them. Just the sound of the paper bags got their attention. I thought that was another highlight while here at Kiddie Zoo.

There was no actual circus tent nor any circus shows. No flying high above the wire acts, but they did have clowns walking around offering balloons made into animals and overflowing amounts of cotton candy and carnival food. That is the best part of any amusement park, isn't it? The different smells of food and the sounds of laughter. There was one man who stood out that I remember from Kiddie Zoo. I would not say that he was the circus master since there was no circus tent, but you could hear his voice throughout the park, welcoming everyone and always wishing people to have a great day and "that's any order," followed by his belly laugh. I thought to myself what a cool job to have, making people smile and telling everyone to have a great day! I could tell people to do that.

"We have to go" were the words I kept hearing my father call out to my mother. "Joyce, we have to get on the road if you want to spend some time with the boys." You see, today was the day my brother and I were going to our first sleepaway camp, Camp Cedar Lake, Jericho, New York. To this day, I have no idea where this camp was located, but I do know that it was Upstate New York, passed my uncle's Zalkin's Birchwood Lodge area. We had two small steamer trunks and a few small suitcases filled with clothing and whatnots my mother felt we would need at camp. Everything you could imagine was packed. I think we had enough bug spray to last a year, shorts, T-shirts, socks, underwear, rain gear, and more. One thing about my mother was she knew how to send us everything we could possibly want or need for this four-week camp trip.

I can still picture the entrance. A large hanging sign made from limbs and lumber displayed the words "Welcome to Camp Cedar Lake!" Okay so far, right? My brother was in the next age bracket up, so his cabin was located closer to the main area. Cabins were made of wood, wooden floor, and bare walls. There were three sets of windows on the front and back sides and two windows on the sides. Since there was no air-conditioning, the windows were kept open so that the constant breeze would come through. It was a nice breeze, except when the wind would come from the east. You see, approximately three hundred yards on the other side of this area was a field. A field filled with rolling hills and cows. Not just one or two cows but a field with dozens of cows and a few bulls. The farm next door had an agreement with Camp Cedar Lake to allow their campers access to that area. How the scent would come right through the cabin windows sometimes made for some nighttime sheet cover-ups to get through the nights. This was a large camp with a huge lake separating the boys from the girls' camp. I recall that there were some wonderful trails where we picked fruits and acorns from the trees. We would hike for hours before returning to have cookouts at the large firepits. The food was always amazing. Well, at least I thought it was great food. The sing-alongs were okay, but after about one week, I was done, ready to go home.

I was big on writing postcards to my parents and sent them daily. My mom kept almost every postcard I sent, and from what I was able to read later in life, I really wanted to go home. I was done with Camp Cedar Lake. Reading these postcards, you cannot help but laugh. I did almost anything imaginable one could write to try to get your parents to come pick you up early. And I mean almost anything. One letter said that I was having a good time, but one day, when I was walking in the camp, I heard my name called out. It was my brother yelling out to me from a window in the camp's infirmary. Seems my brother ended up with a bad cold and fever. So what was I to do? I wrote another postcard telling my parents they needed to get here quickly as Chuck was in a hospital screaming out to me. Of course, without really thinking, my parents called the camp to find out that Chuck had a simple cold. Oh well, I tried.

Other postcards I wrote to my dog Tippi, the family miniature toy fox terrier, asking her to tell Mom and Dad to come and get me. Remember, I had a wild imagination (still due to a degree) and used what I was thus far taught to my advantage. No such luck. I ended up spending the entire four weeks at Camp Cedar Lake. As I looked back on this young adventure, my parents did right by sending me (us) there. I learned quickly what it was like to live with those you never knew, how to make lasting friendships, how to survive in the wilderness if needed, and most importantly, how to share. At Camp

Cedar Lake, it was not about getting away from home as it was about understanding what makes up part of our world. Easier times back then, that is for sure. A small self-promotion. Look for my book *Letters from Camp Cedar Lake* coming out shortly.

I was six years old when the first test of resistance came upon me. I remember my father sitting with both my brother and me down at the kitchen table. It was one of those techno round tables, with medal curved legs, a Formica speckled top, and vinyl-covered chairs that were always cold when you first sat down on your legs felt the cool, stiff plastic. So this was usually done when something big was about to happen. With anticipation and bated breath, Dad directed us to understand and agree that the basement was "OFF-LIMITS" to us until he gave us the ok to return. Now the door leading to the steps going down into the basement was no more than a few feet from right where I was sitting with my brother and father. Boy, I remember that the door started taking on its own formation. Looking at it, I could already visualize a solid steel frame with a solid steel door secured by a very thick chain and metal lock.

"Steve...STEVE!" my father called out to me. "Promise me that you will not try and go down into the basement."

With a scared promise, I chose to follow his demands and not make any attempt to crash through that imaginable steel door. However, for the next two months, the basement was off-limits to my brother and me. Mind you, my mother had full clearance since the clothes washer and dryer were in the basement, allowing her clear passage for the sake of clean clothes, towels, and bedsheets. For us, it was completely off base, and we adhered to his demands.

The countdown had begun. Now three months later, it was a Saturday afternoon. Chuck and I were standing just on the other side of the basement, waiting anxiously for that word from my dad. As we stood waiting, that seemed to have been hours rather than just a few minutes, I remember saying to my brother, "Chuckie, what's that sound coming from the other side of the door?" Squinting our eyes thinking that would give us additional hearing power, we just could not identify what it was. At one point, I thought I heard a train whistle, but that was quickly put to rest that it would be impossible to get a train in our basement. Then those words came through as if Moses was parting the sea. ENTER! A voice was heard coming from the other side of the door. That is all that was said. Anticipation was huge. I placed my hand on the doorknob and quickly turned it so that all I then had to do was pull it wide open with ease.

The basement at the bottom of the stairs was dark and still. Suddenly, there were lights flashing and the sound of engines and whistles blaring. As we made our way down the stairs, I looked toward the right and saw the most incredible sight any six-year-old boy would love to see. There were trains running in all different directions, whistles blowing, lights flashing along the train tracks, and I remember seeing small boats in what appeared to be a huge lake in the middle of what was a large layout of Lionel Trains. Complete with waterfalls flowing running water, four separate trains, buildings, cars, trucks, and people figurines, it looked just like a town and a countryside. The layout was quite large. It contained six pieces of plywood, secured to wooden horses, and took up half the size of the entire basement. Just from the smile on my dad's face, I knew that he was bursting with pride for being able to build such a layout with assistance from my uncle Eddie next door. They both worked on this project every day for almost three months. I wish I still had those Lionel Trains. Today, some of those engines are worth thousands of dollars. Back then, who knew what their values would be fifty years down the road? I remember when we were starting to pack for our family move to Holmdel, New Jersey. My dad asked me what I thought we should do with all the engines, train cars, buildings, etc. This thought stayed with me even till today.

Without coming up with an idea, Dad said, "How about we donate them to the Fair Lawn Orphanage Home so that other children can enjoy them?"

As I recall, without hesitation, both my brother and I agreed. The day we dropped off all the boxes filled with time, energy, happiness, love, and offerings, I, for the first time, felt a warm glow come upon me. It was warm, calming, yet filled with happiness as many of the children from the orphanage surrounded us cheering and clapping for what they were about to receive. I think that was the first time I saw my father wipe his eyes. Being concerned since this was a new sight for me, I asked my dad if he was okay. His response, still to this day, means so much. With a happy tear in his eyes and a smile on his face, he looked down at me and said, "Son, always remember, when you do good to others, it'll come back twofold. Yet again, lessons taught, and lessons learned. Another important ladder to what someday would be part of my success in life. The last thing I recall was my dad calling one of the older boys over to the driver's window and my dad reaching out and placing the engineer's cap on his head.

"You're now the engineer, so yell out, 'All aboard!'" my dad called out as we waved goodbye from the car pulling out of their driveway.

I found that doing good to someone other than yourself for no reason is one of the best feelings anyone could possibly have. Another lesson, another chapter in life.

There were other times when I would just sit back and observe. Even at a small age, I witnessed and fully understood right and wrong. Today, I can say thank you to my father for the certain things he taught me.

Holmdel Township, New Jersey, was an upscale town. Still consisting of a full country flare, there were many working farms. Allocco Farms was one place in particular—strawberry fields, pumpkin fields, apple orchards, lemon and lime fields, Jersey corn, and Jersey tomato fields covered acres and acres of land in Holmdel. Being able to grow up in my teenage years in Holmdel was a wonderful experience. True, it was much quieter and slower than any city would be, but we still had some of the best restaurants, drive-in movie theaters, and of course, the Jersey Shore. Personally, I would not trade my upbringing to live anywhere else. You see, where one lives and is raised plays an important part in developing one's skills, attitudes, and wants. This was something I will always be thankful for from my parents.

Our move to Holmdel, New Jersey, was the only actual move I can recall—that is because I was fortunate to be in a family that made the choices that they made.

"Plant your feet and build around yourself," my father would always teach me.

We went from a comfortable, moderate three bedroom, two bath home to a newly constructed large fourteen room house with three large bedrooms and a master bedroom that took up the entire back and length of the house, a beautiful brick fireplace, and a large enough backyard to play football and build a custom pool. Now when I say land, let us not get confused. I am not talking acres and acres of land. It was more like one and one-fourth acres, which, to me, seemed to be larger than life back then.

The rooms were huge, and there were various levels throughout. We were shy four feet from putting in a bowling lane in the basement. My parents were avid bowlers, but unfortunately, it was just a little too short. So instead, my father had the basement completely tiled to include two shuffleboard courts designed directly in the tile and a ping pong table. Being in the fifth grade now, I was able to start understanding family status, and of course, then "mine is bigger than yours" saying came into play. Not just by me but by my new friends here in this quiet thoroughbred horse and farm town. Holmdel back in the early '60s was filled with many active farmhouses and some serious horse training facilities. For many years, Holmdel, New Jersey, was considered one of the elite places to bring your horses for racetrack training. The grazing and hills were a perfect setting, rich in soil and vegetation. You have heard that saying, "There's nothing better than a Jersey tomato." Or "the sweetest corn is Jersey corn." Yellow or white, it doesn't really matter as long as they are from New Jersey. I can still see us driving over to Allocco's Farm every weekend to pick up our fresh vegetables and fruits. You see, Holmdel was not a bustling town and not any type of city.

I lived in a town where people never locked their front doors. We were able to walk anywhere at night without the concern for our safety, and most importantly, we respected each other. We had the best volunteer fire department and a police force consisting of Chief Joseph Phillips, his son, R. Bruce Phillips, and cousins Tom Durdack and John Cavallaro. Headquarters was in the basement of their four-room Town Hall Building. At night, the police department was never manned by an officer (since there were only four), and they used to have metal handles that they would turn on to send all calls to Monmouth County, State Police Headquarters in Freehold, New Jersey. For calls, the dispatcher would then radio one of the four police vehicles to advise when they were on patrol. It wasn't like Mayberry with Andy and Barney, but we sure were a tight community.

Since we had moved closer to the New Jersey Shore, it was too difficult for Lulu to go home every weekend. She decided that every five weeks, she would take the bus back up to Patterson to see her family. My father would then pick Lulu up on his way home from work on the following Monday. When my father would pick Lulu up, it was a complete scene. Here comes my father, driving either a Cadillac or Lincoln Continental. You remember those huge boats on wheels? Quite large and filled with every new gadget that came out for cars at the period. Dad was known as Da Man. The patrons of the bar and upstairs residents would see my father's car come floating down this small, congested street as if it appeared to be this huge frame. "Lulu Bell!" some of the patrons would shout out in the direction toward the second-floor windows. "Da Man is here for you! Let's go! Lulu Bell Gandy, you hear me shouting! Da Man, Da Man is here for you!"

Dad would sit in his car with the front passenger's window down as he would have some banter and laughter with this group. Lulu held court among this very tight neighborhood. Patterson had many areas that had serious reputations of violence, and this happened to be one of the worst. I learned really quick that no matter what the surroundings are, being the one in charge is very important. No matter if it is a legitimate business or the corner bar running numbers, if you are one of the elites in the group, they all have your back. They would sell their soul for their number one. Some businesses are like that even to this day. Lulu and my father were each leader in their field, and I knew for a fact, early in my life that my father was very well respected wherever he went. I saw that as being very cool. The definition of coolness has many reasons. You learn them as you grow no matter what your background is.

THIS LIFE OF MINE

On Saturday mornings, Mom and Lulu (if she decided to stay for the weekend) would have a breakfast of scrambled eggs with bacon and toast, orange juice, and a tall glass of cold regular milk ready for us before the weekend chores were tackled. I do not know how it was for you, but for us, we always had a set of chores to do that my father planned out for my brother and me. As far back as I can remember, my dad had planned out a scheduled sheet of what chores had to be done outside the house. You know, the flower beds are kept clean and fresh. Any weeds found had to be immediately pulled. Lawn to be cut and bushes trimmed if needed. I remember watching my dad when he had Sears & Roebuck's Company deliver the new sit-down lawn mower. Six horsepower with five gears! We were as excited as he was. Of course, I barely got to ride it since I was the youngest. So I kept to the weed pulling.

Riding the mower changed quickly. You know the saying "When your dad's away...." So my brother and I marked out an eight-figure course alongside our long driveway. Grass had not been seeded yet, nor have any trees been planted. There it was, the ideal place for the Holmdel Figure Eight Speedway! We had soft-to-medium dirt and two-dirt speed bumps. We knew this was not a clever idea, but we wanted to see just how far off the ground we could race this mower. Even when my dad asked me about this track, I said we were just riding slow around it, especially over the bumps. Taking the turns sharply, we were eventually able to create a lot of dust in those turns. We would be covered from head to toe in dust when we finished. That lasted a few months, and we got away with it until winter set in. What were we going to do with the riding mower now? I thought. No problems.... My father had Sears deliver the snowblade unit that was made for this model as well. The mower portion would be released and stored so that it could become the Sears snowplow!

It had weights for the rear wheels, chains as well, and this incredible snow blade, controlled by the pulling of different levers while seated inside a canvas-covered cab. Those times were fantastic knowing that we were outside in snowfalls, fully protected by this clear-covered canvas while plowing the snow off the driveway and circular driveway. Just thinking about it right now fills me with those adolescent memories. I then came up with the idea of Steve's Snowplow Service for the Hills of Holmdel. That was the name of the development we experienced. None of these driveways had short drives. They were all a good length, and I knew people would jump at the thought of not having to go outside to shovel, blow, or plow. They had Steve to do it! And to plow I did. To me, it was easy money, and I was having the time of my life. That was my start at producing ideas to make a dollar and enjoying it while I did it. I did not need a driver's license because it was not a pickup truck. It was just Steve Wallach, riding from house to house on his father's sit-down mower/snowplow, checking on people to see if they wanted their driveways plowed. This was the start of my snow calendar, which was simply made up of the names of my repeaters that would be listed for any snowfall over an inch or so. The Repeaters Club has started. That Sears six-horsepower sit-down mower stayed with me for many years after Holmdel, New Jersey. It made it all the way to my home in Nashville, Tennessee, where I kept it busy for another eight years. I was taught that if you take care and maintain, items can last you for years to come. I still practice that belief to this day. Unfortunately, that sit-down tractor was destroyed in a fire and just could not be rebuilt. Boy, I can still picture me riding it wide open and being able to use it in Nashville.

Our home in Holmdel had a circular driveway paved into the front of the house so that we could take advantage of having a loop driveway rather than just your street-to-garage driveway. It was great, and it was easy to unload the car with packages, plus back then, having any additional driveway gave the impression that the home was bigger than life. My father had beautiful boxwoods manicure along the outside of the circular and gas lanterns that the reflected a very nice ambiance at night.

But no matter what was written on the "to-do list," there was always something that we had to do before any playtime could exist. I guess this was the time for me to figure out how and when deployments come into play in our lives. The excuses I was able to come up with were quite impressive. I found myself sometimes believing them myself. I now can recall hearing my father say with a slight sound of laughter in his voice, "Forget it, Steve. I've either tried or heard every one of them." I would stop and think for a second and realize that I needed to come back to reality and just get the wedding staring up at me. As I grew and continued with the chores, it gave me the opportunity to carry them over for many years to come. Thanks, Dad, for another learning experience. I still hear my father say, "If you don't take care of your own home and show it the respect it deserves, your life will become as stale as how you've let your home become." True words by a very wise man.

Another thing I realized was that these "chores," or I should call them, our Saturday morning chores, taught me something at an early age that I found myself carrying through for my own weekly chores or given to others. Once I was cleared from my detail by the grounds staff sergeant (Dad), it was on and upward to see what the day had in store for me. On to conquer something new or fall into a routine that seemed to have been working. Either way, the flashbacks are instant. I laxed in teaching my own son the importance of doing outside chores. He knew that *if* he did not weed the flower beds properly, I would eventually take over. Sometimes, his attitude would be direct, but he did do his best not to take care of the grounds with me. He, for most times, always got the best of me. One must remember, my son was the most important person in my life. He was not just my son; he was my best friend growing up until his late twenties.

Many events were celebrated during our time in Holmdel, New Jersey. Both my brother and I had our bar mitzvah while living in Holmdel. My parents were standing members in many organizations, clubs, synagogues, and society events. I did realize that I was fortunate with who I was and who I was becoming. Not so much on my own but through my parents' involvement with others, including positions within our community and with me. I was taught right from wrong; I was taught to respect one's elders, respect the police, my teachers and friends, but most importantly, myself. My mother would say to me, "Stevie, for others to like you, you must show them that you are a straight-shootin' person. No lies, just the truth. You are who you are."

From my first school in Holmdel, I knew right away that this area was not city-like. In fact, it was quieter than Fair Lawn and had way more open fields of corn, strawberries, pumpkins, vegetables, etc. It was much more laid back. Why did we move there? I recall my father telling me that he wanted us to be raised without the hustle of being close to New York City or even New Jersey Cities like Newark, Elizabeth, Union City, and others. The peacefulness was something he wanted for my mom as well. So we made the move.

Centerville School, located on Highway 35, Holmdel, New Jersey, consisted of four rooms in a two-level old brick building. There were two bathrooms, one on each level, one for the girls and one for the boys. Each room had windows that contained the old, wired windows. The front windows could not open, but the side windows allowed for cross ventilation, which sometimes allowed the scent of cows and horses from the Allocco Farm located just up the highway to seep through. One water fountain is located on the main floor of this building. The backyard was more dirt and grass. We had a section right outside the back door that had three or four picnic tables and then our famous baseball field with four soiled bases and a shy line of white powder outlining the inner field. Surrounding the field and school was this dirt drive, which allowed the two school buses and cars to ease in for drop-offs and pickups. We had our baseball diamond, and this is where decisions were made, not by the teachers but by the students. Remember, Centerville School was for fifth and sixth graders. Decisions insofar as who were the cool kids, smart kids, goofy kids decided where we belonged and with whom.

Being the new kid on the block, I had to prepare myself for, well, almost anything. Will they like me? Will I like them? These were questions that had to be answered quickly. Walking to class, I was welcomed by the fifth-grade teacher, Mr. Summers, the first African American teacher I ever had. I immediately took a liking to him as his demeanor was that of a happy person who only wanted us to better ourselves. In class, I knew exactly who stood out and who did not. I took my seat and did what I was taught by my father to sit, be quiet, and observe. Get to know your surroundings, especially the other students.

Playing baseball during recess was an hour of pure fun and laughter. The girls would take their places at the picnic tables, cheering on their classmates. Well, most of them. Remember, even back in the '50s, there already existed different personalities for us all. My first time at bat, I hit a grand slam. That baseball had traveled so high in the sky and so slow that the moment felt as if it would take hours before the ball would come down. That was my initiation to the Boys of Holmdel.

This medium-sized guy that you were able to see worked out approached me with a smile on his face and said, "Welcome to my school. I'm Jimmie Mauro."

So from there, it started. I also believe that if you surround yourself with names of those already with a reputation, it will carry over to you. Okay, sometimes the reputation of a few may not be the kind that is positive, but it is then up to you to make the decision for yourself. Now, at that age, I only compared it to a good reputation. Later in life, I became fully aware of the phrase guilt by association. But at that time, it did not matter. Jimmie introduced me to "da boyz" and "da girls" who made up the cool kids of Centerville School. Mr. Summers, who we later referred to as Mr. Chumley, was one of the best teachers I can remember. His caring and attention to each of us is what made him so unique. His smile was contagious as was his laughter. Another teacher there at Centerville was Mr. Kent Bry, a stocky short man who had an incredible stomach. He would refer to his belly as an educated stomach for his own happiness. Of course, we all knew what that meant. His taste for beers when not working showed off his appearance, but he was still a great teacher. This was the school I was so glad to have attended. It taught me many things that one needs when growing up. I will always be thankful to Mr. Summers and Mr. Bry for helping with a portion of my growing years.

After just two years at Centerville, it was time for us to move to another school. There were two other elementary schools in Holmdel: Indian Hill School and the newly constructed Holmdel Village School. It was sad to have to say goodbye to some friends made at Centerville since they would be going to Indian Hill. I was scheduled for the new Holmdel Village School, entering the seventh grade.

Laurel Ave was a long straightaway that had rolling mounds all up and down the street, giving many drivers the desire to race. The best part was seeing if you could get lift off on the last roll as it quickly came upon a train trestle crossing over. Most of us always had that rush of excitement until that one day when someone chose to see just how fast and how far they could jump that last roll. Many of our friends had older siblings, so we usually found someone who would take us with them when heading out to Laurel Avenue. Unfortunately, I recall the day when the emergency calls rang out; that one car was traveling too fast. The car in front of us hit the trestle at the base of the front window shield and peeled off the entire roof of the car, as well as decapitating its driver. That was the last time anyone ever tried to take Magnetic Hill at top speed. Within days, the township of Holmdel chose to flatten that final roll and make that portion of the road surface almost level. To this day, I can still see the destruction in my mind.

Magnetic Hill, which was the name Laurel Avenue was known as. Why? I believe there is a Magnetic Hill in many small towns throughout the United States. It is a road where we know takes you on an incline, yet you could place your car in neutral and be pulled all the way back to where that accident occurred, at the trestle. It was as if that driver was pulling everyone to him. So you can imagine how far and wide that story went about the accident, Laurel Avenue and magnetic hill.

I remember my father having to travel for business. Whether he was developing another shopping center or freestanding department store, there were times when it was my mom who ran the daily routines in the house. Even though we still had Lulu Bell, my mom was a hands-on mom. Always there for us, whether it was something from school or the scouts, my mother made sure we always knew she was there. When I moved from Centerville Hill to the Village School for my seventh grade, I thought, *Wow*! This was a new school with more advantages than we had at our four-room school. In the main area, the back of the school had full-length large glass windowpanes.

I never saw such large glass windows before. In the center of it all, they had a two-pane window glass door that allowed students and teachers to pass through from the grassy areas and the concrete slabs making up an outside area with tables and benches. I remember that the outline of the windows and glass doors contained a metal frame. Seemed legit until the accident. The bell rang, and all of us were either running or quickly, walking to get back inside. It was as if there was a race for first, second, and third place.

As I was about to make it to the door, I remember being pushed from behind and then turning to see who pushed me and falling directly on my lower spine. I know the push was accidental. It was just another student wanting to get inside for that prize winner.

Stars, stars, and more stars were all I remember. When I landed on the sharp metal, it had severely bruised my lower back, which caused me to lose feeling in my legs. As panic set in, I recall Ms. Gilmarten (teacher) calling the office and having them call for an ambulance. It was protocol back then. As panic set in, I could not help but notice in the sky above me, a circle of clouds had formed. A calmness came over me as I remembered very clearly, my Nanny's voice telling me that everything was going to be okay. This was not a forced sight. I can recall this even to this day. Her reach out to me was as if she was extending her arm and hand to me. Within seconds, she was gone again. It had been years since I received any indication from her. Yet here she was, consoling me and letting me know that everything was going to be okay. Long story short, they took me to the local hospital where I was finally released by my mom with a badly bruised lower back and buttocks—embarrassing to say the least, especially surrounded by my friends and others. All I know is that I was back at school a few days later. So many of the students welcomed me back. The student who accidentally pushed me made sure to be one of the first to say he was sorry. "Hey, no big thing," I said to him. In my mind, I already knew it was all okay. My Nanny came and told me so.

The only thing I can think of that happened at the Village School for my one year of attendance was that we had this one substitute teacher one time. She was not your everyday-looking teacher.

She was extremely old and had been substituting teaching in Holmdel for many years. I would not be surprised if she was at the dedication ceremony of Centerville School when it was first built. This "sub" had a problem with sight and sound. I remember she would talk endlessly about nothing. She would get on to a subject and talk forever about it and not any subject that was part of our learning curriculum. When we knew she would be our substitute teacher on a specific day, we made sure to bring "The Buzzer" to class.

The buzzer was a battery-operated device that sounded just like the classroom phone. Every few minutes, someone would press the buzzer and watch Ms. Gilmarten walk over to the phone to pick it up. "Hello," she would say repeatedly. "Hello. Can I help you? I can't hear you." As soon as she would hang up and get halfway back to her desk, the buzzer would go off again. While this was happening, at each buzzer, two students at a time would quietly make their way to the closets that lined the one inside wall of the classroom. This went on until there were just a few students still in the seats. Ms. Gilmarten never missed any of the students. In fact, she never knew we were not in the classroom. The bell would ring, and the class was dismissed. Full attendance was marked. "School's over for the day," she would say as most of us were already gone. Still, she was a very sweet lady.

My final eighth-grade year was at Indian Hill School, located on Holmdel-Keyport Road, still in Holmdel. Indian Hill was an older built school that was closer to my home, allowing me to bicycle or even walk to school rather than take the school bus. I can remember those wonderful and clear days, so many of us would ride our bikes or just meet up along the way and take the walk, cutting through the backyards of the homes in what was called Old Manor—another built area of the same type of homes. Those were great days and times. There was an old cemetery that dated back to the eighteen hundreds, and we would always take the time and pick up any trash that ended up blown onto the graves or tombstones caused by the natural weather conditions. We knew no one that was buried there, but because of its age and long-term wear and tear, some of the stones were illegible. Nonetheless, we felt obligated to keep it clean. Even though I was taught by my father that entering the grounds of a cemetery was not allowed under Cohan Jewish Law, I felt it was my responsibility to help others in keeping this area clean. I saw no harm in what I was doing.

Our eighth-grade homeroom teacher was Mr. Kaufman. A short stocky man who had a nervous twitch that some took advantage of. We found that if you tapped Mr. Kaufman on the shoulders from behind, he would spin quickly and put up his fists like he was getting ready to fight Muhammad Ali. It was quite amusing to watch this. Sometimes, we would get caught, but other times, he would just stare at us, wondering who the culprit was. He never told us why his reaction was always so aggressive. I do not believe any of us got the answer.

Most of the students that attended Centerville are now together again at Indian Hill School for our final year in grammar school. Between the reputations of the Mauro Brothers, the Wallach Brothers, the Miller Brothers, the Hill Brothers, and a few stand-alone eighth graders, we made sure we were involved in sports, after-school events, and the most important, girls!

Ah, the '50s and '60s were incredible years to grow up in. The clicks that we formed in grammar school carried through into high school, college, and even into the present. We all have stories about school, and yes, so do I. Just off the cuff, here is one I recall. We were in homeroom class with Mr. Kaufman. We had a code that most followed. You know, a hand or face motion. It would only go to those what were part of this, the boys group. Remember, there were so many groups in every classroom. When an immediate meeting was called, the meeting point would be the hall bathroom, of course, depending on the gender of the "group" members.

One day, the discussion during lunch had to do with blowjobs. That's right, blowjobs. Who is best at it, who has already experienced it, and most importantly, who's willing to give one on a dare? It was odd. As I recall, none of the boys would give their names, but most of us already knew who we could include in this list. This conversation started because Jimmie Mauro started telling us that he got head from Debbie M. Debbie had a reputation as being "easy" when it came to going out on a date with her. So the talk was getting heated by some. Laughter and call girl shouts filled the echoed bathroom.

"Come on. I dare anyone to give me a blowjob!" Jimmie Mauro yells out. "You give it to me, and I'll give it right back."

There was a lot of teasing going back and forth, and out of the chuckling came a voice that said, "Okay! I'm game!"

Now imagine if you could, there were, I believe, four or five of us in the hall bathroom. "Okay, Jimmie." We hear this recognizable voice say, "Let's go!" Here stood Paul, a guy with a face full of freckles and bright red hair. Paul was a character in himself. always there for a good laugh, whether about him or someone else. So here stood Paul and Jimmie facing each other with just a couple of feet between them. The rest of us were standing around them, coxing them on.

"Let's go, Paul! Don't you chicken out!" someone calls out.

As the banter became louder with laughter, plain as day, I could still hear Jimmie tell Paul, "Come on, you go first."

Two seconds later, Paul kneeled over and took Jimmie in.

"Holy shit!" were the two words from all of us.

I will never forget the words that, to this day, will live on forever. Paul stood up and tells Jimmie with a smile on his face, "Your turn!"

Without hesitation or delay, Jimmie's infamous words can still be heard in every bathroom stall at Indian Hill School, Holmdel, New Jersey: "Get the fuck outa here! Not a chance!"

As we heard the bell ring in the distance, that was our cue to return to Mr. Kaufman's science class, hoping to keep this, our little secret. So the saying, "Saved by the bell" carries a lot of weight among the few.

Those days of neighborhood walks to school and home are no longer with us in most areas. What ashamed that what was once part of our heritage to the American family has been turned away by the majority. To me, it was so cool to walk the few miles to school because meeting up with your friends along the way gave you the opportunity to plan most things out. Who are you going to have lunch with? What are you doing after school? Hey, did you hear Paulie gave Jimmie a blowjob in the boys' bathroom.

The girls of Indian Hill consisted of many of the girls we spent the last four years in school with. We had some hot ladies in the eighth grade. Just to name the ones that stuck out to me, there were Donna Welle, Kathy Noweski, Linda Festa, Michelle Ford, Sharon McCormick, and the one girl every school had, our easy-to-score Debbie Mooney. Now granted, those days were complete once you said you "scored" with one of them. Now the term "scoring" was used way too easily back in the '60s. Everything from kissing to "copping a feel" to going "all the way" and other title claims meant you scored. When we heard that someone scored with someone, it was acceptable to believe whatever you wanted to. Were you going to be told the truth? Most likely, no. Remember, you had some of these kids that would play it out like this: "Hey, man, I heard you had Mary under the bleachers. You score?" Well heck, most of us would not hesitate to say, "Hell yeah, man! I scored big time!" You know, even in the eighth grade, it was important to keep your image up. I remember that was when you were working so hard to be who you wanted others to perceive you as. Or was it already starting to form a falsehood of who you are? It was important to be seen by your friends and peers as someone who "stands out" above the rest. I noticed at an early age that my father was one who had everyone's attention when he walked into a room. It was amazing to see and even feel just a little what it was like to hold. There were some of us that definitely held that position. At this age, I do remember learning that I represented the name Wallach and while out in public, I carried myself properly. It never swayed me from not doing something. I guess it was due to how my manners were continuously being built and knowing that *if* I did do anything that would cause embarrassment to my surname, my father would whip my ass with a belt. "Plain and simple," he would say, "don't embarrass who you are and where you came from." I fully understood this lesson at an early age. Now mind you, I got my ass whipped more than one occasion. It is not something I am proud of, but it is something that became a part of me, in my heart, mind, and soul.

The staff at Indian Hill School was predominantly white. We had a few black, Asian and Latino teachers and very few ethnic students. There was no reason as to why. Holmdel just did not have many ethnic families living there. Our principal at Indian Hill School, however, was a tall masculine man names Gregory Robinson. Mr. Robinson was a black American, who had an extensive educational background. Well-educated and one of the best influences I had in my early year at his school. He stood with such a stance that if you had to speak with him, he would tower over you, causing his appearance to make him look even larger than he was. A fair principal who refused to tolerate juvenile antics and made us all aware of what the rules were in "his" school. When Mr. Robinson laughed, it would come from deep down inside him, and it would roll out with this force of power. His laugh was addicting. The best way to describe it was that it sounded like a loud roar. Now, on the other hand, it took much to see this man get upset. For the few times that I personally witnessed his temper, I would have to say that even today, I would still fear him.

It was a cloudy morning. There was Kenny H., Carmella S., and a few others including myself who were at the corner of Telegraph Hill Road and Overlook Drive. Our house was on Overlook Drive, five houses up on the right side. Each home sat on a minimum of one and a quarter acre, so there was a distance between each house. The day at school went fine other than our outside recess time was cut short due to a heavy rainstorm that blew in. The rain stayed with us for the remaining school time and even on the bus ride home.

As the bus turned around and came to a stop to let some of us all, everyone saw that Lulu Bell had come to the bus stop with a large golf umbrella to protect me from the rain. Everyone in our neighborhood, the Hills of Holmdel, knew Lulu Bell. So many of my friends would come to our house to swim, play, or just stay and talk to my mother (she was known as Momma J to all the neighborhood children). As the bus came to a halt, Kenny yells out, "Look at the nigger picking up Wallach so he doesn't get wet. What a baby." I sat for a few seconds, trying to comprehend what I had just heard Kenny say. And again, this idiot shouts out, "Go ahead, little Wallach baby! Your nigger will keep you dry! Look at that golf umbrella!" It took what felt like an hour and seconds for me to respond. You see, we were raised by my parents who there was no such thing called racism in our family. This was instilled in us as far back as I can remember. I mention this now so that you can understand why I reacted the way I did. This comes solely because of my upbringing.

Back on the bus, without giving up more than a few seconds, I grabbed Kenny by the back of his neck, and as I proceeded to slam his face down onto the medal bar that outlines the back seat on most school buses, I yelled out, "Don't you ever call her that word again!" All I remember was walking off the school bus to an open umbrella. Seeing Lulu standing there with her huge gold-toothed smile, she and I walked back up to the house. I was furious, yet I felt a power of performance and protection for someone who was not there but was being treated with such disgust. I felt fine. No mention of this to either of my parents, and Lulu assured me that she wasn't going to say anything.

Dinner at our home was a tradition known as family time. This was the one time where we all sat around the kitchen table, enjoying a wonderful meal prepared by either Lulu or my mother. Like it was yesterday, I can still hear the ringing of our telephone. You know, the old-fashioned ring that clangs and clangs until someone picks it up. As I looked up, I could hear my mother say, "Hello, Gregory. How are you?" Then the typical noises of agreement would be heard until I saw the look on her face as if she were just hit with a flying ball. Her voice became louder and louder as she called out, "What? Are you sure? It was Steve? I don't believe it!"

"Expelled?"

I can remember Mr. Robinson calling my mother at home on various occasions since she was president of the PTA for years. That was one thing about my mother. She was extremely active in our school and local charities. Her final words to the conversation were, "I will be there in the morning. Thank you. Bye-bye." As she came back to the dinner table, I could see that all eyes were upon me. Do I make a run for it, or do I first see what the telephone call was all about?

The kitchen table was round so that everyone sitting at the table could see the faces of all. The thought was that we would each be able to connect directly with the person we were talking about. It was the time my father wanted us all to be present for. Everything from each of our day would be told. I see now that this was a wonderful way of keeping in contact. Made sense. As I grew in age, I also grew in thought. The question of the whys was soon being answered either through my own experience or from being taught family responsibilities.

All I had to do was look at the expression on my mother's face as she eased herself back into her chair. "You have anything you'd like to tell your father and I?" were the words that first came out from my mother, not in a melodic tone but rather in a tone that seemed to be holding itself back from gaining strength. Dare do I look over at my father. I knew that *if* I even glanced his way, the magnetic strength of his face would pull me toward him, and I would be completely trapped. Would I mix up the words that I had already started to form in my mind for all the questions I was about to hear? No. I decided to take it directly on. Face-to-face, I was taught, was the best policy for discussion; therefore, I planted my feet firmly under the table, one hand on my leg to keep it from shaking and the other hand resting on the table's edge, gently tapping my dinner plate.

As I glanced around to confirm that my bearings were set, I noticed Lulu quietly walking out of the kitchen backward. For years, it always bothered me why she chose to do that until I finally asked her, and without hesitation, her response was simple and direct; "That evening, Steve, you became a bigger man." Now I know exactly what she meant by that. There were sets of rules that my brother and I had to follow. Respect for yourself, respect for others, manners, no lying, no cursing were just some of the rules. As time went on, more rules were always being added.

My story started simple and direct. My voice was one tone and mild as I looked directly at my mother and said, "Kenny said something on the school bus about Lulu. He wouldn't take his words back, and he said it again, so I hit him."

As my story unfolded, I could see my mother's eyes open wider and wider as if she just stomped her toe. "Look at your father!" were the words now coming from my mother. And then I heard the one word that said it all, EXPELLED! I hesitated to think it would just go away for that split second. That was not the case.

As if there was a powerful gust of wind bellowing through the streets, I could hear my father say, "Steven," (when either my brother or I were called by our formal first name, there was a problem) "I'm waiting for an answer."

As if the trees were uncontrollably swaying as if there was a tornado, it immediately became calm and quiet. Not one word was being said. As I sat there looking at them both as if I were at a tennis match, I picked my head up and, in a firm, yet somewhat shaken voice, I said, "I can't tell you what he said."

The silence this time became eerie. It was as if we knew there was a bomb, but we had no idea when it would explode.

Going back and forth for what felt like eternity, I looked at my father first, then turned to my right, and without further hesitation, I said, "Mom, Kenny called Lulu a nigger!"

You must understand that from the time we were able to comprehend at a very young age from right and wrong, both my parents instilled in us to always respect others through race, color, heritage; marking certain words such as *nigger*, *kike*, *ginni*, wop were words that if they ever heard us say, the consequences we would have to face would be a painful punishment. Not only were we told never to use them, but my parents explained to us what those words' meanings were. So you can imagine how I felt having to tell my parents.

As I waited to feel the wrath of my father's backhand, I was surprised when I heard my father say, "Good boy, son."

Wow, I thought for a quick second. My father and mother were not upset with me for defending what I was taught to do.

"I'm going to phone Gregory back to tell him the real truth of what happened on the school bus," preached my mother to us all.

"No!" I yelled back.

There was no way I was about to tell Principal Robinson, a black man, the *N* word. That was not going to happen for any reason. My imagination began to run wild. Here I was standing in the principal's office and using that *N* word to a huge black man. Even though hearing my mother at first demand that I tell him the truth, then in a more subtle, caring voice, I still refused.

By now, it felt as though I was sitting there for days. It was only about ten minutes. I thought I had this won. I wasn't being pressed by my mother anymore. The room became more peaceful, it seemed, since all that could be heard was the ticking on the wall clock. Suddenly, getting up from behind his desk, Mr. Robinson came around his huge oak desk and sat on the corner of his desk, facing me.

As he leaned down toward me, I could see his demeanor become relaxed as he leaned toward me and said, "It's okay, Steve. What did Kenny say that was so bad it caused you to hit him on the school bus?"

I felt as though the pressure in my head was about to burst. Not able to contain it any further out of being scared, I looked over to my mother, who was sitting next to me, and then looked up to meet Mr. Robinson's eyes, and I said, "Kenny called Lulu a nigger!"

I felt myself duck down as if I was in the middle of a boxing ring getting ready to be knocked out by my opponent and heard these exact words from this giant of a black man.

"That's my boy! Joyce, under these circumstances, Steve is not expelled, but Kenny is suspended for the week."

These were the words that I was hoping to hear. Once again, a child's upbringing is the most important part of one's life. For without the traits that I was raised on, I never would have been taught right from wrong.

I was never faced with racism. Sure, like most, I knew it existed, and I never knew why it existed. It seemed anything related to it only caused emotional hurt and physical pain. Why did people hate each other because of their skin? My upbringing never allowed such hate, especially in our home. I believe that I was fortunate to have had parents who instilled in me at a very young age that all people were the same. Different in lifestyles, but I was never to think one race was better than the other. My questions seemed to be answered as I begged to understand, but then again, not really. The questions

THIS LIFE OF MINE

remain to this day, but the subjects have far outgrown more than they should have.

Every year during our Passover Jewish holiday, my parents would invite a few non-Jewish people to come and celebrate our weeklong holiday. I remember at one time having Mother Hildegard, Father Bernard, Sister Francis, Gregory Robinson, and others over the years. You see, there was no difference between any of us. To this day, I will always feel blessed that my parents raised me with such strong beliefs and traditions. I continue to carry out this fine tradition on behalf of my parents, and yes, myself to this day. Certain Jewish Holiday dinners, our guests come from many different backgrounds.

A Jersey hard roll. Sound familiar? If you were not from Jersey, you would have no idea what a hard-buttered roll was. Not a Kaiser roll nor a soft roll. This was the most incredible hard roll you ever put in your mouth. Baked with a hard crusty shell and an inside that was this soft white cooked dough. Depending on the time you went there, you were sometimes fortunate to have your buttered roll still steaming hot. With a cup of hot chocolate or coffee, every Jerseyite knew what a Jersey hard roll was, and we were proud to be known for them besides our reputation of having the best Jersey corn and Jersey tomatoes.

The teenage years kept me busy with so many things I was involved in. Working part-time jobs to make some weekend money play, meeting up with the boys at the Bethany Sweatshop or Luigi's Pizzeria, we liked keeping busy. We had no computer games. Hell, we did not know what a computer was back then. We had four channels on the television. I remember when my father brought home our first colored television with a remote control that made the loudest clicks when changing the channels. Then there was *Pong*. The first video tennis game made for TV. We thought that was the next best thing to sliced bread. Who knew that that was about to take us into another zone, far away from what we were imagining?

My father traveled to many real estate conventions throughout the year. One was the ICSC (International Shopping Centers Committee) in Las Vegas, Nevada. From memories of each past year, my father came home tired but happy. Maybe it was the business side or his casino winnings or both, but whatever happens in Vegas stays in Vegas has been a true testimony about that magical place also known as Sin City.

Nero, Penny, and Cindy were the names of our in-house AKC Registered German shepherds. The bloodline was important to my father since he was planning on mating Nero and Penny since their combined bloodline was filled with many famous world-champion German shepherds. They were also trained as protection for our family and property. Each, having their own personality and disposition, were always entertained by them as they became family members. Cindy was my father's pride and joy. She could do no wrong in my father's eyes. She was a fantastic, well-trained shepherd.

Picture this. My father was away on a business trip (Vegas), and he had telephoned my mother to let her know an insurance agent was coming to the house that early evening to drop off papers for him. Seemed simple, with no special instructions. My brother was upstairs in his bedroom, and I was sitting on a couch in our den. My mother had gone to the store, and I was waiting for her return. It had started to rain, I recall, as the sky became darker caused by the thickness of the clouds. From the corner of my eye, I got a glimpse of headlights coming up the circular driveway. All three shepherds were with me, and when they heard my mother's car, their excitement could not be contained. Nero had the tendency to want to jump up on you when you first came home out of excitement. No matter what you may be carrying, Nero was going to jump. Mind you, this was a 120-pound solid dog. His excitement was a happy sight no matter how you were feeling or carrying. He obeyed all commands with the exception of no-jump-when-coming-home rule.

I heard the front door open hearing my mother's voice greeting the dogs.

"Hello, babies," my mother calls out. "Okay! Okay! Don't jump! Stop jumping!"

Nero's mighty jumps were too much for my mother to hold up. As Nero and now Penny's facial licks and barking continued, my wonderful mother lost her balance and fell on the Italian marbled foyer. My concern was making sure that she was not injured. Now remember, all three large dogs are in the foyer now, barking with excitement, thinking my mother is on the floor to play with them, and I am now leaning over my mother, wrapping my arms around her to help her stand.

At the same time, my brother heard the commotion and came down the stairs to investigate. As Chuck turned the corner on the landing, he could not help but see me standing over our mother. Rather than question me, he assumed that it was I who pushed my mother down. As I felt a hand grab my shoulder and another punch to my face, I recall shouting to him, "What the hell is wrong with you? The dogs knocked Mom down, you idiot! I was trying to help pick her up!" Wanting to break away from his grasp, I picked up the '60s/'70s-style footstool that I reached for and hit him with it, center face and nose.

By now, Mom was standing. The dogs realized it was not playtime, and me, I did not want to confront my brother again, so in three hurdle-style steps, I raced up the twenty-four steps directly into the hallway bathroom, locking the door behind me. As I paused to catch my breath and digest what just happened and why, I could hear my brother panting loudly stomping on each carpeted step as he made his way to his bedroom located at the end of the hallway.

Only in Wallach fashion (this could have been made into a movie scene), this is what then took place. Picture this: the front bell rang, and standing outside under an umbrella was a man holding a business briefcase in his other hand. The story from my mother was that she welcomed him into our home and told him to please wait there. Not knowing who this man was, the command sent to the dogs was to keep a watchful eye on him and that he was not to move. Remember, I was locked in the upstairs bathroom, my brother was moaning in his bedroom, and my mother, well, she was on the top landing outside the bathroom door, screaming, "Steven! Open this door at once! Your brother won't touch you!" The next few minutes, my mind raced with options. Should I just come out and sit and talk this out with my brother? I just could not come up with what choice would be best for me.

As I stared into the mirror and saw that my nose was still bleeding, this became the loudest boom I think I ever heard. My brother was pounding on the other side of the bathroom door, screaming for me to open it. Not a chance, I thought. Why would I subject myself having to possibly fight with my older brother over something that did not justify the actions being taken.

The layout of this full bathroom was large. Double vanity sinks, a large tub and shower, and the toilet positioned around a small corner wall for further privacy. I knew Chuck was coming through that door one way or another. Would I want to be responsible for having to pay my father for the cost of replacement, or do I take my chance and confront him directly? Looking around the bathroom for ideas, it immediately struck me that I should quietly unlock the door and hide on the other side of the small wall, so when he came crashing through, I would be able to push or hit him into the tub and run.

Run I did! The solid bathroom wooden door was opened as if a gust of wind forced its way through it, and there came my brother grunting like a wild bull. As his profile appeared around the small wall, my time was now to make my great escape. With all my might, I pushed Chuck away, and it was a direct shot into the tub. Wish I had filled it in; nonetheless, there he was, and there I went. I think it was just two steps, and I was down the stairs heading toward the front door. Now there standing in the foyer in front of me was this man in a suit. He had his briefcase in one hand, but the look on his face was as if he, too, were facing the wrath of my brother's temper. Surrounding this unknown man sat Nero, Penny, and Cindy. Still on the marks, my mother positioned for each.

My escape brought me out into the rain, yet I started to run down the street as my brother was now attempting to do his best to catch me. Now one would have to picture this. It is dark and raining, the streetlights are lit, and I can hear my brother yelling at me. What he was saying, I could not make out since he was panting so loud as to jumble any words he was saying.

Next thing I knew, my mother got into her car, which was still parked on the circular driveway, and proceeded to join the chase. My running was more like a jog. My brother had no athletic ability to run at any speed other than picturing someone who had an accident in their pants. I knew this, so I was more like doing small sprints just to aggravate his inability to run fast. As I turned from our street onto Telegraph Hill Road, I was already planning my route back to the house without having to go back the same way I left. On the side property of Dr. D'Agastino's house, there were trees reaching to the sky that stood eighty feet tall. There was a steep hill where my father and other neighbors got together and built a path with steps that would take you back to the top of Overlook Drive. Still not an even walk, but nonetheless, that was the path I chose.

So here I go. Up the cliff by way of the built-in steps, my brother lagged far behind as his pants became louder and louder. My mother, she had to turn the car around and head back up the streets to our home, where a strange man was still standing perfectly still in our foyer, surrounded by three extremely large German shepherds.

I can still see this man's face as I, once again, raced past him and up the stairs to my safe haven in the bathroom. Leaning against the vanity and wiping my face and looking at my drenched T-shirt covered in what appeared to be a blood bath, I could hear my brother finally climbing the stairs and making his way to his bedroom. How long should I wait before the coast clear? I waited until I heard my mother call through the door, "Steven, it's over. Come out and stay in your room till your father gets home." These words to this day still can be pinned to almost every American family…from the '50s, '60s, and '70s. Unfortunately, the great American family started to change to what is has become today. Unfortunately, many children are fatherless in our country, and it is a clear reason as to why the violence across America is so high.

As I could hear my mother apologizing to the man in the suit standing in our foyer, I was able to overhear his words to my mother, "Please tell Mr. Wallach that I don't think our homeowners insurance policy would be a good fit."

The outcome from when my father got home was simple. My brother and I were grounded with no free weekends for the next four weeks. Lessoned learned. Do not assume the worst of something when even though it looks bad. Wait until all facts are told.

Music, for me, was an escape into another dimension. My brother and I were fortunate to be from a family that thoroughly enjoyed the arts. From music to film to those famous Broadway shows, we experienced some of the best creations any child could have. Broadway shows began when I was just five years old. I can remember going with my parents by car to New York City to attend these shows. The noise of the city always fascinated me. Where were all these people walking to? It was as if each one was on their own mission. Looking straight ahead as if people had blinders on, I used to find that specific one in the crowed street who inadvertently would bump into another while balancing their briefcase, corner hot dog, and soda.

Why were these Broadway shows so special to me was because, after each show, we would make the forty-five-minute drive home, and I would make a beeline to the piano located on the inner wall of the living room. The piano was a Schollinger 1952 upright. The tone on this piano was so crisp and on point. I would pull out the piano bench and take my place and proceed to find those wonderful notes that would later become a song from the Broadway show my parents took me to see. I would sit and listen to the music in my mind and would then find their notes on the keys of the piano. I would sit for hours until I was able to play the lead notes. I never knew nor understood what it meant to be a gifted child musically, but as I grew and found my escape in the piano, I was playing Broadway hit songs from start to finish with ease.; at five years old. Thus, "playing by ear" became so natural to me. All songs came to me this way. As good as it was, I regret that I never taught myself to read notes of any songs. Now I could look at sheet music and read the notes from middle *C* to next octave *C*, but any notes higher or lower, I had no idea which ones they were. That never stopped me and to this day, over sixty years later, I am still playing that Schollinger piano in my Tennessee home and my ear to the music.

From high school bands to the town's battle of the bands, there were some great places we frequented for live music. Not to say that being in a band gave us an advantage over the other guys with the girls, but it was "the talk" among the girls in the bathrooms that the laughs and sounds of desire would penetrate the door when the girls talked about being with someone in the band. It was exciting and filled with whatever you wanted to think. The get-togethers after the shows on the Jersey shore, with the ocean's breaking surf as your backdrop, were the icing on the cake. We used to feel that guarantee of lust ran right through our bodies. Sure, even at thirteen years old.

Many different bands were put together by myself and my brother. Most of the time, we played in separate bands except for the one time we tried to make it as a Brother Band. I was backup vocals on my double keyboard Farfisa organ and Hammond speakers, my brother Chuck was playing his Gretsch Drum set and Zildjian cymbals, Blaise Responti was on lead guitar, Moe was on bass, and Jimmie Mauro was our lead singer. The band's name, Grapes of Wrath. We played school dances, proms, swim club nights, private parties. and the most important times were the Jersey Shore Battle of the Bands. Which band was the best on the circuit? I recall that these band battles took place at one particular Jersey Shore Swim Club in Seabright, New Jersey, called Tradewinds. It had a huge room for the dances, plus it was right on the beach. Bands like the E Street Band when Billy Chinook was the lead singer and guitarist, and Bruce Springsteen, who was just one of the guitar players in the band. Surrounded by neon lights and a fantastic light and sound production, we played it every year, hoping to be recognized by some big music producer. Our dreams may have been shattered, but the number of girls we had was endless. You see, the benefits easily outweighed everything else that was important to us at the time and age.

I came to the realization that when you are involved in an industry that primarily lives a fantasy lifestyle, you want that fix to continue no matter how. It is something that every performing musician, artist, actor, television announcer, and athlete cannot admit to; it is that rush when you hear your name yelled out; it is that time someone with excitement rushes over to you and asks for your autograph. No matter what celebrity says otherwise…bullshit. The rush is real. The recognition is supreme.

The summer months were more than just going to the Jersey shore. This was our time to make as much money as possible now that school was through June Six. Some would take jobs working along the shore, possibly renting lounge chairs and beach umbrellas, looking for that quick cash payout, while others would flock to a place called the Garden State Arts Center, Holmdel, New Jersey. It resembled a huge spaceship. With its circular dome-like cover, it had enormous concrete legs holding this utopia up. Beneath the mammoth dome, the land was sloped and manicured from it's perfectly cut rolling mounds to the enormous stage surrounded by lights, curtains, and audio speakers that were cleverly built into the columns on both stages' right and left. The red and gold outlined velvet curtains cascaded on each side of the stage from its hidden rafters to this sleek stage. The seating was designed as a stadium seating chart with the exception that instead of angling up, they angled down, separating the stage from the first row by an aisle. Seating was broken down into sections. Of course, the best seasonal seats were directly centered from Row A up and until Row ZZ. My father always made sure to have the best, whether personally or through business. At least that was how it appeared to me. We had our seasonal seats for over ten years. Located left of the center aisle, row C, seats 1–8. We considered them to be the best seats in a house of thousands. And they were. My father sold his seats for a strong profit.

Every musical artist, band, magic, Broadway show, and who was anyone during that time performed at the Garden State Arts Center. From Bob Hope to Janis Joplin, Tom Jones to Engelbert Humperdink, *Fiddler of the Roof* with Zero Mostel, Judy Garland, Chicago, Earth, Wind and Fire, Liberace, and the list goes on and on.

To work at the GSAC was a summer job so many of us waited for. We would apply in March for employment that usually started at the end of May, Memorial Weekend. The parking lot compared to the Meadowlands/Giants football stadium parking. Separated by manicured lawn mounds and flowers, working this with your colored GSAC vest, walkie-talkie, flashlight, and whistle had its advantages. The salary was decent, and your workload was easy. Pre- and post-shows were the busiest times in the parking lot, especially when over ten thousand cars all wanted to arrive and leave at the same time.

Now on your down time, smoking pot and sex ran wide open. The movements throughout these lots were at a minimum. Everyone was either sitting on the lawn or in their seats.

I chose to work as an usher. Simple gig. Escorting people to their seats became easier over the years. You knew where every seat was in every row and every section. Once the shows started, our jobs allowed us to sit on the steps of the aisles so as not to block anyone's visual view, or we could enjoy walking the grounds surrounded by the lawn sections and the concessions located on both sides of the grounds. The idea was to seat the guests, buy your soft drinks and chips from the concessions, and then find that quiet spot you and your girlfriend could "enjoy."

I worked my way after a few summers to being assigned backstage as a stage assistant. Fancy title, but basically, all I did was escort the celebrity guests from their lower-level dressing rooms to the stage right area. Once the shows commenced, I had a perfect view of both the show and a good few rows of guests seated out front. This was yet another way to pinpoint a pretty lady to get her backstage. You see, it was all in the negotiation. I learned that early in life and found that this, as with other ways, was marking my life's road ahead.

Tom Jones was one of the biggest names in entertainment then, and I was fortunate to be assigned to him for the five nights he was performing at the Garden State Arts Center. Amazing is the only way to describe it. I would always tell him just as he was walking onto the stage, "Hey, Tom, have a great show!" He would smile and reply, "Thanks, mate!" The minute Tom Jones walked out on stage, the screams would overpower even the sound of the band starting his first song. Not only would the screams immediately start, but the tossing of ladies' underwear made the stage look as if it were raining panties and bras. Dozens and dozens would be thrown onto the stage by every imaginable woman of all colors, shapes, and sizes. To see the reactions on their faces, as Tom would often reach out and grab a pair as they were being thrown in his direction, was priceless. His ninety-minute show fulfilled many woman's dreams that night, especially the smiles on so many of their husbands, boyfriends, and partners.

Carol Gilchrist was my first true girlfriend when I was fifteen years old. Boy, did I think I was hot shit! I had one of the hottest girls on my arm, so I guess you can say that she was the first girlfriend I really loved. We were inseparable. Even though we went to different high schools, we would always find ways to see each other on a few school nights, but on weekends and summer, where there was one, the other was as well. Carol's sister Gail was a big fan of Tom Jones, so for her birthday present, Carol and I invited her to the GSAC to see Tom Jones in concert along with my mother. My mother would tell me later that Gail was just beside herself as Tom gyrated on the stage before her eyes. I was already backstage, getting ready for my escort. What was a tradition at the GSAC was that once the shows were over, there would be a wave of people running to the fence line, stage right side, to get the final glimpse of their idol. Remember, the design of this amphitheater was deep in the back; therefore, the views looked down over the rear of the staging area where the tour buses, limos, and production trailers were parked and gave patrons a clear viewing. Many times, there were artists who would run up the hill to get a few quick photos and autographs with some of their fans.

The only problem they had with fans wanting to stay as if they were all "on watch" was that sometimes they would stay well past the time the entire seating area and lawn area were empty. Everyone had left except for these dye-hard fans. So the production staff had to come up with ways to get those fans to leave the area without being forced by the GSAC security staff.

Tom Jones caused chaos after each of his shows. Not deliberately, mind you, only that his fan base was predominantly female, and unless they knew Tom was no longer backstage, they would wait and wait and wait and wait. On that Friday night after Tom's incredible performance, Carol, Gail, and my mother made their way outside to get a position alongside the fencing, waiting to get that last glimpse of their star. As Tom appeared to come out from the backstage area, wrapped with a white towel over his head and shoulders, the scream coming from the hillside filled the air once again. "Tom! Tom! I love you!" Gail screamed out as she waved her hands uncontrollably to get his attention. There were screams by every female standing alongside, soaking in every glance they get back from him.

Recapping what happened next was confirmed by both my former girlfriend and my mother. My mother looked over at Gail and said in a whispering hand motion toward her ear, "Gail! Gail! Who are you waving and screaming at?"

"Oh my goodness! It's Tom! It's Tom Jones!" Gail yelled.

My mother again asked her as she held Gail's arm, "Gail! Gail! Who are you waving and screaming at?"

After a short pause, Gail turned toward my mother and her sister and, with a look of sadness said, "Oh no…. That's not Tom. That's Steve Wallach."

As the three of them burst into laughter and walked away, Gail realized that she had forgotten that Carol and my mother had both told her that I would be making the fake departure as Tom Jones. It was great. I would wait at the backstage door with a towel wrapped over my head and shoulders, and when told, I would exit the stage door, waving at the crowds above and jump into a waiting limo that was positioned and ready to exit. As we pulled away and into the overflow parking lot, we would make our way to an area of the unlit parking lot and wait out until my radio informed us to return. The backstage artist parking area was always cleared, and the venue staff would sweep for any of the remaining patrons. I found Tom and his entourage relaxing before loading up their tour buses and limos to make their way back to their hotel. I learned during this time that it is okay to hide under another's persona if there is no hidden negative agenda. It was just another piece of my living puzzle.

I started writing songs during my band member days more as a release for me than anything else. It was and still is a great way to express and put words to any feeling. This band was complete with members Bobby Mayo, Carol Mayo, Steve Anderson, and me. Our band name was Waterproof Candles. Why that name? I thought that nothing could stop us from being a success with a name like that. You cannot put out a waterproof candle; therefore, you could not stop our success.

We were playing at the Middletown Swim Club on this one Saturday evening. The club was known for some of the best parking lot live shows. Easily, the area, even with parked vehicles, was able to hold some five hundred concert goers. You must understand that the shows here were in the back parking lot, right behind one of the six sections that housed four large cabanas. I remember how large these were: an outside area with a table, two lounge chairs, and two standard chairs. The covered area had a shower stall, a small kitchen area, and an ice cooler. All the comforts of home during those summer months.

"Hello! Ciao! My name is Franco Grasso," this gentleman said with an Italian accent. This thinly built man, wearing a nice pair of creased slacks, Italian-made shoes, and a long-sleeve silk shirt buttoned halfway, showing off the three gold chins perfectly fitted around his neck, not to mention with his sleeves perfectly turned up, said while he extended his hand for a gentlemanly handshake. As I extended my hand in return, I could not help but wonder, *Could this be him? Is this our calling card? Maybe this guy is a music producer.*

"Hello, I'm Steve. Nice to meet you," I said.

Once again, he repeated his name but tagged it with, "I'm president of New Start Records. Years ago, many major record companies had smaller independent labels which were part of the Warner Brothers Conglomerate of Record Labels."

Me, I had no idea, but I chose to play along and see just what this was all about.

Long story made short, we made some noise in the music world with our hit song "Freedom" and B side, "Everything's Free." Our group, High Society, enjoyed playing throughout the East Coast states. Not bad being just seventeen years old, I thought. The recording studio was in Middletown, New Jersey, on Route 36, not in a bustling business district but rather in a freestanding building with a pebble driveway shadowed by a perfume manufacturing warehouse behind. At first, we thought that this was an odd place to record, but our concerns were overshadowed by the promises Mr. Grasso was telling us. The outcome of this was that High Society did make the charts, and we enjoyed our success, as small as it was, in some positive ways. I know I walked away believing that what seems to be odd can be a stepping stone for other plans that have already been partially carved out for your future.

My songwriting increased, and I had some strong inquiries back in the late '60s. I recall taking the train into New York City from the Hazlet/Keyport, New Jersey, train station to meet with a few music publishing companies. On this one trip, my mother asked me to join since she had some shopping to do in the city.

"Sure Mom! No problem," I called out, glad that she decided to take the forty-minute train ride with me. Making appointments with music publishing companies was made easy since most of the top publishing agencies were in two major buildings in New York City. One being 1619 Broadway and the other located at 1900 Broadway. Both buildings stood tall, just as powerful as the decisions that were made within the walls of these two buildings. These buildings contained some of the biggest music publishers in the country. I can recall riding the elevators and sitting in the waiting rooms of some of these publishers with the likes of Barry Manilow and Bette Midler. This one particular time, my mother had some extra time, so I invited her to join me on some of my meetings and cassette drop-offs. That was the term back then: drop-offs. That was when you were making a cold call, hoping to get your songs in the door and listen to them. It was a shot in the dark, but it did work for some. That was one of the only ways to get your music listened to. My mother was Julliard Music trained, and she was an excellent pianist. Again, another reason why my blood ran with music and piano. Not like today, every CD or stick that comes into a record label is not your old drop-off routine. Labels will not accept unsolicited material. Different times and different structures today. A far difference from years gone by.

It was midmorning, and we just arrived at 1600 Broadway. The building itself stood tall and strong. The buildings built back in the '30s and '40s were mighty just by their stance. The elevator door opened. We stepped inside along with another gentleman dressed in a suit, wearing a starched white buttoned-down shirt, and wearing one of those skinny ties that never really matched any suit jacket or shirt. As the door closed and all faces resumed that glazed look as we so often do when riding in an elevator with others, I heard my mother say, "I don't believe this! Can this be? Is your name Arthur Kent?" As the man raised his head to meet up with my mother's eyes, he tilted his hat on his head with his free hand and replied, "Well, yes. My name is Arthur Kent. And you are?"

"Arthur"—short pause—"It's Joyce Wallach!" she said with a positive melodic tone. "Remember you tried to teach my son Steve how to play the piano years ago in Fair Lawn, New Jersey?"

You could see that this man in the elevator, standing within feet of my mother, had an expression of wonder as his eyes looked up and his mouth twisted in thought. "Oh yes, I do remember you, Joyce. How are you and how is Steve doing? You know, he just didn't want to learn the basic steps of reading music for the piano," he said as my mother grabbed my hand as if to stop her from laughing.

"Steve's doing great! He stayed with the piano and has become a wonderful pianist and songwriter. In fact, Arthur"—as she brings her arm up and extends in my direction and says—"by the way Arthur, let me reintroduce you to my son, Steve."

My mother had the largest grin from ear to ear I had ever seen before. She was glowing in satisfaction, just as a proud momma would do to her cub. Arthur Kent and I spoke for a short minutes until he reached his floor. It was more like a few seconds of cheers than anything else. As he exited the elevator, he shook my hand once again and wished me luck. What more could I have asked for from the man who said I would never end up playing the piano? Today, I continue to play that Schollenger piano proudly.

So once again, I am being taught that no matter what anyone else tells you, it is up to you, as an individual, to decide what path you want to go down in your life. No road is an easy road, as I learned quickly. Every portion of my life thus far, I have learned some of life's important teachings. Some, I had to learn the hard way, but I was able to walk away knowing that I did my best and will take with me, all that I have learned.

Over the next few years, my outlook changed. I was now seventeen years old, and I thought I was indestructible. I was sneaking into nightclubs when I was eighteen, and groups of us started forming clicks. Not against each other, but when we traveled from club to club, we did it together. There may have been six or eight of us traveling together. Two carloads, three carloads, it never mattered. Wherever we went, I was automatically considered the head of my group. How I got myself into the highest position was never clear to me. Maybe it was because my last name was so very much respected in many of the surrounding towns in Holmdel. The more I think of it, my name stretched from northern New Jersey to Southern New Jersey as well as areas in the city (New York). My father had developed so many shopping centers and freestanding commercial buildings. The older I became, the more I realized that my father had an incredible reputation all over. People knew my father through various businesses and many from a personal level. It continues to amaze me through life that my father busted his ass professionally and succeeded with everything. He was a man determined to obtain the best in life—in his life and my mother's. I never met a couple that was so deeply in love with one another.

For years, my parents would take my brother and me on a ten-day vacation to Florida. We would stay at the Colonial Motel on Collins Avenue, Miami Beach, Florida. The best way to describe the Colonial Motel was that it was built in the shape of a horseshoe, with the base of the horseshoe being that of the front lobby facing the circular drive and busy Collins Avenue. This was your typical Miami motel, those rocking metal chairs and laminated chairs of multicolors lined the porches of these motels. Their guests, many elderly people, would sit in those chairs for hours just to watch the world go by. I recall just like my uncle Robert's, Zalkin's Birchwood Lodge, the same entertainers from the Borsch Belt (New York) were on the Miami Beach circuit. Shecky Greene, Jackie Mason, Steve Lawrence, and Edie Gormet were just some of the headliners we saw at the Colonial. Great memories. It had this enormous swimming pool in the center of the motel that had the ocean as its backdrop. Lounge chairs in both areas were abundant. Never a problem finding a place to sit and relax. This motel played a huge part in my life when I was eighteen. I will cover it further in this reading.

Lincoln Boulevard was the main shopping street in Miami Beach back in the '50s and '60s. Everything from men's clothing to ladies' fashions, some decorative pieces, to over-the-top items could be found on Lincoln Boulevard. Bathing suits and souvenir stores were side by side. There were more souvenir stores than you could ever imagine. I guess there was a need for them since these stores would be busy all day long. So many of these stores had huge display windows in their storefronts. Just the sight of some of these items acted as a magnet, drawing you into their store, hoping that you would make that purchase. Most times, it worked.

Jimmie Archer and I went to high school together at Croydon Hall Academy. There were plenty of times Jimmie and I would get together after school and on weekends to ride down to the shore or meet up to hang out at one of our favorite spots. Jimmie was of Irish descent with a fair-skinned complexion covered by freckles. What I remember about Jimmie was his innocent smile. He knew how to tilt his head to the side, and with his even closed-lip smile, he could get anyone to say yes to him. He was our player for getting us the most of, well, anything.

My parents would sometimes take a road trip up to Mt. Snow, Vermont, where they had their winter cottage. More like an A-frame, the cottage consisted of three bedrooms, a kitchen, two bathrooms, and a living room with a wood-burning fireplace. I do not recall spending a lot of time there, but I do remember going there with another one of my later girlfriends, Susan Lanning. Susan eventually became my wife, my first wife. That is an entirely new story that I will touch on later. But this A-frame was the first place my father literally caught me literally, with my pants down. My dad happened to walk in on Susan and me while we were in a heated moment. Still, under the covers, but he was not too happy with what he saw. I guess many of us can relate to our own time in memories. You can imagine that the three-hour-long ride back to Holmdel was quiet except for the small, little remarks made by some.

The reason I brought this up was because the following month. My parents decided to go up to the cottage for a quick weekend getaway. It was the same weekend that my girlfriend (at *that* time),

Carol, was going to Miami Beach to babysit her niece. What to do…? My folks were away, my brother had his college roommate visiting for the weekend, and me, I was looking at a very bored three days.

"Hey, Jimmie!" I said when Jimmie Archer picked up his home telephone. "Got any plans for the weekend?"

With a chuckle in his voice, Jimmie responded, "Nah, nothing planned. Why? What ya wanna do?"

Without skipping a beat, I said, "Come on. Let's fly down to Florida for the weekend. Carol is babysitting, and I have a plan."

Next thing you know, Jimmie and I were sitting on an Eastern Airlines flight on our way to Miami, Florida. Prior to leaving, I wanted to at least let my brother know what I was doing, but unfortunately for me, Chuck had gone to the store and left Don, his old college roommate, back here at the house. Thinking that Don would be cool about it all, I explained that Jimmie and I were flying down to Miami, Florida, for the weekend, and he was to inform my brother of this. To tag this made-up concocted story, I told Don that if anyone were to ask where I was, I was staying with some friends a mere few towns over Freehold, New Jersey.

It was the middle of winter. The trees, streets, and highways all had those dirt-colored stains left behind in past snowfalls. Our only way to get to the airport was for me to use my mother's Buick GS440. Two-door car that did pass as a muscle car in its time. You see, my mother had an incredible urge for speed. When she and my father would go car shopping, it was always at Charles Schwab's Dealership in Hazlet, New Jersey. The largest car dealer as you came off the New Jersey Garden State Parkway, Exit 117, they had a front row to every vehicle from that one exit. My father was always dedicated to any company that treated him a little special. There were businesses throughout parts of New Jersey where I would immediately notice that they knew of my father or were associates.

As if it were yesterday, we arrived at Miami International Airport and took a taxi directly to Colonial Inn, Collins Avenue, Miami Beach. Dropping us off in front of the Colonial, I felt that stomach rush come over me. Filled with excitement and nervousness, we planned our surprise. All along Collins Avenue, the motels and hotels were side by side. They would each use every portion of their property to get what they considered to be complete satisfaction. Even if it was a simple one-foot extension from their driveway, it was theirs. Directly next to the Collins Motel was a simple, cheap, not-so-attractive motel. It sat two levels high all with outside room entries and those air-conditioning units that were mounted directly into the building's walls. The sounds of these units would keep anyone awake at night if they had to listen to that.

We had this all planned out. I was to go into the lobby of this motel and register for a room under my name. You see, when I checked in, I did so as a single occupant. Whatever money Jimmie and I could save, we cut corners as best we could. I had the key in hand and made my way around to the double glass doors that let me to the outside walkway on the first level. Even the first level was higher than the ground level. It seems that this portion of this wing of motel rooms may have been built to a higher grade since beneath were huge rocks positioned on that side of their parking lot, looking back toward the beach and ocean. I remember there being a wooden rail separating the walkway and below. Made sense since it would have been a possible nasty fall if one stepped off inadvertently.

So here I am, standing on the walkway outside our room, looking over the rail at Jimmie and saying softly, "Come on, Jimmie! Jump up! I'll help you under the rail!"

You see, if Jimmie walked through the lobby with me, we would have been immediately questioned on the number of people staying in that one motel room. Our room is decorated in what would be called "art deco" today. Nothing matched. The sofa looked as though it came from a mix-and-match warehouse. The pillows on the bedspread had no matching colors found in the bedspread itself. The walls were painted in a faded light blue. A bathroom with just the essentials. Nothing fancy. Everything was white, from the tiles on the walls and floor to the sink and toilet. Even the towel sets were those generic white towels and the hand cloth and wash clothes over each other in perfect dimension. But the number one thing that stood out over the rest was that the bed was not your typical queen size bed. *This* bed had a coin-operated aluminum-colored box sitting on the nightstand. My curiosity got the best of me, as did it to Jimmie. We both made our way to the side of the bed and read the advertised print. ENJOY YOUR VIBRATING BED! I have heard of these beds before but never in the position to try it. Well, try it, we did. There was a slot that said, "Quarters Only." We took turns lying on the bed to see just what all the hype was about these beds. We heard that these beds could be found in many of the "ladies of the evening" bedrooms. Just a rumor, mind you. At that point in my life, I never experienced hooking up with a "lady of the evening." Never had to. Thirty minutes later, the bed stopped gyrating, and we realized there was only one bed in the room. "That's okay, Steve. I'll take the sofa the first night, and then we can switch," Jimmie said. That was fine with me.

So now we are standing in the parking lot next to the Colonial Inn, pondering our next move.

I said to Jimmie with excitement, "Follow me. I got this."

We both made our way into the hotel lobby, where I asked the front desk clerk, "Where are your house phones?" The clerk looked up and pointed to an area that had two hotel phones. I picked up the phone, and it automatically rang the front desk. I know that because as the phone rang through my telephone handle, I also heard it ringing at the front desk.

"Can I have Carol Gilchrist's room, please?" I said in a formal-sounding voice.

"I will connect you," I heard the clerk say both through my telephone sound piece as well as from across the lobby floor.

"Hello," I hear this beautiful voice say.

"Hi, Puna," I said into the mouthpiece in a quiet and happy-sounding tone.

"Hi, Steve," came the words from Carol on the other end of the phone.

"Where are you?" she questioned with a surprising sound. Rather than say anything over the home, I do recall saying, "Can you come out into the lobby? There's something at the front desk for you."

It did not take much coaxing for her to come out. I will never forget the look on her face when she came around the corner and saw me standing there with Jimmie Archer. From the sound of her shriek that filled the quiet lobby for a few seconds with the sound of a trumpet, Carol ran to me in what seemed like in slow motion. I threw my arms around her waist and picked her up as high as I could, spinning in circles. Once we regained our composure, hellos were said, as were hugs and kisses, and Jimmie then decided to go for a walk on his own.

"Great time to check out the area," Jimmie said. "I'll be back later on."

"I can't believe you're here!" exclaimed Carol with pure excitement.

It was hard to believe that I decided to come to Florida and see her when she was babysitting her niece. The plan was when Carol was free during the day, and some late evenings, we would meet up and find fine things to do. Finding things to do was not the problem. Continuing, the secret of my presence was almost uncovered many times. Thank goodness, it was never discovered by her aunt or uncle. We had two fantastic days and nights. Walking the streets in Miami Beach along Collins Avenue was historic in today's times for many of us. We can look back and remember things that will never be forgotten. They were part of my memory bank that will live with me forever.

All good things must come to an end. This was another one of those times. Our funds were running low, and we were at the point where our return plane ticket was for Sunday afternoon. Do you recall a moment in your life when something sticks with you no matter what? This is one of those times.

"I'm having way too much fun to go home, Steve," exclaimed Jimmie.

It seemed that Jimmie was really enjoying the beach, the ocean, and the ladies. Thinking that he wanted to get back to reality was the farthest thing from his mind. "So what are you gonna do, stay longer with no money?" was my reply.

"Yup!" Jimmie shouted back. "In fact, I'm gonna call my mother and tell her where I am."

"You can't do that!" I shouted back to him as we walked along Collins Avenue.

"Oh yes, I can, and I will. I'll just tell her that I will never come home if she yells at me or doesn't wire me some money."

I stood silent for a moment, letting this all sink in before I said anything further. "Jimmie, you're nuts. She'll never go along with it. A few hours later, I said my goodbyes followed by a long kiss with girlfriend Carol. I remember telling her that I would see her in a few more days when she got home. As her eyes filled with tears, we said our farewells as she headed back inside the Colonial.

As the taxi pulled into the parking lot to pick me up, I looked back at Jimmie and said one last time, "You sure about this? You still have your plane ticket for today."

"Nah," said Jimmie with this great big smile on his face.

"I'm all good. I'll let you know what happens when I call my mother."

That was the end of it. I was on my way back to the Miami International Airport, flying home on Eastern Airlines from a quick weekend getaway I had no business doing.

As we were landing at Newark International Airport, Newark, New Jersey, it was quite noticeable that we were landing in the middle of a snowstorm. Seems that the heavier snow started falling within minutes of our arrival. I found my mother's GS in the short-term parking lot already covered with snow. Without gloves, and did my best to uncover the rear and front windows and made my way out of the parking lot. I knew this ride home was going to take a lot more time in the snow, but I had no choice; I had to get home now since my parents were due back home that evening from their Vermont getaway.

The road conditions on the New Jersey Turnpike and Parkway were passable but the conditions of them were getting worse. I thought to myself, I better not have any issues getting this car home in one piece. I knew from experience that when I exited off the Parkway at Exit 114, the road conditions would worsen since these roads were less traveled than the highways and interstates. Even though it took me some extra time to make my way to the house, I felt some ease come over me. I made it and no one knows anything. As I made the approach to our home, I saw that the coast was clear, no cars on the driveway. All is good. Making that right turn into our driveway and heading up the circular was as if I won first place somewhere. I was home in one piece with no incidents.

Driving up the circular portion of the drive, I noticed, further up on the right side, the front solid wooden door opening. As I came closer to the stopping and center point, the door did, in fact, open, and standing dead center on the other side of the fully encased glass door was none other than my father with his arms crossed and my mother to his left and brother to his right. Have you ever felt as though all the blood in your body has rushed out of your body, and every nerve throughout your body commences to shake uncontrollably?

"Oh no!" I said out loud as I brought the car to a stop.

No one is moving. Everyone in the doorway is standing perfectly still. I thought to myself for that moment, Hey I'm cool! I was in Freehold for the weekend. No worries from my end. I got out of the car with my partially glowing summer tan (in the middle of winter, right?) and came around the front of the car. The snow had stopped as if a lid was put on the sky in that minute. As I stood on the front side of the car, the glass door opened widely, and out came my father, followed by my mother and then my brother. At first, I thought this was just another family welcome home, but it was not that cut and dry.

"Hi, guys," I called out when we were all standing outside in the cold on this late Sunday afternoon.

"Where were you, Steven?" my father immediately called out to me in a very stern voice.

You see, anytime either of my parents referred to me as Steven, I was either already in trouble or headed that way. Again, I immediately thought I was good. Spent the weekend in Freehold, so there was nothing for me to worry about. Right? Wrong!

"I was staying with Alan Winik in Freehold," I replied. "We had a blast! Just hung out at his family's home." I tagged back.

Now my father had a great poker face, but if you were part of the family, you knew damn well what the "Wallach grin" was all about. Anything having to do with our immediate family, *if* by chance there was an untruth or an attempt to skirt the truth, this grin would appear on my father's face, and within the next few seconds, be prepared for his wrath. That expression many parents still use to this day.

"Before you answer me, know that I already know the truth."

Well, once again, I thought for a second, I hoped that my brother had my back on this.

"Freehold, New Jersey, is where I was," I said as I stood in front of them knowing my body was about to go into a shake mode.

I will never forget what happened next. Within a second of me saying Freehold, New Jersey, my father immediately looked right at me and said now in a much deeper and sterner voice, "Ya know, son, I've been all over the world and have visited most of our states in our homeland. And with all the times I've been there, I never knew there was a town named, Freehold, FLORIDA!" as his voice hit those high angry notes.

Next I knew, I was picking myself off the snow-filled driveway on the opposite side of the car. My father's contact with my jaw sent me flying over the hood of the car and into the snow. Lying there for a split second, I realized that I was just hit by my dad.

"Oh shit!" I yelled out as I started to regain my balance to stand up.

"YOU'RE GROUNDED! GET YOUR ASS UP TO YOUR BEDROOM! I'LL DEAL WITH YOU LATER!" were the words my father shouted out to me as I made my way past my mother and brother.

As I sat on my bedroom bed, I started to think, *How could my story get to this point?* After pondering this for only a few minutes, I realized one thing: my brother's college roommate, Don, was not downstairs when I came home. In fact, as I walked into the house foyer, I looked both in the formal living room on the left and the den on the right and saw no one except the dogs, who seemed to be taking their cover in the den as my father was yelling at me. Now I know what happened. It had to have been Don who said something. How else would they have known? Could my brother have been the one to tell my parents where I was? All I knew was that Don was nowhere to be found.

After the dust settled, there was a knock on my bedroom door.

"Come in'" I called out.

My brother opened the door and stepped inside. In a quiet voice, Chuck said, "Stevie, it wasn't me who said anything to Mom and Dad. It was Don."

I thought my head was going to fly off when I jerked it back to face my brother.

"What?" I called out.

"Yeah, I didn't even know until after the fact that he went and told on you," Chuck said.

It seems that Don was nothing more than what we called a stoolie. He ran and told on people looking to gain acceptance from his peers. Acceptance? What an asshole he was! The following morning, Don packed his suitcase and drove back to Charlotte, North Carolina, never saying goodbye to me. I wonder why. I never laid eyes on him again after that. Even when I accompanied my parents to my brother's college graduation, I was hoping to run into him. I am sure my brother gave him the heads up that I was coming and that it would be best (for him) if he was not in the same general area as we were. Smart move on my brother's part.

The general mood at my home for the next few months could only be described as walking on eggshells. Things between my father and I were not going well. I felt that no matter what I did or was planning to do, it was always taken negatively by my father. What I learned during this time was that the differences between my father and I stemmed all the way back to our Fair Lawn, New Jersey, days. Though stories told to me by my mother, relatives, and a few close family friends, I never knew (but I felt it) the separation between a father and son. As I looked back over those years, I realized that we had a problem among us. Stories would be told to me and later confirmed that my father had a stronger relationship with my older brother than me. If things went wrong and it involved both my brother and me, I would be the one who was either spanked or grounded, not by my mother but by my father. When I say some things, I am really saying most things. That is just how it was during these years. My brother was my father's favorite, and I was my mother's favorite. Our relatives saw this, as did our close neighbors. This carried through from Fair Lawn to Holmdel. Many years fell under this, and for many years, I suffered from this. Mind you, not to my knowledge, but as I aged, I came to realize this more and more.

This one occasion where I again was caught doing something wrong (in my father's eyes). As I came around the front of my car, a 1970 gold Plymouth station wagon, decked out with curtains running along the windows on the rear sides, a great sounding 8-track tape player with custom speakers and, of course, lights, I was again met by my father. I really do not remember what the actual problem was, but I know my father connected with another hit to my face and sent me back over the hood of this being the second car I flew over. The only difference this time was that my father came around the car and continued his efforts in hitting and screaming at me. For once, I decided not to allow myself to be beaten by this man. As skinny as I was, my defense training came into play. I had taken lessons from a friend of mine, Nathaniel K., a student attending the same high school, Croydon Hall Academy, who held a blackbelt seventh degree in a style known only in his country. Taishea was a hidden family style he taught me that had to do with pain and destruction of parts of the human bones. I learned from him for two years. Not only was he a great friend, but he was also my teacher of martial arts and taught me quite well. His training gave me the ability to use it toward my advantage for personal protection services years later.

As I was scrambling to regain my balance, I ended up now on top of my father. What was I going to do? Could I physically strike my father with a closed fist? Should I follow my training and strike him at his weakest point to defend myself from bodily harm?

Within seconds, I jumped off of him, landing above him, and on my feet, I screamed down to him, "You need to stop hitting me all of the time! I'm done with it! All you ever want to do is hit me!" I remember these words because, at that moment, my life took another turn, which I believe was one of the ingredients that made me who I am today. As I ran past my mother, heading toward the safe haven of my bedroom, I could hear my father yelling at my mother that I was her problem now. He was washing his hands with me.

Within twenty minutes of this father-son altercation, I looked out of my bedroom window and saw a Holmdel Township Police Car come up the circular driveway and stop. There stood Chief R. Bruce Phillips, a tall and well-built man with jet-black hair, came out from the car and was met by both my mother and father. With my bedroom window slightly open, I could hear my father telling the chief that he wanted me out of his house. He did not care if I was arrested or not, but he wanted me out of his house. It is important to understand that I was not the easiest child to raise. I never got into any serious law-breaking crimes growing up, but at times I should have thought things through and asked myself that same question that should be back in today's adolescence: What would my parents think of me doing this? As I heard his words, I could visibly see my mother's facial expression. Fear filled with tears running down her cheeks, Chief Phillips entered through the front door and called out my name. "Steve, it's Bruce Phillips. Can you come down here, please? I'd like to talk to you."

Knowing that the chief was there, I felt that it would be safe to meet him since I seriously doubted that my father would strike me in front of the chief of police. Once again, it is important to note that my father's reputation in our hometown of Holmdel received huge respect from mostly everyone who worked for Holmdel Township. My mother, being the head of the PTA, and my father's contributions to police department, first aid department, the road department, and stood and backed his favorite police chief. He never had any concerns about his requests not being met—by anyone in Holmdel.

"Steve, your father wants you outa the house," were the words said to me by Chief Phillips.

As I stood there in pause, I looked at my father for that one split second and then focused my eyes on my mother as I saw her tears continue to stream down her face.

"Steve, come over to my house and stay there for a while so we can see what's best," the chief said to me.

You have to remember that Holmdel was a very small town by population but had some of the largest and best crop fields and horse fields in New Jersey. The newer homes being built in Holmdel were highly priced homes.

"Go inside and get some of your things while I wait here for you," Phillips said still in a firm but gentle voice.

Within a few minutes, I had gathered what I felt I needed for a few nights, came back downstairs, kissed my mother on her cheek and said that I'd give her a call later and proceeded to get into my car. A car that I had to buy from my father a few months prior. But I did buy it and paid every penny for it.

Being sent to the Chief's home to temporarily stay was not a thing that happened in most towns in Anywhere, USA. Holmdel Police consisted of four related police officers. There was Chief Joseph Phillips, the father of R. Bruce Phillips, who started as a patrolman and worked his way up through the ranks to eventually become chief of police. Then there was Tom Durdack. Tom was married to Bruce's sister and, finally, Dominick Cavallaro, who was Bruce's first cousin. Headquarters was down a set of five concrete steps leading to an old solid wooden door that had been painted over a dozen times. Once inside, there was a room with a desk sitting on a makeshift riser where an officer would sit *if* there was someone extra on duty. To the right, there sat the one jail cell. *The Andy Griffith Show* had nothing on this police department. The one jail cell had its open no-top, one-piece aluminum toilet and sink combined and an old-looking sleeping cot. The only room was the chief's office, which was a room about ten-by-ten with an old wooden desk and an old wire-covered lamp with a thinly faded shade of green. The one thing I remember from the first time I visited (on my own) or because I had to drop off papers for my father was this outside-covered phone box used by telephone repairmen when they had to work on the phone lines. But the closer I looked, I saw that it was not meant for that at all. When you opened the door cover, inside was this good size arrowed toggle switch. The left was marked with a decal that read HTPD for Holmdel Township Police Department, and on the right side stood a bright yellow and blue decal that read MCTY, which stood for

Monmouth Country Dispatch. We were one step above Andy and Barney's Courthouse when it came to police communication. If there was no one at headquarters to answer the phone for an emergency or general call, they would do so in our absence. Throw that switch! Doing so would then send all calls directly to the County's Police Dispatcher who would handle the call.

So as you can tell thus far, my family and Chief Phillips's family were close. After spending the first night being spoken to by Chief Bruce, I was still shocked that my father tossed me out of the house. Never expected it. Come on, I never killed anyone or robbed anyone with a gun. This was way over the top, even for my father. By my third day at Phillip's "hideaway," I decided to begin my journey and head further south along the Jersey Shore to Brigantine, New Jersey. One of my old friends had moved there with his wife and children; however, his marriage fell short of just eight years when he was given custody of his two young boys and a dog named Heinz. The breed of this dog had a mixture of, you guessed it. Over four different breeds just from looking at her.

"There was no other name that would fit her," said one of the boys as they welcomed me into their home.

My plan was to get a job at Resorts Casino Hotel, located directly on the famous Boardwalk in Atlantic City, New Jersey. Resorts were still being built in the later part of 1978. Most of both buildings had been completed, as there were only a few floors still under construction for completion.

Jim's house had no air-conditioning. It was the middle of a Jersey summer heat where the temperature itself was in the nineties during the day with only a slight breeze, and the night's temperature concentrated on staying about eighty-nine degrees Fahrenheit. Every window was open, and every entry door was either propped open or secured, trying to catch any of the breeze that might head in its direction. They were kind enough to give me my own room. Well, it was actually the oldest boy's bedroom, but he and his younger brother preferred to sleep in the bunk beds that the youngest had in his room. So sleeping at night, well, let's just say it had its issues. It had major issues. The dog had free rein throughout the house. That

I had no problem with as our German shepherds ran freely in my parents' home as well. It was that Heinz liked to play outside in the marsh and come back in the house either covered by the wetlands or covered in these small little stickers that would have to be manually taken off. Heinz's favorite escapade was when she would race through the house after one of her swamp rat moves and see how many beds in how many bedrooms she could destroy in one sweep. Mind you, it was not that the beds in any of the rooms were made each morning with a bedspread and pillow ensemble. I know, in my room, all I had was the top sheet to spread across my bed. Done! I noticed at times during the night. I would wake up only to find a tick crawling on either my leg, or my arm, or even my back. The first few nights, I was like, okay…not a big deal. Pull them off and get some more tick spray in the morning.

After the third week of living there, still with no job and these kids running around the house as if there were ten of them, it was starting to wear on me. Now mind you, patience was never a forefront runner for me. I never caused a scene when my patience ran thin; however, I made it well known that IF whatever it is, is not handled shortly, I can assure you that I will scare the living shit out of you. Did not happen often, but when it did, it was remembered by all. What nailed the final brick was when I found about seven to ten ticks crawling all over me. Some were on both my legs, and some were in my hair on my head. But the two I found walking through my private area were too much to handle.

After I was done with my screams, I stood up and said in a loud and authoritative military-sounding voice, "What the fuck! I can't sleep like this anymore! Can you please keep the dog off my bed and out of my bedroom and the couch in the living room? I've found ticks there as well!" stunned, as the expression on my friends' faces.

He clearly looked over at me and said in a calming voice, "My dog can go anywhere she wants in the house, and that's how it is!"

As I stood there actually dumbfounded, he abruptly said to me now in a raised volume, "In fact, my dog can stay, but I want you out of my house now! Not tomorrow, but now!"

As I stood there, thinking of a quick game plan, I chose to stay in my car, which I just moved away from his house.

It was not comfortable that night. Even with that skinny camper's foam mattress, the night's air was damp and humid, typical for Jersey Shore marsh areas. I had to sleep with the windows all around open to allow for any breeze, but again, another still night; only mosquitos, flies, creek frogs, and the faint howling of dogs could be heard in the distance. But there was one thing for sure. I was not going to wake up with ticks on me!

By the second night, I was already starting to think of places to stay. I had to think really quick because that morning, I parked my car in a tow-away zone, and unfortunately, my car was towed to the Atlantic City Impound Lot. Since I was so short on money, there was no way for me to cover the costs of the tow and storage, so there sat my car in a secured parking lot nowhere near the Boardwalk, and me, walking the Boardwalk in Atlantic City.

I kept myself busy by walking throughout the entire resort complex. I looked at all the slot machines, the card tables, patrons sitting in the bars drinking and laughing, couples holding hands, and many people dressed in the resort's uniforms that clearly said security staff. I probably walked in the same areas at least five times. Each time, I would come across the same security officer. I would turn my head so as not to be recognized. Later that night, I had to find somewhere along the Boardwalk to sleep. It was a quick hit of reality. Here it was, a young man who came from a very well-respected family, and now I'm looking for a place to sleep on the damn boardwalk in Atlantic City. As I walked and kept my eyes peeled for something, anything that would be to my advantage, the mist turned into a light rain, but based on the clouds and the ocean's powerful waves, there were some downpours. Just as if it was tunnel vision, my eyes clearly locked directly on the white wooden lifeguard's rescue rowboat, which was carefully turned over in the sand midway up on the beach, nowhere near the tide's highest point. This, I know, was the policy for all lifeguard rescue rowboats along the beach coast. The inside of every lifeguard rowboat was fully protected against any inclement weather. *Okay, Steve*, I thought to myself. This may be the best place for me right now to get out of the rain and wind. Looking toward the left and right of the guard tower, there was no one in sight, so I made a quick dash to the right side of the boat. Since the boat had settled into the beach sand, the only way possible to get inside was to dig a portion of the sand away. Without any hesitation, I made a small hole, and underneath I went.

Granted, it was dark inside, but the protection of the weather was fantastic! Since the inside depth of the lifeboat was over three feet deep, it did not take me long to push some of the sand away, so I had a place to lie down. Looking back, I cannot even imagine that that was me back then. I came from a very well-established family and finished school, yet here I was, having to rest my head and body under a lifeboat on the beach in Atlantic City, New Jersey. If I could write about my experience with this, then it meant something very deep and special to me. I have always believed that you remember both good and bad times so all future encounters may be things that you have experienced and know what would be best. That first night of four nights was not what someone my age should experience, yet I did.

If I was awake and out of the rowboat by six o'clock in the morning, my cover would be solid. You would always find a few joggers running the tide line each morning. Of course, on any clear day, usually by seven-thirty, people would start arriving to make their secure spot on the beach for the day. The only difference was that this was not during the summer. The New Jersey Fall Season has already started, with temperatures dipping well below the summertime months, and the rains were more frequent. I knew that my new "residence" was well-protected since lifeguards were no longer in the towers. Summertime fun on the beach has come and gone.

I ran into an old friend from up north, who turned me onto a bookie.

"Hey, Stevo, maybe you can be one of his runners while you're in AC," I will never forget him saying to me.

So I did what I had to do. I started running numbers for the guy. Even continued doing it when I left Atlantic City. It was always something new. Most times, it was easy, but then when you are asked to collect, it becomes a bit more involved. The one and only time I borrowed from a bookie is the one and only time I ever did it. I fell short of repaying my debt and saw how quickly it could add up.

I tried to make the best out of what I had. Every few days, I would telephone my mother to keep in contact during this time in my life of despair. I had to call midday as I knew my father would not be home and we would not be able to speak freely. My mother was my savior. At least once a week, I was able to go to the Western Union to pick up money that my mother would send me. It was not a lot of money, maybe $25 or $40, but it was enough for me to eat and do some laundry.

I can still hear my mother's words, "Steve, I wish I could do more, but if your father found out." Her voice would break apart and I could tell she was holding back from crying.

I remember that two days after finding my rowboat shelter, the weather worsened. The rain was now falling almost sideways, and the winds became like the sound of howling dogs. Returning to my lifeboat by the sea, I found most of my belongings dry but knew that it was only a matter of time where the tides would rush in. The sand became soaked, which led to the runoff seeping under the lifeboat. What to do was my initial thought. I knew I had to go somewhere to get me out of this horrible weather. As I made my way back onto the boardwalk, I used a plastic garbage bag to cover my head and shoulders as the rain continued to pour down. As my eyes wandered from side to side, trying to seek out another location, directly in front of me stood the resorts hotel and casino. With its flashing red and yellow lights showing off welcome signs of enjoyment, I made my way through the double glass doors to the inside of the casino. As I pulled off my homemade rain cover, I began my search for another idea as to where I could possibly spend the night.

I remember exploring resorts hotel and casino. From the largest casino floor in Atlantic City, I knew where most of the doors led to.

There's nowhere I can think of where I could find a room, I thought to myself. There are so many people, casino staff and security staff throughout the entire area. Twenty-three hours a day, this casino was open, so trying to find somewhere was virtually impossible. As I stood looking lost, a little bell went off behind me. As I turned to see where it came from, the elevator door opened as if it was sent for me.

With no other people looking to take a ride up, I stepped inside and watched how the door quietly closed. For a brief second, I was confused as to which floor I should request. Eight looked like a good floor to push, so eight it was. Within seconds, as the elevator slowly and quietly made its stop on the eighth floor, I simply stuck my head out to see if there was anything that would warrant me to step off. From looking to the left first and then to the right, it had the look and decor of any typical long hotel room hallway.

"Next!" I called out, knowing that no one would hear me. I decided to go higher, so fourteen looked like a good number. As the floor button lit up again, *swish*! That elevator took no time to deliver me to my next desired floor.

As the elevator door opened, my sight immediately aimed at the notice taped on the wall. Apparently, this floor was still under construction by the signs of construction materials and unfinished walls and ceilings in the main area. The floor looks like it was being constructed to have conferences and seminars, since the configuration did not resemble sleeping rooms. My luck brought me to an area located on the left side before the entrance to this extra-large conference room. Oh, I thought for a minute. It seems this is going to be a future coat-check room. The layout was simple. There was a door that went inside to a long (what appeared to be) narrow walkway. There even was an open area next to the door, which would allow staff to take coats and check them in. I thought this would be a great place to stay at night. Warm, dry, and somewhat out of the way. Mostly, every place on this floor was still under construction, and with the stoppage of work here for unknown reasons, I knew the area would not be open to daily traffic.

As I made my way into the coatroom, there were a few chairs and folded small tables piled high up against the wall. As I made my way further inside, I could see that there was an area that was fully protected and hidden. Looks as though it was being designed for filing cabinets or a desk of some sort. So I decided to rebuild the stacked chairs and tables by stacking the chairs and tables in a more suitable area for my needs. The small items I had been carrying, I chose to leave behind, and in my newly established residence. This would be the test to see if this area was being ignored for whatever reason. I checked the doors for the eighth and seventh floors to make sure I would still be able to get inside. I had no idea if this floor would be locked off for no access. Just as if I were living in a high-rise apartment building, I pushed the elevator button and patiently waited for the lift.

"Going down?" I said to the couple already inside.

With a smile and a quick nod, the lady replied, "Yes, we are."

The couple chuckled for a moment. As I made my way inside the lift, I could not help but let out a very faint snicker as my reply.

It is simply amazing how much information one can gather from others inside a talkative elevator ride. This couple had been guests of the casino and were now leaving to fly to Las Vegas, Nevada. Once again, luck was on my side. As I bid them both safe travels and enjoy Vegas, the gentleman leaned over to me, and with an extended hand, he firmly grabbed my hand and said, "Here. Go enjoy yourself for a few days."

As he let go of my hand, which now felt as though it went through a vice grip, I found four complimentary dinners and lunches for some of the finest restaurants in resorts. By the time I realized what he gave me, they were inside this limo stretch and on their way.

The next few days were great. I was sleeping in my own suite, away from everyone, and had been eating fantastic food for both my lunches and dinners. Thank goodness, I had a few changes of clothes with me. You know, I did not want people to think I was a "boardwalker" and had nothing going for me. But again, I guess that was what I had become.

On the third night in my private room, I was exhausted, so I remember turning in roughly around nine o'clock in the evening. Immediately falling asleep, I was awakened by the sound of furniture being moved in front of me. I knew if I turned and put my back toward the person, hopefully, they would not see me. As I could see the shadow of a man looking inside, all I could do was start thinking of what I was going to say to him. It was obvious what I was doing there. I just did not want to be caught. As his two-way radio was sending him a call, he immediately left with a "ten-four central" and walked away. A few seconds later, the ding of the elevator went off, and he, too, was gone. I ended up staying in this room for another three weeks without anyone ever noticing me. It seemed construction on this floor was completely stopped, with no signs of a restart date. I was not proud, but I had to do what was best for me at that moment. I remember living there for about twelve days.

It was a few weeks later that my mother talked my father into allowing me to come back to their house. It was not important as to how she did that, but the bottom line, I was able to make headway with my father. My mother wired me the funds to get my car out of the city's compound lot, which I immediately did. I began to feel somewhat relieved. As I first sat down inside my car. It would have been too long without it. I was able to plan what I was going to do on my two-hour drive from Atlantic City to Holmdel.

After the first few days at home, my mother started receiving a telephone call every two days: someone looking for me. They would never leave their name but always ended the call with, "Let Steve know it's his friend from Atlantic City. He needs to call me really quick." On one of these calls, I was outside at the pool when my mother received another call. This time, I knew who it was and started pacing the pool deck in complete disarray.

"Don't tell him I'm here," I said.

My mother was the cool one most of the time, and this one time, she was fantastic!

"Oh, I'm sorry. Steve is not here, but as soon as I see him, I will have him call you. Are you sure you don't want to give me your name? Steve might respond quicker."

There was a pause, and then I heard my mother say, "Thank you, Angelo. I will have him call as soon as I see or hear from him."

Once she hung up the phone, she immediately turned to me and said (I will never forget it), "Steven, what the fuck is going on? You owe this man money or what?"

Without missing a beat, I looked at her and said, "Mom, when I was in AC, I needed money, so he covered me. I just haven't paid him back yet."

"So how much do you owe him?" she angrily asked. "Right now, it's about thirty-two hundred dollars."

Without saying another word, she picked up the phone, and all I could hear was her side of the conversation. It consisted of numbers, and a few yesses and my name. When she hung up the phone, she said in her stern voice, "Get in your car and go down to my bank. They're expecting you."

"I replied, "Okay, but what am I going for?"

"You're going to get cash to pay this bookie off," she said, "and then you're going to promise me that *if* this shit happens again, you're on your own."

My mother, once again, got me out of a situation that could have turned ugly for me. Oh, and to date, I have never asked a bookie for a penny.

No one could negotiate a deal better than my father. Hands down. I have heard about and have personally witnessed how he works with some of his negotiations. It was like a play, performing before my own eyes. As to this writing, I cannot help but smile at the memories of him doing this.

"It is so important that you focus on what you're trying to succeed at," I can still hear my father say to me. "Focus, mark your mark, and follow through."

These were the words of my father. Now I did not agree with him on everything. There were times when we bumped heads (not literally of course), both of us set in our own ideas to ever think about a change. There were times when we each apologized to each other, and that was what made our talks exciting. Again, I truly believe I was taught by my father (and of course, my mother as well), and I have made some very good decisions. Of course, as with anyone, you are faced with situations that could very well affect your business, so as with any sole owner of a business, you will do just about anything to protect it.

At first, they were just telephone calls to my father. To get to my father, you had to go through a person who had a voice so chipper that each time you called, her responses sounded as if she was singing to you. But bottom line, it was this angelic voice that would decide if you spoke with my father or not. For months, I didn't know where this easy-listening voice came from. What she tall or short? Did she have short or long hair? Hmmm, I wonder what color her hair is. Sure, as any young man would do, I pictured this woman to have a body that would just make any man fall to his knees. Were her breasts petite, or were they voluptuous? Eyes…what color were her eyes? It really did not matter. I wanted to see the body that went with this penetrating voice.

I remember the day when I had the opportunity to visit my father at his office. If I recall, I volunteered to bring some business papers to him that he left behind at home that morning, giving me my first chance of an introduction to "the voice." To this day, I can still picture myself walking toward the end of the corridor where my father's office was. As I came toward the desk of "the voice" it was as if everything turned into slow motion. Just like in the movies, seeing her for the first time sent chills down my spine. The look of me portraying a warden-like surface, when I first entered an area I was not familiar with, I felt myself just melt in my tracks.

"Hello," she said as she raised her head up from what she was doing. "May I help you with anything?"

What felt like an hour was just a millisecond as I leaned forward with a smile on my face and replied, "Hi. You must be Susan, my father's private secretary. I'm Steve. Steve Wallach here to see my father."

As we shared a smile, it was the first time I ever had such a feeling come over me of excitement with this adrenaline rush. Never once showed my emotions on the outside, but I can, to this day, remember just what that feeling was like. What was to be, I thought to myself.

Here sat Susan Jane Lanning, staring up at me. She stood up to greet me, it was so obvious that this lady had the body of a model. From her long-chiseled legs up to her incredible face, Susan was, at that time to me, the most beautiful lady I had ever seen. As she extended her hand to me, I could not help but feel the softness of her skin as she grasped my hand as if she were extended pure satin.

"Well, hello," was my response in the sexiest, soft-spoken, deep-toned voice I could come up with.

"Your father is expecting you, Steve," she said as she led me into his office. "It was very nice meeting you, Steve," she said to me as she turned and walked away.

As I returned my compliment to her, I felt the muscles in my face pull as I gave her the biggest smile I had ever had. My eyes followed her out of the office. As she turned to make her final exit, she looked back, and our eyes met, sealing our first encounter.

"Don't even think about it!" were the words that filled the office. As I turned back to my father, I could see on his face that his 'not gonna happen' expression was full-on.

"She's off-limits!" my father said with a traditional smirk on his face. This smirk became my dad's trademark to mean quite simply, "You are starting to piss me off, and this is just to let you know it's not sitting well with me." Basically, in layman's terms, not a good idea.

One thing led to another. Susan and I did, in fact, get together and kept it a secret from my father for almost six months. Her family knew, and my mother knew. Finding the best time to tell my father that I'm having a love affair with his secretary, and we love each other. Well, that day came fast. We had to face my father. We both knew my father would never object to us being together. What was his concern was that it now mixed business with personal, and this would have my dad placed in a precarious situation. It did for the first few months. You see, when my father came home from work, he was a different man at home. Yes, it was still a strict upbringing, but for him to feel that he had to be in "boss mode" even in his own homemade things difficult.

Now in a six-month relationship with the boss's secretary, people were seeing this was getting serious. Under the circumstances, Susan felt as awkward, so the best advice was for her to resign and take another job at a completely different company; one that was not associated with my father. Six months later, we were married in front of approximately 150 family and friends. We spent our honeymoon on a cruise aboard Home Lines' *Oceanic*. Sailing from New York just as my parents had done, I felt so proud of where I was in life. Always remember that Atlantic City lifeboat.

Almost everywhere I would go, I would come across a piano. Sometimes in a storefront or in a common space inside a shopping mall, a school, or anywhere. If I saw a piano, I wanted to play it. I was fortunate enough to come across a piano aboard our honeymoon cruise. I knew that was a way to show my affection, as what woman would not want to hear romantic music performed just for her? My father told me many years ago.

He said, "Son, when choosing an instrument to play, it's always best to go with the piano.

I clearly recall asking him why. His reply even to this day, some sixty plus years later, is quite simple, "Most of the homes you will enter to pick up your date, have a piano. There is nothing better than impressing anyone [parents included] tickling the ivories. What would you do? Ask them if they had a saxophone?"

As I sat down and began to play, I did not realize that a small crowd had begun forming. As the crowd became larger, I sat longer and continued to play. Hearing the applause after each song only made me feel that much better. Seeing the expression on my wife's face said just what any young married man would want to feel. It is going to be a great afternoon, and looking forward to getting ready for dinner! As I finished playing after close to thirty minutes, a man approached me and commended me on my playing and passed on the name of the booking agency that booked all the entertainment for Home Lines.

"Anytime you want a job on a cruise ship, use my name and call this company when you get off this cruise," sputtered from the cruise director, Eddie Dawson.

I said thank you, and we continued on our way enjoying all this wonderful ship had to offer.

Married life was great…at first. Sure, we did what every newlywed couple does. We moved into a beautiful apartment. We played house, received a rescued Afghan puppy, went food shopping together, and had a wonderful marriage. We enjoyed spending our time together.

It is hard to pinpoint what just went wrong in our marriage. We can use the excuse that we grew apart, but only being married for less than three years, I can look back now and easily say that our young ages played a major part in the breakup. We were both only twenty-one. Energetic with a large amount of testosterone, we both made mistakes from the start. It would not be fair nor truthful not to say that we both shared our breakup. Maybe me a little more, but no matter how we each felt, it was best to divorce and go our separate ways. Did it hurt? I would have to honestly say at first, no, it did not. But as time moved on, within the third month, I started to feel ashamed that I could not make this marriage stay together. Years went by before we spoke with each other. To be exact, thirty years went by before Susan would accept my messages or texts. I had been trying to reach out to her for years, but to no avail. The power of laptops and cell phones has come a long way. It was for no special reason except to say hello and say what you have been up to for the past thirty years, and I was sorry if I brought her pain and sorrow from our divorce.

During my marriage to Susan, I chose to go into criminal justice. After attending the Police Academy for the Port Authority of New York and New Jersey Police, I graduated with the rank of police officer—a position I held with the highest respect. I asked my grandmother (father's side) if she would come to my graduation in a few days. You see, my grandmother was the final matriarch on my father's side. Therefore, her acceptance of me was important.

Immediately, she said, "No!" Now it is important to note that her tone meant she was not happy with my question.

"You should have become a cobbler," were the words repeated twice as she looked away from me.

Officer Steven Wallach, Port Authority NY/NJ Police

"Nanny," I said, "I don't want to be a cobbler. I'm going to be a police officer and you should be proud for me."

"No!" my grandmother abruptly said back to me. "I do not want to see you in a uniform. If you don't want to be a doctor, then you should be a cobbler. They will never not be needed. Everyone needs good shoes on their feet!"

How can I rebut knowing that no matter what I said, she was not going to join my parents and brother during my graduation ceremony? As we walked out of the door, I could hear my grandmother say, "Good luck, and I love you." That was all I needed to hear. Her approval was secretly in her words, and that let me know that it may not be what she wanted me to become, but I still gained her respect and approval.

I thought I was going to be the one to change the world when I became a police officer for the Port Authority of New York and New Jersey. Dealing with the airports in both states, the tunnels and bridges that connected New Jersey and New York, and all three commercial airports like Kennedy Airport and the infamous Port Authority Bus Terminal, never made my job boring. Being a cop in these areas had its calm and daily duties, but there were many times that your authority would be put to the test. Maybe it was saving a life or taking a life, but decisions had to be made in a split second. What we, as police officers, had back then, unfortunately, is forgotten nor appreciated in today's times. All the hardworking people, children, and elderly had one thing in common when it came to the police: respect. It is so unfortunate that this was not only lost but has been taken away from the men and women of law enforcement.

Working the midnight shift at the New York Bus Terminal was never a dull moment. Millions of people pass through the New York Bus Terminal yearly. It is one of the major transportation hubs in North America. Those who chose to call the bus terminal their home were known as skells. These were the people that used the bus terminal to live in, whether on a bench, the floor of an enclosed telephone booth steps leading down to the bowels of the exhaust-filled parking spots where the busses would be lined up waiting to take thousands of patrons away from this city, or any corner they could call their own. I saw every type of skells there was. Some were covered in filth, showing signs that they had been on the streets for a very long time. Others were wrapped in clothes that were obviously taken from trash receptacles. Some were even barefooted, showing signs of skin diseases. Many showed signs of mental illness as well, but there was nothing we could do except round them up and put them outside of the terminal in any weather conditions. Helping those with medical issues was never at the forefront. As many skells were picked up every night, there was twice the amount find a place inside the New York Bus Terminal (BT).

Police officers working the BT, as it was referred to within the department, had to put up with a lot of situations of loitering. There was one officer whom I was assigned to use his baton to wake those skells who were sleeping or blocking clear passages on the stairwells. No matter how kind you were, some of them would turn to spitting at you or wanting to fight you if you approached them in a mild manner. We used to play foot-golf. When the ones that refused to wake up and leave, they would be hit on the bottom of their feet with our batons as they slept and ignored our calls to leave the BT. Imagine being hit on the bottom of your feet by a full-swing police baton as if you were teeing off. They would jump up so fast out of pain and shock, but we had no alternative. We never wanted to touch them as they were covered with the stains and smell of urine, and so many were covered in body soars that we felt that our safety was in jeopardy. But we did keep the BT fairly clean of skells and those looking to cause harm to others or even themselves. Public and safety were the two words that meant something back then. It may not have been the most proper way to get their attention, but you have to remember, this was the New York Bus Terminal, and for health and safety, we did what we were instructed to do. Keeping ourselves from harms was either physically or for health reasons.

I was assigned to various areas throughout New York, Long Island, and New Jersey that were manned and operated by the Port Authority Police. Years ago, being assigned to posts at major airports like JFK, LaGuardia, and Newark, or tunnels and bridges like George Washington Bridge, Holland, and Lincoln Tunnels. The assignments at the airports far outweighed any posts at these other locales. At least at the airport, you were assigned to a sector car or had an easy post at each of the satellite terminals, supervising the checkpoints.

A post I will never forget was being assigned to the World Trade Center, Lower Manhattan, during its lengthy construction. I recall being assigned to the 110th floor. Coming off the service elevator into an area that was still very much under construction, all I had was a chair that had seen better days and construction lights hanging from the steel bars that aligned the entire floor area. On windy days, you could hear the sound of the wind as it rushed through the walls and windows that were not nearly completed. Without the wind, you could hear a pin drop late at night. Nothing was moving at three o'clock in the morning, so the night shift did go slow, but you made the best out of it. Surrounding this torn-up old chair were magazines scattered on the floor, so there was always something to read. *Sports Illustrated*, *Playboy*, hard-core porn, and old newspapers made the time go faster. Some of us took advantage of being able to go outside of the towers. The most incredible views you could ever imagine. You could see well into New Jersey, Long Island, Staten Island, and all five Burroughs. The views were breathtaking. The memories I have of standing on the "Top of the World" is something that I will cherish for the rest of my life. Here was a landmark taken away from the American people and that of the world by a group of hateful and despicable people still trying to destroy the free world. I will never forget the feeling when standing at the highest spot in all of New York, yelling at the top of my voice, "I'M KING OF THE WORLD, MOM!"

Her name was Ingrid, and she came from Sweden. She lived in the same apartment complex as I in Avenel, New Jersey. Once married to a friend of mine, their divorce was short and sweet. Her ex was an entertainer whom I had the pleasure of working with at various times. Ingrid and I would get together for drinks and would sometimes go out for dinner. On many evening talks, we would always come back to our exes and wonder about the what-ifs and the why-nots of our marriages. On one occasion, we decided to drive back into New York City and go to Windows of the World for dinner. This five-star restaurant sat on the top floor of one of the towers and had the most spectacular views of any restaurant anywhere in the world. The maître d' was a dear friend of mine, so I knew our service would be impeccable, and the final bill was heavily discounted. Sitting there dining on filet and lobster, drinking some incredible wines from their thousand bottle wine cellars, helped set the mood for where I was hoping to take this. After dinner, I asked Ingrid if she'd like to take a walk and see the most spectacular views ever seen before.

"What can be more spectacular than this view?" Ingrid asked in her Swedish accent shared by a smile.

"We're not on the top of the world yet," I said, "not yet," as I pulled out her chair out.

Arm and arm, we left this wonderful restaurant heading toward the elevator. As the elevator door opened and we made our way inside, I remember pressing the top floor button as I leaned over and gave her our first kiss. Hoping I would know what police officer would be sitting when the elevator door opened, I had already set the mood for possibly a new and exciting encounter and chapter. Thankfully, I knew the officer working on the top floor, so the clearance was a sure thing. Making a quick informal introduction, we then made our way to a door that was marked in bright red: "Caution! Hold Door When Opening." There was another sign on the door that read, "Welcome to the Top of the World!" To describe the view can only be said in one word: spectacular! Every person having the privilege to see this firsthand will remember it forever.

Ingrid and I both had an expression on our faces just like that wise saying, the cat who ate the mouse. As I held the door firmly and opened it, it led outside to a sky filled with the brightest of stars as if we could reach up and grab them. The sky was a fantastic deep blue, the stars were shining bright, and we each had a glass of wine in our hands, and that is all it took as if it was a movie featuring a man and woman throwing their arms up and embracing each other followed by a passionate kiss surrounded by a deep blue sky and stars that filled the sky. Let me just say that the remainder of the evening, until we were able to see a sparkle of the sun piercing over the horizon, was fantastic. We spent hours under that sky, making love to each other and wishing things were different back home. It was truly an amazing evening. As the sun began to rise over the horizon, we made sure our clothes were properly attired as it was time for us to leave the top of the World Trade Center and make our way back to the car for that drive back to New Jersey, filled with memories that will last (at least me) a lifetime. Knowing me, I could not resist. As I was about to step through the construction door, I looked up at the sky and yelled, "I came on top of the world!" as if I were James Cagney all over again.

During my time as a police officer for the Port Authority of New York and New Jersey, I was assigned to numerous locations. Without a permanent assignment, all police officers were placed in what was referred to as the PA Pool, and you were assigned based on the facility that needed the manpower. Sometimes, we would not know where to report until six hours before duty. My last assignment was for the Holland Tunnel—one of the worst facilities to deal with. Thousands of vehicles and trucks would cross through the toll bridges daily, leaving the exhaust of pure filth. So many of us were assigned posts that we could not help but breathe the fumes in. To this day, these posts are still manned by a police officer and officers are still getting sick from the carbon monoxide. My final year came quickly. In fact, it came without me knowing it was coming. This was an immediate decision made solely by me. All I know, after I left for what was called injury on duty, I wanted to pursue my next adventure. I wanted to pursue my work on a luxurious cruise ship as an entertainer. Why not? I played a great piano, and my voice was still able to punch out song after song after song. I never thought that the decision to resign would be forced on me for an injury on duty. Still, I was not planning my exit as a police officer quite yet.

From time to time, I would sit and look at the photos of my honeymoon cruise. Not for any reason, but it brought happiness at the same time bringing me the sadness of a failed marriage. I found myself coming home from my shift, and without even changing out of my uniform, I would pull out the photos I still had in my possession just to look at. Sentimental, sure, but it gave me more of an education than I had ever thought.

This one time, when I pulled out the photo album, that handwritten note by Eddie Dawson, cruise director of the *Oceanic*, fell out. Facing toward me, I reached down and picked it up only to read what was written on it: Branson Entertainment, Broadway, New York, owner: Efrem Abrahmson. Ask for John. It had the phone number listed as well, but that was over forty years ago! Knowing that I would be working the BT for the next coming shift, I decided to act. I made an appointment for the following week with both John and Efrem to audition as a solo piano player or band musician. Like it was yesterday, I can still picture myself parking my patrol car directly in front of the building on Broadway, flashers on, and calling out for lunch break. As I entered the building in full police uniform, I said my hellos to others, and I made my way into the elevator and up to the floor of what I had hoped to be a very successful audition.

The face of the receptionist was priceless.

When asked why I was there, I replied, "I had an audition appointment."

Her look of confusion said it all. Over the intercom, I could hear her tell Mr. A, "Mr. A, there's a mister, um, police officer named Steve Wallach who says he has an appointment with you."

With her expression going from puzzlement to a grin, she hung up and said, "Officer, they're waiting to see you now. Please go ahead."

As I walked into this room, a room surrounded by glass windows on two sides, one could not help by admire the view from such a high level.

"Mr. Abrahmson, hello. My name is Steve Wallach. I'm here to audition for a piano-playing position with Home Lines. As the room went silent, I knew I had to do something to break the ice. I saw this upright piano in his office, so I made my way over to it, sat down, and started to play song after song for the next few minutes. As I hit that last note, you could hear a pin drop in the room for the next few seconds.

"Wow!" is what was blurted out from both John and Efrem. That's all it took: a position as a piano player was offered to me, and I jumped at the opportunity. The ships for Home Lines now stood out in my mind. "*Oceanic* and *Doric*, here I come!" My plan was going into effect. I had in my mind that being an entertainer aboard the ship gave me an advantage in applying for a position on the cruise staff. In time, I moved from being a lounge piano player to the assistant cruise director under who else but my new friend, Eddie Dawson.

My first contract was on the *Doric*, making weekly cruises from New York to Bermuda during the spring and summer months. It was one of the best times I can ever recall from my past times aboard cruise ships. Met some wonderful people that, to this day, I keep in contact with, while others unfortunately passed on. Social media outlets have made it much easier to contact so many, somewhere in the world.

My only dilemma prior to signing with Bramson Entertainment was where did I plan on finding the time to work on a cruise ship and continue with my duties as a police officer. It was quite easy. As a Port Authority New York and New Jersey police officer, we were given two options for our overtime pay. First being paid for the overtime and second placing the hours earned in what was called a comp bank, enabling officers to continuously add hours to their bank and then using those hours to take time off. I always preferred the latter because I would use my comp time to time off where I would then go over to the cruise lines to work. I made more money with my time on the ships than I would have by taking the hours saved in pay.

Times on cruise ships back in the '70s and '80s were far different from what they are today. Back then, the ship's administration ran the ships while the corporate offices ran the company from marketing to reservations. In those early years, working aboard gave those in a position to make great money. Once you made it to the senior cruise staff level, most cruise directors would always offer extra money made from onboard games and activities with their staff. Remember, I said most of the cruise directors. As in any business where cash is made readily available, there were people like Eddie Dawson, Frank Dorman, Ray Rouse, Allan King, Adam Weir, Ralph Michelle, and a few others who knew that the monies taken in were from the actions of their cruise staff. Why should they not be given something to show their appreciation? Then you had cruise directors like Everett E. Everett and Stanley Kane, who would make it a point to let you know how much money they made for that cruise, but for you, nothing. Those were the cruise directors who eventually ended up with no ship when some of these companies closed and/or had issues with their own staff. Do not get me wrong, EEE was truly one of the greatest cruise directors back then. His problem was he was extremely cheap to his staff.

"Be thankful you're working on a cruise ship," EEE would tell us. "The free cruise is rewarding in itself."

Did he really expect us to buy his reasoning?

Working on board ships back in the late '60s and throughout the '70s and '80s was far different from what cruising has become. Years ago, the clientele was different. Most of the passenger guests were upper-middle to first-class economically. The cost of taking cruises was by far more expensive than attending a beach resort along the eastern coastline. You would see women boarding the ships dressed to the max, with furs and jewels, while the men portrayed themselves in the stylist fashions trending at that time. Remember, years back, cruise ships were designated either First or Tourist Class. As more ships came into the market, the prices reflected a strong competition among those cruise lines marketing for first place. Nonetheless, cruising during my employment time was an entirely different place to vacation. To be served by waiters carrying silver trays filled with some of the most incredible cuisine found in even the best hotels, entertainment, and production shows, and always seeing the ship's officer's dressed in their tightly starched uniforms made every cruise even that much more a memory of greatness for me. I can still see myself sitting in one of the forward lounges, waiting patiently to finally be cleared by US customs. Staff and crew could not wait to get off the ship while in home port. It was our only time off, and we spent it either shopping, doing laundry, or visiting family and friends. I was fortunate enough to have my parents come into the city every other Saturday to pick me up to spend the day with. No matter what we would do, it was always something that I looked forward to.

So are the rumors all true about working and living on a cruise ship? Well, it depends on who you ask. For me, I loved it! Meeting new people from all walks of life and we did have quite a mix of people. Were there single people on board? Absolutely! Whether they were traveling as a group or even with their parents, there was never a shortage of energetic young people looking to experiment and/or find that special someone. From mingling during the day out by the pool or meeting up during the evening in their dressed-to-kill outfits, people were always 'hooking' up while on the cruise. And why not? If we (cruise staff) played low-key while working on board, the after-hours and the island nightlife left little to the imagination when meeting up with a guest. It was clearly stated in crew contracts that there was no mingling with the passengers, but that did not have to do with the cruise staff or officers. It was our job to mingle and make each guest feel at home. We did! It became a game of strikes for many of us. How many ladies did you bed down this week? It was as if we were living life to its fullest. Studio 54 and Forty Thieves were true examples of how the sex games played into so much. People just carried themselves in so many fashions.

The first night of every cruise was like a market of women on display. Every senior officer would be out mingling among the guests, trying to mark which ones they would plan on approaching. It was like a game. If an officer had his eyes set on one, other officers and cruise staff would go after the same guest. It was like the best man gets the gift. That could either go two ways: one being best for the suitor or the officer losing out but making the life of "another" difficult. Human nature in the beast I would guess. And yes, it came out often—every seven days.

The travel talks aboard the ships were handled by the Cruise Directors. There was no outside company onboard back then. The stores throughout the islands were secured by the cruise directors. The deals made with every store varied and they, too, were set by the cruise directors. I found that this could virtually be some serious cash money, but it would have to be set up without shoreside knowing. This was quite an easy task. The corporate side shoreside never really knew what the cash potential was from island shops, so they left this up to the cruise directors. For example, I had five stores per island stop that I would promote in my daily travel port talks with the passengers while cruising to each island. Every cruise itinerary stopped at four ports, enabling me to have twenty stores per cruise. Without going into a financial breakdown, cruise directors were making large amounts of money. We had a fantastic thing going on when it came to having avenues to make expected earnings. These earnings were not acquired in the United States nor were we paid within the boundaries of the US. For years, this was the way most cruise directors made their side small fortunes.

We also had the onboard games that consisted of the famous horse racing! There were various games with horse racing, one being the roll of six dice in a handheld wired container with miniature horse figures all lined up on a painted canvas rolled out on the pool deck as the passengers would place their wages. The money cage was manned by someone from the casino staff, but the proceeds were controlled solely by the cruise director. In fact, the bidding to "own" one of the horses could cost as much as $500 to $1,500. It all depended on how much money the passengers were willing to spend on a wooden handmade horse. The passengers would bid against each other to own the rights to call the horse their own and to decorate the horse in any manner and receive a percentage of the bidding cost if it wins. The rules were that your horse had to be with you every minute you were away from your cabin, thus, meaning that no matter where you were on the ship, the horse had to be with you. The more outrageous the horses were decorated, the more attention they would get from all the other guests. Usually, on every cruise, one of the horses would be 'kidnapped' and held for ransom by another player's team member. One would be amazed at the amount some people would pay to get their horse back. A kidnapped horse means the horse would be out of the race, and all money spent to buy it would be lost. I can only think of a few times in years this happened. People were there for great times, no matter what the cost was.

Then there was bingo. A cruise ship's number one favorite! The amount of money passengers would spend on bingo cards was unbelievable. The true bingo players would purchase ten cards to play at the same time. These were the people you pretty much stayed away from during the game. We had little-known sayings for some of the numbers we would call. "B4! 'Before' you have bingo, you must have B4," you could hear myself call out to the crowd. Their passion was sometimes worn on their very short sleeves. Cruise directors always made money from these games. It was part of the job. Bingo is still played on every cruise ship today. It will always be a true moneymaker, but now more so for the shoreside than when I was a cruise director.

I will never forget that final sea day when we had the famous White Elephant Sale! This was a chance for all passengers who purchased items throughout the islands to get rid of them so they did not have to carry them home. This was fantastic! We had passengers bringing us items that they had no idea as to why they purchased in the first place. From clothes to swimwear, from little island trinkets to handmade carved-out bowls, necklaces with a fish tooth to monkeys playing the drum, there were so many items on each cruise that made their way to another's home.

I guess that's where the saying, "One person's trash is another person's treasure."

But again, the cruise directors always included the chief purser and another superior officers in the split. That was not uncommon back in the sixties through eighties. It ran smoothly until corporate found out about it and decided that not only did they want in on the action, but they wanted the entire agreement made between the Island shops and them, pushing out the middleman, the cruise director. I will never forget when word came out that Stanley Kayne, who worked his way up from comedian to cruise director to executive corporate cruise director, was the one who ran to the Home Lines' Office thinking he would be seen as the proud one for turning this financial adventure over to them. All it did was make him turn out to be a backstabber who lost out once Homes Lines closed their operation. Served him right for wanting to cut out the cruise staff and officers. He was a great comedian, but as the head cruise director, he ended up with a less-than-a-proud reputation in my eyes and many others.

I spent many years on the high seas as a musician, entertainer, cruise staff and even cruise director over the next number of years. After Home Lines, I was fortunate enough to find myself with Holland America Lines. Truly an older crowd, even back in the seventies, Holland America Lines was known as your grandparents' cruise line. I decided to leave the New York Ports and make my way down to Miami, Florida, where I first experienced Carnival Cruise Lines. I was fortunate to land a gig aboard the Carnival Cruise Lines' *Mardi Gras*, the first of many ships to sail under the carnival logo. Only after a few weeks, I was transferred to their new and exciting ship, TSS *Carnival*, a larger ship for that time frame but still with the same basics as we had on Home Lines.

My introduction was brief since I was already familiar with *Carnival*'s policy. One thing that still stands out was when I was introduced to a gentleman from the dining staff. I believe his name was Masimo, and he was one of the headwaiters, overseeing quite a large staff of waiters and assistant waiters. It became obvious that he was much more than just a head waiter. I noticed that many people working on board treated him with a little more attention than the other head waiters received. After a few days, I came to find out that it was Masimo people who went to see when they needed some 'assistance' with another crew member or even island connections for the crew. The more I paid close attention I realized that Masimo was their Don. For me, no issue. I got along with Masimo from the minute I arrived on board until the day I signed off. Anything and everything that went on was the way of ship life for the crew and some officers on this particular cruise ship.

I clearly recall an evening where one of the kitchen crew had a physical altercation with a dishwasher crew member. Plates were thrown, glasses were smashed into shattered pieces, and it was apparent that this was more than just a typical argument. As quickly as the fight broke out, it was immediately stopped when Masimo walked into the area. The next morning, you could not even tell that a dish was ever broken, never mind a serious fight between two crew members. When asked about how things ended up, it was as if it never happened. The one who started the fight was no longer there. He was no longer anywhere! In fact, he was no longer listed as part of the crew! It was as if he had never even existed! We were out at sea for these last two days. You thinking what I thought? That moment on, I made sure to keep my mouth shut and my ears and eyes open in crew areas.

I was aboard the TSS *Carnival* when we received word that Elvis Pressley passed away from a drug overdose. The word of his death spread throughout the ship in minutes. In fact, the captain and cruise director made a full shipboard announcement over the ship's PA system that the king was dead. I was standing out on the aft deck with a few others when the announcement came out. You could hear others calling out in disbelief as others began to cry, looking for someone to hold onto for comfort. Yup, you guessed it! My initial introduction to this incredible-looking lady standing in front of me, hoping that I would reciprocate with a hug, was the start of yet another chapter in my life aboard the ships. We ended up going back to my cabin and making sure that I was there for her during this time of emotion and comfort. I ended up comforting and supporting her emotionally for the remainder of her cruise. Every night and sometimes even during the day. Just another perk that came with the territory, I guess. Even with a cabin mate, the hook-ups between so many were no big deal with having someone else in the cabin with you. Sometimes, the only thing you would hear is someone telling you to keep it down; your voice, that is.

After my contract, I ended up traveling to Gross Pointe Park, Michigan, to meet up with this lady who invited me to keep in touch from the ship. Why not take her up on it? I remember flying into Detroit and being met by this incredibly attractive long blonde lady driving to a vet. White with a red interior, it screamed sexuality as we embraced and kissed each other hello. She had been on the ship two months prior, so I was concerned that the attraction was still there. It was! Once we got back to her place, we never left the bedroom for two days. They were two of the most incredible days of my life again.

Once our levels came back to normal, we sat and discussed what we should do with our affection for each other. Keep in mind that most of our time together has been for sex. Sure, we would have some conversation, but usually within a few minutes, we were at it again. Being in your midtwenties sure did enable many of us. This fairy tale lasted the week. As the week ended, I realized we had literally, nothing in common. All she wanted was for me to stay with her. I did not need to work; I did not need to do anything as far as she was concerned. "Just be here for me, Steve," she would say to me. "I'll take care of all the finances." As good as it sounded, there was no way I would ever not work for my own money. Sure, I could become the gigolo of St. Louis, I thought to myself. Sure not! Two days later, I was off to Miami for another gig on a ship, any ship.

After another three-month ship contract as a lounge piano player, I did what I always do. I hooked up with another lady. This one came from Detroit, Michigan. Here I go again, I thought. Where was I going to go when my contract was up? I know. How about landing in Detroit? She wanted me to come see her, so now I was able to. Well, I needed to. I had no other plans to live, and the thought of having a roof over my head with a beautiful lady was just what the doctor ordered for me. My bags were packed, and off to Detroit I went.

After a couple of days of never leaving her apartment, I decided to find myself a job playing piano in a lounge a few nights each week. This gave me a chance to get out and enjoy myself. I came across a piano gig in a bar not far from her house. The Purple Orchard was where I ended up working, Thursdays, Fridays, and Saturdays, letting me make just enough money to help with the essentials. I did not want her to feel as if she was having to cover my expenses while I was there. Things were going great. I was playing to make money. I also had the fortune of meeting a gentleman who also played the piano and wanted me to join him in a studio to record dueling pianos. This other pianist who had written some incredible dueling piano songs wanted to market us as an act. We got this idea after listening to the Mark and Clarke Band, a band consisting of two pianos and two voices with a unique blend. They had a huge orchestra playing with them. We became fairly well-known in the Detroit/Gross Pointe Park area.

Things were great until the word marriage came into play. Not expecting this, I immediately began to question her reasoning, and the more I asked about it, the more upsetting she would become. It became apparent after about five days of this that she had no desire to agree with me. She wanted to get married, get pregnant, and live happily ever after and not have to work. Do I need to go on? This came crashing on Friday, and by Sunday midday, I was already on my way to the airport, heading back to the ships. You see, I felt the ships were my safe haven.

With no plan in the works, I arrived at Miami International Airport with everything I owned. Two suitcases and a backpack filled with all my personal belongings. I completely forgot to find a place to stay so for the first night. I checked into some dive motel. I needed a quick plan, and I knew that without it, I was set to fail. I recall having some relatives on my mother's side who lived in Hallandale, Florida, so I made it a point to reach out to them the following morning. This is where I set up temporary residence while I tried to make the best out of what needed to be done. I had left my car in the parking lot of a hotel that was kind enough to allow me to park there when I was out of town.

It was obvious within hours of my arriving to my cousins, Bernice and Bob, did I immediately notice they were having trouble with their son. Seems that the son was refusing to take his medication and was running around with a less-than-desirable group of people. He had not come home for the past three days, and they were beside themselves. One thing I am still to this day proud of is how my mother instilled in me to have compassion for others, and my father taught me that you never turn your back on the family. Knowing just how distraught my cousins were, I promised them that I would go out and look for him. They gave me an idea as to what areas he frequented, so those were the sights I went for.

On the second evening, having spent hours already searching for him in parking lots, shopping centers, I came across my cousin in an alley hanging out with another group, all dressed in filthy torn clothes that it seems they've been wearing for weeks without washing them. I saw some people stretched out on the pavement, with needles still in their arms, passed out as if they were tossed aside like old clothing and others talking just to hear the sounds come from their mouths. Half of them not making any sense, yet they were arguing with themselves. I grabbed my cousin and pushed him into my car.

Slamming the door, I could hear him shout, "I'm not going home!"

Nothing was going to convince me to drop him off at the next corner.

So now I am driving back to cousins Bernice and Bob's home with him in tow. I looked over at him and said, "Man, what the fuck has happened to you? Ya gotta talk to me, cuz. Look, what the fuck you're doing to yourself and your family."

Dead silence fell inside the car. Nothing was said. It was as if no one was even in the car. Not one sound was uttered as we both sat, looking straight out the front windshield.

As I was about to turn into his driveway, he said to me, "Hey, man, don't pull in yet. Can we drive a bit and talk?"

"Absolutely," I said back to him. "Let's take a ride."

Immediately, he went into explaining why he is the way he is, and from the sound of his voice, it sounded as though he was calling out. That short ride turned into close to one hour. Many things he opened up to me and spoke freely while there were some things he kept closed to his chest. There was no breaking him into letting me hear more. I was thankful for what he confided in me.

At first, I really thought it would take me some serious time to get him to respond to my words, but within that hour, I recall him looking at me and saying calmly, "Thank you, cuz. You probably just saved my life."

With that, I drove us back to his parents' home, where they were both anxiously waiting. I probably did save his life. Last I heard, he was married and living somewhere in Texas with his wife and two beautiful children.

Shortly thereafter, I received a callback from one of the cruise lines I applied for after I returned to the Miami area. Royal Caribbean Intl asked me for an in-person interview, which I gladly confirmed for the following day. No mention of my piano playing came up. Rather the conversation was for a cruise staff position. I thought hard about it for a few minutes, and next I knew, I was boarding my first Royal Caribbean ship, *Nordic Prince*. Being a part of the cruise staff was exactly how I envisioned it to be. Free movement throughout the ship, with an emphasis on mingling with the passengers, made the time go by. Schedules and Shows had been set for the season; therefore, I was merely keeping things running smooth and adding my own touches. It was a very happy cruise staff.

At night, once we were basically through with our programs, making our way to any bar was next for most of us. Years ago, we were able to really set our sights on the next encounter. Just like past ships, it was still the same routine when it came to striking up conversations with an attractive single lady. And yes, it was the exact same on the first night of these cruises; the senior officers were out in their best-dressed whites on the hunt for the weeks' findings. It became a contest with many of us on the cruise staff to see who could win a lady's hand before the other. Sure, many of the women I have spoken with have said when asked about this that there are those who would do just about anything to be with a man in uniform, especially someone with another accent, dark tan, and "not from around here."

Cruising was allowing fantasies to be brought out. That saying was still around the ships from years gone back, a girl in every port; ahhh, shipboard romances.

Going into my second contract, I found myself back on the *Nordic Prince*, but I am now the assistant cruise director under Cruise Director Dave Barrett. Dave was an English chap who had the style of a true comic. Dave was always on que and was able to adlib any comment or question whether he knew the answer or not. A funny disposition whom I had the utmost respect for long after my association with Royal Caribbean. Dave Barrett passed away at a young age in his late forties or early fifties from cancer. Truly a man who always had our backs, even when he knew otherwise.

New passengers were starting to board the *Nordic Prince* for another Caribbean seven-night run. As assistant cruise director, it was our responsibility to be at the gangway welcoming each and every passenger aboard the ship. The smiles and excitement on the faces of our new passengers were what stood out the most. Well, to me and a few other senior officers, setting our sights on the ladies is what made the gangway time go fast. That extra hello or that direct smile started the game.

What I found to be interesting even today is that ladies coming on cruises all the way back to the '60s and '70s and throughout now had the same thought process of meeting someone aboard the cruise that would give them this fairytale time of meeting that man in the uniform or that immediate rush leaning over the balcony looking deeply into the ocean below. The romance of the century. I think I (like many others) had that romance of the century a few times while working on board a cruise ship. Now I know of many officers and crew who met their wives aboard a cruise ship they were working on and have had many years of matrimony to show for it. And yes, from those, there have been no such great memories of couples lasting, but again, that is part of human nature throughout the world, or should I say in most countries where women and men are treated as equals.

It was aboard Royal Caribbean's *Nordic Prince* on a new Eastern Caribbean itinerary, where I saw the face of (another) angel and the smile that was bright and inviting. I, like the three other senior officers standing next to me, returned smiles to her, hoping that she would acknowledge at least one of us. As they all reached out to welcome her, I chose not to extend anything more than this incredible smile I had on my face. It was like slow motion, frame by frame, when her eyes met mine as if we had known each other for years and today was the day we reconnected accidentally. Sure, it sounds great! I reached my hand out to introduce myself. She chose to follow suit where upon our hands met a second before we both tried to introduce ourselves to each other.

"Hello, I'm Steve. Your assistant cruise director. Welcome aboard!" I said in a very melodic tone.

As my hand escorted her into the lobby area, she grasped my hand as if silk was just draped over my hand and said, "Hello. I'm Bunny. Bunny Hager."

Needless to say, the entire week was filled with my usual routine of mingling, hosting bingo, opening some of the secondary shows, and most importantly, spending as much time as I could possibly do with Bunny. The only problem was that there was another senior officer setting eyes for Bunny. You cannot go any higher than this officer. Who else but the captain of the *Nordic Prince*. Oh well, Houston, we have a problem.

The cruise was sensational, and Bunny and I spent every available time together. She ended up spending her nights with me in my shared staff cabin. It was an actual passenger cabin, so the design was nice, and it had your basic cabin steward assistance. The only concern I thought I had was that I shared a cabin with another staff member. As awkward as it may seem, this never stopped most of us finding that "love connection" with someone. This was a part of shipboard life.

As this cruise was coming to an end and it was the end to my contract, I had two months off facing me before deciding if I wanted to return. Where to go?

As Bunny and I were looking out over the ocean right at sunset, I turned to her and said, "Bunny, how'd you like some company for the next week or so?"

As she gazed back into my eyes, I could see her smile getting bigger and bigger. As she threw her arms around my neck, she said, "Okay, now to convince my parents."

The day of disembarking as crew can go smooth or sometimes real slow. Today was the day of the turtle. Everything was running slow. From passenger baggage to the sign-offs, I finally told Bunny to go with her parents I would take a taxi once I cleared the ship and US Customs. For a quick second, I thought to myself, "I wonder if she gave me her correct address?" I have always needed to see both sides of everything I was involved in. The advantages and disadvantages were and still are part of my character. I was taught at a young age to weigh out every possible scenario before deciding.

Life at the Hager house was short-lived. I do not even think I made it there for a full seven days. For no other reason except her father had this real Marine-like attitude with his wife and Bunny. Oh, and now me, he thought. Rather end up with a confrontation with him, I chose to stay at a hotel back in Miami Beach before plotting out my new adventure.

After each cruise contract, I would fall into the same routine where I would recontact the cruise lines with an updated résumé, looking for that next ship. With my formal background, I was able to fall into a few strong categories, so my time ashore was as short or as long as I wanted it to be. The next number of years I spent traveling throughout the Caribbean and many parts of the world aboard some of the finest cruise ships of that time. From a world cruise to the Mediterranean and Caribbean with Costa Cruises and Italian Cruise Lines to Bermuda and Caribbean runs aboard Home Lines, I always found that these were some of the best years of my life. I cannot help but go back in my memory to relate to a story with every ship that I was on.

I met my father and mother at Pier 52, New York Harbor, on a Saturday when Home Lines' *Oceanic* tied up to disembark another group of satisfied cruise passengers. With just a few hours off the ship before I had to report back for my gangway duties, my parents wanted to spend a few hours with me. On city visits, my parents always made their way to see their personal jeweler of many years. Max was his name. Max stood roughly six feet three inches and always looked as if he had just come back from sunbathing on an island. Evenly tanned in a deep goldish Mediterranean tone with his pearly white teeth, Max always had a smile on his face when my parents visited. No wonder my father would spend an absorbent amount of money on jewelry my mother set her eyes on. My father took great care of my mother in every way imaginable, and she was his number one in everything, as he was to her. Truly a marriage like no other. But while we were there, I spoke with Max about becoming his traveling salesman. With no idea thought out, I started to hopefully convince Max to let me have some of his jewelry and start selling it on my own. I knew that the cost of jewelry in Bermuda during the '70s was high, and I knew that I could easily offer friends any of my personal pieces of jewelry at prices lower than what the islanders were paying for retail on the island. Even though Max at first had doubts, he decided to take a chance on me as long as I signed for each piece of jewelry I took, knowing that I was fully responsible for every piece of jewelry I had in my possession.

To this day, I can still hear Max say, "Steve, I'm doing this because of the love I have for your family. They have been great customers of mine for years."

From the moment I signed our agreement to our hug and handshake, I felt good about my accomplishment. The kiss on each cheek confirmed it, As Max pulled me closer to him, he whispered in my ear, "Famiglia vegliata per la famiglia. Inteso?" which said, "Family watches out for family." We sat and chose which pieces I would be taking back with me. Let me say, it was a huge amount of worth I was now in possession of. Like my father, I was continuing to build my own reputation; even through some of his contacts, it was still a commitment I had to make sure people felt and respected me for.

Word spread quickly through the ranks of the officers aboard the ship. From the captain to the staff captain, including the chief purser and other officers were asking me if I had this style or that style ring. Even on bracelets or pins, my business just on the ship kept me busy with this side profession.

I knew that from my father's teachings, he would say, "You should always consider going that extra mile for your boss. It could pay off in the end."

He was so right. Once again, I made sure to always handle the captain's requests. He always had first choice. He appreciated that from me and followed the traditional, "Famiglia vegliata per la famiglia. Inteso?" Being on a full Italian speaking ship of Home Lines, it became obvious very quickly to me on my initial contract with them, that Home Lines is a family, a very tight family.

My friends in Bermuda consisted of many wonderful Bermudians. From tour excursion company owners, restaurant owners like Anthony of Forty-Thieves to hotel managers and nightclub managers, to Manny, the beach supervisor at Elbow Beach, and the list goes on and on, I had some fantastic friends there. Every week when we would return to New York, I would go see Max and complete our week's paperwork. I started bringing more and more of Max's jewelry with me. This was listed as my own personal jewelry, and at times, if I chose to sell some of my pieces to friends, there was nothing to stop me.

It was a Monday morning, the S/S *Doric* had just docked on Hamilton Street, Bermuda. The sun was out, the waters were calm, and the ship's shore excursions were starting in a couple of hours. I, as my staff, under the direction of Cruise Director Eddie Dawson, had assignments to be with the passengers departing the ship for their excursion. I always enjoy having the terminal's top steps as my position. The location is where I would see each guest as they left with smiles and excitement on their faces. More importantly, it gave me a chance to send out special hellos to some of the ladies. Two hours later, the tours were gone. The terminal only had a few scattered passengers walking between the ship's gangway and Hamilton Street. I could not wait to get back to my cabin, change into a pair of shorts and T-shirt, then make my escape on my moped headed over to Elbow Beach for relaxation, swimming, and games. Chief Purser Roberto Arena and I would usually spend time sitting up on the concrete tide wall overlooking the pink sands and the waves as they would crash down offering all shades of blues and aqua blues. It was here where we played our ritual game of backgammon. Roberto Arena was from Italy and had been working on ships for a few years. He had one thing in common with a celebrity known worldwide. He looked identical to actor Peter Sellars. In fact, anytime you saw Roberto, many of us would whisper, Peter Sellars and this enormous smile would appear on his face. Truly a very respected man with a great sense of humor. As of the writing of this book, Roberto lives in Florida with his family and is now retired. We keep in touch through social media and look forward to the day when we can meet up with one another.

This cruise for which I completed my terminal excursion duties, I went immediately back to my cabin to change because I was anxious to get to Elbow Beach to meet with friends who had wanted to purchase some of my personal items. As I went to unlock my cabin door, I found that my door was ajar. My immediate thought was I was robbed while I was out in the terminal.

"Oh shit!" I screamed within myself.

With that, I pushed my cabin door open to see if anything had been disturbed in my cabin. As I opened the cabin door completely wide open now, I was able to see the chief purser, the ship's security chief, and two other gentlemen seated on my bed and sofa. The gentlemen seated on my bed consisted of a police officer from Bermuda and a slightly built man wearing his blue Bermuda shorts, high-stretched black socks, and a light-colored blue shirt, showing me his badge and ID card stating that he was a lieutenant with the robbery division of the Bermuda Police. As I glanced at his badge and the faces of the others, I could not help but notice that most of my jewelry had been placed out on my vanity. Not saying a word, I had the strongest feeling I was in serious trouble. For what? I had no idea. There was no law that said I could not carry my personal jewelry with me when I traveled. But still, being met in your cabin by two senior officers and the police was not taken lightly. The plot was getting thicker.

The questioning was done by the detective while the others sat and listened and never uttered one word. I was asked why I carried so much jewelry with me, and without hesitation, I said that I had a fetish for jewelry. I purchased a lot as an investment but also enjoyed wearing most of the pieces as well.

"Tell me, Mr. Wallach," said the detective, "how can you wear eight rings at a time?"

Clearing my voice, I clearly said without pause, "I like changing my rings when I change clothes. Same thing with my necklaces and bracelets. I have purchased all this over the last few years."

"There was a robbery on the island last week," said the detective. "A jewelry store in Saint George's was broken into, and over one hundred thousand dollars in jewelry is now missing."

I could tell by the way they were both looking at me, they were hoping to see some kind of a reaction. The only reaction I felt inside me was a sigh of relief. I knew the bottom line was that I was not involved with this robbery.

The detective then said, "We need to take this jewelry down to the station and compare it with the photos of the stolen pieces. Here is a sheet with all of your items listed."

For a moment's pause, I did not know whether I should agree, knowing that I was in no way involved in their jewelry store robbery investigation or just hope for the best. Chief Purser Arena convinced them that I would immediately follow behind them and make sure I report as directed. Both police officers agreed. Having to leave the ship with the police would possibly have caused questions to become public, and Chief Purser Arena felt it best not to cause a scene. I forgot to mention, but both ship's officers had purchased jewelry from me in the past and on this sailing, I had diamond engagement rings another senior officer was hoping to buy. They knew, as I, that I had nothing to do with this, and they would make sure the matter does not leave the ship. Rather than force me to walk out with them, they allowed me to follow five minutes later. I had no choice but to go. They had my passport as assurance, and I had their inventory listing of every piece of fine jewelry that now had.

As I disembarked the ship to make my way to the station house, I reflected on what I was prepared to say and not say. In the palms of both hands, I could easily feel the buildup of sweaty palms as I walked into the station and asked to meet with the detective.

"Walk through those double doors. You'll find him on the right side down the hall," the police officer said to me.

Walking into the room, I was met by other the detective and the same police officer. This time, they had smiles on their faces, and they immediately broke the ice by offering me a glass of water.

As I took my seat, the detective spoke in a quiet tone and said, "There was a misunderstanding."

As I looked toward him over the brim of my water cup, he said, "Seems we were looking at the wrong individual. You see, Steve, the jewelry store in St. Georges was broken into last week, and over $100,000 in jewelry was stolen. Your name was mentioned to me over the weekend while I was at Elbow Beach. I noticed a friend of mine who is the beach supervisor at Elbow Beach had a beautiful thick gold rope chain on his neck. When I asked where he got it, he clearly said, 'I got it from that cruise director guy, Steve.'"

The detective immediately thought that I was part of this jewelry heist in Bermuda. Once they realized they made a mistake and admitted that I had nothing to do with the heist, they returned all my personal jewelry and handed me back my passport. However, before I left our meeting room, I noticed that the detective kept looking at this one gold necklace I had. So it wouldn't be a total loss, I made him a deal he couldn't refuse. He purchased a gold chain before I left. Everyone was happy; especially me.

So, you see, once again, what could be seen as wrong turned out to again be fine. Life has many ways one can learn from. Believe me, I learned my lesson that time. Always make sure your papers are in order whether needed or not, for the day may come when those papers could be needed for your welfare. I knew I had nothing to worry about with respect to the ship and officers. I was somewhat curious as to how the captain would confront me, but in the back of my mind, I knew that the turquoise and diamond ring I had in my cabin was for his wife. Therefore, I was not that concerned or worried.

The first stop I made upon my return to the ship was to the nearest ship's telephone. Twenty feet inside the shell gate, I immediately phoned the bridge to speak with the staff captain and to say that I was back on board, and everything was fine.

"The captain wants to see you," said the staff captain.

I immediately responded with your typical innocent reply, "Why?"

Without a direct response to my question, the staff captain said sternly, "'Cause he's the captain."

Without any hesitation, I decided to take a detour before going to the captain's office and headed back to my stateroom to pick up the ring that I promised I would have for him. You see, business is business, and if my showing him the ring immediately following my return, it may calm down any matters being addressed. If you know what I am referring to?

As I approached his office door, I noticed that only the curtain covering the entrance to his office was closed, allowing him to hear every noise or movement outside his office. As I came closer, already feeling dry mouthed in anticipation of what was to follow, I clearly heard the words as if I could hear them today.

"Stefano, prego entra."

"Si signore capitano, volevi vedermi? I replied.

My first thought was that everything ended up okay and that I was in no way involved in any jewelry store situation in Bermuda. It was a complete and coincidental mistake.

"Yes, Steven you are correct," now in a broken Italian and American accent, the captain replied back. "I received a telephone call from the detective who explained that you had nothing to do with their situation." With a huge grin on my face, I looked up from the chair I was now sitting in in front of his solid wooden desk and said in a melodic tone, "Ah, but look what I have for you." The captain leaned forward and, with his outstretched arm, took the open ring box from me and said, "Per me?" (For me?). The lighting could not have been any better. As I passed the ring box over to the captain, the sun's rays from outside magnified through the large porthole window and made the ring sparkle that much greater.

"Sensazionale!" (Stunning), were the captain's words to me. Just to make sure he was happy, I took another $50 off the price of the ring, hoping this would soften anything that I may be receiving after today's events. We did our business, and as I was preparing to stand, Captain leaned back in his reclining chair, placed his arms folded high above his head but interlocking his hands on the back of his neck, and said, "This little thing today"—long pause—"I will keep here on the ship. It will go no further."

With a grin on my face, I clearly said back to him, "Grazia, Capitano Grazia."

Another sale complete! Hmm, I think it's time for dinner, so I made my way down to the dining room to meet up with my staff members for a very relaxing dinner.

Home Lines' new S/S *Oceanic* was the most prestigious ship at that time. The M/S *Queen Elizabeth* was the only other ship that people compared her to. Different in their own unique ways. I preferred the *Oceanic* over any other ship. The full Italian officers and crew, the ultradeco design, and the cuisine is what made the *Oceanic* the number one sailing cruise ship for many years in a row. More importantly, it was the officers and crew that made it the best. Home Lines had the highest percentage of repeaters of any other cruise line worldwide. At the time, Home Lines was closing her doors. They had an annual 87 percent repeaters program in place. More than any other vessel of its time. Guests would book back-to-back cruises during our Bermuda season from New York City. The same guests would also be booked on the *Oceanic* and *Doric* during the winter months when she sailed from Florida to the Caribbean waters. People just loved Home Lines. For me, it was another memory. As I could relate to, for the first time, I became familiar with ships, especially Home Lines. As it was the Homeric, my parents first introduced to me.

I feel another story coming up. I think this is a good time to make a few comments so that to explain my life. It was not a life with different women, involving incredible sexual encounters, champagne, and caviar or traveling the world with your home being a luxurious cruise ship. Well, the more I write that out and say it, the more I realize that yes, my life has truly been great.

My father always said, "Bad things are never really bad in business. Those decisions allow you the ability to learn and grow from them."

The following week, Eddie Dawson (back now as cruise director), said there was an outside company coming aboard the *Oceanic* to shoot various commercials and still shots. This was the memo we received one week prior to this event. Many different companies and clubs would bring large-size groups on for various reasons. Sometimes, private events like weddings, anniversaries, and birthdays. During the morning's turnaround day, we always had a staff meeting. This one was different. Eddie Dawson kicked off the meeting with, "There will be a modeling agency coming on board for the duration of the cruise and the models would be wearing skimpy outfits and modeling a bunch of new bikinis and two-piece bathing suits. I expect you all to assist when needed and not push the envelope!" Laughter broke out among us.

"Awe, come on, Eddie!" one voice yelled out.

Me, I sat there for a moment and just thought to myself what it would be like to "hit on" a model. That day was just around the corner. *There goes my mind*, I thought.

Our first full day aboard this cruise was spent at sea; filled with travel talks, sunbathing, cooking lessons, dance lessons, bingo, and doing simply nothing at all. I was in the Orpheus Lounge, getting ready to have that simple all-time favorite, pass the potato game—a very simple game where people keep their arms and hands behind them as they attempt to pass an uncooked baked potato from one person's neck to another person's neck without dropping the potato. If the potato falls, you have to start all over. As I was explaining the rules and called out, "Okay, folks, who would like to play? I need two teams of five players each." As people raised their hands and others came running to the stage to be chosen, one person stood out as they came up to the stage.

"I'd like to play!" said a voice to the left of me.

Yup, you guessed it; it is happening again!

Walking directly toward me were the legs of someone who was (again) the most beautiful girl I had ever seen! Tanned and chiseled legs that were a mile tall, followed by a walk only a model would be familiar with. Each step was as if a musical note was leading the path to something special. Her name was Traci Scoggins, and she worked as a full-time model and actor based out of New York City. She was joined by other beautiful models on board to shoot a commercial for a clothing and bathing suit company. As I tried to continue with my introduction to a passenger game I was about to go over, I could not help myself as my mind wandered and my concentration on the game was tilted. Game? What game? I completely lost my train of thought. Here stood (again) one of the most beautiful ladies I have ever seen (again) here directly in front of me.

As I extended my hand to welcome her, this melodic voice said to me, "Hi I'm Tracy. Can I join in the fun?"

Without skipping a beat, I looked directly into her eyes and responded with the most welcoming tone I could do and replied, "But of course, you can join me. I'm your assistant cruise director, Steve."

As our hands touched and I felt her warm smooth skin lay within the palm of my hand, I could not resist but tell her, "You, my dear, is simply gorgeous! Where have you been my entire life?"

As I felt my smile grin larger, she looked at me and said, "It's great to me you."

This was what I wanted to be, the start of yet another chapter in my life.

My mind was racing. *Holy shit*! I thought to myself.

This woman was a goddess. Every portion of her incredible body was chiseled to perfection. Her smile was contagious as her lips drew your eyes closer to her. For the remainder of the cruise, Traci and I spent as much time together as possible. We were both there for work. It just happened to be in two completely different fields of employment. I was there to entertain the guests who paid money to cruise to Bermuda, and she was there to fulfill her obligation for a photo shoot. No matter what we did during the days, we knew that the evening hours would be spent getting to know each other. I was so looking forward to arriving in Bermuda because the only hours I had to work were on our initial arrival and assisting with the shore excursions. Once that was finished, I was free to enjoy Bermuda and a full beach day with Traci. I could not wait for us to jump on the back of a moped and ride off, heading in the direction of the famous Elbow Beach and Hotel—a day I knew would be fantastic. Elbow Beach is a place where we tell our guests to come and enjoy. The food and beach were always kept pristine. They had fantastic-tasting hamburgers, and their fries were always hot and crisp. Time was spent with some of her crew as well as mine. Laughing, drinking, eating, and enjoying everyone's company was great. There was a nice buzz going on among us, and it felt right. At one point, Traci and I decided to take the traditional "couple walking hand in hand on the beach." From what I remember, it was a wonderful talk and walk. This beautiful lady with me was so intelligent and focused on everything in her life, except there was no man. You know me, I say and ask what I want.

"So, Traci, can I ask you a question?"

With a nod and smile, she said, "Yes. Ask away."

"As we continued to walk hand in hand, I asked her, "So there must be a man in your life, right? Or are there men in your life all wanting to walk side by side with you?" I thought I might as well get this out of the way before it does or does not go any further.

"No, Steve," she said to me. "I'm completely single! I just haven't met anyone that I feel attracted to in all ways. I've come close, but they only ended up wanting to date a model. You know, the same nonsense it usually is."

I know what you're thinking. Stop it! Whatever it is, you are wrong. I was a bit nervous in this entire situation. Wow is all I could think to say to myself, repeatedly. By the third night of the cruise, my cabin became her cabin. Well, sort of. She never really moved her belongings in, but we spent every night together. Our attraction to each other was magnetic. I will never forget our first time or every time. Traci was every man's dream as far as I was concerned. Her personal and emotional side were truly inspiring. She said she learned so much through her mother and father, as I did and continue to do.

"My parents are both lawyers, and I had an amazing upbringing," she said to me.

There was a tone in her voice that just had this way of bringing you into her personal space. Me, I loved it. It was a feeling of calmness and a hug, an invisible hug you could actually feel take you over.

The remainder of the cruise was fantastic. The passengers were happy as we headed back to New York filled with purchases from Bermuda, items from the ship's gift shops, and those cardboard cases of purchased liquor. The prices for booze (even to this day) are quite reasonable aboard the ships, and when the bottles are duty-free, guests load themselves up with cases. They'd rather pay any tax for purchasing over the limit, so they use this as an excuse to buy as much as they can carry off.

Saying goodbye to passengers became a ritual at the gangway. As the passengers disembarked the ship, we thanked them for joining us and told them to have safe journeys home. Meantime, in the back of our minds, we were already on the next cruise, planning the times for the coming weeks' activities. Me, I was in a state of I'm in love—in love with a gorgeous woman that I just met on the cruise. Like so many other cruises, many of the officers and staff would keep a running log in their minds of what escapades we did on the last cruise. It was like a scale, with the center being the starting point. If the needle went toward the left, it meant that the last cruise was fair. If the needle went to the right, then it was a good cruise. If the needle went all the way to the right, then it was a fantastic cruise! The meter reader was a true part of our fun.

Saying goodbye to Traci, the other models and their crew were quick. Once they were cleared, they had vehicles waiting at the entrance to the port for them. We gave each other a quick kiss and exchanged telephone numbers. Remember, cell phones were not even thought of in the mid-'70s. It was either landline calls or mail for all communications. Or of course, what is the best would be, in person. There is nothing better than meeting someone face-to-face and exchanging the proper greeting. Me, I'm a hugger and kisser. Hey, it comes from being my father's son.

The next cruise, I felt empty. The girl whom I fell hard for was gone, and all I had were the memories we made. Granted, thinking back on everything we did gave me incredible memories that I cherished throughout my years. It had to mean something if, after all these years, I could recall every encounter we had.

The following Saturday, upon our return after another successful cruise, I stood in the crew line to disembark the ship for a few hours in New York, and who do I see in the far distance of the pier was hot-looking lady in a Supergirl kind of outfit. I spent the entire week thinking about her. As a path led between us, her entrance was on a pair of roller skates. It was as if she was gliding through the air brushing from side to side. Coming to a halt directly in front of me stood this angel.

"Surprise!" Traci called out as she leaned forward, bringing her lips to mine. I could not help but react as a child to winning a prize.

"Wow, I can't believe you're here! This is unbelievable!" were the words I yelled out.

Standing in front of me, I felt a chill run down my spine. My fingers and arms made their way around her tiny waist, interlocking as if I never planned to let her go.

"I wanted to come down and surprise you this morning," Traci said to me. "I hope it's alright." There was nothing in my mind that told me to react differently. I was so taken aback that she, Traci Scoggins, would take time out and come see me when "my ship came in."

Traci and I spent time together on Saturdays for the next few months. With my contract in full swing and her commitments to her career schedule, we knew it would eventually become difficult. Time moved on, and we both went from passion to realization that it was become harder to say goodbye each Saturday afternoon at four o'clock. And I started thinking during my time away from her, can we both survive being separated for long periods of time? I knew right then that there was a concern by me thinking, what if we get really serious and she meets this other guy at a photo shoot or movie set and dumps in publicly? *Hell no! I was not about to let that happen to me*, I thought. Break things off before you get hurt. That was how my mind went. Here, before is the most beautiful woman I have ever met and had sex with, and I'm afraid she'll meet another actor and bon voyage my ass to see (I should have been a screenwriter). It broke my heart saying goodbye to her the last time. Watching her walk away truly was another time of romance that I will always think bout.

Throughout the years, I tried on a few occasions to contact Traci, but to no avail. I know she continues to speak at various organizations and continues to make a few cameo appearances on television and in the movies. I do not know if she ever married or had children. I guess I will leave it as that. As beautiful as she was on the outside, that is how beautiful she was on the inside. Truly an incredibly special caring soul.

I guess as with any job, people can walk away with memories that will last them a lifetime. My years on the ships were incredible. I could go on and on with stories. Being able to decide which ones to reveal has been made using a strong method of choice. Simply said, whichever stories pop up and I can think of as I am writing, I will include. Not all stories you think of are made for print. In fact, most short stories should be kept within one's own thoughts. To share is letting the world see inside some of your thoughts. No matter how deep or emotional they are, always be proud and stand for what you allow others to read. You may walk away with the same thoughts as the writer tried to portray, or you may have your own ideas. Either way, they are shared stories.

My final romance at sea during this time was with one of the hairdressers from Steiner & Co., which controlled the majority of salons aboard many of the ships worldwide. I had just completed my contract on one of the ships, and she still had two months left on her contract. Jennifer Simpson was her name. English, she came from a small town called Glossip, which was just outside of Manchester, England. A former UK *Playboy* Bunny, Jennifer had long curly hair that shined over her well-tanned and fit body. A size 2, Jennifer knew exactly how to make heads turn when she walked into a room. Great smile, green eyes, and a body that screams HOT!

By this point, we had been together almost four months already. I found what it was like to be on the receiving end of my relationship. I was now on the shoreside, and Jennifer was still on the high seas. For the next two months, I would fly to an island where her ship would be arriving so that we got to spend a few hours together. Sure, most of the time, she would meet me at the gangway to sign in as a visitor, and we would make a dash to her cabin. We had to keep in my mind we only had a few hours together before she had to go to work, so time was precious to us. Seven nights is a long time to be separated.

By the end of Jennifer's contract, she, too, had had enough of ship life for a while. People do not realize the hours staff have to put in while working. Every job consisted of seven days a week. We had no days off—only a few hours here and there each day. It was a trying job that lasted anywhere from three to ten months. No days off, nothing. Many staff and crew would burn out after one or two contracts, so the turnover on cruise ships back then was plenty. Unless you were a true sailor and came from a family of sailors, contract after contract was difficult for many. By the time Jennifer completed her term, she was ready to come off and try something different with me.

I found a place called River Ranch Resorts, located in Lake Wales, Florida. The newspaper said they were a full resort offering a sleuth of activities, including an Olympic-size swimming pool, horseback riding, evening activities, trails for exploring, and even a weekly rodeo put on by the locals in the area. They marketed themselves as a resort with a Western flare. They even had their own private runway. The paper said they were in search of a new entertainment director and a hostess for their new program. What better timing, we thought. We contacted River Ranch Resorts, and after our initial telephone interview, they offered us the opportunity to be included on the ground floor of their renewed resort. I purchased two one-way tickets from Miami to Orlando, where we were met by one of the staff employees from River Ranch Resorts. Introductions were made, and we were on our way to this newly designed resort, western style.

The driver's name was Red. That's right. Red.

"I never go by my real name. Everyone just calls me Red, so that's what I use," said our young driver, who may be seventeen years old at the most. "This your first time to River Ranch?" Red called out as he lowered the volume on the radio. "I hear you folks are the new people coming in to work with us."

I recall Jennifer and I looking at each other and shrugging our shoulders. I looked up and caught Red's eyes in the rearview mirror and replied, "I guess we are."

It felt as though we were driving for hours. Lake Wales, Florida, was in the middle of Florida, northwest of Orlando. At that time, nothing was really built up in the area. It was more of forests and fields with fewer and less houses marking the roadside as we went further out of what I considered civilization.

"Hmmm, I guess this resort is far off the beaten path," I asked Red as he glazed into the rearview mirror at us.

"It's not too much further. That is why when people go food shopping or to the general store, they make sure they get everything on their first run because if not, it's about a forty-minute drive each way."

With that, I replied with just a one-word response, "Oh."

"Most people coming to the resort fly in with their own plane. It's kinda a family place," Red said in a smirking sound.

As we pulled in on this gravel-grated drive, we noticed the landing strip to one side. "So is this where they fly their planes into?" I asked.

It was a small single-surfaced asphalt runway. There was no tower, just a small one-level building sitting midway down the runway.

"Yup," Red proudly called out. "This place will be filled this coming weekend. Wait and see,"

"Wait and see what?" I called out.

We did not even know if we were taking the jobs or not.

As we walked into the lobby and set our bags down, a tall gentleman came out from the back-office area and introduced himself to us as the manager. He welcomed us and made small talk, waiting for others to join us. This was our person-to-person interview getting ready to happen. As we were waiting for the others, I could not help but look around and see what was there. The main building was quite nice. Very rustic. It was a large log cabin building with huge windows and an entry that you could drive a tractor through. The inside had a stone fireplace, which reached up to the top of this eighteen-foot ceiling, oversize leather-covered couches and chairs, bare wooden tables, and your typical table lamps to match the decor of the furniture. There were magazines scattered on some of the tables outlining the events of River Ranch Resorts.

As I gazed over to one area, I could see a piano inside the room. "I see you have a piano," I called out.

"Yeah, that room is a lot bigger than what you're looking at. It's our lounge and bar area," he said proudly. "It's usually packed on Fridays and Saturdays. Come on. Look inside. This is where your office is."

Before I knew it, Jenn and I were being escorted into the lounge, hoping that our response would be positive.

The room was quite nice. There was a huge bar along the side of the room. The bar looked as though it came from an old Western town, taken down piece by piece and rebuilt here. There was a stage, a dance floor, and rows of tables and chairs. Neon signs dressed the walls and dated posters were on display as well. From the size of the room and how the bar was stocked, I had to believe this place was busy on weekends.

"So the reason we are so happy to have you both here is because we need people like you," said tall walkin' manager Keith. "The others that tried to run our lounge just did not have any idea what they were doing," he claimed. "At least you both have worked all over the world, so we really feel good about bringing you both here." Before I could say one word, Keith introduced us to the resorts accountant, who was also his wife, and said, "Look, I know we probably can't pay you as much as you both are used to, but I can tell you both that there is money to be made here." I thought for a minute and kept my mouth shut to hear what offers he was about to make us. "Your pay is done weekly in cash plus a percentage of what you bring into the house." Percentage brought into where? I thought for a moment what he meant by that and then realized they are wanting Jenn and me to design the entire program for their upcoming season. They were looking at us to design the season's events and activities.

"Look, Steve," Keith said to us, "most of our clients are families coming here to experience a bit of country Western living. You know, like working on a ranch but not doing the work, just enjoying everything it has to offer." Keith said in his best, convincing voice, "But before you both give me your answers, let me take you for a ride through our property so you can see firsthand what River Ranch has to offer."

Next thing I knew, Jennifer and I were in an open-top old army-styled jeep with Keith getting ready to explore this place called River Ranch Resorts. I remember my father telling me that there would be times in my life when I may have to start off low to reap the rewards from my efforts later down the road. The salary was fine since it was paid in cash. I was more interested in the additional monies to be made.

As we pulled away from the main house, we could see a small single-engine plane approaching land.

"Here comes the first of about seven planes arriving for the weekend," Keith called out. "On our weekends and every other Wednesday night, we have a lot of activities for our guests. On the first and third Saturday of every month, we have a live rodeo here." As Keith was pointing things out to us, we arrived at their rodeo ring. This was an authentic ring with its own set of bleachers on one side and gated pens on the other for what I expected to be for horses, bulls, and cows.

"This is where we keep the bulls and where the rider's 'git' on 'em for the rodeo," Keith excitedly said. "Your job will be to keep the guests here and build up their excitement until the final ride."

My job? My guests? Keep them excited until the final ride? Who were they thinking we were? We just came from luxurious cruise ships, not some dirt-filled stable.

We continued in the jeep through some beautiful back-wooded areas and drove alongside the riverbanks. There were horses, donkeys, cows, and even a few bulls just wandering around on the grounds, which made this place like a typical ranch. What did we know? We were both city slickers and never once stayed at a dude ranch or anything near to it. But as my father always taught me, "Son, it's a new thing to do, and you're not familiar with it. Make the best out of it, and do your best at it." And that is what Jennifer, and I did. Being dropped off in our room, we said we would see them for dinner.

Our dinner was huge: whipped potatoes along with fresh cut green beans, dinner rolls, and a huge T-bone steak times two. The steak was cooked to perfection. The vegetables were steamed, and the potatoes were perfectly whipped. We had a pleasant dinner with Keith and his wife and started to feel comfortable here at River Ranch Resorts. Even Jenn could not help but comment just on how good her meal was. Our good night and thank-you were made, and Jennifer and I headed back to our room. Exhausting day of travel and a site inspection. My head hit the pillow, and within minutes, I was fast asleep.

The next morning after breakfast, we decided to dive right into making this one fantastic resort filled with great activities and events. Many of the events were already scheduled for the season. They just had no one that was able to make it run without any hiccups. I had some great ideas, so I chose to incorporate some of the ship's activities with a land venue.

Two nights after our arrival, Jennifer was welcoming the guests into the lounge, and I was tickling the ivories at the piano. Ended up being a great night.

One guest said, "That was the first time anyone ever touched that piano that knew how to play it."

That made me feel good, especially not knowing if my song choices would be a good fit with the room. It worked, and the tip jar worked extra hard that night. Keith was extremely impressed, and before the evening ended, she was all thumbs-up.

The next few days, we had all the activities and the staff prepared for the guests. It became the norm where we had events on certain nights, and of course, there was a famous rodeo every other weekend. Guests would fill the bleachers, as would the residents. People came from all over on rodeo night. This was becoming the place to be on Wednesdays and weekends. By the end of the first month, we had everything running smoothly, and the guests were really pleased.

After two months, I could tell that Jenn was feeling as though this was not what she planned for. We spent the next week working and talking to each other and going over the pros and cons from being off the ships. I was overworking on board. I wanted to find land employment that would keep me going without giving up so much. Even though we were making some decent money, Jennifer was missing her home back in Glossip and really wanted to go back. I could not leave. I made a commitment as she did, but I was not willing to break mine without having something guaranteed to go to. Another week had gone by, and the tension was just building between us to the point that we chose to go our separate ways.

I remember driving her to the airport and found myself standing there with her, thinking of every possible thing to say to get her to change her mind and return to the resort with me. There were no words to convince her otherwise. As I held her in my arms, I knew she could feel my heart pounding through my chest. I was never one for good goodbyes. As I gazed into her eyes for what I felt would be the very last time, I told her I loved her and wished her the best. My last words were that I hope that our paths cross again as I turned and walked away without turning back, for I knew if I did, I would get emotional and run to her, asking her to stay. That was something that I just would not let myself do. My heart was (again) crushed.

I ended up staying three more months at River Ranch. I set up bingo, horseracing, and even family activities good for entire families to participate in. Just like on the cruise ships, the racehorse actions brought in a lot of money, as did bingo. I called some of my friends who were solo performers and convinced them to come perform at the resort. We were packing the room with shows, bingo, and special events for eight weeks straight.

Midway through my remaining three months, as I was driving in the adjacent field next to the airstrip I watched two Cessnas, single prop planes land on the resort's airstrip. As both planes came to a standstill, the doors opened, and you could see a couple of outstretched arms reaching up into the sky as if to give praise for a safe flight. The remaining window changed into the small door that all passengers exited from. As they each exited their planes, the smiles on their faces expressed pure happiness as they waved from the makeshift tarmac to where I was parked. There were six in total: four men and two women. They all looked too young to own these airplanes, so my curiosity built stronger with each beat of my pulse. As we were introducing ourselves to one another, I found out their interesting story of coming to River Ranch.

"These are our four top students, hailed one of the two pilots. They ranked the highest in their classes. Our school always takes the highest ranked on a trip. This year, we chose River Ranch Resorts."

Hearing a strong French accent coming from each of them, I knew they were not from the States.

"Where did you fly in from?" I called out.

"We came from Montreal," called out the pilot.

"Montreal, Canada!" I shouted back to them.

With a nod of a head, I became impressed with such a long flight. It's not that we are right next door you know, was my first impression. Making my congratulations, I made sure to make eye contact with each one of them when I spoke. It is always a great impression when you speak directly to someone by also looking at them. By the time I reached the third student, I was taken aback by who the student was. A beautiful mid-twenty-year-old young lady standing before me, with beautiful green eyes that stood out from within her headgear. A smile that portrayed her beautiful straight white teeth. She slowly removed her helmet and began to shake her head back and forth so that her shoulder-length hair could fall into place. You know, just like those commercials where a beautiful lady is taking off her glasses and moving that head back and forth in slow motion.

She then reached up and removed her sunglasses in a slow seductive motion and looked directly at me and said, "I'm happy to meet you. My name is Marie" (here I go again). As I could not help but stare into her eyes, I thought to myself, *You are a single man, Steve. Go for it!* Where this inner voice came from, I have no idea. But what I do know, I took the advice and knew I had only a few days to be with her. I had time to think as the lodge had sent over the shuttle van to pick up the guests and their luggage.

"Can I ride back with you?" Marie said in an anxious-sounding tone.

"Sure, I'd love it! Come on, hop right in," I said.

I know what you're thinking; And you may be correct. But as far as I am concerned, I am just being hospitable to one of our guests.

They were there for only three nights, so I knew that I would be able to speak with her at the different activities scheduled or during any off time. I was one of the easiest people to find when a guest asked for me. Let's just say my phone rang often with requests from one particular guest. As they say, always make sure your guests leave happy. Our time spent together was happy times. I made sure to that. It was during her visit that I realized this really was not the place for me. I knew being here in the middle of nowhere would not give me any opportunities to find permanent work and, most importantly, someone I could start to spend the rest of my life with. Saying goodbye to Marie that following Monday was sad, but at the same time, if it weren't for our meeting, I may not have ever thought further about finding what I wanted in life. To just exist had no foundation for me. I wanted to leave my mark, as my father has done, somewhere where people would remember me for what I gave and was and not what I did just for myself.

There's a saying that reads, "Once you go to sea to work, it's hard to ever come back to reality." There is a lot of truth to that. I have been going back and forth on ships for so many years. When I think back over the years, I realize that I had spent my time on many ships, including many that are no longer operating. With Home Lines, I enjoyed working on both the *Doric* and *Oceanic*, Holland American Lines offered me a world cruise aboard the *Statendam*, Costa Cruises' *Carla C*, *Amerikanis*, and *Flavia*, Italian Cruise Lines' *Marconi*, Carnival Cruise Lines' *Mardi Gras* and *Carnival*, Royal Caribbean's *Nordic Prince* and *Song of Norway*. This was yet just another time I turned to do the same thing. So off I went back to Miami to try my luck in regaining a position on a cruise ship—any cruise ship.

I contacted a dear friend of mine at Norwegian Cruise Line to ascertain whether she knew of any positions within her company. My timing, once again, was spot-on.

"Steve, be in my office tomorrow at eleven in the morning," Jackie Johnson said to me. Jackie was senior vice president for all sales and charters. "I have a meeting with the entertainment director, and it would be perfect timing for you to come in to see me. I will instruct my secretary to let you right in when you get here. Make sure you walk in right at eleven o'clock."

Well, that was easy, I thought to myself. I ended up checking into the Holiday Inn in Downtown Miami. A good night's sleep is what I needed so I could be awake and fresh for my midmorning meeting the following day.

I arrived a few minutes before eleven o'clock as was ordered, and I made my way up to Jackie's office. My timing was exact.

I walked over to the secretary's desk and said, "Good morning. My name is Steve Wallach. I have an appointment with Jackie. I believe she is expecting me."

My tone was direct, calm, and I completed it with a smile.

This very attractive secretary stood up and said, "Oh, Mr. Wallach, we were expecting you. Please follow me."

That's all it took.

I worked as assistant cruise director and acting cruise director on ships within the Norwegian Cruise Line Fleet. I was known as a floater, going between ships where staff was needed. I continued aboard the ships for the next few years before I chose to finally give in and retire from the sea. So I thought....

I decided it was time for me to turn my attention on a new and exciting time in my life. I chose to move back home to New Jersey and work directing my inner thoughts to a more desired profession. What that was going to be so the real question. If I go back up north, my only escape would be to try to find a position in my other true desire, which was in entertainment. Now for granted when you say entertainment that can cover a mass of avenues. Did I want to pursue my talents in live events, music tours, music publishing, songwriting, or was I just grasping at straws since I really had no professional training in any of the professions? I thought to myself that it really did not matter if I was proficient in one particular field. I had no professional training in working on cruise ships, so I was determined to use the same approach as I did and had success with over the years.

Arriving back in New Jersey, I found myself relying on my bank account to keep me sane. Since I had money in the bank, I really did not focus on what or where I wanted to work. I found myself meeting up with old friends and making new friends. My focus was turned to Atlantic City, New Jersey, again. Gambling was in full swing compared to when I was there in my earlier years, so I still had contact with a few people. Finding myself back in relationships with a few less desirable people, my attitude and priorities started to revert back to a more laid-back attitude. What this meant was simple; I was becoming lazy with each passing day that turned into each passing week.

On one occasion, I recall going to a branch of my bank and drawing out some additional funds so my party times would continue. It was on this one occasion that I realized there was something wrong. I was running out of money. My bank account kept dwindling down until there was no more money for me to withdraw. I had come to once again feel that emptiness in the pit of my stomach as I realized that I was falling back into the same laziness that I faced some years back. But did that stop me from having good times with my drinking, gambling, and freestyle lifestyle? The answer, unfortunately, was no. I continued as if I had not a problem in the world. This continued for a few weeks until I realized that not only had I run out of my own funds, but now I had gone to a few people to borrow money so that I could try to keep up with my image. Image? Hell, all I was trying to do was continue with my carefree ways. I never thought for a second what the outcome would be if everything came to a halt. Not for a minute did I think that would happen to me again.

I ended up feeling that all I would need was a good run in the casino to get me back on track. On track to what? I guess I thought that *if* I was able to make enough money gambling, all my troubles would be behind me, and I could continue with my life of partying. I started to plan out what it would take for me to pull myself out of this financial lull I was in. I knew of someone who was always willing to loan others money. The reasons never mattered even though this gentleman always wanted to know when he would be paid back in full. With me, it was simple. I needed money to make money, not by working at a job every day but by turning my mind to gambling. Now I was not thinking about slot machines or even some of the table games. I was concentrating my thoughts on one particular game of chance, blackjack.

"Come back here at ten o'clock tonight. Capisce?" he said to me.

He, who has a name, Anthony was your averaged-size man in his forties. Built solid, Anthony had been the man on the boardwalk. He travels between New York City and Atlantic City every week. To say Anthony was connected would be like saying I love milk with my cold cereal. If Anthony was paid on time, he would be your best friend. Having a delay in payment would lead to another "fee" and a stronger and firm conversation with Anthony. I tried never to go past my delivery date and time. Only once did that ever happen.

I used to watch my father play blackjack. He was known as a heavy player, but he was also known to be sharp when it came to playing this game of cards. Rumor had it that my father was a counter. A counter was one who could count the cards as they were dealt, hoping that he would know when to double or even triple his bets. My father was exceptional at this. Unfortunately, I was not. I had no idea how to count, when to count, when to double my bets, and especially when to walk away. A professional gambler knows when to walk away. I was not that fortunate. I found myself sitting at tables and praying for my next hand to be a winning hand. When I lost that bet, I will make excuse after excuse as if I need to convince myself that the next hand would be a winning hand. The convincing took over my mind. I became completely hooked on a game that I had no luck or professional training on, and I should have taken my loss and moved on. The last time was always the last time. I would continue to borrow and pay back, borrow and pay back Anthony, thinking or should I say believing that the next time would be the time for me to make that big hit.

On a rainy night in AC, I had a meeting with Anthony. Nothing of any concern, I just wanted to make sure that I always had an open line to him. On this visit, Anthony had someone with him.

"Steve, let me introduce Angelo to you," Anthony said with a grin."

"Steve, I'm Angelo. How ya doin'?"

Anyone's first impression of Angelo was someone you would think was probably a security man or bodyguard for the mob—definitely a bodybuilder, if not both. Just from glancing at him, you either felt completely at ease and safe knowing he had your back, or you were petrified from what he could do to you. I must tell you, though, Angelo had a heart like a puppy. He was kind and generous and would give you the shirt of his back if needed. If you were fortunate enough to be able to be on his good side. It was more important to know that when it comes time for business, the friendship is set aside, and the business side comes out.

"Always remember one thing, Steve," I could hear Angelo say to me as if it were yesterday, "never take an act of a promised deal and turn it into a chase. The hare will also outrun the turtle."

Angelo definitely was not the turtle. So as Angelo was my banker at times, I made sure that the return was never late, except this one time.

I came back to my parents' house for a visit. Still playing piano at a few lounges and a few dive bars, the visit was nothing more than a well-needed family connection time. My father still left the house at eight in the morning for work, and my mom would be planning out her day. My father was still not happy with me, but he tolerated and accepted that I would hopefully become someone of strength and respect. Me, I decided to put my bathing suit on and make my way out to the backyard and enjoy and relax at the pool. Beautiful area, with a large inground rectangular pool surrounded by a well-designed concrete type of deck. The area at one end of the pool offered plenty of room for a few chaise lounges and a four top table and chairs. Of course, there was a large umbrella keeping the area shaded on those hot New Jersey summer days. It was nice to be able to just relax and enjoy my time at home.

The atmosphere was calm, and it was just about lunchtime when I heard my mother call out, "Lunch is ready. Come in and fix your plate."

Already tired from the sun's heat, going inside was a grand idea, especially knowing how cool it would be inside the air-conditioned house.

As I made my way onto the patio, I could hear the sound of the telephone ringing. "Hello," I can hear my mother say, "Who's calling?"

By the time I heard my mother say hello, I felt this thump in my chest. It was as if someone pushed my stomach in with a blunt instrument. I quickly made my way into the back kitchen door and looked directly at my mother, waving my hands uncontrollably for her to look at me.

I was mouthing the words, "I'm not here! I'm not here!"

Hoping I caught this in time, I was waiting to hear my mother's next words. "No, I'm sorry Steve isn't here right now. Can I take a message? Yes. Okay, I'll let him know. Goodbye."

As my mother was hanging up the telephone, a sigh of relief came over my body, but in a split second, I had to come up with why I acted like a lunatic waving my arms and hands all over.

"Steven!" I can still hear my mother say to me. "What is going on? Who was this Anthony guy?"

I could not just come out and tell her that I owed my bookie some money, so I invented another story by saying. "Oh, I just didn't want to talk to him right now. Just too tired."

My making light of this was to not put any emotion in it so that there would be no questions coming from my mother. Lunch was served. It was fantastic, and once finished, I cleared my plate and went right back outside onto my waiting chaise lounge. The telephone rang a few times throughout the early afternoon, but since I never heard my mother repeat a familiar name, I paid no attention to them.

The New Jersey sun can still be seen in the sky, and the heat was just as strong, if not stronger. It must have been close to two thirty in the afternoon. My mother was outside sitting on the patio, and me, I was still enjoying my lounge time when the phone rang once again. Still with that small tint of a twinge when I heard the ring, I still ignored it since the last number of calls that came in, all were general calls I assumed my mother received daily.

"Oh, hello, Angelo. Yes, this is his mother."

I can hear as if it roared through the sky above me. I never felt tunnel vision with just a voice. Nonetheless, I knew immediately who was on the phone that then caused me to sit completely erect from my chaise. Looking sharply at my mother as my head went side to side repeatedly, my arms began to wave helplessly in the air, hoping she would continue with the story that I was still not home.

"No, I'm sorry Angelo. Steve has not been home since your last call, but I'll make sure to tell him when he gets here. Is there any message I can give him?" I heard my mother then say. "Okay, I'll make sure to tell him. Thank you. Bye-bye."

As relief came over me for that split second, that would be short-lived as now I hear my mother call out to me in an obvious "who done it" mystery sounding tone, "Alright, Steven, what's going on here?"

First, let it be known that whenever my parents called me Steven and not Steve, I had an invisible amber glow come over me, letting me know that whoever was talking to me was starting to get really aggravated with me. The tone and manner in their voice would always change, and when the Steven came out, it was not a good sign. Prepare to defend myself, I thought to myself.

And defend what I did or attempted to do. "Mom, it's nothing," I said. "I did some work with Angelo a few weeks ago, and he wants to finish the deal. Nothing to be concerned about. I'm just not in the mood to talk to him right now."

As I believed in my mind that it sounded good enough that I would have believed it myself, my mother gave me a look, paused, stared, and said, "Okay, as long as there's nothing to worry about."

"Nothing at all, Moms, straight up!" I quickly reiterated.

So now my mind started to do its thing. I could feel the cells in my brain start to flutter as I was searching for that one idea to say in case he calls back. First, I thought, I just won't let anyone answer the phone. That lasted only three seconds until I realized there was a telephone in almost every room in the house. What was I to do? Race around and collect the phones? Sure, let me make it more obvious that I was trying to avoid speaking with Angelo. I had about another thirty minutes before the sun would fall behind the tree line. I chose just to lay back down and let my brain start to plan. I did some of my best thinking under pressure. Once again, I had to sell myself. Never a dull moment.

The day was coming to an end as the change of scenery filled the sky. The brightness of the sun and the heat from its rays had changed into a partially darker sky with a bright deep orange and red sky and the glimmering of few stars as they take their mark in the night's sky. I gathered up the little that I had outside with me and made my final way into the closed screened porch. It was always a good place to drop your things off before making your way into the kitchen. The cabana outside had a bathroom, two changing rooms, and a shower. Grabbing a robe and towel, I enjoyed the next twenty minutes feeling the beads of water massage me, hoping for me to set a plan in motion on what I would have to say if confronted again by my mother or anyone regarding Angelo.

Not thirty minutes went by when the house phone rang again. I knew deep in my heart that the person on the other end was Angelo. We already knew that I preferred not to talk with him, so I immediately looked at my mother and mouthed the words, "I'm outa here," as I could start to feel a slight body tremble. "Tell him you gave me the message, and I said I would call him later on."

So without even pausing, I could hear my mother say, "Angelo, I gave him the message, and he said he would call you later today. No…he already left here."

One thing I knew I had always on my side was my incredible mother. Not that I was someone who was always in trouble or breaking the law, but my mom and I had something special. A friendship for each other that grew for many years to follow. Actually, till death do we part.

As my mother hung up the phone, I heard that angry tone of hers, "Steven, enough of the bullshit! What is going on, and who the hell is this, Angelo? The last call this man didn't sound so happy. I need some answers now!"

What could I do except be truthful with my mother and hope that she has an idea how to handle it. There was one way, but I really did not want to ask her for money. She would have to get it from my father who in turn would go through the roof if he knew I was dealing with anything with a bookie. especially a known bookie as Angelo was. But I had to be truthful with her. She was the only person I trusted enough to share this with.

"So listen, Mom," I started out with, "ya know, sometimes when I would run a little short in money, I was able to call Angelo and borrow it from him."

As I stood there looking at her, knowing that I was not too sure I pulled this off, like it was yesterday, I can hear my mother say, "Steven, I want the truth. How much money are we talking about here?" were the words I could hear her say. The look on her face made me know for a fact that she was about to verbally tear into me.

"Okay! Okay, so I borrowed some money from him, and I haven't paid him back yet! I plan on it! I just don't have it right now." I called out to her as I shuffled my legs and repositioned myself for the long haul. "Mom! It's okay! I got this!" I remember my mother stopping in her tracks and calmly saying to me in her "everyday" soft-spoken voice, "Okay, let's get real. You borrowed money from a bookie, and you're past due paying it back."

After what seemed to be an hour pause, my mother rephrased her words and said, "How much money are we talking about?" in her caring and concerned motherly voice.

I cocked my head to one side like a dog's head being told he was going outside, and I said in a quiet voice, "Five thousand dollars, Mom. And if I don't pay him back"—with a pause as if time was standing still—"I'm afraid it's my ass!"

The wildest of things were going through my mind. If Angelo finds me, am I met with a beating, maybe I'll be tied up and tortured with pins under my fingernails. I had no idea what to think except I knew other times when Angelo had to collect his way. Maybe I was not quite sure what my mother's reaction would be since I was never faced with this type of situation, so I was hoping she would be understanding.

I was left standing in our den in front of the stone fireplace, feeling as empty as a fireplace without any wood in its mouth to burn. Having left the room, my mother calmly returned with her hands and arms extended behind her, not uttering one single word. You could have heard a pin drop. Even our four German shepherd dogs refused to move as each was positioned sitting in place. They each were stretched out on the oakwood floor, each not moving an inch. They sensed something was up, and they did not want to be any part of it. Even their breathing calmed down so that you could hear a pin drop. I felt as though I was about to be taken down (not physically) by my mother. I realized I had to go with it no matter what. I was still waiting and hoping for her final words.

"Call him back and tell him you have his money," my mother said to me. "I do not want to find my son lying dead in some ditch. But, Steve," she said in a voice that sounded broken and was on the verge of a stutter, "I am warning you for the last time. If you ever do this again, you are on your own. I do not want any part of it. Do I make myself clear?" her voice blurted out as if this was her final way of saying, "Take it or leave it."

I took it. It was the best and only choice I had. Angelo got his money. I made a promise to my mother that I would not use a bookie for a loan ever again, and more importantly, I understood the position this put my mother in with my father. My parents were a team, and nothing would nor could ever come between them. Truly a power couple. The look upon my face was not a look of ease or contentment, yet I was able to extend that onstage smile so my mother would not think I was not thrilled right now. I knew the final straw was going to be the biggest hurdle. How do I keep this from my father when he returns home from work?

"Oh, and by the way," my mother whispered to me as she walked by, "Don't worry about your father. I will deal with him my way," she said. "No need to say one word about it."

End of discussion. Bottom line, I paid Angelo back, and I always assumed that my mother was able to keep this away from my father. The matter never came up.

Over the next few years, I primarily made a moderate living playing piano at different lounges, piano bars, and private parties. A favorite place I enjoyed playing at was the Orchid Lounge on Sip Avenue, Jersey City, New Jersey. It was exactly like one would picture a lounge with satin sheets on the walls, drop lighting that barely shined much light over this dimly old room. But the place had a reputation. A great reputation where many in the surrounding towns beside Jersey City knew about the Orchid Lounge. I can still smell the stale beer and cigarette-filled room. No matter how it looked and what the odor was that night, the Orchid Lounge and I would pack them in on weekends. Some wonderful memories looking back.

I started concentrating more on my music. From songwriting to poetry, I found myself more mature than during my New Start Records days, so I wanted to look further into writing. From my days of touring, I became a little familiar with Nashville, Tennessee, home of country music and some of the most talented songwriters. Maybe it was time for me to move on again—find another place to call home and make my mark. I think Nashville was calling me, but first, I needed to visit and see just what Nashville was all about. That is Nashville, Tennessee, not to be confused with Nashville, Indiana.

It was February 1981. There still were signs of winter with snow on the ground, the sights of bare trees and covered swimming pools. The temperature was somewhere in the forties when I decided to fly down to Nashville and see if this was somewhere I wanted to attempt to settle down. I received an invitation to join the Nashville Songwriters Association International. Just what the name said, it was an organization made up of songwriters from all over the world. It was not just for country music songwriters. You see, this organization known as NSAI was the backbone of every songwriter all over and still is. This organization was put together by some of the biggest names in country music and run by a dear friend of mine who first invited me to Nashville.

Maggie Cavender was the president of the NSAI, and she was one of the known people in country music who made sure to put songwriters first. Maggie would always say, "It's the songwriter who makes the music and the artist who makes it a hit." Maggie was probably a lady size zero. There was nothing to her. Standing maybe five feet two inches with straight dyed red hair that she wore down to her shoulders, Maggie Cavender was every songwriter's mother. Truly a wonderful lady and way ahead of her time.

After I arrived in Nashville for the convention, I chose to stay at the Sheraton Hotel, Broadway. This enabled me to be close to the Nashville Convention Center where NSAI was holding their annual event, and it was in walking distance to the famous Music Row, a marked area where all of the music publishing companies, songwriting institutions like NSAI, ASCAP, BMI and SESAC, recording studios, record labels, managers, and agencies with the likes of William Morris Agency, Creative Artists Agencies, the list goes on and on. With the amount of people attending this convention, I knew it was somewhere I needed to be. I was very successful, and I was fortunate to meet and write with some very talented people over time. While at the hotel for an afternoon break, some of the people I had met were also staying at the Sheraton, so we planned to meet and relax for approximately the two hours we had off. I had room service deliver plates of appetizers and beer. Roughly thirty minutes later, my telephone rang in my hotel room. Nobody knew I was staying here, so who could possibly be calling me?

"Hi, this is Judy Hall, the sales director here at the Sheraton Hotel," was this voice that came through the phone. The voice had a smooth and sweet Southern accent. Judy continued with, "Apparently, someone phoned the front desk and said that they smelled cannabis in the hallway of their floor and wanted us to be aware of it. Do you know anything about this, Mr. Wallach?" said that Southern voice on the phone.

I said without hesitation, "They smell what?"

And without another second going by, I could not help but chuckle, Ms. Hall said, "Look, if y'all are smokin' pot, then blow it out the window. Don't be so noticeable."

"Okay, thanks for the call," I said, trying to keep from laughing.

When I hung up the phone, I had to laugh and tell the others.

Getting ready to go back over to the convention, I picked up my hotel phone and pushed the button for the sales office.

"Hi, this is Judy Hall. May I help you?"

"Hello," I said. "Where is your office?"

"It's on the right side of the front desk. Why?" was her reply.

"I'm on my way down to say hello and thank you," I said in a very calm tone.

Within seconds, I hung up the phone, told the others I would see them back at the convention. In the lobby, I followed the signs that directed me to a glass door that had the words "Sales Office," etched in gold decal. I was now intrigued to see who owned this voice on the phone.

As I pushed open the door, there on the right side behind a waist-high divider sat this woman with shoulder-length brown hair and the phone receiver up to her face. As I waited patiently, I could not help but noticed her posture. She sat with her back firmly against the back of the chair, her legs firmly crossed, allowing one's imagination to run as they glanced at her legs underneath her slit skirt. As my mind started to race, I thought that I would be on my best behavior when I introduced myself to her.

As she hung up the phone, she turned to me, smiled, and said, "You must be Mr. Wallach?"

We made our informal introductions, and I was already looking forward to meeting her after work for cocktails and hopefully dinner (not again?).

The night's events were great. I met Judy for drinks and dinner, and we even shared a toke or two afterward. She was someone I found quite interesting and appealing. Only problem was I was leaving in less than forty-eight hours, and there was no way I could get together with her that quickly. She was not a one-hit wonder.

This was the last day of the convention, and I was on my way out to Los Angeles to market a friend's tour bus company. Buddy McKensie was his name, one of the best-known coach drivers during this time. Buddy had been the driver for Kenny Rogers, Alabama, Chicago, Dolly Parton, and the list went on and on. This time, I met Buddy at the convention, and he wanted me to join him in promoting his buses to the West Coast people. Buddy's company was well-known among the few top country artists, but he really wanted to pursue his goal in becoming one of the top bus touring companies nationwide. I decided to make the trip with him. There was nothing holding me back here in Nashville. I was offered a place to leave my items securely locked up at Buddy's warehouse, so without any further reasons not to, I boarded this incredible designed coach, and we set out for Los Angeles, California.

The trip cross-country took us three days. Even with a few stops along the way, we made some incredible time.

"Ever drive one of these before?" Buddy called out to me.

"Hell no," I said without missing a beat.

"Well, ya think you could drive one?" Buddy laughingly said.

"Hell yes," I quickly said before he could even catch his breath. "Just tell me what to do, and I'll do it," I said as my voice shook in excitement.

So right then and there, Buddy stands up from the driver's seat and says, "Come on, son. Take the wheel," and moves over to one side.

You have to remember, the bus is still moving down the highway at seventy miles an hour. Continuing down the left lane as if there was nothing abnormal about the drive, calmly as I could, I slide in behind the wheel of this massive bus, put my right foot on the pedal, and made like I was a full-time tour coach driver.

"Damn, Buddy! I'm drivin' this bus!" were the words that came out of my mouth.

The excitement on my face and the feeling of driving this was incredible. Something I always wanted to do, and now I was doing it. It was a great run out to Los Angeles, California.

Buddy and I kept in contact throughout the years. Not hearing from him for some time, I searched social media and found his wife, Wanda. We exchanged messages, and she sent me her phone number. I, at once, reached out to her.

"Hello," I could hear a voice say on the other end of the phone.

"Hi, Wanda. It's Steve Wallach."

"Oh, Steve, it's been a while," she replied back. Before I could say another word, all I hear was, "We lost Buddy in the middle of a tour while in Toronto, Canada. Buddy failed to pick up his artist at the venue. They found Buddy dead from a severe heart attack, an attack he apparently had in his hotel room."

I was shocked to hear this. Everyone loved Buddy McKenzie. He will always be remembered as a dear friend.

We made it to Los Angeles and checked into the Downtown Sheraton Hotel on Lower Wilshire Boulevard. That became our home base for the next five days. The hotel was kind enough to make room for the coach right in front. Many hotels will allow us to park directly in front as a sign of promoting their hotel as the place where the celebrities stay. I remember the hotel distinctively because it was there on our first night the news came out that Natalie Wood had died from a boating accident. Many people were talking about her death in the lounge. Over drinks, it seems that it is a wonderful crutch to lean on. So when I heard the news and saw her photo on TV, I could not help but think of Judy. You remember Judy Hall, sales director from the Sheraton Nashville? Filled with questions, I started thinking about her. We really hit it off together, I thought. We laughed, got high, drank and joked with each other as though we have been friends for years. I did what I thought was the next best thing. I called Judy (here we go again!).

After nearly a three-hour phone conversation, I went into romance mode (again) and said to her, "So listen for a moment, please. You have a round-trip plane ticket with your name on it waiting for you. Your flight leaves tomorrow morning, and I will have a car pick you up at the airport."

I hung the phone up without giving her a chance to respond. Seriously, it was an immediate reaction to what I had said. If you ask any other, I think they would say that I hung up so abruptly because I was afraid of rejection. If that were the case, I guess the answer would be known fourteen hours from now. Will she be at the airport arrivals tomorrow late morning? Your guess is as good as mine was. Thinking repeatedly about Judy and the air ticket. *What if she's not there when the plane lands?* I thought to myself. *Better yet, what if she is there? Did I do something I'll regret?* I really knew nothing about her except from the small talk we had before I left Nashville. I always like a challenge, so tomorrow will bring me yet another that needs to be conquered. Well, maybe I should not say conquered. Call it what you like. I have released the challenge. We will know tomorrow.

I finished my evening in the hotel's lounge sipping Absolut Vodka on the rocks with a splash of Sprite, finished with a twist of lemon. I enjoyed listening to the voice of a pretty little lady tickling the keys of the ivories. She had a smooth sensual voice that grazed those in the lounge like honey on a bee. She looked as good as she played—excellent. Right away, be honest with yourself. You immediately thought it was getting ready for (not again) to now happen the night before Judy arrives at eleven-twenty tomorrow morning.

The following morning, I made sure to wake up early enough to have a shower and an easy breakfast in the hotel's dining room. The sun was out, the skies were clear, and the shade of blue made you feel like you were in California with the California weather. I checked to see if I had any messages; there were none. Was I thinking there might have been a message from Judy saying thank you but no thank you? Honestly, yes, I thought as my mind began to wonder, picturing her arrival.

After arriving at the airport with about twenty minutes to spare, I stopped by one of the concessions, where they had fresh flowers for sale. Being the romantic I thought I was, it was a perfect fitting for me to have a boutique of long-stemmed roses waiting for her. I wanted to make sure she felt as excited as me. When she appeared, walking around the corner to clear the secured area, I was standing with bated breath, hoping to contain myself from not acting as if I were a twelve-year-old boy getting a bicycle for Christmas. I felt something come over me (okay…again!).

This was the start of a sixteen-year marriage filled with your normal, everyday escapades. I would have to say that most of our years together were good. In fact, they were great. As with any marriage, you sometimes fight mentally hard to make it work. A good marriage takes a lot of blood, sweat, and tears. Those of us who are married realize this. Maybe it is realized too late, but we all fully understand the good, the bad, and the ugly.

I had taken a job as road manager for country artist Tanya Tucker. It was mid-August, your typical humid-filled summer day in

Nashville, Tennessee. Leaving your home to walk to your car parked street-side, you had to go back and shower again. The humidity was high, to say the least. I was hired by Beau Tucker, who was Tanya's father and her personal manager. All decisions about Tanya's career had to be approved and cleared up by only Beau.

Beau Tucker's background consisted of farming. He had no idea what went into managing a country music artist, never mind his daughter, who reached top status with her first hit single, "Delta Dawn." Beau had a short temper when it came to all the incidents Tanya would get herself into. He had some of us searching her hotel rooms and her private bedroom on the bus. Granted, Tanya partied her ass off. There were more powder runs and sushi runs at every venue. Most knew of Tanya's highly respected slogan, "It's Tanya Tucker Can You Fuck Her, Tanya Tucker, Tanya Tucker!" Whether people believe any rumors about any celebrity, you need to know that the majority of the rumors are actually true, to a degree. They have always been and will always be "the party girls."

Let us take a moment to reflect. This is not a kiss-and-tell storybook. I am writing just as if I were speaking directly to you about not only my years on tours but my entire life—both the good, the bad, and the boring. Everything I wrote about my childhood through my teens and now my adulthood is a fact. It was an experience I will always be grateful to, and my thanks to those that believed in me during my life, thank you. Buckle up that seat belt. It's going to be an interesting ride.

So here I am, boarding an American Airlines flight headed to Los Angeles to be picked up at the airport and driven to Tanya Tucker's California residence for the start of her nationwide concert tour. Not a bad gig, I thought to myself, as I could hear the landing wheels come down and lock in for our arrival in Los Angeles, California.

Arriving lower-level baggage area, I, at once, drew my sight on a man standing off to the side, as not to be in the path of the passengers scurrying to find their luggage, wearing a black suit, white shirt, and tie. He was holding a sign that read in bold letters: "STEVE WALLACH."

Before I could even pick out my luggage, this man approached me and introduced himself, "I'm your driver. They call me Hollywood!"

Well, okay, Hollywood, I thought to myself as I returned my introduction. "Hey, Hollywood. I'm Steve."

"Just wait over here, Mr. Wallach. I'll grab your luggage for you. How many pieces?"

"Just two, please," I called back, thinking that I could have grabbed my own luggage. But I will take it this way.

My luggage was retrieved, and we made our way into the lower parking lot, where all the limos were perfectly aligned, waiting for their calls to pick up their clients. Hollywood had it all down to a science. He knew how to pack the luggage; he had cold bottled water waiting for me in the cup holders between the seats in the rear of the limo. The air-conditioning was blowing cool air through the vents in this stretch, and I had already reclined myself as if this was something I was completely familiar with. I was not, but who needed to know?

Some forty minutes later, I pulled up in front of a house and was met by a girl in her twenties who said, "You must be Steve? I'm Karen, Tanya's personal assistant."

I already knew that she was extremely difficult to deal with, especially when I and our production manager needed to have production and venue talks with her. Her name was known as the bitch. I came to find out she was Tanya's yes-girl. Anything Tanya wanted, and I do mean anything, she made it happen. Store runs, pharmacy runs, man runs, dope runs, food runs, liquor runs, she handled it.

As Tanya's road manager, I was given the title of being forced to find out about most things. Tanya was sly, and at times, between she, her assistant, and her bodyguard Ted Walker, they did their best not to keep me in the loop. Introductions were made, and I was told to come inside.

Once inside, I could hear a voice talking to someone who must have been on the phone because I was able to only hear the one-sided conversation. Coming down the stairs was a woman in her late twenties, wearing light blue jeans, and a white-and-red blouse.

As this woman came to the final landing on the house steps, she looked over at me and said, "You must be Steve."

Before I could even respond, she said, "I'm Tanya Tucker!"

At the same moment she introduced herself to me, around the corner coming out of the kitchen came a man who extended his hand and arm and said, "Hi! I'm Glen Campbell!"

Now I felt a small rush come over me. Standing directly in front of me was the legendary Glen Campbell. I threw my hand out to shake his and firmly shook as I wanted him to know my presence was there. It was a great introduction.

First impression of Glen was that he was this happy man who spoke and smiled a lot. Tanya, on the other hand, started yelling at her assistant over what seemed to be a scheduling problem. Watching her assistant do her best to calm the situation down, I just stood there, taking it all in. *Hmm*, I thought to myself.

"She's a handful, alright. Time to make my mark present."

I immediately said, "Tanya, let me look at this scheduling. I'm sure I can make this all go right. We will go over it in the car."

In the meantime, we are pressed for time right now because we have to be at Magic Mountain by three o'clock for your soundcheck before tonight's show."

Not skipping a beat, Tanya called back, "Okay, good. Let's get going."

So Tanya, Glen, Tanya's assistant, and I climbed into the back of Hollywood's limo, and off we went on our way to my first show with Tanya Tucker and Glen Campbell.

The hourly ride gave us the opportunity to get to know each other. Tanya did most of the talking, directed only toward Karen, never once asking me anything or Glen. Glen, on the other hand, was simply Glen Campbell, a funny man. He was telling me story after story. In fact, after about twenty minutes into the ride, it was obvious that both Tanya and Glen were as high as a kite. Never-ending gibberish, it was quite amusing to see these people who are loved the world over as high as they were. I would say from my own unprofessional opinion, the cocaine had a home with Tanya and Glen.

We arrived at Magic Mountain, where I was introduced to Tanya's band members and her production team. Most were from the West Coast, but a few of her musicians hailed from places including Nashville and Oklahoma. As we entered Tanya's dressing room, I noticed Tanya make a beeline for the bathroom, at the same time calling for her assistant to join her. Glen took a seat for a quick minute and then got up and went over to the bathroom door, where he gave it a quick knock and walked right in. That was odd, one toilet bathroom with three people in it. Yes, questions came to my mind, but again, I was here to make sure Tanya performed and got paid. The manner to which people use the restroom was no concern of mine. So I thought....

As the band was preparing to take the stage, Tanya and Glen were standing just outside the green room when we were able to hear their voices getting louder and louder. At first, I did not pay much attention to it. The music was playing, so I just thought they were trying to talk over the sounds. I never knew what their conversation was about, but all I knew was that their conversation got louder, and the barrage of foul language echoed throughout the backstage area. Finally, I had to take the initiative to stop them and have her refocus on the stage. This bullshit was not going to happen on my watch.

Tanya walked out like a pro and held the audience immediately. One thing about Tanya Tucker, she knew how to work a stage, and work it she did. Glen, on the other hand, was handed his guitar by his tech and began doing riffs as if he was in front of the crowd.

"I still got it," Glen called out.

He was a fantastic guitarist and could make any guitar sound incredible. Glen and I smiled at each other, and as he was about to take the stage as well, he turned to me and said, "Thank you. You done good."

I now had Tanya Tucker on stage doing a duo with the renowned Glen Campbell. You could not help but feel the energy on the stage and in the audience as screams, cheers, and stuffed animals were being thrown up on the stage by many of her fans and his.

"Welcome to country music," I said as I grinned, escorting them both back to her dressing room.

After the show, her show went off great, and we prepared to meet some of her fans at the meet and greet, an event most promoters need after every show.

THIS LIFE OF MINE

On the way back in the limo, Tanya shouted out, "Who wants sushi?"

Immediately, her assistant and Glen said, "Sure! Sushi sounds great to us!"

"There's a favorite place of mine off Sunset Boulevard," Tanya called out. "We can park in the alley and go through their kitchen door."

And that is what we did. Hollywood knew of the location, and he positioned the limo at their kitchen employee door. You see, one of the perks of working with some celebrities, you get to have a little bit of clout, so parking, entering, and being serviced usually runs smoothly and fast.

This was my first experience with sushi. It was also my last. I just could not find myself eating any raw fish designed in any shape or form. Sushi and I just did not get along. I ordered myself a bowl of steamed white rice, which was needed to hold me over until we were able to drop them off at her residence and head over to my hotel. As we were exiting the restaurant by the same route we entered, Tanya was met by a couple in the rear of the kitchen. A small hug and kiss and a quick handshake between Tanya and her friend, where a small folded paper was handed over by Tanya. It was none of my business, so I did what I knew to do—nothing. As Hollywood was about to speed off, a man came up to the limo to speak with Tanya. I will always remember this man.

As he and Tanya talked through the car window, he handed a cylinder tube to Tanya and said, "This is the last photo I took of Elvis during his last performance. I want you to have it."

The man holding this was one of Elvis's personal photographers. Sean Shavers introduced himself to me as I reached out for the cylinder. I offered to give it to Tanya as we drove off.

"I don't want it," Tanya slurred her words to me. "Throw it in with the other stage items when we get back to my house."

By the time we arrived back at her house, it was obvious that Tanya's condition worsened, and her drunkenness took center stage.

"Where do you want me to put this cylinder?" I asked.

"Oh, fuck it," Tanya spurted out. "I don't want another photo of Elvis. You can have it."

And have it is what I did. It hangs proudly in my game room at my home. In fact, I have been offered some serious money to sell it, but right now, I will keep it with my other photos of another king: Michael Jackson.

Arriving back at Tanya's house, I carried some of her belongings into the kitchen area and waited to see what our next move was. Glen had already disappeared in the house, and Tanya's assistant was already on her cell phone in the corner. Me, I decided to ask Tanya if there was a place we could go and have a sit-down.

"I'd like to go over your schedule as we prepare for your tour," I said.

Grabbing my carry bag, I followed Tanya into what appeared to be her dining room. There were papers scattered all over a long rectangular dining table. The papers seemed to be in no actual order as there were stacks upon stacks upon stacks.

"I see you have your hands full," I said in a joking manner.

"Not really," Tanya called out. "Between you and my assistant, I know you'll have me covered."

As I glanced at the dining table, I could not help but notice her assistant looking away and not really paying any attention to what we were discussing.

"I want a bodyguard," Tanya blurted out to me. "Find me a bodyguard that I can rely on. You know, rely on for everything" (with an emphasis on everything).

I thought for a moment. I had met a man while I was in Nashville, staying at the Sheraton Hotel. His father was the piano tuner, and that was how we had met. I was playing the piano in one of the conference rooms when he escorted his father over to the piano.

"My dad's here to tune this piano," this deep voice called out to me.

As I turned from my piano bench, I extended my hand and said, "No problem. I was just killing some time. I'm Steve Wallach."

Now picture this young guy holding his father's arm: he was tall with a solid build, who fit the part, looking like he worked security. His hands and fingers towered over any normal set of hands.

"I'm Ted Walker, and this is my father, Ted Sr. My dad tunes the piano here every few months."

Without hesitation, I stood up and moved out of the way so he would be able to do his work.

While his father started to set up his tuning bag, Ted and I had a small conversation.

"Yeah, normally, I handle security and bodyguard work out at Country Music Fan Fair every year, plus I handle security at a lot of the major recording studios. I'm the one who keeps the fans back," he said, laughing as if he meant that he was the one in charge. "It keeps me busy."

I had no idea what a fan fair was but refused to let him think that I was in the dark. I came to find out that the fan fair was a five-day festival where thousands of fans could get up close and personal with their favorite country music artists. Not familiar with this event, I just played along as Ted described all that takes place during this music festival.

As I arrived back in Nashville from my first Tanya Tucker meeting, I immediately thought to myself, *Hey, call that guy Ted Walker and see if he wants the job as bodyguard for Tanya Tucker*. First, I had to run it by her manager, Beau Tucker. It was Beau who called all the shots, and if I stayed on his good side, things hopefully would run smoothly. It was not for me to make the decision about hiring additional road crew, especially her bodyguard.

After speaking with Beau and Tanya, it was decided that Ted Walker would be Tanya's personal bodyguard while on tour. I offered Ted the job, and he immediately accepted, thanking me for giving him the chance at this. I hired Ted for another reason besides his size. I needed someone close to my artist to report back to me any out of the ordinary things that she may do.

I recall Beau phoning me the night before we were to fly back out to California and said, "This new guy Ted, you better let him know I want to know whatever my daughter is up to."

At first, I was somewhat puzzled by Beau's statement, but over time, I realized that Tanya had a problem. Not just any problem, Beau let me believe that his daughter had a cocaine problem. Never seeing her snort a line of cocaine, it was difficult for me to say I had. Granted, her behavior over time gave it away to everyone. Plus on some occasions, Tanya would appear with a white powder at her nostrils. I seriously doubt it was powdered sugar.

Tanya was going through thousands of dollars weekly. How do I know? I was the person who carried all the travel funds needed to keep the tour running. The venue payments for Tanya's shows were paid either in cash or by check, always with complete and approved receipts. I knew there was a problem when Ted came to me telling me that Tanya wanted more money. Hey, it was not my money to decide. I was there to make sure she got paid for her performances, the band and entourage were properly paid, and all expenses were paid along the way. I did, however, make a note of the times Tanya wanted money. Again, it was not for me to deny any cash to her. It was never an exuberant amount of cash. It was twenty-five hundred today, thirty-two hundred the next week, so on and so forth. When it started reaching five thousand, I had to question Ted about it. As dedicated Ted was to Tanya, he knew it was I who gave him this touring chance, and at least he felt obligated to pass on some information to the one question.

"Is Tanya using the float money for coke?" I asked.

All it took was a nod from Ted. I knew what I had to do next.

The shows went great. Most of them were sellouts, so handling the collection after each performance was easy. The only problem we had was when Glen Campbell would join us on the road. The tension backstage would become tense. The crew would be sitting and waiting for Tanya and Glen to explode and start throwing and cursing at each other. To this day, I never knew what their fights were about. As long as Ted was keeping an eye on her, I thought it was covered. Ted was nothing more than her "yes" man. No matter what Taya asked for, Ted would come to me saying he needed more money for her. It got to the point where I started demanding Ted call Tanya's father and fill him in.

THIS LIFE OF MINE

We were flying from Nashville to Lake Tahoe for shows at Harrah's Casino/Hotel. Every time I flew with Tanya, I always had a first-class seat as she and Glen did. Oh, let us not forget about her assistant. Whatever class Tanya had, she did as well. So here we all are, seated in first class, and the band was on the coach. Our production crew had already made their way to Tahoe by means of our coaches and semitrucks. Tanya traveled with a fairly good-size production back then.

Not thirty minutes into the flight, Tanya made her way to the bathroom in first class. Not five minutes later, Glen gets up from his seat and makes his way to the same bathroom, lightly knocking on the door. Two seconds later, the door to the bathroom opens, and Glen steps in. Now both were in one of the planes' first-class bathrooms. Without exaggeration, Tanya and Glen stayed in that bathroom for well over an hour of the flight. In fact, I can honestly say that neither one of them came back to their seats for half of the length of the flight. Back then, flight attendants never hassled an entertainer during a flight. In fact, most of the time, they allowed us to move freely. For the five hours thirty-minute flight, two hours and thirty minutes, Tanya and Glen both occupied that one bathroom.

Tanya Tucker and Glen Campbell finally made it out of the bathroom and returned to their seats, laughing loudly. They continued to laugh out loud and speak to each other without any concern for those around them. You see, it was as if there were no other people in first class—just the two of them. Their boisterous laughs finally came to a halt as we made our final approach. Hello, Reno, Nevada. Tanya Tucker and Glen Campbell have arrived.

Throughout my time working with Tanya Tucker, it was obvious that her relationship with Glen Campbell had serious issues. From their name-calling and their use of vulgar words like that of a sailor, they made quite a name for themselves. From reports and news outlets to the print in many good publications and that of the newspapers known as the rags, both names appeared in their publications for obvious reasons.

Another time was when we arrived in Shreveport, Louisiana. We arrived at approximately ten o'clock at night. The night's air was hot, but the humidity made everything feel sticky. We were glad our long road trip was finally over, and we would soon feel the water from our long-awaited showers and a fresh clean bed to sleep in. Our three tour buses were all lined up in the hotel's parking lot. I made my way into the hotel's lobby to begin the process of checking in the band and road crew, as most of them were already filling into the lobby area. Not five minutes, Ted, Tanya's bodyguard, came into the hotel lobby and called out to me and said, "Steve, they're at it again!" Making a motion with his hand that Tanya and Glen were still on their bus, I asked Ted what the issue was. "All I know is that Glen is now standing outside the bus in the parking lot, preaching words from the Bible and calling Tanya everything from the devil's wife to a slut. They're not settling down!"

I came out to see just what was going on, and I did find Glen Campbell standing outside the bus door, Bible in hand, and he was screaming what he said were quotes from the Bible. As I tried to open the bus door to see if I could get some handle on what was happening with Tanya, Glen called out, "She's locked the door to hell! No one can enter! No one can leave!" Each time Glen would start to preach, he would again point to scriptures in the Bible. "I demand of you to open this door," Glen screamed out. Hearing silence, Glen took his fist and continued punching the glass window on the bus door, causing the glass to finally crack. *Oh my gosh*, I thought to myself. I must get inside this bus and calm things down before it gets further out of hand and the police come. Too late, as I turned to look at Glen and Ted, two police cars pulled up. I thought that we were busted for sure and that there was going to be an arrest. As Ted tried to calm things down with Glen, I introduced myself to the officers and explained that there was a slight altercation and misunderstanding between these two people, one being Glen Campbell and the other Tanya Tucker. When celebrity couples fight in public, it is always called a misunderstanding so that no one person gets the fault thrown at them. It seemed to be working.

As the tone outside calmed down, Tanya unlocked the bus door, and she and her assistant exited, asking me, "Steve, where's my room?"

I had Ted escort her into the hotel lobby and directly to the waiting elevator. I stayed behind with Glen and the officers. I assured the officers that I would make sure things stayed quiet, and there would not be any further incidents involving either Tanya or Glen. Glen signed a few autographed photos for the officers, and off we went in the elevator to the third floor, where the hotel rooms were waiting.

"Glen, promise me there will be no screaming matches once you go inside," I said to him. "We were lucky that no further action was taken by the police. Now promise me you'll go to bed. We have a show the next day, and we're all tired."

Knocking on the suite door, I was hoping that Tanya would open it and all would be back to normal—normal being no screaming and nothing being thrown.

As if nothing ever happened, Tanya jumped into Glen's arms, and they both went into their suite, closing the door behind them. Ted and I looked at each other and thought. Finally, it is quiet. We said good night to each other and made our way to our assigned hotel rooms. Finally, we made it to Shreveport, Louisiana.

As I was about to start dreaming of walking along the ocean beach on a Caribbean Island, a loud pounding was heard on my door.

"Steve, they're at it again! Glen ripped the sink right off the fuckin' bathroom wall, and he's standing in the middle of the suite, reciting scriptures from the Bible."

I made my way to get partially dressed and went to see what happened. Walking into the suite and trying to assess just what happened, Tanya approached me and said, "Make this go away! I am not dealing with this now!"

Knowing that the police were probably on their way back to the hotel, I immediately had Ted keep Tanya in her suite, and I took Glen to an unoccupied room we had on the floor.

"Glen, please don't come out of this room! I don't want to have to bail you out of jail!" I yelled out, trying to keep Glen's attention.

As I closed the door behind me and stood in the hallway on my way back to Tanya's suite, I was met in the hallway by the same two police officers. After doing my best to convince the officers that no one was pressing any charges and that I would make restitution for the damage caused in the suite, they both agreed, and that evening's smackdown was finally over.

"Mr. Wallach," as the one officer began to say something, "if we must come back here tonight over this same incident, I promise you, someone is going to jail. Do I make myself clear?"

Immediately, I said, "Oh yes, Officer. Thanks, I really mean it."

The following morning, I met with the hotel manager and gave him all our business information with the assurance that we would cover any damage done to the suite caused by either Ms. Tucker or Mr. Campbell. What was strange, Glen had no recollection of cracking the bus window nor cracking the porcelain sink and pulling it away from the wall. Further in the day, we had a great soundcheck, the show went off without any incidents, and we were all on our way to the next venue.

Further on in the tour, Tanya had a performance at the famous Billy Bob's in Fort Worth, Texas. Bill Bob's was a huge country bar and dance hall. They have had and continue to have top headliners performing there, and Tanya was a favorite there. Glen had left the tour for other obligations, so it was just Tanya that Ted had to deal with. The two sold-out shows were incredible. The fans loved it, and the promoter was happy knowing that he just made a small fortune at the ticket door. Once the two shows were complete, Tanya had a backstage pass list that had a sleuth of names on it. Probably twenty names appeared on the personal backstage pass list, most of them being male. You see, Tanya had a reputation for enjoying herself with men. One of the favorite saying's was (and still is), "Hey that's Can Ya Fuck Her Tanya Tucker." Now I am not saying that she was promiscuous, but let's just say most men that came out of her dressing were walking with huge smiles on their faces. You could hear some of them say, "Man, she was incredible!" What was incredible? Her show or her after-show? It was obvious and known that Tanya was a party girl, and many men would share their personal experiences about her. Hey, that was life on the road with Tanya Tucker and, sometimes, Glen Campbell. Vegas, here we come! Well…almost.

Before I confirmed the job with Tanya Tucker, I had told her father that I was getting married in September this year and that I would need to leave the tour for this special moment in my life. Getting married for the second time, I wanted to make sure that I covered my bases and that my job would still be there.

"Beau, I'm gonna fly back to Nashville right after we finish at Billy Bob's," I said over the phone. "In fact, I'll bring back the monies I took in from the last set of shows we did."

I knew Beau would not object then especially when he knew there was quite a large amount of money. Beau even made it easier for me. "Just meet me in Paul Moore's office at William Morris Agency the following morning you fly in," Beau said. "We can settle up then before you head back out."

I knew I only had a few hours in the morning the following day before I had to meet up with Judy Hall for our wedding vows. I got up early the next day and made sure I was at Paul's office right when they opened. Judy was already nervous about the wedding. We had planned a two-event wedding for us. Well, it was a one-wedding ceremony with two separate receptions. One was to take place in Nashville with Judy's family and our local friends and the other in New Jersey at my parents' home for my family and my parents and other friends. I only had four days to make this all happen. We had two full days of rehearsals coming up in Reno, Nevada, for Tanya's television special that I could not afford to miss. There was too much involved.

I met Beau the following morning. Settlements were made on the shows, and Beau made it a point to tell me that he was concerned about his daughter.

"Concerned about what, Beau?" I asked as he sat across me in Paul Moore's office.

He and Paul looked at each other and then looked over at me.

"Steve, I think Tanya may be doing drugs. You know, drugs like cocaine," Beau said in a determined tone to find the truth.

As I looked directly at both Paul and then Beau, I could not help but feel a bit taken aback. As if Tanya was my blood, I felt that

I had to do my best and watch over to see if there was anything to be suspicious about.

"Beau, I really don't know what to say," I said in a compassionate voice. "If I see anything, I will definitely let you know."

Already having a strong idea that Tanya was doing blow, my thoughts were confirmed when I spoke directly to Ted over the phone about the concern Beau had.

"Ted, I'm telling you that *if* Tanya is doing anything, you best bring it either to my attention or call Beau and let him know. I'm not here to babysit anybody, especially Tanya Tucker."

I hung up the phone and directed my full attention to my marriage needs with Judy.

I recall what led up to us having two receptions for our wedding. The running joke was that they wanted to make sure the north and south did not meet. In fact, our actual wedding ceremony was held in my rabbi's chambers, and we only had our two other witnesses with us. We had both been married prior, and we felt it was not necessary to have only those in Nashville attend. Our wedding ceremony was quiet, and we sealed it with the breaking of the glass, calling out the Hebrew word for congratulations, *mazel tov*. The southern reception was complete.

Having less than a week to complete the remaining wedding reception in New Jersey, it was long ago decided that my parents would hold the event at their home. My parents' home, as you know, would make for a wonderful and beautiful venue for our northern reception. It was not overly decorated as my parents' home was already a showplace, but my mother made sure there were plenty of wedding decorations abound. The backyard was beautifully decorated in white roses, and the lighting used for this evening affair accented the manicured grounds. Even the area by the pool was covered with plants as well as lighting. It truly was a very comfortable and beautiful place for a celebration. It truly was a wonderful reception in both Tennessee and New Jersey.

One thing that stood out was when Judy asked, "Why are there so many limos parked on the circular drive? I thought that was a bit odd. I did my best to introduce Judy to our northern family and friends during the reception. There was Hiam, Gino, Izra, Antonio, and a few others who never left their limos. It was as if they were on the "get ready and go" tour. We had a very eclectic group of friends and business associates. There had to be at least 150 people at the house. A beautiful affair my mother designed and made happen.

Sunset for sleep. Sunrise to catch a flight back to Nashville to prepare for my following flight back out on the road to join Tanya's tour in Sparks, Nevada.

It was a long flight to Reno, Nevada, especially having to change planes along the way. I had so many flyer miles built up that I chose to cash in some of my points to upgrade to first class since traveling without Tanya did not allow me the perk of flying first class. At least traveling in the premium class gave me the additional space that helped with my long legs and a nice, cool blanket and pillow in case I chose to sleep. Being it was a day flight, the best part of traveling first class was keeping the booze flowing! I had over four hours to play the role.

Arriving safely and meeting my driver in the baggage area, I was ready for the ride to Sparks. It was not a long ride, but I now had to spend more time in a car, counting the minutes when I would arrive at Harrah's Hotel/Casino. Tanya's headlining concert was nightly for four nights. Our preproduction was to last for the next two days, watching the carpenters, electricians, sound technicians, and lighting crew all work vigorously to keep in their allocated time. It was total chaos on the stage. The venue had to be set exactly, the sound had to be impeccable, and the lighting had to be spot-on. They were filming and recording both Tanya's new album as well as portions for her television special. Now I had to deal not only with Tanya but Beau, the record producer, the producer from ABC, her clothing guru, and the list went on and on.

"Steve, we need you to do this," I kept hearing Beau say to me. "Where's Tanya? Now you best make sure she's ready to go when they call for her!" Beau would repeatedly say every fifteen minutes.

"Not an issue, Beau," I would say.

I knew it would take me a few extra minutes to make sure Ted had her ready to walk toward the stage. And on the stage, Tanya did walk. Her first full dress rehearsal went great, and the day was called.

Later that day, some of us decide to try our luck in Harrah's Casino. The casino was filled with people looking to have that one special luck run where all their financial troubles would disappear from their jackpot winnings. Walking through the slot machine area, you could not help but hear the bells and whistles of the winning machines. Screams came from some of the lucky winners. One would think they won a million dollars. No, not really. It was for a measly $35 win. Still, watching the faces of these people gave you a feeling of possibly being the next big winner. It was time to make the casino work for me. I wanted to be the next big winner. Doesn't everyone?

I am primarily a blackjack player when it comes to the casinos. Going back to my first desire to play the games of chance, I used to watch my father play. The older I got, well, you know what happened if you have read my book up to this point. But I felt that that was years ago, and I believed that I had a firm grip on gambling. Throughout the years since my late teens, I have been able to take my chances at the tables, but I also only sat down with a set amount of money. If I win, then the better for me. If I lost the bankroll I had set out to play, then that was the end of that play. There was no more banking to add onto the deficit. I was to get up and walk away from the table and head to the closest exit and say to myself over and over, if necessary, "I'm done for the night."

Within the first two hours of play, I had accumulated a good-size profit. I started with $500, playing at a $25 minimum table, seated at my favorite position, third base. The positions of seats at a blackjack table consist of seven spots. The first seat being called first base, the middle seat going by second base, and the third seat holding down the table for the final betting decision was third base. Each base was followed by another open seat. If you went by the terms of a baseball diamond, these seats were referred to as the short-stop seats. Over time, playing, watching others play, reading books, and playing blackjack, it was common knowledge among strong players that third base can either save the table or break the break, causing most players to lose that hand, giving the best option to the dealer. I was pretty good at following the blackjack book rules. Sometimes, I would bend the rules to hopefully suit my win, but most of the time, I was known as a book player.

By my third hour, I could not believe how much I had in front of me. It was well over my initial $500 investment. Do I leave the table and count my winnings, or do I stay and play a set amount and see what happens? I didn't want to break the motion at the table, so as I continued playing, I counted my winnings and saw that I had made in excess of five thousand dollars. I believe it was exactly $5,300, not including my initial $500 buy-in. Not a bad hit, I thought to myself. Should I get up and walk away, or should I play a little bit longer? You see, this was routine. I would try to convince myself to walk away, but that devil on my other shoulder was telling me to continue playing. *What to do*? I thought to myself as I now have cut far back on my initial bet of a mere $50. I set aside $4,100 and chose to play with $1,300 of my winnings. Feeling as though I was on a great winning streak, I started making between $200 and $300 bets. Craziest thing was that I was winning almost every hand.

I remember, at one point, I had a $300 bet on the table. My first card was an eight, and my second as an eight. The dealer had a six showing. The blackjack player's book always tells the player to split a pair of eights, knowing that the odds of the next few cards could determine you a strong winner or lucky player for that hand. The odds of losing the hand were low. As any skillful player would do, I split my eights and double up on my bet. So now I had $600 on the table. The dealer pulls out the next card from the card boot and flips it as she drops it down on the first eight. A three appears now, giving me eleven. A perfect opportunity to follow the rules of blackjack and double down on the eleven, hoping for a ten or equivalent thereof, so in total, I would have twenty-one. As the dealer flips over the last card for that play, my dreams come true.

"Twenty-one!" the dealer called out, and the entire table of players cheered out. It was not onto the next eight. Dealer flips the card, and out comes an eight.

"Hmmmmm," I recall making that sound as I reach for another three hundred dollars in chips. "I'd like to split these eights," I said to the dealer as she smiled over at me and mouthed the words, "Good luck." On the first eight appeared a two.

Dealer calls out, "Ten. Would you like to double down?" she said to me.

Without skipping a beat, I said in return, "But of course!"

With a smile from ear to ear, the dealer deals me an ace. "Twenty-one!" I called out as the others at the table cheered with excitement. The dealer then pointed to my last eight as she flipped my next card. As if the cards were turning over in slow motion, I could see from its side view that the card was another three. As if my arm movement and my breathing were in sync, I pushed up an additional three hundred dollars in chips, hoping that my winning streak was still on target. That final card came out of the card boot as if it were in full, slow motion again. Finally, the dealer flipped the card in the air, and as if it fell, I could not help but see that it was a picture card. A card is worth ten!

"Twenty-one!" everyone shouted from the table. What a huge hit.

I recall keeping my cool and not reacting like the voices over near the slot machine wins. I sat quietly at third base and counted in my mind just how much I won in the hand. In total, my bet was $1,800. In return, my winnings totaled $3,600. So when I combined my winnings for the day, I walked out of the casino with over $7,700 in my pocket. Now minus my total winnings from my initial buy-in of $500, I ended up winning over $7,000 for about five hours of casino play.

Lying on my bed in my hotel room, thinking of my winnings, my production manager called and said he needed to see me. The tone in his voice was concerning, but I was still on such an emotional high, I said, "Well, come on over. Let's have a beer and talk." I had not hung the phone up, and there was a knock on my hotel room door. *That quick, huh?* I thought to myself.

I opened the door and found my production manager standing in the doorway, arms crossed, and said to me, "We got a problem."

Trying to keep my composure, the first thing I said was, "Yo, bro! I just won a shitload of money downstairs in the casino! Check this out!"

As I began to fan a stack of hundred-dollar bills in front of him, he waved his arm at me and said again, "Steve, we have a problem! There's money missing from the draw."

As my joy turned to concern, I asked him what he was referring to. "Well, I wanted to pay the band and the crew their per diems so I wouldn't have to worry about their money," our production manager said to me. "But when I went to the casino cage to sign out the $6,000, I was refused. Steve, they said that there was already a six thousand advance given out, and I would have to get approval from the entertainment department. Even though our shows were in the showroom of the hotel, all agreements, paperwork, and funds were handled through the casino."

I told him that I would call the vice president of entertainment to find out what was going on with our account.

After placing a call and leaving a message for the vice president of entertainment to please phone me back, I sat down in the chair by the desk in my hotel room and started to open my tour book to see if there were any other direct contact telephone numbers. While I sat and reviewed, there was a pounding on my hotel room door, and before I could not even get up to answer it, the door flung wide open in a fury, and standing in the middle of the door frame was Beau Tucker looking as mad as can be. I never had to invite him into my room. He barged in and began screaming and ranting. His screams were as if someone had a bull by his balls, and he was barely making any sense when he yelled.

"You stole money from me," he repeated a few times in his rants. "I know you stole my money and lost it all at the tables in the casino!"

I could not help but change my demeanor to now reflect myself in a defensive stance. I looked directly into Beau's eyes and yelled back, "What the fuck are you even talking about? Have you lost your mind?" I shouted as I was now concentrating directly on Beau.

Remember, I was still sitting in my chair when he came crashing through the door. "Either you give me back my money, or I'll take it from you!" Beau yelled out, now in a complete emotional wreck. Next thing I knew, I could clearly hear Beau yell out, "Fuck it! I'll kill you myself!"

The next thing I witnessed was Beau pulling out a pocketknife from his front jeans pocket. As he continued to rant and rave, I kept my eyes firmly glued on Beau's hands as he opened the knife at me. Within seconds, Beau lunged at me with his knife. As I came out of the chair and performed a roundhouse kick, I made foot contact with his shoulder, sending me back into the chair behind him.

"Beau, you've lost your fuckin mind!" I yelled out. "I never once stole a penny from you, and for you to accuse me…go fuck yourself!" Beau refused to listen to a word I was saying to him. "The only money that was taken from the bank was to pay the band and crew their per diems. The entourage had not received their per diems for the past four days, and they were starting to get upset that the office had not sent this money to them. Usually, the office would cut me a check for all per diems, and I would pay it out in increments so the crew would not spend it all at one time. Some of the crew on this tour would go through their per diem of the week in two days.

As Beau regained his balance and stood in front of me with his little helpless pocketknife as if it were a machete, I told him for the last time to put the knife down. When he refused, I knew that if he came toward me again, my training would want me to take him out in a matter of seconds. Beau was about to lose his life if he came toward me with that knife over something I had no idea what he was referring to. Here standing in front of me with the smell of stale alcohol reeking from his breath, I told him that if he took another step, it would be most likely his last. What else was I to do? I did not want to hit him or hurt him as I knew I would have crushed him, so instead, I picked up the hotel phone and dialed 911. It was time to put this matter to bed, not in my bed either. Beau finally left my hotel room upon the arrival of the police. He was later arrested for assault and battery and for verbally threatening to kill me.

Suit was filed, and the matter was later settled out of court. There was an order put on the suit that the findings of the court would not be discussed or made public. It was agreed to, and as far as I was concerned, the matter was over with. I was cleared of any wrongdoing, and the matter was settled through mediation. That was the last time I worked for Tanya Tucker. I was just building my reputation while she was destroying hers. The fights between her and Glen Campbell only got worse as their names made the tabloids almost on a weekly basis for months to come. Long after that tour, Glen Campbell had asked me if I would testify on his behalf for the sleuth of trumped charges pending against him from Tanya.

"It would be my pleasure, Glen," I said back without hesitation.

This was the one tour that I learned from; the ability to work hard and honest and know how to cut through the bullshit when dealing with an "easy" outgoing artist or their dumb-ass manager/father.

My time with Jersey boy Eddie Rabbitt started in 1982. Eddie was a country music legend during his time. Always headlining his own shows, he performed at, I was recommended to Eddie's manager, Stan Moress, by both Sonny Nell and Paul Moore, two of the top booking agents for the William Morris Agency's office in Nashville, Tennessee. Because of my work ethic and early reputation, they felt that I would be a great person for Eddie's upcoming national tour. I met with Stan Moress, a tall, thin man who relocated from Los Angeles to Nashville and had an incredible reputation in the "biz." Stan and I both had the same demeanor; we thought we were great. From our looks to our clothes, Stan reminded me of me. I think I wanted to have the same respect within the industry that Stan had built over the years. Stan Moress's name touched so many, so why not? I liked where I was headed. Over time, though, when you work for Stan Moress, it is on his terms with very little room for negotiations.

I met Eddie at his home in Franklin, Tennessee. It was a modest colonial house that sat back from the street but was no different from any other house on the street. There were no markings of celebrity status—just a house on a hill, a pregnant wife named Jeanine, and a daughter named Demelza. I remember his daughter's name because it was not an ordinary name. Very pleasant as was his wife. However, I was forewarned from the beginning that Jeanine could be a handful. *Come on*, I thought to myself as I made my way into a back paneled room where a worn-out couch was against the wall, a table centered on the couch, and an upright piano. It was not a new piano. In fact, from the wear and tear on the piano, you could tell that it was used and most likely misused and abused at various times. The wood frame had scratches in it, and there were other markings that showed its misuse.

"It's in tune, so don't go by what it looks like," Eddie called out to me.

Walking into the room from the kitchen was a tall, built man with wavy thick hair, a beard, and a smile that would go on forever.

"Hi! I'm Eddie Rabbitt," he said as he extended his hand.

I immediately turned to him with my hand now extended and returned the greeting by saying, "Hello Eddie, I'm Steve Wallach. I'm your new production manager."

Our mutual greetings had some similarities; we both talked about the piano. So right away, I felt completely relaxed. Both of us hail from New Jersey. We had things in common to talk about.

Eddie was the type of man who was pretty much set in his ways from the minute you met him. He was straight up about what he wanted when it came to his stage performance, yet he always came across as one who would prefer to be easygoing than demanding. Eddie had an incredible band, Hare Trigger. Impressive musicians in their own rights. Jimmy Hyde (drums, vocals), Don Barrett (bass, vocals), Gene Sisk (piano, vocals), Lee Garner (guitar, vocals), and a few others. I met Eddie before I met his road manager and confidant, Bill Rehrig. Bill was more of a quiet man that fell into any crowd he was in. From my point of view, Bill was more than just Eddie's road manager; he was Eddie's right hand for everything. Whatever Eddie wanted Bill was there to make sure he got it. Eddie was not one who would be on time for anything if it were left up to him. From soundchecks to performance times, in almost every situation, I had to do my best to speed Bill up to get Eddie there on time. It usually always

THIS LIFE OF MINE

worked. Well, sometimes, maybe a few shows, he ended up being a few minutes late. Besides playing road manager, Bill Rehrig was also an incredible fiddle player. Truly an expert at his craft. Every performance Eddie would call Bill out on stage to play "Orange Blossom Special"—always a hit at every show. At this writing, I had come to find out that Bill Rehrig had passed away at age seventy-five.

Eddie Rabbitt was a lady's man both on stage and off. Not any fault to him, mind you. Women just loved him, and no matter where he was or who he was with, many ladies would always stop for a quick photo or autograph. The cheek kisses were his best. Eddie would cock his head to the side, and his renowned smile would be huge as he displayed those pearly white teeth. I do not recall Eddie being promiscuous on the road. The only hang-up and addiction he had was watching porn, preferably with animals. I do not understand what he found in these videos, but it was his choice. Admittedly, we all sat around and watched them too. Once we saw it one time, it was enough. Not for Eddie Rabbitt. Everything from some long-haired gorgeous blond jerking off a horse or a woman spreading cream cheese on herself and letting her dog have a field day. I just, for the life of me, could not understand what the thrill was. But hey…to each their own.

I was with Eddie during the time of his son Timothy's death. There is nothing that can ever be said to a parent when they lose a child. Eddie and I had this in common, so yes, I was there to help him out any way I could. All I can say is that it was devastating to the Rabbitt family and especially my friend, Eddie Rabbitt.

Eddie's shows were always sold out. Eddie, along with Hare Trigger, always made sure their audiences saw truly a great live show. Every show was made up of music, songs, stories, jokes, laughter, and special guests. During my touring time with Eddie, one of his no. 1 hit singles was "You and I," a song he did a duet with Crystal Gayle. The song was a huge hit and still is played on both country and easy-listening radio stations. I recall when Eddie would go into a story about how the song was written and performed. While he would be speaking, production would wheel onto the stage, a reflective-looking screen facing the crowd. Eddie would start "You and

I" and would sing the song with such emotion as the lights would set, creating a romantic mood in the air. When it was Crystal's turn to sing, she would appear on the screen as if she was standing right there, next to Eddie Rabbitt, and singing their no. 1 hit song. The crowd would stand and scream for a few seconds, which was how strong a hit it became. Every opening act would stand and watch in awe as to the response. The song was very moving. Eddie (and Crystal Gayle) offered a fantastic way to show off this hit single.

The incredible comedian, the late Gary Shandling, was our opening act throughout the tour that year. With Gary's HBO Special and his appearances on many of the evening talk shows, Gary had a great following on his own. Joining Gary and Eddie was an easy sell to promoters, and their shows were complete sellouts. William Morris Agency was their booking agency, so the match was easy to negotiate. The best thing was that Gary had no real stage prep, a tall wooden stool (no backrest), a small table for his bottled water, and a towel. There was also a mic stand and a mic, and that was it. Amazingly easy yet so powerful.

Gary, off stage, was like he was on stage. His daily antics with Eddie, the band, and crew became a routine. We always expected something from him. We just never knew what or when. I recall arriving the day prior to a show at this one venue on the tour, and Gary asked if it were possible for someone to take him over to this shopping mall that was supposedly just a few minutes away.

"Sure, no problem," I remember calling out. "I'll get the production car, and I'll go with you."

So off we went on a trip that would turn into one of the funniest clothing store runs I was ever part of.

It was a chain department store called Penny's. Back then, Penny's could be found in every major town or city. I still had no idea why or why Gary wanted to come here.

I remember asking him, "So, Gary, what do you need to buy?"

As we continued to walk through the parking lot approaching the entrance doors, Gary looked at me and said with a large smile, "I need a wig and a dress. Not just any wig and not just any dress. A wig with really had long black hair and a sundress."

What on earth can you be up to? I thought to myself.

The first department as we entered the store was the ladies' department.

"This is exactly where I need to be!" Gary called out.

"Ladies! Are you nuts?" I called out to him as he approached one of the sales ladies.

"May I help you?" the saleswoman asked. As Gary stood there, you could see on the sales lady's face that expression that asks, "Don't I know you?"

I decided to just stand there and let Gary handle this. "I'm looking for a long-hair wig and a sundress," Gary explained. I need it for a show I'm doing."

The sales lady then called out, "Wait a minute. Aren't you that comic guy? You know, Gary Shandling?"

I just stood there with a simple grin as I again thought that Gary had this all figured out and did not need any assistance from me. As Gary explained he needed it for his show that evening, the sales lady did her best in showing Gary so many sundresses that after the first three, it really did not matter, but Gary let her continue, only every few minutes asking her, "So do you have a long hair wig?"

Never getting a straight reply, I finally told Gary I was going to look around and see if I could find a long-hair wig. My mission was to get a wig. But a wig for what?

After a few minutes, I could hear Gary's voice and the same sales lady, getting closer to where I found myself, in the girl's teens department. As Gary came around the corner, I was pointing up toward a lady mannequin that not only had a dark brown long hair wig but one of the ugliest sundresses I think I have ever seen, even to the day of this writing. It was primarily a medium blue and yellow-and-white starburst all over it. The sleeves were short but ballooned outward, so the young girl wearing this would have upper arms like Popeye the Sailor.

"That's exactly what I am looking for!" Gary called out. "I need a size large and the same wig as on that mannequin."

"Oh," said the sales lady in a baby-like voice now. "I know we don't have that exact sundress and we don't sell wigs like that."

Right away, Gary's mind was thinking. He put his hand up under his chin, squinted his eyes, puckered his plump lips, and said, "You don't have tickets to the sold-out Eddie Rabbitt Show…do you?" Gary makes a quick glance over to me. I was already on the riser, taking the sundress off the mannequin, and Gary was pulling the hair from the wig, ready to catch it as it fell. Dress was off, and wig was off, and I was writing down the lady's full name and giving her four complimentary tickets to this evening's performance with Eddie Rabbitt and opening act, Gary Shandling. Both wig and dress were placed in a bag, and we said our thank-you and goodbye and made our way out into the parking lot, not saying a word but looking at each other as we walked away…quickly. We both got into the car and broke out laughing so hard. As our laughter became louder and more uncontrollable, it dawned on me. *What the hell was so funny?* I thought.

"Okay, so why did we do what we just did?" I asked Gary. "What the hell are you up to?"

Gary looked over at me, and all he could say was, "You'll see. You'll see."

That evening, Gary opened the sold-out show, and Eddie just took the stage. The show was going great. The sound was perfect, and Eddie could not have sounded any better. As I could hear Eddie starting his story about the next song, it was time once again to make sure the screen was ready to be wheeled out on the stage. This time, who walks over to me on the side of the stage but a lady wearing a blue sundress with colorful bursts. She had the longest hair next to Crystal Gayle's I had ever seen, I thought to myself. I thought for a second and called out, "Oh no!" This person is not a lady at all! It's Gary! Just from the look on his face, I knew he was up to something. I just knew it. As they began to wheel the screen out onto the stage, Gary got behind and stayed hidden while it was out there. By this time, all I could do was watch and see.

As Eddie sang this beautiful song, we all waited with anticipation to see what Gary had planned. As Eddie finished his first lines and the music climbed for Crystal's portion of the song, out came Gary Shandling, dressed as if he wanted the audience to think it was Crystal Gayle. Well, not really. No one could ever take the place of Crystal Gayle. Not then and not now. The audience went wild. They were laughing so loud, applauding, and standing in their seats to get a better look at the outfit Gary had on. You see, this was what concerts are all about. If you just want to hear the music, buy a CD or download it. You attend a concert to see the performance of the artists and the musicians, highlighted by an incredible sound and light show. That is why it is so important to continue attending live performances of all music genres. It took Eddie about one minute into this three-plus-minute song for him to realize that the crowd was cheering and laughing, not at him but at what was going on behind him.

As Eddie turned around to see what the laughter was directed at, his eyes immediately fell upon this figure of a "lady" standing there, holding a microphone and lip-syncing to Crystal Gayle lyrics. At first, I did not know what his reaction would be, but it was easily seen within seconds that Gary's comical stunt went over with genuine laughter coming from Eddie Rabbitt. Just from his body functions, Eddie was laughing with such force, as seen from his facial expression complete satisfaction.

"I cannot believe you pulled this off!" Eddie shouted over the microphone. "Ladies and gentlemen, please make some noise for my friend, Gary Shandling!"

The crowd was on their feet! Not only were they applauding and screaming for Eddie, but they also began the traditional "ladies" panties being thrown up onto the stage—something that happened at many of Eddie Rabbitt's shows. As Eddie continued laughing along with Gary, he let the crowd know, "Hey, paybacks are a bitch!" The crowd roared; the venue lights became bright as the stage lights dimmed. This truly was a fantastic Eddie Rabbitt Concert.

As the panties and many stuffed animals were swept into a pile center stage, one of my crew brought out two plastic bags; one, of course, for all the stuffed animals and the other for. Let us just say, our traditional garbage file. One thing that Eddie did after any show where items were tossed was he would see which ones he wanted to bring home for his children and the remaining we would always dedicate to the local children's hospital. You see, Eddie had a tremendous heart for children, especially those who were suffering from medical issues. He made it a point to see that these items were delivered, and confirmation came back.

As emotionally strong as Eddie was for children, he was not that way when it came to his parents. Eddie had decided to move his parents to Nashville, Tennessee, as they began to age.

"I wanted my parents near me," Eddie explained to me when he started asking me to handle some things for them. Of course, I said, "No problem, Eddie. Just let me know what I can do for them."

As I thought about what I just said as I said it, I came to realize that I may have opened myself to be the errand boy Eddie really wanted for them.

Without any hesitation, I quickly said, "But, Eddie, I don't mind bringing things out to them from you, and I'm not here to be on call for them."

As Eddie looked at me, he quickly nodded and said, "No worry, Steve. It's just that they don't drive, and it's hard for them to get out."

Again, I stressed that I did not mind helping a few times. "Let me have their address, and I'll drop these things off to them on my way home," I said. "I'll also need their address."

"Oh, that would be great, Steve. They live not too far from you," Eddie said as he handed me a few items.

When I looked at the address, I paused to think where it was. Eddie had said it was off Whitebridge Road and was in an apartment complex. Thinking the key word was apartment complex, I was thinking it was an actual apartment complex where there were many buildings looking the same, a pool, management office, etc. Boy, was I ever wrong. Tucked way off the road from Whitebridge Road were two buildings side by side, each with their own door entry protected by an old and bent aluminum color faded canopy. There was an old cracked concrete walkway, wide enough for only one to pass, ending at a step up to their door. I thought as I made my approach, damn, this is one nasty place to stick your parents. I was right.

As Eddie's father opened the door, I introduced myself as he said with excitement, "Please do come in. We don't get many visitors."

As I stepped inside, I could see that this was a very old and broken-down apartment. The wear and tear on the color-faded walls, the old linoleum flooring in their very small kitchen, and the faded and stained carpet showed that this was no place for any elderly to live that had a child as a top celebrity. Basically, what a shithole. As I stayed to talk to them, they kept repeating that they were so proud of "their" Eddie but continued making excuse after excuse as to why Eddie did not come to visit.

"Thanks, Steve, for bringing us this food and other items. You realize that Eddie is just way too busy to come here himself," the senior Mr. Rabbitt said to me more than once.

"I understand," I called back to him as I was making my way out their door. I got upset that someone making incredible money like Eddie Rabbitt was, would place their own parents in a rundown apartment building. What I do recall was that when I saw Eddie the following morning, I saw him in a different way now. I will leave it at that.

We were on a six-month touring schedule, which kept us away from home for weeks at a time. The shows were running into each other as we would have to cover hundreds of miles every night to make our next venue. The last show on this leg of the tour was at the Orange County Fair, Costa Mesa, California. This was a huge fair back in the '80s. Artists from all genres of music would perform here. I worked at this Fair when I was with Tanya Tucker the prior year.

Our arrival by coach was on the morning of our show. The sky, I recall, was heavy with dark clouds, and the chance of rain for this day was high. As my crew met with the local stage crew, we came to begin the process of loading in with our equipment. The stage was already live with other acts as we set our equipment in line to be next. During our load-in, it began to rain lightly. That was not any issues. We have set up and performed in the rain before. Just so long as everything was properly grounded, I always allowed the band and artist to take the stage.

Like it was yesterday, Hare Trigger was already on the stage, instruments in hand. I made my way over to our private touring coach to let our road manager Bill and Eddie know we were ready.

Eddie came out from the rear of the bus with that traditional huge smile and said to both Bill and me, "Okay, boys…let's go kick some butt!"

The rain was still coming down lightly but steadily as we made our way up the backstage stairs, stage left. We could see from the side of the stage that the rain had left a few small water puddles on the stage. As the stage crew ran out and began to sweep the water off the stage, the stage manager for the venue came over and said that they were going to hold off, taking the stage for about five minutes. With our coach just twenty feet from the stage, Eddie chose to return to his bus.

Once we were inside, I turned to Bill and asked, "Bill, what does the contract say about outside shows and rain, lightning, and thunder?"

I could see Bill cock his head to one side with that look of doubt and said, "I think I'll call Stan and see what he says."

Bill had to leave him a message to call us. I needed to go back out to the stage, so I asked Eddie and Bill to just sit tight until I could ascertain what the status was. The rain still had not let up as I made my way to stage left, where the stage monitors were already under plastic coverings to keep from getting any moisture. It seems that while we were on the bus, heavy rain, along with thunder in the distance showered the area. Only half the crowd was protected by the aluminum framed roof. Yet the others in the crowd chose to stay and hope for the best, and that was to see their favorite country artist, Eddie Rabbitt. One thing about Eddies fans is that they are dedicated.

"Hey, Steve, from Bill," I heard coming over my radio. "Please come back to the bus."

As I walked across the stage, I could see that there was a lot of water that had collected in various areas on the stage more than before. As I made my way into the coach, Bill handed me his cell.

"Hello, this is Steve," I said.

"Steve, hi, it's Stan. We spoke for a few minutes, and he said that Eddie was not to perform if there was lightning with the thunder and the rain looked like it was going to let up. I agreed and immediately went back to the stage to make my determination.

The rain had stopped, and the production crew began uncovering the amps and drums and making sure things were properly reset. Once again, Hare Trigger took to the stage and immediately went into Eddies introduction. As I opened the bus door, there was that huge smile looking down from Eddie.

"Okay, okay…let's go kick some butt!" I called out.

We made our way onto the stage, where Eddie did not even wait to be introduced. "Ladies and gentlemen, this is Eddie Rabbitt!" could be heard throughout every speaker in the venue.

Eddie grabs his guitar and throws his strap over his shoulder as if he had rehearsed this for years; he has. He and the band start to play as they make their way to their mic stands. As Eddie belts out his first word, he grabs the mic stand, only to be electrically shocked. At the same time, when his front band members went to begin their vocals, they, too, were jolted by what now seems to have been an electrical shock. I immediately ran onto the stage and pulled Eddie's hand off the mic stand that he was still holding. I could see from his expression that he was still shocked.

The band members unplugged their instruments and those able to walk off the stage with them did so. Our drummer, Jimmie Hyde, just grabbed his sticks and said in a very frustrated tone, "Steve, get this figured out!"

As I made sure Eddie was fine, he and Bill made their way back to the bus. I know they could hear me saying that I was going to pull this due to weather in about ten minutes unless this local production manager could assure us of what the problem was and if it could be corrected. Never had I experienced dealing with pulling a show due to weather, but I was prepared to do what was best for my artist and band.

As I watched with concern, the stage crew was doing everything to not only sweep off any water remaining from the storm but to ascertain what the hell went wrong with the power. Standing waiting to hear an update, the production manager came by and said that he "believed" he was able to get things corrected. This time, I went out on the stage and grabbed the mike. Rather than grabbing the mic, I gave it a smooth and slow movement of my hand across the metal stand. In return, it seemed to be fine. No shock or even a trickle came from it. The show was now ready once again. I radioed Bill to bring Eddie out, but this time, Eddie and all of Hare Trigger took the stage together. The first song went off without a hitch. The only matter was it began to rain again, and all eyes immediately went to the stage production manager standing now stage left by the monitor boards.

Eddie was about to finish his song when he grabbed for the mic and again, a shock came through the stand into Eddie's hand.

"That's it!" I yelled out. "This show is done! I am not taking any chance that anyone is going to get electrocuted!"

I called the band off the stage and told Bill to get Eddie back to his bus and that I would handle this. More panic on the stage as the stagehands did their best to attempt to keep the stage dry, but to no avail. Finally, when I saw the stage production manager place large, carpeted floor mats in front of each mic stand and tried to explain to me that "this" attempt was to control any shock, I looked at him as if he had lost his mind.

"Eddie Rabbitt is canceled!" I yelled out. "We will not take a stage that is so unsafe."

With this, I explained the situation to both Eddie and his road manager and felt that as his production manager, I could not take this chance for the third time today. It was agreed, and we packed our equipment, and that was the end to this portion of the tour.

That evening while traveling on the coach, Stan Moress, Eddie's manager, finally called us back, and I explained why I chose to cancel the day's gig at the Orange County Fair. Thinking Stan would also agree, he instead chose to scream and shout into the phone, telling me I had no reason to cancel without his approval.

"Hey, Stan, you knew what was going on, but you were not around to take our calls about it," I called out into the phone. "What? You wanted Eddie to take the damn stage and, this time, get electrocuted? I decided to make the call after I told both Bill and Eddie what the conditions were," I said back with anger.

All I heard in return was Stan yelling that he would see me once we got back to Nashville. I wiped the sweat from my forehead, turned to both Eddie and the band, and said, "I'll take that cold one right now."

Our return to Nashville was easy. We dropped Eddie off at his home on the way back to Nashville, and once we made it back to our starting point, we each went our own way as this was the end for this leg of the tour. Without going into detail, I met with Stan Moress the following day, and after all the yelling back and forth, it was decided. I made the right call after all.

Eddie Rabbitt truly was easy to work with. He was known to be cheap, but that was okay. For the time I was with him, Eddie and I were just two Jersey boys doing what we both loved to do. Eddie passed away from lung cancer at the young age of fifty-six, and that once again made me realize just how short life could be. Rest in peace, Eddie Rabbitt, and it was truly my pleasure to work for you. He, too, taught me reasons why some things happen the way they did. The only thing I could not get over was how Eddie allowed his parents to live out their lives in such a run-down apartment.

I was home for a short period when I received a call from a man named Al Bunetta. Al was this short stocky Italian man that had a balding spot on his head. When you first meet Al, he comes across as this typical New Yorker, accent and all. Al talked with his hands (as I do), but with Al, it was overexaggerated. Al was looking for a road manager/production manager for his artist, John Prine. A name not familiar worldwide back in the '80s, but a name that was known among Americana Music throughout the world. Probably one of the best storytellers through music, I landed my next tour with this man. To date, John is the most laid-back artist I ever had the pleasure to work with. Before being accepted, I had to meet John's business manager, a man in New York named Sy. Who was this man who had a lot of control over John's affairs? He was his financial manager, and if your job consisted of handling John's money, Sy wanted to make sure he had someone he could trust. Needless to say, Sy and I got along fine, and he actually welcomed some of my ideas for keeping the accounts for John while on tour.

John's entourage was simple: John Prine (guitar, vocals), Phillip Donnelly/deceased (guitar, vocals), and Rachele Peer-Prine/deceased (bass, vocals). Yes, John had his girlfriend, who later became his wife in the band. Rachele did not join us on every date in the beginning. It was on the dates where the venue lent to a larger sound. Most times, in the beginning, it would be myself, John, and Phillip. John and Phillip together were magical. The sounds they produced truly were unique, and I still think that is why John Prine and his music were welcomed by so many. The songs were real; the words were as true as anyone could get, and John had a very raspy voice, which set him aside from any other singer. Willie Nelson once told me that if you can hear the B side of any record, and just by the voice alone, you know who the artist is; that makes a hit artist. Well, no matter if you heard the A side, B side, or just a recording of John Prine, you would know immediately who it is. John Prine was able to stand alone and be fully recognizable up until his untimely death from COVID-19. John lost his battle at age seventy-three on April 7, 2020.

Traveling with John and Phillip had some incredible memories filled with stories that are still told to this day. Almost everything surrounding John Prine was mystical in some form or another. I remember we were doing a show in Steamboat Springs, Colorado. We had to fly into Denver, where there was a driver/van awaiting our arrival. We made our way into the van and began the long drive to Steamboat Springs for our show the following evening. As our ride took us through some incredible scenery, the climb through the mountains became that much more exciting as it began to snow quite heavily. As each minute turned, the snow kept getting deeper on the roads and surfaces. Signs began appearing on the highway that snow chains were allowed on all vehicles. Snow chains? Seriously? I have not seen snow like this anywhere. Sure, the East Coast got the amounts of snow when I lived there but nothing like having four feet or more. Along the drive, our driver informed us that he would be exiting to attach his chains as well. As we came off the highway, we saw there was a McDonald's and asked if we could possibly stop there to pick up some burgers and fries.

"No problem," our driver said, and with that, we made our way into the parking lot that had already been plowed once. Looked as though they would need to plow again as this snowfall was huge. As we exited the van, I could not help but notice that it was as though they just dropped this McDonald's and these two other stores smack in the middle of nowhere, only a highway that passes through. I saw no other roads leading here or away. We make our way inside only to find a line of people waiting to place their orders. As a gentleman and what appeared to be his two daughters ahead of us approached the counter to give their food order, I could see John tap the man's shoulder and called out, "Hey, Doc, what'd ya doing here?"

I could not believe my eyes nor my ears as this man turned around and said, "Well, hi, John! Strange seeing you here."

In amazement, John turns to us and tells us that this man was his doctor back in Nashville, Tennessee. Here we are, miles from nowhere, in the middle of a snowstorm, standing in a McDonald's somewhere in the hills of Colorado. This can only happen to someone like John Prine. We all said our hellos and goodbyes and made our way back to the van. We finished the ride and ended up at this beautiful ski resort where we were performing. Our stay was impressive. I recall relaxing in a large outdoor hot tub as the snow fell with flakes bigger than I had ever seen.

John had a strong following in Canada, and Al Bunetta made it a point to lock in some wonderful venues there. On one occasion, we were staying at a very exclusive hotel in Montreal. John, Phillip, and I all had separate rooms, so I made sure that the rooms were next to each other. You see, Phillip Donnelly had a habit of always finding "happy trouble" if given the opportunity. John was a close tie-in, all in a friendly manner with no ill intentions.

On this specific date, here we were. Three grown men are always on the prowl for "something" to do. After close to three hours and many Geneses, Phillip was his usual happy drunk state, and John was right there with him. You see, one of us had to be sober, and being the only one out with them, it was my responsibility to make sure all went well. As the van was, I believe, a few blocks from our hotel. There, standing on the street corner, were two beautiful ladies.

I say ladies because I knew they were "ladies of the evenings" there to make any man's evening quite pleasurable.

"I'll git out here," Phillip called out to the driver.

"Wait a minute," said John. "I'm going with you!"

As Phillip and John stepped out of the van, Phillip turned closing the door and said with a grin in his Scottish accent, "Tanks alut! Tanks! We're good from here!"

He closed the van door, and as I started to leave, I could not help but watch Phillip and John go directly over to the ladies. Yes, Phillip Donnelly and John Prine have left the venue. This was not the first time for them. John and Phillip were as close as two brothers. They had each other's backs, most of the time, as brothers would say. I headed back to the hotel, where I went over some papers for the next day's show. You see, knowing how easygoing John was, he was able to go freely without causing any fanfare. After about an hour, I decided to call it a night.

It had to be about three hours later that I heard a knocking on my door, and that distinguished Scottish voice called out, "Steve! Steve! You awake?"

As I sat up from a deep sleep, I rubbed my eyes and went for my shorts, as I slept in the raw and still do to this day. I looked through the peephole, and there on the other side of my hotel room door stood Phillip, with his shirt completely unbuttoned, John standing there with a grin on his face, along with the two ladies that they stopped off to see.

"Steve," Phillip said to me now with a thick Scottish accent, "John and I need some help here."

As I saw that Phillip's hotel room door was open, I suggested that we all make our way inside and out of the hallway area before anyone saw us and complained. Inside, I find that these "ladies" speak no English, only French. In fact, trying to talk with them was not only difficult but amusing. You see, after their "get-together," it was time to pay. Problem was, they would only take Canadian currency. I could not stop laughing when John and Phillip were pulling out currency from the United States, pounds from England, pesos from Mexico, lira from Italy, and more.

"Steve, come on, man," Phillip would say. "How can we convert what we have into Canadian currency?" I could not help but laugh because to see this in front of me play out would make for a fantastic comedy skit. "I even called the front desk to ask what the exchange rates were for the money I had," Phillip said.

It was a brilliant idea, I thought. Maybe they will just take the money knowing what the total would be. They did not. Next thing we knew, there was a loud knock on the door, and there stood a large man, a very large black man. All I can recall was that "Mr. John" was there to make sure his ladies were properly taken care of. Long story short, I went into my room and took out enough Canadian currency to pay for their bill. Picking up a few hookers was not what was storytelling; it was the way these two drunk musicians were standing in their hotel room half-dressed, trying to use a calculator and do exchange rates for their money.

Then there was the time we were riding on our tour bus heading between cities. Inside the bus were me, John, Phillip, and Rachele. Buddy McKenzie was our driver. A hell of a nice man. Buddy and I worked together on many tours throughout the years. It was sad to learn of Buddy's passing from a heart attack while he was sleeping in a hotel in Canada. It was raining outside. The sky was dark, and there was some fog, but inside the coach, we were all seated around the table, drinking whatever was our pleasure at that moment. During this time, our conversation took a turn, and John held the floor by talking about his father. John's conversations were never light. They each had some type of meaning that we each took away with our own understandings.

Many times, John spoke about mystery and psychic happenings. He said that he felt the presence of a man and saw a man outside the window of our bus in a side profile stance, wearing a fedora pulled down over his forehead, a scarf that was open, and a trench-type coat. Never really questioned him because I knew John was very spiritual in his own way. As John continued with his story this time about his father, I recall him looking up from the table and outside the window across us. With only a dim light inside the bus and the darkness and rain spots on the outside, a light would flash through either from another moving vehicle, streetlight, or something else. Suddenly, John reached for the camera that was on the table, raised it quickly, snapped a shot, and said, "There's a man outside the bus window watching us."

"What?" I called back. "What are you talking about?"

The bus did not stop. In fact, we were traveling over fifty miles per hour, so how could there be a man outside the window of our moving coach?

"You take this film in tomorrow when we stop," John said to me.

The conversation got exceptionally quiet for a few minutes, then one by one, we took our turn heading back to our individual bunks.

As morning arrived, we were just pulling into our hotel. "Remember, once you get us checked in, go drop this film off to be processed," John said.

"No problem, John," I called back. "Let me get you all checked in first."

There was a photo store one block over. I dropped the film off and was told I could pick up the photos in about two hours. When I returned for our photos, I quickly stood there, anxiously waiting as I flipped through the beginning photos. I came across two dark photos that were taken from inside the bus. They were the same; the profile face of a man, wearing a fedora pulled down over his forehead, a scarf that was open, and a trench type coat. I never doubted John Prine from that day forward.

Another time, John decided he wanted to travel to a place to write. Not alone, mind you, he had in mind that he, Phillip, a master songwriter named Roger Cook, and I would find a place off the beaten path. As I looked over our future dates, there was one date that stood out—a place I had never been to and heard so many great things about it. Would this be the chosen spot?

I called out to John, "John, I think I found just the place."

When we arrived at the airport, we were met by the promoter and owner of the venue we were to perform at. Even though we were in a snow-capped town called Jackson Hole, Wyoming, the locals and visitors knew how to enjoy themselves to the max. From horse-drawn carriages that were always filled with people to the venue we were playing at, there was something for everyone. Knowing that we were there almost two weeks before our performance date, the promoter was willing to go the extra mile.

"Anything you boys need, just let me know," exclaimed the promoter.

"Well, we'd love to go snowmobiling," John called out.

"Not a problem. Let me get you settled at your home away from home." The man who arranged all this for John Prine.

I thought I would have learned my lesson by playing venues in the snow, but this place was like no other. Surrounded by some of the most majestic mountains, each covered with what looked like a pure ivory snow blanket, covered as far as the eyes would allow. You could see the actual mountain peaks as they rose out of the snow, reaching for the sky. John had this idea that we would find a place, and after seven days, he would invite Roger's wife, Vickie, and John's wife, Rachele, to join us. The first seven days were for writing.

As we made our way through the well-maintained streets that have been perfectly plowed and salted, making them dry in the strong Wyoming sun, we made our way to our retreat. To give you some idea of just how deep the snow was, the snowbanks on either side of us were taller than the van's roof we were in.

"I can't believe how deep the snow is here," I called out. "Any idea how deep it is?"

Through the chuckle coming from the promoter, he said, "The side banks are about eight to ten feet."

That was insane to us. We all could not believe just how high these snowbanks were. Phillip chuckled with his Scottish sound and said, "Wouldn't be good to have a little car here. Hell, if the snow falls, you wouldn't find them till spring!"

As we came around another snow-banked corner, there stood in front of us, a spectacular homemade from wood and glass—lots of glass. The front of the house was beautiful, offering so many things to look at. From a ten-foot entry door to these large windows on both the first and second floors, the house was beautiful. As we each made our way into the foyer, we could not help but notice the jaw-dropping view out of the back. Almost the entire back of the house was glass. Huge glass windows enable you to see everything as if you were standing outside. What stood taller than any other mountain from this view were the famous Grand Tetons. I was amazed at the beauty that stood in front of me. They stand 13,770 feet and are the second tallest mountain in Wyoming. I was already imagining waking up each day for the next ten days seeing this view. The area itself gave off a tremendous vibe. You could feel it just by standing there.

"I can already see that we're gonna write some great songs here!" John shouted out.

And they did. Between John Prine, Roger Cook, and Phil Donnelly, a few songs did end up on some of John's recordings.

The house was well-stocked with the essentials, such as Heineken, Absolut Vodka, and an array of other drinks and food. The promoter followed our Ryder and had most of the requested food and drink items delivered. We were set. We thanked the promoter, and as we closed the door to begin our new chapter, I could see Roger Cook coming into the living room, carrying what I assumed was his famous ukulele. The uke he has written every one of his hits, including "I'd Like to Teach the World to Sing" (Coca-Cola's theme song for over forty-plus years), "You've Got Your Troubles," "Green Green Grass," and a sleuth of others. So here stands Roger Cook and now John Prine in front of me, looking as if they ate the mouse.

"Okay, what's up?" I asked.

So Roger begins to talk in his thick British accent and says, "I understand your birthday is in a few months."

I stood there, thinking, *Wait, my birthday isn't for another four-plus months.*

"John and I thought that since you have shown such interest in my uke, we would have one made for you."

Both John and Roger opened up the box and brought out this brand-new custom ukulele, made by famous ———, Brazil. I was dumbfounded. I stood there in disbelief that they, anyone would go to such extremes to buy me my own instrument, never mind it being this ukulele.

"Holy shit!" I yelled out. "I can't believe you guys did this for me!"

And this is how this writing retreat started. Not only do I have a new uke, but I'm sitting here with the man who has written hit after hit on his uke and the number one storyteller in Americana music, John Prine. To this day, I still play my ukulele, and every time, I still think of that time in Jackson Hole, Wyoming. After working with John Prine for two years of touring, I decided to adventure out and look for another tour after a few months off.

During my months off, I spend my time at home in Nashville, Tennessee, with Judy (my wife at the time) and, of course, my pets. I am a huge dog lover and have also become a cat friend. After John's touring, my wife and I decided to go house hunting. I remember it vividly; it was New Year's Day, 1984. It was bitterly cold outside, and I was already perched on the couch, waiting for the parades and football games to start. The phone rings, and I can hear Judy saying, "Hmmm, let me check with Steve." As Judy walked into the den, she said that the realtor found us an incredible house, and it's available today just for us before they put it on the market. As much as I just wanted to stay curled up on the couch, I decided to agree to go look at it with the understanding that this was not going to be an all-day event.

Our realtor picked us up, and away we went. It was close to where we were already living. As we drove down this beautiful treed road, I could not imagine us being able to afford anything in this neighborhood. The homes all had huge lots, many of them with huge trees. As we drove further down this road, I looked up toward the right and saw this beautiful house sitting high above on this large hill.

"Now tell me that's the house we're going to see, and I'll tell you we have a deal."

Knowing that there was no possible way it could be that house, I already set in my mind that this was a wasted trip.

"Well, actually, Steve, that *is* the house we're going to," my agent said. "I know the bank that is holding the deed because the former owners were relocated, and the bank took the note."

I could not believe what I was hearing. As we drove up this winding driveway, we came up to what is still my home. Part of my divorce settlement from Judy was that I was able to pay her off and keep the house. February 14, 1984, we moved into the house, and five weeks later, I was on my way on the next tour.

I met a man during my previous tours by the name of Jack Nance. Jack was a tall, thinly built man, smoke cigarettes constantly, but had a great background in music and touring. I remember Jack telling me that he was at one time the drummer for Conway Twitty and cowrote, "It's Only Make Believe" with Conway. The song was a huge hit and is still heard on the radio to this day. But Jack was more than a drummer and songwriter. His road took him into the management side of artists. I thought, *Why not? Let me reach out to this guy and see if he may know of a tour coming up.* And he did.

It was May 1984, I found myself sitting on a plane with Jack, flying to Los Angeles, California. I was anxious and excited as we discussed business for the next five-hour flight time. We arrived at LAX and were met by a limo driver named Hollywood. Our luggage was gathered, and off we went to check in at the Hilton on Sunset Boulevard.

Jack phoned my hotel room and said, "Let's meet in the lobby in thirty minutes, and we'll head over to the rehearsal building."

I hung up the phone, and within ten minutes, I was sitting in the lobby, anxiously awaiting Jack. Twenty minutes later, we were in the limo and off to what will become my next tour.

As the limo pulled into this well-guarded building, I could not help but feel excited about being here. Credentials were shown and displayed, and we made our way into this huge rehearsal warehouse. The stage was massive, and the lighting rigs were outrageous. The backline equipment that filled the stage was enormous—larger than any other backline I had on any past tours.

As I stood there, other individuals were brought in, and introductions were made. Because of my background in policing and being a so-called bodyguard with some of the past artists I've worked for over the years, Jack felt my expertise would be beneficial to Bill Bray, the security director for the group that is here. The door opened, and out came an older man wearing a fading brown fedora-type hat.

"Hi, I'm Bill Bay," said the man standing in front of me and six other large black men.

Skin color was not important to me, as you all have read here, but I thought it was a bit odd that I was the only white male standing with what would become a strong and professional security team. Other members of our team were commissioned police officers, former police officers like me, bodyguards, and martial arts instructors. Bill Bray was extremely strict on keeping the names of the bodyguards away from print. Out of the numerous Tour Books available, there was only one full color program souvenir book where our names were permitted to be included. It was the last printed booklet, so it was a nice gesture to include us.

The stage doors flew open, and out walked five men—five brothers, to be exact. Yes, I was about to meet the legendary Jacksons.

Standing now in front of me were Tito, Jermaine, Randy, Marlon, and Jackie Jackson. As everyone was being introduced, Bill Bray began the introductions with, "I don't know who will be assigned to whom, but we will work on that."

Next thing I knew, Tito Jackson decided to take off and climb the steps in this arena. As everyone else just stood there waiting for I would assume directions, I immediately took off after Tito and allowed him the run up those steps, but I made sure I was right behind him all the way. We got to the top of the arena and made immediate eye contact with each other.

"Damn, you're good," Tito said with a smile on his face. "Glad to see there was someone who had the sense to come after me. You're my man. What's your name?"

"Steve. Steve Wallach," I replied.

"Heck, when I saw you take off, I felt it was only the proper thing to do. So I chased after you just to make sure all stayed the same."

"That's exactly what I was hoping for," Tito replied.

That was the start to an incredible relationship, both professionally and personally. We returned to the others, and it was settled.

I was assigned to Tito Jackson, and the other men there were each assigned to the remaining Jacksons. While each of us began gathering detailed information from each of the Jacksons, the backstage door opened again, and out came two huge black men followed by the one and only, Michael Jackson. Honestly, I was blown away! Here I am, standing not ten feet away from the famous MJ. It was immediately noticeable that Michael was shy as he only waved and said hi as he took to the stage. But the minute he hit that stage, it was like dynamite! He became what everyone would say: that's Michael Jackson!

Then a voice yelled overall, "Okay, boys, take the stage, and let's get this going!"

As I took my position on stage right where I could keep an eye on Tito primarily but also the others on the stage, I could not help but feel euphoria as I was standing right there with Michael Jackson and the Jacksons. The band consisted of some incredible musicians. Some that I recall were Rory Kaplan and Pat Leonard (keyboards), Gregg Wright and Dave Williams (deceased, guitar), and Johnathan "Foot" Moffett (drums). Of course, the frontline musicians were Randy Jackson (vocals, percussion, keyboards), Jermaine Jackson (bass, vocals), Tito Jackson (guitar, vocals), Marlon Jackson (percussion, vocals), and Jackie Jackson (vocals). Jackie was only able to perform in a few shows as he was recuperating from a broken leg. And let us not forget Michael Jackson (vocals).

What can I say? This was one of the most intense tours I have ever worked on, even to this day. There were private jets, private artist coaches, and over a dozen semitrucks carrying not one but two identical stages and production, enabling this incredible crew to be able to piggyback the shows so they were always able to be set up and ready for the next venue. Nothing was left undone. Everything had a purpose and a place. If things did not run like clockwork, there were the voices that could change that. Everyone is replaceable and we each understood and accepted that.

The details involved in moving the Jacksons was an enormous undertaking. The security involved for that time frame was strong. There was never a time where any Jackson was left unattended by either their bodyguard or another body. The crowds at every hotel we stayed at were jammed with hundreds of fans from the world over, trying to get one glimpse of Michael and/or any of the brothers. Not only would we have our team, but the local police departments were also involved in our security details.

After weeks of rehearsals, we arrived in Birmingham, Alabama, at our first hotel, where the crowd was enormous. Police cars were lined up, making a path for our entourage to enter. People were screaming for Michael. Michael Jackson! Michael Jackson! As the entourage pulled up to the main entrance, each of us was able to properly secure the area so that each of the Jacksons would be able to have a clear path into the hotel, through the lobby, and into waiting elevators to take us to our secure floors. It was routine for us to arrive at the band hotel, where we would have at least two floors totally closed off to others. If Michael was staying at the same hotel, there would be another top floor added.

Steve Wallach Tour ID Passes

Like I said, this one particular hotel we came to, we secured Michael and the brothers in the hotel rooms. Security was stationed on each floor at the elevators, and some of us decided to go down to the lobby and watch the madness. There were people all over. Many with signs, others dressed like Michael, and others just standing there, hoping for any glimpse of the superstar. Wearing our lanyards advertising the Victory Tour, it was simple for us to be approached by so many. Whether it was requests for an autograph or concert passes, the offers were, let's just say, everything. I believe that every sexual fantasy was offered to us. As many were fulfilled, I can only talk about what I was a part of, and some will be left up to the imagination.

After about ten minutes of sitting in the lobby, we can hear a commotion taking place outside the lobby doors. As we watched to see what was going on, the lobby doors flew open, and there were two burly men pushing their way through the crowd, making a path for what appeared to be Michael Jackson.

"Holy shit!" I yelled out. "I thought MJ was already upstairs in his suite!"

Without further hesitation, one of our bodyguards, James Anderson, ran to get the elevator. The others and I made a beeline to help get Michel safely inside an elevator and up to his floor. The elevator door opened, and we just made it inside before the crowd came around the corner.

Inside the elevator, I recall leaning over and saying to Michael, "Boy, that was close! Where's DeBias?" (Chuckie DeBias was Michael's personal bodyguard.)

There was no answer, which immediately sent up a red flag as far as I was concerned. I kept looking at Michael and these other two men and realized one thing: this WAS NOT Michael Jackson! This was an impersonator who did his best to make an attempt to get to Michael's hotel floor and suite. I have to say. This was one of the best we have seen so far. From his hair curls to his loafers, including a Michael Jackson jacket, sequined glove, and the famous fedora, this guy really looked the part. I immediately leaned forward and pushed the button for the next floor. The elevator door opened, and I called out, "This is not MJ!"

Without any hesitation from the other bodyguards, we physically tossed this impostor and his two men out, leaving them with our traditional saying, "Fuck off!" I remember Charles Lee, Randy Jackson's bodyguard, turning to me and saying, "Damn, that sure looked like MJ." We learned yet another important task: do not trust what your eyes see until you see its truth.

Another time, we were staying at the Adams Mark Hotel in Dallas, Texas—a beautiful hotel located with suites that overlook the downtown area. Directly across the street was a Mercedes-Benz dealership. Some of the Jacksons already had fleets of Benzes, but Jackie Jackson wanted yet another one. So when Jackie and his bodyguard decided to go car shopping, I was busy setting up Tito's keyboard rack in the living room of his suite. My phone rings, and it's a call from the Benz dealership. It seems Jackie was set on purchasing this brand-new Mercedes, and his bodyguard called me, asking what he should do.

"Hell, let him buy the car," I said. "It's his money."

Each of the teams carried plenty of cash on them in case their "client" wanted to make purchases. Jackie did not have his credit card with him, so he called Tito about it.

Tito hung up the phone, turned to me, and said, "Steve, go across the street to the Benz place and handle this for Jackie."

I made my way across the street, briefcase in hand, and negotiated the deal for Jackie. There is nothing better than cash when it comes to negotiating. Done. The Benz will be shipped back to California, and Jackie becomes the new owner of a new Benz.

We were off to Jacksonville, Florida, to Gator Bowl Stadium. When we arrived at the private airport in Jacksonville, there were two beautifully appointed tour coaches waiting for us delivered with drivers from the charter company, Florida Coaches. I do not recall what brothers were on which coach, but I do remember that Tito and I had a great-looking female driver. Having been used to SUVs, vans, limos, and jets, climbing aboard this coach and having this hot-looking driver was perfect. We had a good distance ride ahead of us, mostly on the interstate, and at this time of night, the highway only had a few cars and trucks, so virtually, we were running wide open. About one hour into the ride, Tito had taken over the navigator's chair, so not only did he have a clear view of the highway but also a spectacular profile view of our driver. I think her name was… well, does it matter now? She had on tight jeans and a company polo shirt that outlined her oversize breasts. Were they natural? Did it matter?

Then I heard Tito ask, "Hey, can I drive? You know, can I drive the bus?"

My immediate thought was, *Here we go*.

"Have you ever driven a bus before?" our driver asked.

"Sure! Many times!" Tito said back.

Next thing I know, our driver goes to stand up while still moving down the highway and says to Tito, "Okay, then…let's go! Come on over and take my seat and grab the wheel."

Before I could even respond, nor anyone else inside the bus that was awake and watching this, Tito slipped into the driver's seat, and away we go.

Tito was doing an excellent job of driving. In fact, he even picked up the CB radio to call one of our other coaches.

"Ah, breaker one-nine, breaker one-nine. How 'bout that bus behind me? Got your ears on?"

As many of us started to laugh, my laughter was more like a nervous laugh. I knew Tito and knew he was up to something. As the other bus pulled alongside us, we were parallel to each other, taking over both lanes of the two-lane interstate. When I had a clear view inside the other bus, I could not help but notice another brother had commandeered their bus. Picture two buses heading down the highway with Tito Jackson driving one coach, and (I think) it may have been Jermaine driving the other.

"Let's race!" Tito shouts out over the radio.

That is all it took; the race was on.

Hitting speeds up over eighty-five miles per hour in a half-million-dollar bus on a dark highway, the cheers now coming from others seated inside the coaches made this look as though it was a race to the finish!

Finally, our driver stood and said, "Okay, I think we're done here. Let's bring the speed way down, and I'll take over."

As Tito let off on the pedal, I could feel our bus easing back into a normal, steady pace. As Tito stood, the others on the coach applauded as if he had just won at the Indianapolis 500.

The owners of Florida Coach were two identical twin brothers, Jack and Jerry Calhoun. Now when I say identical, I mean identical. When they both walked into a room, you could not tell them apart. Their coach company sat on over seven acres. Not only were the Calhoun brothers the top charter celebrity coach company at the time, but they also had a few private small aircraft. The hospitality was fantastic. The Calhouns opened up their beautiful place for all the brothers and immediate staff. Well, except Michael. Michael never traveled with his brothers. We would always meet him, Chuckie DeBias, Bill Bray, and his massive entourage either at the hotels or venues. So given the opportunity to ease up and allow the brothers to enjoy themselves, that was something that I recall made things run calmly.

When the brothers heard that the Calhouns had their own planes, Tito was the first to call out, "Come, let's go fly!"

Most of the brothers chose not to, but of course, here's Tito first to jump at the chance. It was Marlon, Tito, me, and Jerry Calhoun who climbed aboard.

"There's no way I'm gettin' my ass in a small plane," James Andersen, Marlon's bodyguard, called out.

He was lucky the plane was a Cessna 132 and only had room for four. Off we went into the wild blue yonder.

The entire flight time, both Marlon and Tito kept saying they wanted to learn to fly and get their pilot's license.

"Not a problem," Jack said. "I'm an instructor, so after the tour, come on back as my guest, and I take care of it for you."

Tito and Marlon both were thrilled. Did they ever return after the tour ended? I doubt it. That was okay, though. At least they experienced getting in the pilot's seat at least once.

The coaches were there waiting to take us back to the hotel. Everyone boarded, and off we went. As we were heading to the hotel,

I could not help but hear Tito and our sexy driver laughing during the drive. You know, it was the kind of laugh that sounded a bit mischievous. Next thing I knew, we were back in our two-bedroom suite when there was a knock on the door.

Making my way and looking through the peephole to see who was there, I broke out laughing as I opened the door and said, "Well, surprised to see you here."

Standing before me was our coach driver in her tight jeans outlining every inch and every form of her butt and her legs. She was now wearing a fitted tank top, which was incredibly revealing.

"Hello," I said in a whimsical tone. "Come on in, and I'll get Tito for you."

As she made herself comfortable on the sofa, I walked into Tito's adjoining room and just smiled at him. "Who was at the door?" Tito asked. "Is it the driver?"

Just from my expression, Tito already knew the answer. As we then entered the living room area, I made sure to continue my walk to the opposite end of the room and took hiding in my own adjoining room.

"Have fun!" I chuckled back.

About fifteen minutes later, "Hey, Steve. Hey, Steve," I can hear from the other room. "Come on in," Tito called out.

For no other reason, I had to respond; he was my client, and safety always came first (chuckle chuckle). When I walked into the room, there was no one there. Puzzled, I stood for a second when I again heard Tito call out, "Steve, we're in here." Hearing that the voices were now coming from Tito's bedroom, I walked in only to find them both on the bed and, well, having the time of their lives, it seemed.

"She wants you to join in!" Tito blurted out.

Next thing I knew, Tito and I once again enjoyed our romps with this eager-to-please young coach driver. What could I do? Here was my boss telling me to join him. I had no choice (chuckle chuckle). Some call them perks of the road. I just called it job-related. The following day, the concert went off without a hitch from our point, and we then said our goodbyes and climbed aboard our charter flight, headed for New York,

Since we were performing at the Giant's Stadium in New Jersey, I recall us flying into and arriving at the Hemsley Palace Hotel and then going to a Brooklyn warehouse for another video shoot. From the outside, it was your typical brick-layered building with old wooden framed windowsills. The only difference was that these windows were covered and completely blacked out. Inside, there was a huge room already designed for the video. There were dancers all over the place, dressed in the smallest of outfits, and each one looked better than the last one. It was a very busy place, with music blaring, manufactured smoke filling the room, and lasers flashing. We ended up staying in New York overnight since we did not leave Brooklyn until late that evening. Next morning, we were back at the airport heading back to meet the tour.

Days ran together. Nights ran together. It got to the point on some days that we were traveling a thousand miles per hour. There were interviews, children's hospital visits, PSAs (public service announcements), and meetings after meetings after meetings. The further into the tour we went, it seems the more problems occurred. Problems between the Jackson brothers and Michael amplified. Our promoter, the infamous Don King, and most of the Jackson brothers did not get along. In fact, the managers of both Michael and the Jacksons were having serious problems with King. It was also known within the ranks that Michael had only reluctantly joined his brothers, who needed the income while he did not.

We were performing at two or three sold-out concerts at Giants Stadium (now referred to as Met Life Stadium), East Rutherford, New Jersey. We had been staying in New York City at the Helmsley Palace Hotel for almost ten days. The downtime for the brothers made daily trips out on the streets of New York City. Okay, not that we really walked anywhere substantially since we had an SUV and driver at our beck and call, twenty-four hours a day.

"Hey, Steve," Tito said over the hotel room telephone. "Come on over. I have an idea."

Follow orders, so I grabbed my radio, and off I went. Tito was already standing at his room door with a shit-eaten grin on his face.

"Okay." I chuckled. "What are you planning?"

We walked back into the suite and waited until the door closed. No sooner than the door latched, Tito turned to me and said, "Hey, Prince's new movie, *Purple Rain*, was just released in a few movie theaters. Man, let's go see it." My expression was that "are you serious" look. Before I could say a word, Tito was holding up the theater section of the local newspaper and said, "We'd never be able to do this here in the city, but we can go to New Jersey and see it. I found where in Jersey its playing." As he was waving this paper in front of me, I could not help but think that this could be fun. I found the closest major theater, located at the Paramus Mall, Paramus, New Jersey. We followed procedure and advised floor security. We were going shopping, and off we went. New Jersey, here we come.

Arriving at the theater almost at showtime, I suggested we wait until the movie starts, and I would get the manager to let us sneak in and sit in the back.

"Sounds good to me," Tito said.

I made my way to the box office window, and the man seated at the booth was the manager, so the timing was perfect.

"Hi, my name is Steve Wallach. I have a client that would really like to come in and see this movie," I spoke.

"Sure, just buy your ticket and get in line. The line moves fast," Mr. Booth Man said.

As he smiled and stared, I then said, "No, no, you don't seem to understand. I have one of the Jacksons with me, and he'd love to just quietly sneak inside and sit in the far back without making a fuss. You think that's possible?"

The man did not know how to respond except by tilting his head to one side and making a statement that was more like a question. "Come on. That's impossible. Here…at my theater? Okay, so let me meet him, and if it's really one of the Jacksons, I'll just bring you right inside the side door." No further action was needed. We walked over to the SUV where introductions were made, and inside we went, finding the entire back row empty as if they knew we were

THIS LIFE OF MINE

coming. To cap it off, the manager even brought us popcorn and lemonade.

Bill Bray, security director, made it clear that under no circumstances were we to leave with a brother without clearing it through the proper channels. After time on the road, you realize that that sometimes is not the best for the artist's movement, especially with such an artist(s) in high demand. But then you must make it a production to do something like being low-key and not drawing attention. The Jacksons PR firm always wanted action and drama. It was great for the read they said. Tito and a few other brothers would handle their own affairs through their own staff, making our movements like a game to see who could get away without anyone knowing. I understand that Bill Bray wanted to know every movement of every brother. Honestly, Bill Bray had his hands full with Michael, and most of the team had a handle on their artist.

Tito and Dee Dee (Tito's wife) always wanted to hit the streets of New York. My attitude was that if we don't attract attention, we should be able to walk without any concern. Tito wore a jacket and always had one of his many baseball-style hats on. We usually had someone with us to help Dee Dee with all the shopping bags. Thousands of dollars were spent on clothes and other items throughout the tour. Dee Dee was a smart shopper. Tito loved to spend.

The down days in New York City also gave Tito and Dee Dee time to make new friends. One floor below us was Eric Estrada and his lovely wife, Peggy Lynne. As we approached their hotel room door, you could not help but smell fresh tomato sauce with garlic and other herbs cooking from within their door. You need to understand that many of the suites in the Helmsley Palace Hotel contain small kitchens where guests on their long stays can enjoy their own home-cooked meals when desired. This was someone's home-cooked meal.

Eric Estrada was performing in an Off-Broadway play and had invited Tito and Dee Dee to attend the following night. I, on the other hand, made sure they made it to their seats and were properly escorted back out to where I was waiting for them. Eric had invited Tito and Dee Dee back to his dressing room, where they then decided to have a very late dinner at the infamous Russian Tea Room.

As our SUV stopped and I made my way around to the other side of the vehicle, Eric put his arm around me and said, "Steve, you come in and eat with us also."

Tito chimed in and said, "Yeah, Steve. Come on inside and eat."

Heck, I wasn't about to turn down an invitation to dine in the Russian Tea Room. And yes, it was an excellent dinner and some wonderful people. The Estradas and the Jacksons became very dear friends years after. But with so many divorces, friendships end abruptly or fade away, and people change and set out for other reasons, and this was no different. I know, as of this writing, that Eric and Peggy Lynne eventually divorced and have since moved on. I know that Dee Dee and Peggy Lynne became very close friends up until the murder of Delores (Dee Dee Jackson) by a former lover/friend. I continue to keep in contact with Peggy Lynne as of this writing. Now living just outside Nashville, Tennessee, Peggy and I do enjoy our text get-togethers.

Michael traveled with his own personal chef. First, there was Remi, and then Mani Niall joined in somewhere during the Victory Tour. Michael loved shrimp, and he was always asking Remi for shrimp. Since I am originally a Jersey boy, my parents' home in Holmdel, New Jersey, was only about forty-five minutes from New York City. In one of my telephone conversations with my mother, I asked her if she would possibly do me a huge favor and bring Michael some fresh shrimp. Now this was not just any shrimp. These were the ten- to twelve-count shrimps—huge and so tasteful.

"Sure," my mother said. "How can I say no? I'll bring up a couple dozen for you."

"How 'bout tomorrow? You and Pop will come into the city and then I'll take you over to the stadium for the show. You'll ride over with all of us," I said with excitement.

"Great! Dad and I will see you and Michael around three o'clock," she, too, said with excitement.

I said, "Okay, sounds great! Do me a favor, though. Bring an extra dozen in a separate bag for me. I'll never see one shrimp once I bring it to Michael's chef."

THIS LIFE OF MINE

The following day, Michael had a feast with one of his favorite dishes, shrimp and me, I got to spend some quality time with my folks and dined on my own bag of chilled shrimp.

The day prior to the start of our sold-out concerts, there were transportation meetings throughout the day. During these briefings, Bill Bray made the team aware that there would be a huge entourage of limos, sedans, and SUVs making the drive from Midtown Manhattan through the Lincoln Tunnel along Route One until we reached the exit ramp leading us into the stadium. NYPD handled our police escorts through the city, but once we reached the tunnel, it was then under jurisdiction of the Port Authority of New York/New Jersey Police. Having been a police officer for the Port Authority Police years prior, I wanted to first make a few telephone calls and see if they would be willing to help us. I had an idea that I felt was the most suitable idea to make this run without incident.

The entourage was planning to leave the hotel within thirty minutes. There were limos and SUVs already in position, anxiously waiting at the main hotel entrance. There was an NYPD–marked police vehicle in front, followed by Michael's SUV, followed by another security team vehicle, and more. As we gathered Michael and his brothers and made our way to our waiting elevators, the ride down was quiet as it usually is during this movement. The elevator doors opened from the two elevators we had commandeered, and we made our way down the hallways through additional doors leading us directly into the kitchen. Security had cleared a pathway, which we followed onto the loading dock and to our waiting vehicles. Doors could be heard slamming shut, and faint sounds of a few tires squealing as we made our way up the ramp and out onto the streets of New York City. The only difference was we left from the opposite side of the Helmsley Palace Hotel. While most of the paparazzi were out front, only a few caught us leaving from the opposite side. With sirens blaring, our entire entourage was making our way through the streets of New York, having to cut in and out of vehicles that could not understand to move to the side when you hear a siren, but we now picked up a sleuth of paparazzi cars trying everything to get that one million shot of Michael and the Jacksons.

As we were making our final turn onto the entrance to the Lincoln Tunnel, I could see the flashing blue lights just ahead. As we made our approach, I knew exactly what to expect. Traffic cones were set out to close off one complete lane going into the tunnel and throughout the tunnel. On the New Jersey side, the cones continued completely around the loop until we were no longer in Port Authority of New York/New Jersey jurisdiction. At that line, we were met by two New Jersey State Trooper vehicles that escorted us the remaining drive into Giants Stadium. No time in the history of the Lincoln Tunnel have they ever closed any lane with the exception of the president of the United States. I was honored that I was able to accomplish this for them, but at the same time, I was slapping myself on the back and giving myself nothing but coos. Before I forget, when Michael Jackson got in his SUV along with Bill Bray and Chuckie DeBias, they headed out in another direction. His SUV made its way to the New York Heliport on the East River, where a chartered helicopter was waiting. Michael and his team flew directly over to Giants Stadium, but this was never brought out publicly until days later.

There were many celebrities that came to the hotel for the preconcert parties, and some actually rode over with the brothers. One of Tito's good friends, Magic Johnson, and his wife joined us in our van. I will never forget how pleasantly shocked and thrilled Magic was for how I was able to pull off such a stunt.

"Hell, no one closes the Lincoln Tunnel!" Magic cheered us out as we were making our way through the tunnel. "How did you do this?"

As I turned over to Magic, I said with a smile, "Stick with me, Magic. I'll get you where you need to go every time!"

Another reason why I'm grateful for the knowledge I gained from my father. "Where there's a will, there's a way" was one of his sayings. To this day, I still try to follow that throughout my life. The Giant Stadium Shows were a great success.

The tour continued with its New York City date at Madison Square Garden on August 4, 1984. It was like a who's who when it came to the celebrity guest list. It was completely out of control insofar as everyone thought they were far more important than the others and expected to be able to take center stage backstage: Elton John, Billy Joel, Donald Trump, Liza Minnelli, Eric Estrada, Quincy Jones, and many others. I recall having to escort Dani DeVito backstage.

As we were walking toward the back through the maze of pathways and curtains, for some unknown reason, I turned around and looked down at Danny DeVito and said, "Boy, you sure are short!"

I finally understood years later that if looks could kill, I'd be dead. Mr. DeVito did not find that funny, or was I trying to be funny? I just could not help but notice just how short he was standing next to me at six feet four inches. Well, I didn't expect to be on his Christmas card list anyway. As the general lights dimmed and the stage lights and sound began to take their cues from some of the best techs in the industry, it was showtime!

The rigging alone for our Madison Square shows was intense. The huge sides were able to hold up the mass of speakers and lights were amazing. So much how to go into the construction of every portion. The rigging hanging overhead was the largest I'd ever seen. Tons of lights and more speakers, hanging with 100 percent assurance that they were tightly secured.

By this time in the shows, I took stage left since it was me that Michael would toss his personal Fedora Hat to after his first song. Tito's stage side always had the monitor boards, so there was enough personal security on that side. Bodyguards and local police officers protected every portion of the stage. Bill Bray made sure that the stage was put at ease for the brothers.

By the start of the third song, I could not help but notice a movement out of my side view, coming from the stage left columns. As I glanced straight up, I immediately saw the figure of a man high above moving his way to the front. Without hesitation, I began to climb the tower quickly but safely to make contact. As I approached this unidentified man, I called out for him to immediately stop. My approach high above the stage was quick. I questioned the man immediately and then demanded that he start working his way back down. In the meantime, I had radioed my other team members to have someone meet us when we came down. And coming down was a venture in itself. The height was over fifty feet, and now trying to climb down was a bit harder than climbing up. Apparently, the man had made his way undetected to the backstage area and had made his way to the rear of the stage. Thank goodness, this was not an actual threat, but we never sat idle when something was out of place.

Our next date was five days away in Knoxville, Tennessee. Bill Bray had called a special meeting together with the team to go over some new details about the update early that morning. When we arrived for the meeting, I noticed Bill was a bit on edge. Anytime Bill would pace back and forth and touch his hat continuously, there was something concerning him.

"I received some information that is alarming," Bill said in his quiet serious voice. "I'm not liking what I have, but we have to get involved with it."

Bill opens a letter that MJ Productions had received. Inside the letter, it clearly stated that there would be a shooting at the Knoxville Show, and there would be tragedies. This letter contained the names of some of the Jacksons, including Michael, and some of their bodyguards. As Bill read from the letter, he called out the names and said, "Steve, you're on here as well."

I thought for a minute and clearly said, "Okay, Bill, what's the plan?"

It was arranged that Michael would be flying in the day of the show and would go directly to the venue. The brothers would travel from their hotel to the venue but not by normal transport. I suggested we use an armored vehicle for the brothers.

"It must be an armored vehicle that has air-conditioning."

There would be no way the boys nor anyone could stand riding inside a closed armored vehicle in the middle of August. I suggested that I could make a few phone calls and see if there were any armored vehicles in Knoxville with air-conditioning. Bill agreed and let me take charge of finding an armored truck.

The closest armored vehicle I was able to locate was in Nashville, Tennessee, not the closest city to Knoxville, but with the time remaining, they could have the truck at our hotel by midafternoon, leaving ample time to get them to the stadium for the show.

THIS LIFE OF MINE

But in the meantime, there was a serious threat that had to be dealt with. Michael's Production Company had been receiving threatening letters within the last few weeks from what appeared to be the same person. When reviewing the envelopes, we noticed that these letters were being mailed from various cities; therefore, trying to pinpoint it was nearly impossible. The last letter also contained a rough sketched-out blueprint of the Knoxville Tennessee Stadium. Every hallway backstage, every passageway around the back of the stadium, and the entire seating chart was included. This had to be from someone who had direct knowledge and/or information on this stadium. Bill and the local police were working hard to track this person down. It was immediately brought to Michael and the brothers' attention.

Bill asked the brothers, "What do you want to do? Should we call and cancel the date for safety reasons?"

Each brother voiced their opinion, and it was decided that it would be left up to Michael to make the decision.

"I am not canceling any show!" we were able to hear Michael yelling into Bill's cellphone. "These people paid good money to see the Jacksons, and that's what they're gonna get," Michael said with great passion.

We outlined our transportation, and it was agreed. The concert would go on as planned.

It was still bothering me how this person had the complete layout not only of this stadium but other stadiums he included with his absurd mailings. I contacted our production manager and asked him if any crew had been fired recently. As I thought, there was one of the flying carpenters fired from the tour. This individual was extremely upset that he was fired and had been escorted from the venue this took place. It was in Dallas, Texas. He was terminated for his drinking and lack of acting in a professional manner. When you are high up in the rafters or climbing a rig, it takes strength and agility, not to mention you best know what you are doing.

The advanced team contacted Bill Bray and said that the entire stadium and backstage area had been swept with no sign of any threat. Then why was this person so adamant about his threats? I wondered.

As we all made our way into the hotel lobby, we were welcomed with this spotless armored truck at the entrance.

"Gentlemen," I said, "your chariot awaits."

You couldn't help but give a slight chuckle as they went to open the side door of the armored truck. I recall Marlon's bodyguard, James Andersen, called out, "Damn, this door weighs a ton!"

And it sure did—solid steel. We each stepped up into the rear of the truck and chose our spot on the wooden benches located on both insides. It may have been in the middle of a hot August summer day in Tennessee, but we were sitting cool inside this armored truck, heading to do a show at Neyland Stadium, Knoxville, Tennessee.

Once we arrived backstage and the boys made their way to their designated dressing rooms, I met with a few police officers and Bill Bray on the stage. Everyone was puzzled as to where his threat came from and was it real. I mentioned to Bill that production said they fired someone a few weeks back and he was not accepting his termination like a gentleman. When we spoke about his carpenter's work ability, we were each scanning the area to see if we saw something odd. As I glanced toward the back of the stadium, I could not help but take notice of this massive crane that was located outside the stadium but with a clear open view from the crane to the inside.

Maybe it was my cop instinct, but I turned to Bill and said, "Bill, I think you have to get the cops to go check that crane out. I have a bad feeling that he may be perched on the crane."

Bill looked at me with a puzzled look but immediately got on his radio and asked that this request be immediately handled. Not fifteen minutes later, we are told that the Knoxville Police did, in fact, find someone at the crane with a high-powered rifle. I never found out if it was our terminated crew member, but I have a strong feeling it was. The show went on without a hitch and we again made history at Neyland Stadium. I recall when I was interviewed by my local newspaper, *The Tennessee Banner*.

When we arrived in a city ahead of the night's performance, the PR team for the tour would usually have either radio interviews scheduled or visits to a children's hospital. The visits would be chaotic because rather than us arriving quietly and going to see all the children, which is why we went, the paparazzi and the television camera crews would be making it more difficult to move through the paths. I always enjoyed going with the brothers. In fact, all hospital visits with every artist I have ever worked for always had me leaving there, looking up at our God and giving thanks.

But on this one hospital visit, in Philly, we were all inside a large room filled with children in hospital beds, IVs in many of them, bandages on some, casts on others. It was truly a wonderful feeling of healing when we saw the faces of these children. It was as if they forgot why they were there and just gleamed with excitement being able to see and possibly meet Michael and the Jacksons. As I watched, I noticed Randy Jackson motion over to the brothers' manager, Jack Nance, and started pulling at his own skin. It was as if he was pinching the skin on his hand. At first, I stood puzzled until I saw that he was letting Jack know there were no black children in the room.

As Jack finally figured out what Randy meant, Randy leaned over toward Jack and said with a very stern voice, "They better go get some black kids in here and now!"

With that, Jack had made his way out into the hallway, and within less than five minutes, another nurse came into the room and called out, "Here are a few more children that would love to see the Jacksons." *Bam*! A matter taken care of without a media breakdown, and most importantly, all the children were so incredibly happy, as were we. I could not help but agree with Randy. If there were a mixture of children of other races, why were they not also in this very special gathering?

In Philadelphia, we just finished another sold-out stadium. We usually never returned to our hotel immediately after a performance. There is always media, meet and greets, VIP green room, and the lengthy list of celebrities, all wanting time with Michael mainly but also with his brothers. We finally arrived back at the hotel lobby to find it was packed with fans. Located in a hotel in downtown Philly, it created pure havoc for the local police and, of course, the hotel personnel. As we made our way through the lobby, the screams and flashes from cameras were enough to blind you. But this is what kept our adrenaline going. Knowing that all these screaming fans were here for the man I was assigned to protect his brothers. It gave you a feeling that, to this day, is hard to describe. Out of this entire packed lobby stood this beautiful girl standing there with this huge smile. Okay, granted it was not only her smile that caught our attention. It was her waist-length blond hair, magnificent hourglass body, breasts that were having the hardest time staying inside her half-buttoned blouse, and the deepest blue eyes. As much as we wanted to stop and talk to her, we were pressed to get the brothers in the elevators and up to our designated floors. I knew exactly what Tito wanted me to do. Once we reached our suite, I made sure all was set properly. I made my way back down to the lobby in search of this blond goddess.

As I came out of the elevator, there she stood, alone, waiting for someone to approach her. And approached her, I did.

"Hi," I said as I extended my hand to her. "I couldn't help but notice you when we came it."

As my hand met with hers, I could not help but notice how soft her hand was. "Hello, I'm Sharon," she said with a seductive smile and nod of her head.

Small talk ensued, and I finally asked her if she'd like to come up and meet the brothers.

"I'd love to," she said in a soft voice.

We made our way to the elevators and took our short ride to my secure floor.

Walking out of the elevator, we were met by floor security, who, in turn, gave us a nod and smile. Most of the suites Tito and I shared had a living room separating the two bedrooms. We always took advantage of this layout because I was able to have Tito's keyboard racks delivered and set for him. Also, it gave us an opportunity to use this middle room as a meeting room, always knowing we had our bedrooms to run back to if we wanted to be alone. Introductions were made, and Tito and I just looked at each other with this child-like grin coming from us both.

"So did you see our show tonight?" Tito asked her to advertise his smile.

"Yes, I did, and it was incredible!" this seductive voice said. "It was the best concert I've ever been to!"

Hugs were exchanged, and the night was about to begin. Immediately, our new friend Sharon sat right up, realigned herself on the couch, and with that seductive smile, she said in a very sensual voice, "Thanks for inviting me up."

Tito stood and said, "It's my pleasure. I must make a few calls, but I'll be back. Anything you want, just ask Steve, and he'll make it happen."

I couldn't help but turn my head toward Tito, smile, and look over to see this playboy-like beauty sitting next to me with a grin that allowed her perfectly straight pearly white teeth shine through and her breasts just about to burst out her shirt. What to do...? What to do...?

I offered my fantasy-wish girl a drink from our stocked bar, as I, too, felt I knew that I needed one. We had the usual conversation that two people meeting for the first time had. I remember her telling me her recent life story.

"I'm married, but my husband is away for some time," she said in a soft-spoken whisper. *Away*, I thought to myself. Maybe he was a traveling salesman or something that would cause him the leave such a beautiful lady. *Hell, it better have been for a huge salary*, I thought to myself. Before I could even ask her, she said, "Yeah, he's gone for about fourteen more years. He's in prison." Without taking a breath, she popped down the rest of her cocktail and said, "I'll have another." As I poured her another drink, I could not help but wonder what she was doing with herself. Seriously, she was drop-dead gorgeous.

As I handed her the cocktail, she refused to take her hand off mine and said, "I haven't had great sex in over a year, and guess what, today's your lucky day."

There is no need to go further into the actual details of some fantastic sex; however, it is important to know that this was only the beginning of what was to be a very long night. I could not help but to go into a state of panic or just say fuck it and let things run its course.

"Listen, let me go check next door and see how long Tito is going to be," I spoke.

As she nodded, I was already across the room and through the adjoining door.

There's Tito, lying on his bed, eating nuts and listening to music. "Hey!" I said in a soft but sturdy voice. "Aren't you comin' back over?"

With his shit-eating grin, he said, "Yeah, I'll be there, but go ahead and get things going. I'll be there soon."

As we both gave out a little laughter, he motioned me back, and I smiled back at him as I closed the door.

As we continued to "getting to know each other," Tito opened the adjoining door and walked in. When I looked over at the door, his expression was priceless.

"Ooh, sorry. I didn't mean to walk in on anything," Tito said with a laugh in his voice.

"Heck, come on in."

Next thing you know, Sharon was reaching her hand out to bring Tito into the group. So use your own imagination because if you do like what you are thinking at this moment, it's a grand slam home run.

Somewhere during our escapade, there was a knock on the hotel room door. Not just a regular knock but a knock the security team produced so we would know who was on the other side of any door. Having to leave our little get-together, I opened the hotel room door, and there stood Randy and his bodyguard Charles L. Next thing you know, clothes were being dropped on the floor not only by Randy and Charles but others, who got wind and came to participate. By the end, a few of the Jacksons (not Michael) were there and their security team. Too many reasons for me not to want to get an actual count. After about another hour, the brothers and their guards left, and Tito and I looked at each other, smiled, and at the same time said, "Good night." And it sure was a good night.

Sharon ended up sleeping in the bed where it all began. Tito and I each had our own rooms on each side of this center room. I remember her saying that her stomach was upset the next morning. Hell, I wonder why. She had to have well over eight people leave their mark. It really did not matter. I then did what Tito asked me to do. I arranged to have Sharon taken to Philadelphia Airport as she asked, and that was the end. Neither Tito nor I ever heard from her again,

THIS LIFE OF MINE

nor did we try to reach out to her. I had her contact information in case it was ever needed at some time, but again, it was just another punch to the belt of touring.

As the tour progressed, Tito and I became what I would consider close friends, not only on a business relationship but also on a personal side. Having to hold the position as his bodyguard and part of the security team, he knew I had his back. This led over to me also overseeing security for his then-wife, Delores (Dee Dee), and his very young boys, Taj, TJ, and Taryll (who are now a Jackson music group called 3 T's. But when it came to traveling at any moment, whether it being part of the tour or personal, I made myself available, even at downtime.

It was now October 1984; the entire entourage had arrived in Miami, Florida. As usual, Michael and his team went to the designated hotel, and the brothers and their team went to a fantastic hotel located in Coconut Grove, Florida, a small quaint town within the Miami area. I do not remember the name of this unique-style hotel, but it was rated five stars, and their hotel rooms were designed with a cosmopolitan European flare. I remember this hotel because I ended up returning here with Tito weeks later.

It was the weekend of Thanksgiving, to be exact. We had a break from the tour so that those on the crew capable of leaving were able to join their families at home for the Thanksgiving holiday. I was looking forward to going home because it had already been a few months since I had been able to get home due to our heavy touring and media schedule. I was looking forward to this time home.

Like it was yesterday, my cell phone rang, and it was Tito on the other end.

"Hello," I said. "What's up, T?"

"You need to get back out here immediately," Tito said in a stern voice.

He only spoke with this tone when he was flustered about something. Without questioning as to why, it was my responsibility, and I had to follow his request. Three hours later, I was on a first-class flight heading to Los Angeles International Airport. I was met by a limo and taken immediately to my hotel, which was located within ten minutes to Tito's residence in Encino. Upon my arrival at the hotel, I checked in and immediately set up my radio connections as I was in the radio range to Tito's home.

"Okay, I'm here," I said into the phone. "What's so important? Are you okay? Is your family okay?"

"I need you to book two first-class tickets from LA to Miami for tomorrow morning," Tito said. "I need the first flight outa here."

I said, "What's going on?"

There was a pause on the phone, which seemed to last a few minutes. Without any words from Tito, just silence, I said I would take care of the fights and would call him back once confirmed. Ten minutes later, Tito Jackson and Steve Wallach were booked on the American Airlines, nonstop flight service to Miami, Florida, on November 24, Thanksgiving Day. What could have been so important for me to be asked to leave my family on America's wonderful binge day, Thanksgiving Day?

The following morning, the limo initially picked me up at the hotel, and then we made our way to the residence of Tito Jackson.

"Morning, T. What in the world is going on?" I spoke.

"I'll tell you in the limo. Let's go!"

Three minutes later, Tito's overnight bag and the two of us were headed to the airport for our five-plus-hour flight to Miami. Still not giving me any information, Tito just made small talk while glancing through the magazines he had with him. Mind you, these magazines were specific, all designed around boating, yachts, charters, etc.

Finally, Tito looked up from his magazine and said, "We're going to buy a boat."

With that known smile on his face, I could not help but first look at him with this dumbfounded expression.

"A boat?" I spoke. "What the hell are you gonna do with a boat in Miami, Florida?"

Tito looked at me and said, "I'm not gonna keep it here. I'll have it shipped or floated to California."

I just sat back in my first-class seat and said nothing. What was I going to say? Here we are headed to Miami to buy a fuckin' boat that he will then have shipped all the way to California. "Tito, you're not even on the water. You live in Encino! On a mountaintop!"

"Oh." Tito laughed. "No, I'll have it shipped to me house in Oxnard, California."

Tito and Dee Dee also had a beautiful home up near Bear Mountain, and it was there he would keep the boat.

"Tito, have you thought this through?" I said. "Dee Dee hates the water. She can't even swim."

"Oh, that's okay. She'll get used to it." Tito returned with, "Oh, and by the way, you have to negotiate this for me."

What the heck do I know about negotiating for a boat?

The following day, our driver picked us up, and we were on our way to buy a boat.

"Where is this boat you so desperately want?" I spoke.

"Oh, it's up in Fort Lauderdale," Tito said back.

Now the photos and information of the boat came out of the folder he was carrying. When I looked at the photos, it really was a beautiful fishing boat, around forty-two feet. It had a great aft deck for fishing, a well-appointed living room, a galley, and two cabins beside the master cabin.

As we were arriving, I said to Tito, "I think it would be best for you not to walk in there with me at first. My thought is that if they know it's a Jackson wanting to purchase their boat, the price will go higher."

"Good idea, Steve. Think I'll just sit in here until you come back," said Tito.

I ended up negotiating a fantastic deal for Tito, not only on the cost for the boat but also for ground shipping it from Fort Lauderdale, Florida, across the country to Oxnard, California. That was what we had to leave our families for—to go buy a damn boat. My immediate thought was that there was no rush for this. We could have handled this after the holiday weekend. No. Tito Jackson, a Mormon, who does not celebrate Thanksgiving holiday nor any other holiday, chose to do it then. Again, it was part of my job performance, and when the brothers called for you, you came.

Coming to the end of this historic tour, we found ourselves at the Los Angeles Hyatt Hotel, Downtown LA, on Wilshire Boulevard. The hotel lobby had been blocked off due to the hundreds of fans that had been created outside the hotel's main entrance. Remember, this was home for Michael and the Jacksons. Each one of them lived no more than forty minutes from where we would end up staying for close to ten days. Securing three full floors of the hotel enabled everyone to move freely between the floors. You needed a security key to enable the elevators to reach each of the floors. Of course, Michael had the top floor to himself, and the brothers were divided up among the remaining floors. Even Reba, LaToya, and Janet Jackson took up residence with the entire Jackson siblings. The brothers' wives and children were there plus the children's nannies and cousins, followed by more cousins and cousins they didn't know they even had.

So many celebrities were stopping by to meet with Michael and the brothers. Most, of course, to see Mike, but then again, some that were there for all. Having the brothers able to stay on the secured floors enabled some of the team crew to assist when needed. Whether it was handling any paperwork or assisting in celebrity escorts, I had no issues playing the part. Tito had his family there, and he planned on staying inside. I knew that if he chose to go anywhere, I would be the first to know.

On one occasion during our stay there, Miko Brando, one of Michael's assistants and personal friend, contacted me via radio and asked me to assist him on an escort. Not doing anything except relaxing in my hotel room, I went up to Michael's floor, where Miko was waiting in the hallway.

"Hey, Steve," Miko said. "Can you do me a favor and take the elevator down with me and bring my father, his wife, and friend up? They're here to see Mike."

"No big deal, Miko. Where am I to meet them?" I asked.

"They should be right by the elevators standing with one of our security men," Miko said back.

So down the elevator we went on our way to meet and escort Miko's father and wife up to Michael Jackson's suite.

The elevator door opened, and standing right there as if he knew it was about to open was Miko's father. In front of me, no more than two feet, stood Marlon Brando. It is important to understand that I have worked with and met with some of the greatest entertainers and actors, but standing before me was my idol.

"Mr. Brando," I said in a quiet voice, "I'm here with Miko to bring you up to Mike."

"You can call Marlon," he said back to me.

Wow, I thought to myself, doing my best to keep my composure. Now Miko had a heart as gold. He was loved and liked by everyone that encountered him. He was a true friend and confidant to Michael but was a real down to earth kind of guy. Miko had a stutter, but that never hampered him at all.

As we were riding the elevator up, Miko said, "Staaa, Steve, do my father."

At first, I ignored him, looking straight up at the lit signage showing the floor numbers race by. But within another second, Miko again says, "Come on, Steve, dooo dooo my father."

Standing still as I possibly could, Marlon pokes me in the side and says, "Yeah, do me."

What was I to do? We had not reached the floor yet, and I was trapped inside an elevator with Marlon Brando, his wife, a friend, and Miko. I turned to Mr. Brando, then looked up at the ceiling in this enclosed box and called out loudly in my Brando voice, "Stellaaaaaaa!"

That was my best impersonation when he starred in the movie *A Streetcar Named Desire*.

Standing there as if I was waiting to receive an Oscar, Marlon Brando laid his hand on my shoulder and said, "Not bad, not bad."

Leaning into to me, he followed up with, "Son, don't give up your day job."

We laughed as the elevator doors opened and Chuckie DeBias was standing waiting to escort Michael's guests inside.

Once again, the shows in Los Angeles were completely sold out. After each performance, the backstage meet and greetings for the brothers were not as chaotic as it was for Michael. Everyone wanted to see him. The celebrity guest list made the New York listing light in comparison. Artists, musicians, actors, managers, lawyers, doctors, and promotors, you think of them, and they were there. I was glad that Tito always wanted to head back to the hotel. This time, it was for his family.

Steve Wallach with Marlon Jackson and Tito Jackson, the Jackson's Victory Tour, 1984

The Jackson's Victory Tour came to an end. What should have been the start of the world tour, heading over to Europe, Australia, and Japan, the tour abruptly came to an end. Michel had announced from the stage that the tour was ending, and he would no longer be touring with his brothers. Rumors still have it that the verbal fight between Michael and his brothers, their managers Frank DiLeo (deceased) and Jack Nance (deceased), lawyers from all sides, both promotors Don King and Rick Sullivan, there had been so much blood spilled. This would be the last stop to ever seeing the Jacksons all together again, performing on one stage.

THIS LIFE OF MINE

Sometime in January or February of the following year, I believe it was 1987, I went out as security director for a Canadian singer, Corey Hart. By the middle of the second week of his tour, which was to include North America, it was obvious that Corey Hart is an asshole. His sidekick road manager William took second place. When we arrived in Arkansas at the Arkansas Fair, we were to perform that evening from a makeshift stage in the middle of a rodeo rink. One hour prior to showtime, we were told that the tour was canceled. The band would return to Canada via coach, and those from the States would return home from Arkansas. This was the best news for a tour that was not worth the time, especially for an artist whose head was bigger than the rodeo rink itself. Back to the drawing board and open those contacts—something I was getting used to.

Before heading home, I had a few days to kick back and enjoy. I had spoken with my mother that afternoon to see how everything was at home.

"Everything's great!" she said in a loud and excited tone. "We're not home. We're in Vegas for another week!" I could hear in her tone that she was having a fantastic time and enjoying the benefits that Vegas has to offer, especially when your treated with full VIP service.

"Mom, I got an idea," I said. "Maybe I'll join you both out there for a few days if you don't mind."

"Me, mind," she says back. "Of course, you can meet us!"

That evening, I was on the next flight to Vegas, using up some of my airline points that I have accumulated throughout my tours.

It was great seeing my folks, and in fact, we made a deal to see each other the following morning for breakfast and some time by the pool. Sounded great to me. I was fortunate that they had a two-bedroom suite, so this became "old home night" but on the road.

The following morning, breakfast was delivered, and we enjoyed our waffles, eggs, bacon, sausage, fresh-cut fruit, toast, bagels, fresh coffee, and a list of so many other things. By eleven o'clock, we were on our way to the pool. The pool was a large area filled with lounge chairs, chairs and tables, and umbrellas enough to go around. We found a great spot with only one row of five chairs behind us and a walkway in front—ample room to stretch out and enjoy the sun and cocktails. I am bringing this up because of yet another story of information I was about to be taught.

The young couple sitting behind us had no idea that we were part of a family. They had thought my parents were there alone and I was someone who just happened to be next to them. As they came around the front of our lounges, I heard the woman ask, "Excuse us. Do you mind if we ask you a question?"

Without hesitation, my mother said, "Of course not. What can we help you with?"

You see, no matter where my mother was, if someone needed anything and she was able to help, she was there for them.

"Well, we've seen you here at the hotel for the last four or five days, and every time we see you walking around, you're holding each other's hand. It's obvious that you're older than us, but are you here on your honeymoon?"

As I began taking my sunglasses off to see the expressions on my parents' face, my mother, without missing a beat, said with a true deep laugh, "Oh, darling, we've been married well over twenty years."

The couple explained they were in Vegas for their honeymoon. That was all my mom had to hear; her jovial sermon began. Seeing the smiles on everyone's faces only shows just how hard my parents have worked on their marriage and their future. The words she shared with this couple had far more meaning than just marriage. Words like respect, commitment, and honesty cover everything we all must deal with. For if not, the reality could outweigh your passion. Is that worth it?

I always wanted to have the same kind of marriage as my parents had. Granted, there were some times when they could have thrown in the towel, yet they continued by any means they saw fit and what worked. My parents had been married for well over sixty-five years before their passing.

After arriving home, I chose to take time off from touring and concentrate on others' interest in entertainment. I became a representative for various artists over the next two years. One being a young man named Jamie Houston. We put together a fantastic band consisting of the infamous bass player Dee Murray (deceased) from Elton John, Chris Golden, Rusty Golden, musicians and sons of William Lee Golden of the Oak Ridge Boys and their drummer. The band was fantastic. I named Jamie "The Houston Project," and we played locally throughout the Nashville area. When it was time to bring Jamie Houston to the labels, I designed a fantastic event and the world's famous Exit/In right in Nashville. Every major label was in attendance, including a few top musicians and artists such as Steve Winwood, William Lee Golden, Michael McDonald, and others. It was a huge success. Jamie was being offered record deals and songwriting deals.

As with a handful of artists in any genre of music, they think and feel that they should outrank other artists working just as hard to get that same recognition. Things just were not going fast enough for Jamie. It became a dead-end issue when the band members one by one dropped out because of his emotional rollercoaster and lack of respect for others. Me, sure, I lost money betting on him, but to me, I was not going to put myself through some artist's pathetic attitude. I released Jamie from his agreement. He moved to California, and he never made it as a recording artist. However, he did go on to be a songwriter for various music publishing companies.

I received a call from a friend of mine, Buford Jones, whom I worked with on past tours, and told me that there may be an opening for the director of security for Pink Floyd. Buford was the house soundman and one of the best in the touring industry. Because the sound was going to be the first for a quad sound, it was a huge undertaking for the sound company, Clair Brothers. I immediately called their manager at the time, Steve O'Rourke, at his office in the UK to ascertain if the position was, in fact, available. After a few telephone conversations, I was hired and on my way to Toronto, Canada, to meet with some of the management team and then to eventually meet up with Dave Gilmore, Steven Wright, and Dave Mason of Pink Floyd. Roger Waters was already on his own so absence from the tour was already known by tens of thousands of fans.

The initial question was where to have rehearsals. The location had to be large enough to hold the entire production. The requirements were massive, and what the production was looking for was going to be difficult.

"Why not rehearse in a hangar at the airport?" I said.

Just giving open thought, I believed if this was possible to do, it would be great. Not only would our rehearsals be located at a facility that was large enough for what we were looking for, but it was also secure from the general public getting any views from what was to be an enormous tour. My idea not only paid off for our rehearsal location, but it saved thousands of dollars paying for another venue in discussions. The icing on the cake was that we were not rehearsing this show anywhere. We were any act without a country. You see, they were able to land all the equipment within the compounds of the airport; therefore, none of our main production had cleared customs. It never left Toronto Airport; therefore, there was no manifest for billing. A brilliant move, if I must say so. We rehearsed in an Air Canada 747 hangar for the next two weeks.

Dave Gilmore and Steven Wright planned on trimming down their weight on this tour, so they were hoping that someone, anyone within their immediate circle, would help them in curving their food desires.

"We can have pasta twice a week," Dave Gilmore announced. "But it has to be homemade."

Well, right up my avenue. I have been cooking for years, and Italian cooking was one of my specialties.

"Hey, Dave, I got this covered for you." I quickly stood out and said, "I'll start tomorrow with homemade sauce and pasta."

This was an easy fate to accomplish. The band had an enormous house where they stayed for the weeks we were in Toronto. Therefore, having a well-stocked kitchen was a perfect fit. I outlined an exercise program not only for them but also a similar plan for their wives, who accompanied them.

I came to find out that Dave Gilmore had his pilot's license and always wanted to get inside the cockpit of a massive jet. This was one of the top subjects Dave consistently had with those who cared to listen.

I recall the time when Steven Wright looked over at me and said, "Okay. They say you can make things happen. Go find him a huge jet to go on."

For a minute, I just stood there, looking directly at Steve, as I was already in deep thought about my new challenge.

"Okay, you have a deal," I laughingly said. "Give me some time, and I'll come up with something."

Not having an idea on what I was going to search for, but I knew one thing was for sure: I was going to find him a passenger jet.

The following morning, I had already come to an idea of what I could get for Dave Gilmore. Remember, this was no ordinary man; this was Dave Gilmore, guitarist for Pink Floyd. Whatever I could do to make this thought become reality, I was going to do my best to make something, anything, happen. After breakfast, I drove over to the airport and made my way through a field of checkpoints before driving to the rehearsal hangar. It still amazed me that we were rehearsing the entire show with full production and lighting. I first contacted our Air Canada representative, whom we have been working with for the lease on the hangar. From the onset, he was very willing to accommodate our requirements and any matters that always popped up in rehearsal settings. My timing was perfect; he had time to meet with me at a specific location within walking distance from the hangar.

As I made my way to our meeting location, I passed a building that I thought looked a bit odd. The building structure stood out from the others. What caught my eye was that there were two (what appeared to be) separated steel boxes positioned on stand-like platforms with cables of some kind running from each box to the building's electrical panel. Interesting since it took on a shape like no other in the immediate area.

As I opened the door of the building, our Air Canada representative welcomed me. Once we said hello, I immediately reopened the door and said to him, "I gotta ask you a question. Can you please tell me what this is?"

"Oh, those are our two in-flight simulators," he said back.

"Simulators? Like actual cockpits for all pilots and co-pilots are trained on?" I spoke.

At the same time, my brain was designing the "treatment" (a term used to give an overall picture of what the storyline would appear like in a movie, video, etc.). "Have I got a huge request!" I said with a sense of excitement in my tone.

We both were now standing outside and walking toward these steel boxes. "Steve, these are the actual flight simulators our pilots are trained on. Every pilot must pass this course with one hundred percent. One simulator is that of an actual 747 and the other simulator, equaling that of an L1011."

Without losing a second of time, I looked over at him with what has become known as the "Wallach grin" first seen on my father's face when he had something not of the ordinary, on his facial expression. I inherited it from an early age since I was always trying to negotiate something and said, "What are the chances we can get Dave Gilmore and the boys in those simulators?"

As we stood there, I could see he was already in the thought of hopefully willing to work with me.

"Steve, let me make a few calls and see what I can do," he said back to me. "It shouldn't be too long until I call you at rehearsal."

We shook hands and ended on a high note. I think I may be able to pull this off, I thought to myself. How cool would this be *if* I could make this happen. I made my way back to the rehearsal hangar in time to see the flying pink pig come down its cable line followed by cheers from the band and crew.

While in the production office later that day, my cell phone rang to find our Air Canada representative on the other end.

"Hello," I said. "This is Steve. Can I help you?"

The first words I could hear coming from the other end of the phone line were, "It's done. It's done! I don't know how we did it, but we did it. I was able to get clearance for Dave Gilmore because he has a pilot's license for single-engine planes."

I was thrilled when I heard this and thanked him for making this happen. "I'll let Dave and the boys know about this," I immediately replied.

"Oh," our rep said, "if any of the other guys have their pilot's license, they, too, can come and try out the simulators. Just let me know what day will work so I can get that time cleared."

I gave my thanks on behalf of myself, Dave Gilmore, Steven Wright, and Nick Mason.

"I'll give them the great news when they finish rehearsals," I ended our conversation.

It was about four o'clock that afternoon. Rehearsals went great, and everyone was making their way out of the hangar to head back to their hotels.

"Hey, Dave," I called out. "Can I speak with you and the boys for a minute before y'all leave?"

As Dave signaled for the others to come over, he said, "Okay, what's up?"

"So I was able to set something up for you guys if any of you would like to give it a try. I need to know now, though, because it'll take at least a full day to set and secure this."

As Dave and the others gave me a questionable stare, I said, "Who wants to get inside Air Canada's actual in-flight simulators and fly an actual 747 and a L1011?"

I really wish I had a camera to capture their facial expressions. The smiles and glows coming from each was something that I will always remember. Dave Gilmore just could not believe I pulled this off.

He kept saying, "You're kidding right? Seriously. No, you're kidding us, right?"

I felt great each time I replied, "Straight up. You asked me to make something spectacular happen, and I did."

I did just for Dave Gilmore, Steven Wright, and Dave Mason.

The following day was an off day, so the timing once again was perfect. I drove over to Dave Gilmore's rented home to pick up him, Steven, and Dave and make our way to Air Canada's rehearsal hangar. There, we were met by our Air Canada Rep and made our way over to their flight simulators. Once inside the building area, we were given instructions by the two Air Canada in-flight simulator training pilots.

"Who's first?" asked the senior training pilot.

Without hesitation, Dave Gilmore shouted out, "Don't have to ask me twice!"

As the door in front of us opened, one could clearly see that we were about to step into the cockpit of an Air Canada 747!

I recall there was an actual step up to get inside. This was because the actual simulator was not connected to the structure of the building itself. Remember, I made mention of these two huge steel boxes that sat balanced on their own individual landings. It was exactly that of a 747. We were told immediately that every switch, button, screen, and throttle found here was the same as those found in a moving 747. Nothing was fake. Everything here could be swapped over to an actual 747 if parts were needed.

After some information was given, Dave took the pilot's seat as the training pilot took over the copilot's seat.

"So where would you like to fly today, Mr. Gilmore?" the Air Canada pilot asked. "Would you like to fly and make your approach to Chicago's O'Hare International Airport? How about you see what it's like flying past the famous Sears Tower in Chicago."

Next thing we knew, the simulator had disengaged itself from the building, and we were virtually flying! It was one of the most incredible experiences I ever got to witness and try. I recall Dave Gilmore was the only one with an actual pilot's license, but Steven, Dave Mason, and I had our own students' pilot license, which meant we were still in training. Still, the training pilot was kind enough to let each of us take a turn flying this 747. Dave Gilmore was the only one who was able to eventually land the simulator with the hands-on assistance from the training pilot. Steve Wright and Dave Mason crashed into the lake, and I took out the Sears Tower. Thank goodness, these were only simulators. This day was a day I will always remember. Huge thanks went out to Air Canada for allowing us this incredible experience.

THIS LIFE OF MINE

Rehearsals went on after this for the next ten days. At the end of one rehearsal day, I received a call from Floyd's manager, Steve O'Rourke, giving me the news that I was not expecting. It seems that Steve chose to replace me with someone the band had worked with for years. Apparently, this person had just completed a world tour with Duran Duran, and they were their first choice for the position with Floyd. So as it happens on occasion in this industry of falsely committed agreements and promises, my gig was gone within twenty-four hours. Bags packed and on my way to the airport for that one flight home. It started to set in that here I was, a new parent with a mortgage and bills and a wife at home taking care of a two-year-old child. I made a commitment to Judy, at the time, that if this tour did not work out, I would come off the road and get a real job. It was time; I had been on tours for over ten years now.

Within three weeks of returning home, I had already spoken with my father for his advice and guidance and had made some active moves to start a new business. As with anything related to a business venture, I always made sure to bring it to my father's attention to see if I was heading down the right path. Why shouldn't I? This man has made some incredible deals and was known as the king of negotiators. Some ideas were not always the best, but this time, with new responsibilities in my life, I wanted to make a move into something that I knew was a great idea and, most importantly, with a future.

My father and I bounced ideas off each other for the next few weeks. Everything from owning and operating coin Laundromats to car parts to home decor ideas, nothing seemed to grab a hold of what I was looking to do. Whether it had to do with bad ideas to locations, we just could not come up with something that we both agreed to. My parents were due to come for a visit the following week, so I knew my father and I would make the best in hoping to come up with a positive idea.

My dad and I decided to go out for lunch and come up with more ideas over a bite to eat. On this day, we chose to go to a very well-established place called Schwartz Deli. Located in the prominent shopping center named Belle Meade Plaza in Belle Meade

(Nashville), Tennessee, Schwartz's had been there for over twenty years. If anything, a good pastrami and corned beef sandwich would fill our needs. And so it was. We drove over to Schwartz's Deli to discuss what I planned on doing for the rest of my life.

Schwartz's was a so-so deli among delis. This was Nashville, Tennessee, in 1987, a place where the culinary cuisine for a good pastrami sandwich was something most Southerners were not familiar with. Meats such as pastrami, corned beef, salami, beef tongue, and chopped liver were words not in the vocabulary of most people in the south. It happens to do with what foods are primarily found in different areas. For example, a deli in the eastern states, such as New Jersey, New York, Maryland, Pennsylvania, Connecticut, and even down to Florida were part of the English language. Delis were an institution throughout these states and every locale was in an area with a medium to higher population of Jews. So when one talks about a real deli in the South, well, it's not something that would equal the high standards of an East Coast deli. True delis, or formally known as delicatessens. These stores concentrated on the foods that coincided with Jewish beliefs and tastes. Just like Italians claim allegiance to foods like pasta, meatballs, tomato sauce, various cheeses, and meats, the Jewish communities do the same with their pastrami, corned beef, noodle kugel, kasha, stuffed cabbage, chopped liver, just to name a few. Along the East Coast, there are delis found almost anywhere there is a shopping center. Many delis all looking to be number one. In Nashville back in the '80s, we were fortunate to have at that time only one deli that was anything close to a real Jewish deli: Schwartz's Deli.

I moved to Nashville, Tennessee, in 1981, and I remember that during the early '80s, there was another deli named Zager's Delicatessen, located in the Green Hills section of Nashville. Zager's had sandwiches that were closer to what is known as a thick sandwich with meat stacked. Unfortunately, by 1983, Zager's Delicatessen had closed after many years in business, leaving Schwartz's Deli as the sole survivor of something close to a true New York traditional deli sandwich.

Looking up toward my father as I was examining the meat-filled (lack of) corned beef and pastrami combined sandwich on tasteless rye bread, I said with the sound of pure determination, "I know, Pop. I'm gonna open a real New York–style delicatessen! You know, something like Carnegie Deli!" You see, the Carnegie Deli was not just a deli. It was the real New York Deli. A place known worldwide, where you walk in and feel like you are living in the hustle and bustle of New York City, where people are calling out numbers like number seventy-five—number eighty-one! As you make your way to the counter, one could not help but view all these fantastic meats on display and in a separate display case, cheeses from all over the world. Hanging from the ceilings directly over the display counters were salamis of all shapes and sizes and flavors. The smell alone could make anyone crave one of their sandwiches.

"Hey, Dad," I said, "call Leo and see if we can meet with him."

I had a relative who was a part owner of the famous Carnegie Deli. Therefore, there was no place else to turn to for direction. We further discussed this deli thought even on the way home in the car. "The more I think about this, the more of a great idea it sounds like," were my words to my father. We had also discussed what the Jewish population was in Nashville. "I really have no idea of how many Jews there are living here, but I know we have four synagogues in Nashville," I said. "There's only one deli taking care of the Jews in Nashville. There's room for another deli. And I mean a real deli!"

As we pulled up my driveway, my father said, "I'll call Leo in the morning."

A few weeks later, I found myself behind the counter at the Carnegie Deli, New York City. People were swarming in nonstop. Voices of all sounds and tones were calling out food orders. You could hear someone yelling, "Number one hundred-eighty-two! Number one hundred-ninety-one! Orders ready! Pickup!" This was every day here at the Carnegie Deli. So I was about to take a real quick course on the workings of a true deli from the inside out. My two weeks were strenuous, not as much of the physical labor as the mental labor in hoping to remember everything being taught or explained to me.

I was taking a six-month course and squeezing it into a fourteen-day marathon. Those days were probably some of the best days I will ever recall. The fast pace and the reliance on others on the critical conveyor belt were what made your team a success or failure.

Returning to Nashville with all this knowledge and information, we finally settled on a location in the thriving Green Hills area of Nashville. I purchased top-of-the-line equipment and refrigerated display counters and was all set to be the first Kosher-Style Delicatessen in Nashville, Tennessee, exclusively carrying Hebrew National Kosher Products; still to this day, one of the highest reputations of being the top manufacturer of their famous Kosher all-beef hot dogs, first-cut pastrami, first-cut corned beef, salami, beef tongue and more. Hebrew National Products would be found in our new and exciting Nathan's Delicatessen and Catering.

The name Nathan's Delicatessen and Catering was named after our son, Nathan Michael Wallach. There is a Yiddish word known as *k'fell*, which means to "show pleasure in the highest manner." This is how I felt being able to name our new business after my son, my only son. Truly a feeling that sometimes cannot be described to its fullest. But here it was, the day before our grand opening. My parents had flown in to be with us for this celebration. Judy's family lived only forty-five minutes away, so we knew that they, too, would be attending. With my touring background, I learned the value of promotion and marketing, both of which I used to our advantage. Judy and I had already confirmed catering contracts with two of the synagogues in Nashville, one being the Orthodox Synagogue, which alone gained us tremendous respect within the Jewish community. That evening, the rabbis from the two confirmed synagogues came to Nathan's to offer the traditional blessings for a kosher-style establishment. Along with our parents, we could not be happier. Nathan's has been blessed. The shelves are stocked, the foods are being prepared, and we are set for our grand opening the following morning. It is important to understand that for any products being kept strictly kosher, they must be prepared separately from any other nonkosher products. This also includes any cooking utensils. Meat and dairy products cannot be stored together or cooked together. That is what was so important, to have established agreements for catering with Sherith Israel and West End Synagogue.

Before leaving on the last night prior to opening, we were waiting for one last bit of advertisement for Nathan's. For some reason, it was delayed. The menus were due here yesterday, so did this have anything to do with the delay? All I was told was that they would be here at seven in the morning. We were there starting at five since there was quite a bit of preparation. Like clockwork, there was a knock on our glass door, and there stood someone holding a box that appeared to be our menus for Nathan's Delicatessen and Catering.

"Thank you! Thank you!" I called out. "You made it just in time!"

With just a few minutes prior to opening, I was only able to take a quick glance at the menu that I designed and drafted. I put quite an amount of time and emotion into naming our combination sandwiches. Just like these famous delis, such as Carnegie Deli, Katz's Deli, 2nd Avenue Deli, their combination sandwiches are named after family and celebrities. We chose to name sandwiches out of respect for both our families. There was the Joyce-Ala (my mother), which consisted of salami, pastrami and corned beef and another called the Dish-Ala (my father), pastrami, and corned beef. There were other names given for sandwiches or dinner plates, but it was just about opening time, so I laid the menu on the counter and went back to preparing to open our doors.

The grand opening was at eleven o'clock in the morning, just in time for those early lunch eaters. Best part of our promotion was that we were offering our famous Hebrew National Hot Dogs for one dollar! We had a food station just for the condiments, such as sauerkraut, relish, chopped fresh onions, onions in a tomato sauce, and of course, your spicy mustard or yellow mustard for those not wanting to venture out of their ordinary. Besides having a line out the door and along the sidewalk, we were packed with customers standing in front of our glass display cases ordering pastrami, corned beef, salami, and homemade chopped liver by the pounds. You see, besides being a deli for the best sandwiches, Nathan's was also your stop for all your salads and the choice of deli meats. The day could not have gone any better. From opening time to five o'clock, Nathan served hundreds of hot dogs and made so many sandwiches that we lost count until we checked the register. Let me just say. It was a great day financially.

As we were just about to lock the door and the end-of-day filled with great success, a friend of mine, Canter Bernard Gutchen, from the Temple (Reform Synagogue), came in and said, "Steve, you have a problem." Not having the slightest idea of what he was talking about, I let him inside. Judy, Nathan, and my parents had already left to go home, and I was going to meet them there after the staff and I cleaned up.

"What's going on, Bernie?' I spoke. "You don't look so good."

As Bernie was looking at me, he handed me what appeared to be one of my own Nathan's Delicatessen and Catering menus.

"What? Yeah, I know. It's my menu. So?"

When I followed Bernie's finger onto my menu, it was like tunnel vision; I saw nothing but the tip of his well-manicured finger. There, printed clearly on my menu, was a specialty sandwich named Lucille, which consisted of stacked fresh-cut deluxe ham and a choice of cheese.

Even as I am writing this, I cannot help but feel anxiety come over me. Here we are, at the grand opening of Nashville's first kosher-style New York delicatessen, Nathan's Delicatessen and Catering; offering kosher products and kosher cooking for all your Jewish holidays and catering needs. I was shocked, to say the least. I had no words. I stood there staring at what I thought was a well thought and planned out menu. I spent weeks working on it with Judy and THIS HAM AND CHEESE was not on the menu I had approved. What was I to do?

Bernie looked at me and said, "Be prepared to get a sleuth of calls in the morning. When people get home and read your menu, those who follow strict Kosher guidelines will be mortified. If they feel for one minute that you are mixing your meats and dairy together, against the laws of Judaism and kosher law, you will be refused by every kosher Jew in Nashville, and those Jews that may not be keeping kosher in their homes but feel insulted by this."

"I will let you know," he said in a soft-spoken voice.

"So you want me to follow you home when you break this to Judy and your parents?" Bernie asked.

"No. Listen, you've done a lot by bringing this to my attention. Bernie, you must believe me," I said softly. "I had nothing to do with this. I never had a ham and cheese sandwich on my menu. Never! You must believe me."

As Bernie, my Cantor from my Temple, put his arm around me, "I do, Steve, but you need to find out how this got on your menu. Then what to do about it? You must address this to the Jewish community before it is seen by all."

I agreed and quietly made sure our first day in business was clean and ready to meet in the morning without the first full day of business.

When I got home, everyone had huge smiles on their faces, dogs barking. Everyone was filled with excitement except me.

"Son, what's wrong?" my father said. "Where's your smile? Today was a huge success! Aren't you happy?"

"Happy?" I said as I tossed the Nathan's menu onto the kitchen counter. "Happy? For what? Look at this shit!"

When my father and the others looked over to the menu, they could not help but see the large red marker I used to circle the ham and cheese. As my father's hand came down to pick the menu up, I could not help but see my father's entire body change form. He went from a relaxed frame of mind to now standing almost at an attention stance with a look of fury on his face. Being a practicing and religious man, I can see that my father did not find this to be amusing at all. Once my mother then saw this, all I could hear were signs of disbelief.

Judy then picked up the menu and said without any pause or change in her voice, "Oh, I added the ham and cheese sandwich and named it after my mother. If you had names for your family, then I wanted them too."

Right away, I knew if I did not speak up, my father was about to rip into her verbally, and this I wanted to avoid as best as possible.

"Judy, what the hell is wrong with you?" I shouted out. "Do you know what you just did? This will probably kill our fuckin' business before we even open!" I was mortified. None of us could explain why she would add ham to a kosher menu. "Do you have any idea what this will do to us?" I asked her.

All she could do was say, "I wanted my family to have a sandwich name after them."

"Fine!" I yelled back. "We could have come up with anything else but ham! And you chose to change the menu behind my back at the last minute?"

By now, it was an all-out yelling match between the two of us. My parents immediately took on the role of calmness, but my father stood with me, being furious with her. We had to immediately send out an e-blast to the entire Jewish community, explaining that there was a misprint on our menu, that we were extremely sorry for any misunderstanding, and that our kitchen at Nathan's was designed with two kitchens in mind. All meat and dairy products are kept separate and in their own specific refrigeration. We have all separate pots and pans, cooking utensils, etcetera. This is a must to be approved by any rabbi as a kosher kitchen.

The aftermath of this unthought-out print did, in fact, hurt our business. We had to reestablish our catering. We did lose the catering business with the West End Synagogue and had to do all our cooking at Sherith Israel, our Orthodox synagogue. Nothing could be prepared at Nathan's if it had to do with any Jewish event. To this day, I still cannot understand why Judy chose to be so ignorant. Here, she had converted to Judaism, studied and past her courses, and yet destroyed the credibility of Nathan's Delicatessen and Catering the day we opened.

For the next two and a half years, Nathan's participated in many community events, including the National Women's Convention held in Nashville, numerous city, and town fairs and events, and won both years for being the Best of Nashville/Eateries. Our lunch business throughout the week averaged that we were making approximately

250 sandwiches per day. Mostly pickup or delivery, but Nathan's was known for their sandwiches, stuffed cabbage, brisket, and selling over fifty pounds per week of freshly made chopped beef liver.

Still, after nearly thirty-one months in business, Nathan's poor parking and lack of backing within the Jewish community (ham and cheese) is what caused the closing of this fine deli and bankrupt pf the company since the debt and taxes due outweighed any profit. With only eighty-nine parking spots available in this center, forty-eight were taken up by employees of all the stores located here. Even with strict parking rules from the landlord, it mostly landed on deaf ears when it came to the parking. In years following the closing of the deli, whenever Nathan's was brought up in conversation, I would always ask a Jewish Nashvillian, if in the conversation, as to why Nathan's was never fully accepted by the Jews of Nashville. And (unfortunately) the answer was always the same. Clear as day, I can easily hear Jay say to me, "Steve, you're not from here. You're a New Yorker. Nashville is extremely clique-ish. You just don't 'fit' in and won't be accepted. And then to have ham on your menu was the icing on the cake." He ended our talk with this, "Don't rely on the Jewish community to make you a success. They never back anyone unless you are part of 'their' clique."

Lesson taught; lesson learned.

It was necessary for me to regroup after that ordeal. Losing Nathan's was as if a part of me was cut out. Your blood becomes your emotions as your nerves become a series of broken roots. It takes time to heal, and I learned that complete healing will never fulfill what was lost. All I could do was focus on what my next steps would be. After weeks of depression and anxiety, I lifted myself up and decided to do what I knew. I made a few calls, and within two weeks, I was back on tour with a new and exciting artist.

I received a call back from a booking agent who said there was a manager looking for a tour manager/production manager for their international artist.

Jokingly, the first thing I asked was, "Does he speak English?"

"A little," chuckled the agent. He went on to explain that this artist is as huge in his home country of Brazil as Michael Jackson is stateside. My immediate thought was that no one can use Michael Jackson as a comparison. Michael could sell out the largest stadium multiple days. So I think there was an exaggeration taking place. "Well, actually, Steve, this artist has sold out Rio de Janeiro, Brazil's, Maracana Stadium five days straight," the agent said.

With a registered capacity of 78,838 seats and three quarters of the field filled with standing fans totaling another 100,000, Milton Nascimento was the most respected and loved artist in all of Brazil.

Milton was about to venture out on his first North American Tour in almost ten years. This time, the tour was to take him to over twelve stateside venues and a few in Canada. Placed in a jazz family of music genres, Milton Nascimento had his very own unique sound and style of music. So this enabled us to perform at the Montreal Jazz Festival, the Atlanta Jazz Festival, Bath Music Festival, Vancouver Jazz Festival, the Playboy Mansion Jazz Festival, hosted by Hugh Hefner, the Humphries Smooth Jazz Festival in San Diego, and many other unique venues. Our stateside shows came first. I met Milton and his band in New York City. They had booked the venue where we were to kick off the tour three days prior, giving them enough time to meet their sound crew and check all the backline equipment that they had ordered in advance. This was probably one of the few times that all the rental gear requested was here. It was not convenient for me to lease a coach initially for the first six stateside dates since the venues were not demographically able to get to via ground transportation. Therefore, fly-ins made it necessary and more convenient. Travel funds were included in most of Milton's North American dates, and using air travel made those expenses less of an issue for our settlements. For a few North American dates, I did lease a coach where it made sense and we were all able to comfortably share as the crew had their own coach.

While we were in Canada, we were going from East to West, and I felt there was no better way to make this trip exciting and adventurous for Milton and his incredible band than by traveling via train. I remember doing a portion of the John Prine Tour by Rail in 1982, so I thought, why not make this cross-country? First, I had to see if this was available and, more importantly, whether it fit into

THIS LIFE OF MINE

our itinerary. Having days between each venue performance, we had ample days to get to our next show. By now, Milton and his Band had full confidence in me. Even though there was a huge language barrier (Milton's band could only speak Portuguese and hardly spoke a word of English), hand motions and facial expressions made its point. During downtimes, it was comical as we each tried to teach the other our language. Within a few days, I was able to remember specific Portuguese words that would make things easier as they did with English. It was still amusing to listen to us all trying to converse. Not Milton, though. He would sit quietly and just watch and listen. Occasionally, I could see his eyes looking back and forth of those talking and this small grin would break out on his face.

"Hey, Milton," I would call out. "You are understanding all of this, right?"

He would just look at me and smile from ear to ear.

The only other person on our tour who was not a musician or crew member was Milton's personal bodyguard. I fully remember him by his size and demeanor. This man stood approximately six feet six inches. He looked like a football player fully dressed in uniform all the time. He looked as though he could stop a train with just his huge hands and biceps. This man looked like a capital V from his waist up to his shoulders. He was built, just like the saying, a brick shithouse. His arms were massive; each was bigger than my legs. His legs were huge, as if they could just knock over-age trees although he had a heart as if he were a teddy bear. He had this incredible soft side that he used when dealing with people. No matter what the issue, if it involved the bodyguard then to watch him in motion was quite impressive. He knew when he had to be soft-spoken and knew when to exercise his position and responsibility. He watched over Milton like a hawk. Milton's every move was handled directly by the bodyguard. They had the most incredible bonding I have ever seen, especially in this dog-eat-dog business they call entertainment.

Our last and final show for the North American tour was in New York City. Saying goodbye to the band members was hard. We had established a friendship that lasted far beyond the tour. Even with broken languages, we were still able to keep in touch. I miss those times. I cannot remember any bad events with these band members. The band consisted of father and son percussionists. Two others were related to them, and one played a guitar as if it were crying out to you. Incredible musicians. Each offered different sounds to make one think there was a sleuth of drums and bongos. Insofar as saying farewell to Milton, well, that was harder to do than I had anticipated. I had worked with some of the biggest names in music on prior tours and our goodbyes were filled with joy and sounds of true friendships made. But with Milton, it was as if we were saying goodbye as brothers.

Milton and I spent many hours talking about, well, everything. We covered history, countries visited, children, and even discussions on health, birth, and yes, even death. You see, Milton had this ability to bring out the best in people. No matter if it was a stranger off the street or someone he had known for years, Milton was gifted with this supernatural power that did wonders for so many. I would hear stories of people back in San Paulo, in Rio, or a small village where people suffered from health or wealth. It would be Milton who would pray with them or for them. Never asked for himself but always asked for the Almighty to grant a wish for whoever he would be with. We would hear a few days later that some 'miracle' saved this person or that person, all because Milton Nascimento laid his hands upon them. This was known countrywide. All of Brazilians and Portuguese people know of Milton Nascimento. His name was as powerful as the man himself. It was he who taught me that we should never demand of the Almighty; we can only ask of him. To this day, that meaning alone has carried me for years.

"Thank you, my friend," I quietly said. "Thank you for allowing me the opportunity to work besides you and for you entrusting your life and profession in my hands for those seven months."

We smiled at each other as we had that final gentlemen's hug and went our separate ways. This truly was a fine gentleman, and I learned so much from Milton Nascimento more than he'll ever know.

Returning home for some much-needed relaxation and, more importantly, to be with my son, Nathan, I looked forward to my time

THIS LIFE OF MINE

home. Judy had gone back to work as sales director of the Holiday Inn Vanderbilt, Nathan was a Temple Day Care, and then my dog, Bagel, a mix between a Catahoula (Louisiana) and Australian sheepdog, was holding down the fort while I was away. Being home was always a wonderful time. It gave me precious time to spend with my son and time to work on my marriage to Judy. You see, after Nathan was born, things between us changed drastically. People would say that the change was due to some medical issues our son was born with, but through incredible medicines and specialty doctors, my son's health took a turn for the better. Unfortunately, our marriage was still not up to par. The only thing I will make mention is that postpartum depression is real and affects so many women after the birth of a child. When one does not recognize it through its symptoms, it is vital that one seeks a doctor to assist, whether medically or psychologically, for it can play the utmost of tensions and eventually divorce worldwide. I only wish Judy had sought the help so many were asking her to get. So we just dealt with it and tried to continue onward and upward.

It was now winter of 1990. New Year's had come and gone, and it was time for me to begin looking for another tour. Winter months were usually down months for touring. Very few full tours would be running. There were, of course, some artists who would perform a single show when the money was right, but overall, that was time for rehearsals and tweaking production costs. I pulled out my directory and began the search—the search for hopefully a country artist who would keep me closer to home. In this industry, I will tell you fact that, yes, it helps tremendously if you know somebody who could make a telephone call on your behalf. Sure, there are those who will say, "Just use my name. If they need to talk to me, they can call me." Most times, when you heard this, it was nothing more than pure bullshit talk. Wanting to make themselves look great and keep contact open, I would say that it was hardly ever done intentionally. They (artist, manager) mean well, but you cannot rely on their words to get you any gig, most of the time.

I had some wonderful contacts at the Country Music Association (CMA). I befriended a lady who was a legend there. Just the mention of her name opened doors that were kept shut. Back in the '80s and '90s, any event that had a country artist was designed and run by the lady in charge, Helen Farmer.

Helen was an older woman who had spunk in every step she took. Every sentence that she spoke was done so in a way only Helen Farmer could direct. She was one of the happiest people I had the pleasure of working with over the years. People from all walks of life in the music world, especially country music, know Helen Farmer or wish they knew Helen Farmer. When Helen spoke, all listened. She just had this way about her. No one could say no to her. Some tried but quickly found out that it was better to agree with the one person who knew best and could catapult your country music career to stardom.

When I walked into her office in April, she was on the telephone, laughing and talking loudly with someone named Jack.

"Hey, Steve, what's the Jewish word for *ball*?" Helen called out to me.

With a puzzled look on my face, I said, "In Yiddish, it's *pilke*, and I think in Hebrew, it's *bol*. But check on the spelling to be sure."

Hellen finished her call and immediately threw me her huge smile and said, "So where's my kiss?"

No one could resist Helen Farmer. She was one of the sweetest and caring people I have ever met here in Nashville. I compared her to another incredible industry figure, Maggie Cavender, Nashville Songwriter's Association International. Both of these women showed the wear and tear work on their faces. They worked effortlessly for the betterment of country music, and because of their efforts, I would say that country music is what it is because of people like Maggie and Helen.

"So what do I owe this unannounced visit," Helen called out to me.

I readjusted myself in her visitor's chairs, and I said, "I want to find a country act that will keep me based here out of Nashville. Touring, yes, but based right from here."

Almost immediately, Helen yells out, "I was just talking to your next artist's manager, Jack McFadden of McFadden and Associates."

As Helen was telling me this, she was already dialing the phone.

"Jack!" she called out. "I have the best person for Bill Ray. He just walked into my office! You'll love him. He's honest, very professional, and happens to be one of me. He's Jewish!" As I am watching Helen's facial expressions, her head begins to nod up and down, and she says into the phone, "Okay, I'll have him there tomorrow at one-thirty. Thanks." Helen hung up the phone, looked up at me, and said, "I think I just found you your next gig. This kid is gonna be huge! His name is Billy, Billy Ray; Billy Ray Cyrus. Ever hear him?"

"Can't say that I have, Helen," I said back in a puzzling tone. "What's one of his songs?"

Helen immediately said, "'Achy Breaky Heart'! It's all over country radio following its video. The video is fantastic!"

Having no clue who she was referring to, I simply agreed and played it out. Helen again reiterated that I had a meeting with Jack McFadden and was to follow up with her after meeting with him. One thing I remember doing when I left her office and headed back home, I turned on country music in my car and hearing it immediately, "Don't tell my heart, my achy breaky heart." Bill Ray Cyrus's single was a huge hit. Radio stations were playing this song five times on each rotation. This song was rocking the sound waves, and it was obvious that this Billy Ray was going to be big. I was looking forward to meeting Jack McFadden.

Jack's name had a reputation within the country music industry as a manager who created stars. In his corral were the names Buck Owens, Keith Whitley, Lorrie Morgan, and others. As I made my way into the office of McFadden & Associates, I was met with an array of gold and platinum NRAA album/CD plaques lining the hallway leading to the receptionist's desk.

I gave the receptionist my name and said, "I had an appointment with Jack McFadden, and he was expecting me."

As she directed her arm toward the direction she was asking me to follow, there in front of me was this solid large oak door as if I was about to enter a mighty kingdom's den. I knocked and heard a voice on the other side say come in.

There sat a heavyset man behind a huge oak desk on the phone talking about who knows what. I noticed right away that he had so much going on with different calendar books opened, a stack of what appeared to be contracts, and a collection of note stickers stuck on every imaginable open spot on his desk. As Jack completed his telephone call, I heard him say, "Okay, Billy, I'll talk to you later." This man reached over his desk and extended his hand and said, "Hi, I'm Jack. Jack McFadden."

Needless to say, I was hired as security director for Billy Ray Cyrus and his personal assistant. Jack felt that since I was there with him on all public outings, it would only make sense that I also handled Billy Ray's day-to-day schedule. There was a sleuth of telephone interviews (worldwide), radio interviews (worldwide), and numerous appearances at every venue that would be listed on his first ever tour. Bill Ray and his band, Sly Dog, were a bar band—period. They never experienced being on any tour, never mind headlining their own tour, nor playing venues from 1,200 seats to 35,000 seats and up.

No matter who I worked for on tour, I always made sure to have direct and personal contact with my artist. These people were putting their lives in my hands and if there were any trust issues or negative vibes, it could cause serious problems for the tour. Remember, case in point, Corey Hart World Tour CANCELED after a few weeks. Billy Ray and I got to a mutual and trusting bond immediately. I really felt inside that this one artist had an incredible manner of being thankful and appreciative for every small thing anyone did for him…starting now.

The tour kicked off sometime in the latter part of nineteen ninety-one or may have been early 1992. The atmosphere with Billy Ray and Sly Dog would change at the drop of a dime. Within a few short weeks, every band member thought they were the stars and deserved to be treated as VIPs. It was not a question of being taken care of. It was more as if they demanded and expected everything to be at their beck and call. Some were worse than others. When they started expecting me to handle them personally, they immediately realized I did not work for them.

"You have any issues, go see your tour manager!" I would say almost daily while on tour.

As I mentioned, some were better than others. I think the worst was Greg Fletcher, the drummer. Fletch had never worked for any established band before. His expertise came from bar bands, and his attitude showed for it. He would scream at production staff, catering, hotel staff, employees working their butts off at truck stops along the way. Then there was Terry Shelton, the lead guitarist. Truly a phenomenal player, but he, too, had a short fuse. He felt that it was the duty of others to handle his needs, no matter what those needs were. Terry and I got along just fine. Most times, I was able to calm him down. Bart Stevens, keyboards, kept mostly to himself. Yes, he would join the others if they were going out somewhere while not performing, but Bart had a way of just being somewhat demanding. Michael Sagraves was Billy Ray's rhythm guitarist and backup vocals. His personality outshined the others even though he was more reserved than the others. Lastly, Corky, Billy Ray's bass player, pretty much stayed by himself. Not into going out and causing a scene, Corky would just either stay in the bus or his hotel room during off times.

When we were playing a concert in Knoxville, Tennessee, for a huge country music radio station contest and local television show, this was close enough to Nashville and Flatwoods, Kentucky, and the herd of family and friends that showed up was in the hundreds. Nonetheless, many of these people attended Billy's after-show meet-and-greet function. Here, it gave the fans the opportunity to meet Billy Ray Cyrus, grab an autograph and a photo, and leave happy. Of course, we had those who felt their time deserved a longer one-on-one with Billy, but usually, I had it down to a system on the meet and greet and getting people to move on.

Prior to the show and knowing that the family would be staying at the same hotel, it was left up to me who (if any) family member would have a room near Billy's room or be placed on a different floor. Of course, Billy usually had the last word on whether he wanted anyone staying near him, but this specific time, Billy called me into the back of the tour coach and said to me, "Hey, Steve, I need a favor, man."

"Sure, Billy," I said. "What's up?"

Billy continued telling me, "So you know that Cindy" (Cindy Cyrus was Billy Ray Cyrus's wife at the time) "was coming to Knoxville, and so was my girlfriend, Tish. Man, you gotta make sure that these two never see each other. They know each other from back in Flatwoods, and it just would turn into a huge fight, and I want to prevent that."

So what does any great bodyguard/assistant do for their artist? I had Billy and Cindy at one end of the hallway, and Tish's room was at the far end. It was only a two-story hotel, so there was no place to really separate them.

"Not to worry, Bo" (a nickname Billy's father had given him years ago). "I'll take care of it and get you both sets of keys."

Did I feel strange about doing this for him, knowing that his wife would be there as well as his girlfriend "of the day or week or month" would be there as well? It was not my problem and the way he or any of my artists conducted themselves behind closed doors, as long as his personal did not interfere where it would bring out negative stories and even photographs. I was not his judge and jury. This was the world of music touring. You see way more than you could ever imagine—whether being a direct part of it or not, this was life on the road. People knew that there was a code, a code of touring ethics: what happens on the road stays on the road, so they say. My attitude is that anything over twenty-five years is fair game. Anyway, most of the stories have been told, maybe in a different way, but the endings are always similar.

I recall a time when I was with Eddie Rabbitt, and one of his guitar players ended up saddling a female concertgoer. Ricky Skaggs and his band were opening for Eddie and had been staying at the same hotel as us. Unfortunately, when Rickie was returning to his hotel room, he saw a girl come out of a band member's room and felt the need to call that guitar player's wife and tell her. Come on, seriously...what did he get out of it?

"Ricky said it was the Lord's wish I tell his wife," said his guitarist. I am glad it was not me having to face this when I returned home. This "tattletale" spread throughout the country, music tours

THIS LIFE OF MINE

like fire on coals. Let it be told, I understand that he and his wife later divorced.

So here we are, Cindy Cyrus is in the star's hotel room, and Billy was with Tish in her hotel room at the end of the hallway. It was obvious that there was something wrong on the home front in Billy and Cindy's marriage, but again, I was not there as his spiritual guru. Merely, a man hired to protect not only him but his public reputation as well. Thank goodness, Cindy and Billy's marriage fizzled out soon thereafter and they were divorced.

Over time, a short amount of time, I was told who Leticia "Tish" Jean Finley was. This would be the first real-time I met her under these circumstances. I was introduced to her when Billy and I were in Flatwoods but was never told of any relationship between the two. Tish had her hair all blown up and teased with at least a half can of hair spray so every hair that was strategically set would stay like that for hours, and her makeup was, well, let's just say, a work of art. Bright white teeth she had a great smile. As the days went on, Bo finally told me about their relationship because he knew that it would be best since I was with him most of the time and that he could trust me. Tish ended up being flown out on various tour dates, but Billy Ray preferred being on the road with just his band, Slydog, and his crew. So rules were set down, and Tish was fine with it. The excitement was just starting.

We finally made our way into Canada for the first set of Canadian shows for Billy Ray Cyrus. The show went without a hitch, but our flight to Toronto was not as fortunate. I can still see Billy Ray, Slydog, our production manager, John and Roger, our stage soundman, and our road manager, Hal Ray. At every airport, I was able to coordinate with the airline that Billy Ray and I would relax in the airport lounge and make our way to the gate within a few minutes of departure. This is saved in case of any fan-related incidents.

I can still hear our road manager call out and say, "Steve, I'm going with the band to make sure they get through to the gate."

"No problem," I called back. "Billy and I will be down shortly."

No sooner were we taking our positions in these comfortable lounge chairs, our soundman John came to the airline check-in desk and asked to speak with me immediately. As I could clearly see John standing there, pacing back and forth, I knew there was something wrong.

When I came up to the desk, I said, "Hey John, what's up?"

John turned to me with sweat pouring down his face and said, "Oh shit, Steve! Hal was stopped at the checkpoint by the police."

Police? I thought.

Okay, something is wrong here. Billy saw us talking and felt, as I did, that something was wrong, and he, too, decided to go with us to the checkpoint. Now it is important to note that all monies from the attendance gates were settled by the road manager, so right now, I immediately saw the brown business briefcase on top of the conveyor belt at the checkpoint holding approximately twenty-five thousand dollars in cash. However, what immediately caught my eye was that on top of the X-ray machine at this checkpoint was what looked like a gum wrapper opened with a white substance block inside.

As my mind started to work fast on what was about to happen, I quickly took the money briefcase off the belt and called out to John, who was already making his way down the tiled floor and quietly yet loud enough for John to hear my voice and said, "John, take this!"

I pushed the briefcase down the tiled floor hoping that John would see this and make his way back to retrieve it before it was noticed by the authorities. As surprised as I was, none of the security checkpoints nor the police noticed this. All John said was that the briefcase was his and it had cleared the checkpoint.

So Billy Ray, Hal, and I were now standing with the police, hearing them tell us that Hal was stopped for possession of cocaine. Thank goodness, I was able to convince them that it was not for resale, but it was apparent that our road manager Hal had a substance abuse problem. We all had an idea of this, but again, Hal, as everyone else, performed their duties on the road. What you did in your own time was not our concern unless it affected the tour. This reflected the tour. The police, along with airport personnel, then had to pull Hal's luggage from the belly of the plane, which then caused the plane's delay. There was nothing I could do but explain to Billy not

THIS LIFE OF MINE

to say a word. Nothing. It was important for me to start making calls and see if there was anything my contacts could do to assist. As they hauled Hal off in handcuffs, Billy and I made our way to the plane's first class, took our seats, and ordered a cocktail.

We just looked at each other and that's when Billy said to me, "Steve, I'm in your hands, buddy. Please make this go away."

One must remember this was Billy Ray Cyrus's breakout tour. The "Achy Breaky Heart" king has another sold-out show to do at the stadium in Toronto, and we did not need this to make it to the media. I am proud to this day to say, it did not. Through my own contacts and associates, I was able to convince the magistrate that Billy had no connection to this matter, in fact, and I asked that any leeway that could be given to Hal be done so that he could return to the States. Hal was terminated on the spot for his possession of cocaine, and I chose not to notify Jack McFadden at that time since I knew we would be seeing Jack in Toronto the following day. When we arrived in Toronto, there was a message on my cell phone that the magistrate chose not to fully prosecute Hal and allowed him to plead guilty to a lesser offense, enabling him to fly back stateside. That was the last time I ever saw Hal Ray. The next morning, Billy Ray and I sat down with Jack and explained what had happened. At this point, Jack asked that I please handle the settlements and finish out the next few dates before we headed back to Nashville for a few days' break.

Billy Ray and Sly Dog are just about to take the stage in Salem, Virginia. It was another sold-out show, and this crowd was as loud as all our past shows had been. During Billy's shows, he would always find someone in the audience whom he would openly flirt with so that it looked as though it was part of the show. I noticed in the audience that this one girl, along with whom I presumed was either her husband or boyfriend, was overly excited every time Billy would look at her. She was very attractive, with long blonde hair covering her voluptuous breasts. She had a wonderful smile, and you could not help but notice just how exciting it was to see Billy Ray paying her some attention from the stage. However, the man with her appeared not as pleased. In fact, you could notice that his actions were tense in comparison to the others in his immediate area. By his constantly grabbing her arm in his attempts to get her to calm down and stop jumping, he looked like a stick of TNT getting ready to explode. Something was just not sitting well with me. Maybe it was my cop instinct. As Billy Ray was about to leave the stage for an outfit change, out of my peripheral view, I saw this man reach down toward his legs, and as he was coming back up, I could not help but notice a gun. As I ran out onto the stage, I called out to Cyrus and his road manager, Al, "GUN!" At that moment, I dived from the stage, landing directly on both this man and the lady, making sure my landing enabled me to grab hold of the *gun*. As we slammed to the ground, the crowd around us immediately assisted me, and within seconds, two police officers were there. As quick as it happened, that how quick the Salem Police Officers came in from the sides and removed the man without incident. Billy had come off the stage for a stage clothes change, and by the time he returned, the audience was back up on their feet, screaming Billy's name as if nothing ever happened. This jealous, worthless, pathetic excuse of a man was charged with a sleuth of charges and was given over twenty years in prison. As far as I was concerned, it was just another day on the job, and I did what I was hired to do: protect the life of Billy Ray Cyrus.

Billy Ray had a way of saying just what people not so much wanted to hear but needed to hear at that moment. Whether it be thanking a fan or signing an autograph, Billy could either be sincere or just full of shit. But one thing I will give him credit for is his love for children. Children were stricken down by any medical condition that would force them into a hospital and, yes, sometimes fighting for their lives. Having lost my daughter, I know that curse, feeling helpless for a child. During all of Billy's performances, it became a tradition for people in the crowd to toss up stuffed animals, flowers, cards, US banner flags, ladies' panties and bras, and much more. After each show, the stagehands would gather up everything that was thrown onstage and place them in large garbage bags. I swear there were some shows where we would have three or four large plastic garbage bags filled. As with any mail, letters, or notes that would reach Billy, I would first go through them to check for any negative or threatening letters. And yes, there were many such letters or notes. Some being your typical misspelled words of jealousy or hate but some that needed a second look at. Those were set aside. I would keep all the stuffed animals in one or two bags and if Billy wanted to go through them in advance, he would ask to. Otherwise, after almost every show, Billy and I would go with our driver to the closest hospital with a children's ward or to a Children's Hospital, where we would then sneak into different areas and introduce ourselves at the various nurse's stations and explain why we were there. Once the excitement of these nurses stared back at Billy Ray Cyrus standing right there in front of them, they tuned in to what we were doing there and would allow us to visit some of the rooms. Billy would take these stuffed animals out, sign them, and lay them on the bed or bed table so when they woke up, they would find this special gift left just for them. One thing I will say about Billy Ray Cyrus, he had an enormous heart when there were children involved. There were times I remember when Billy and I would get ready to leave a child's room, and they would wake up. The older ones would first rub their eyes and look, and all Billy would say was, "Go back to sleep. It's just a dream." To then see this child curl back and close their eyes was something so touching I will always remember. There would always be one or two children who, once awoke, could not turn over and go back to sleep. The excitement of having Billy Ray standing in front of them, in person, was too much so they would just lay there or sit up if able and just say those words, "Billy Ray, I love you!"

Our replacement road manager met us at the Spectrum in Philadelphia. Al Schultz was his name. A tall, medium-built man of German descent had worked with KT Land, another country artist, as her production manager. He fed Jack McFadden a load of bullshit about his past work but the bottom line. He had never worked as a full tour manager before. However, Jack believed his stories, and thus, not only did we have Al, but he convinced Jack to hire his wife in some production capacity, leaving most of the production crew upset, but they knew they had to deal with her, so they just accepted her. She was more in the way than not. Al walked around as though he was Billy's manager and had all the answers: not. Most times, Al was okay to work with, but there were times when he truly carried himself at the venues as if *he* was Billy Ray Cyrus's manager. He had Jack McFadden believing so much of his shit it became a laughing joke on tour among the band and crew.

This one time, Al went a little too far with his anti-Semitic remarks. Al was not pleased with the promotor at this show. I must comment that the promotor happened to be Jewish and had a fantastic reputation in the music-touring community. Very well respected for many years. One of our truck drivers, Ted Walker, overheard Al as he stormed out of the promotor's backstage office make the comment, "Those fuckin' Jews. We should have killed them all when we had the chance." Ted waited a day or two to tell me because he knew that I would become unhinged and would have wanted to confront him right there on the spot. I wanted to drop him like the trash that he was. But I held my ground and waited for the opportune time to have the next move. It was time to bring this to Jack's attention before I went directly to Billy Ray. I was not going to act as though this did not happen. I will say that a few years down the road, Al was applying to work with another management company, which happened to have a Jewish CEO. Word got out to Stan Moress, who passed over him without hesitation. Karma's a bitch, isn't it sometimes? Al was just another wannabe who thought he had more knowledge of how this industry operated.

By this time, Billy Ray had moved up in transportation, and we were now traveling in a chartered six-passenger jet. This was fantastic! Being able to travel home after most shows and flying out for the next was working fine. Billy was happy to be home and I, as well.

Because of the huge success of "Achy Breaky Heart," we had engagement dates in the UK as well as Australia. I will never forget the time we finished a show at Radio City Music Hall, New York, and we then had to fly over to England for a television show. As tickets were being prepped, only the immediate entourage was to join Billy, his road manager, sound man, and myself. Oh, I almost forgot. Jack McFadden made it a point to take the last remaining ticket so he could go. As you can guess, it was my air ticket that Jack decided to take. I can remember sitting in our tour bus at LaGuardia Airport,

New York when he told me he was going in my place. We had a few choice words for each other, but the bottom line was that HE was Billy's manager, and as manager, he called the shots. I did find out from Cyrus when they returned that it was nothing but pure chaos with the crowds of fans, and nothing was kept together. Jack and Al both had no control over the crowds, and it turned into a pure cluster. Underneath, that made my day.

Next, we had a ten-day tour in Australia. The band and crew were extremely excited since they had never left the country before, nor have, they ever been on a plane for such a long flight. Jack and Billy were in first class; Band, Al, and I were in business class; and crew were in coach. When we arrived in Australia some twenty-three hours later, the crowds were just as wild as here in the States. Touring different venues gave us the opportunity to really enjoy so much of Australia. From the Opera House to the zoo, allowing me to hold a koala bear were true highlights of the trip. Being able to swim off the beaches surrounding this magnificent country was amazing. The Gold Coast is simply fantastic. The ocean's surf, the people, the restaurants, the foods—truly a place I will always remember.

While we were playing in Perth, Australia, we had the pleasure of staying at the Burswood Country Club. A five-star hotel and club, it had a very strict dress code such as no T-shirts were permitted, all shorts had to be tailored, no cut-offs, and no jeans on the golf course. Driving up to this grand hotel, I can still hear Roger, our monitor man, saying, "Well, shit, I ain't got nuthin' else to wear 'ccept my T-shirts and jeans." The band said the same thing. One could not help but laugh. If I recall, they let them wear what they had. You know tourists, I thought to myself. There were stares from others on the course, as you must remember that this is one of the most expensive private golf country clubs in Australia. They played, we lost, there was no score taken.

That evening, we all went out to explore some of the sights. We were starting to get hungry, so we chose a Chinese restaurant. Why there? Well, they had this enormous glass window where you could see these large plates of food being served to its patrons so we opted that would be the place to go. In the center of the table sat the largest lazy Susan. Large trays of food were placed, and all we had to do was spin the Susan when we wanted our choices. Everything there was fantastic—the food, the service, and of course, the sightseeing of beautiful women walking by. There were a few girls that, when they walked by, they immediately stopped and stared right at us. We were able to make out the words they were saying, "Billy Ray Cyrus." Thank goodness, we were just about to leave because we really did not want to cause a scene, which was happening wherever we went. When we walked out, autographs began, whispers from Billy to one of the girls began, the next thing you know, I signaled for our van driver to pick us up. It seems that Billy told them where we were staying, so I knew it was going to be a long night.

When we arrived back at the hotel, I could not help but notice an old friend of mine sitting in the lobby, Sir Tom Jones.

"Come on, Bo, let me introduce you to Tom Jones," I said.

The look on Billy's face was priceless. Remember, Billy was not familiar with meeting a sleuth of celebrities yet. He had just started his career and was still starstruck with certain people.

I worked with Tom Jones years back, in the '70s and once I refreshed his memory, he immediately recalled our times together.

Billy and Tom sat for about thirty minutes before Billy said, "Man, I'd love to sit here longer, but I have somewhere I have to be."

Goodbyes were said. Tom and I hugged and said it was great seeing each other after so long, and next thing, I walked Billy back to his suite, where he was met by his lead guitarist, Terry Shelton/Sly Dog, and the two ladies they met earlier.

I just smiled and said, "Please, Bo, stay in, and if you plan on leaving, let me know."

I knew he would not be going anywhere, especially with the sight of these two ladies.

One tour date was in North Carolina, near Fort Bragg. This date stood out because it was here in Fayetteville, North Carolina, when Billy Ray, for the first time, met one of his illegitimate children. Christopher Cody was born after Billy had an affair with his mother, Kristin Luckey, while her boyfriend was in the service stationed overseas. This was the first meeting for both Billy and Kristin since their sexcapade. I was happy to hear that Billy Ray stood up as the father and would make all necessary financial aid to Kristin for her medical bills and a custodial financial payout to Kristin for the needs of raising Christopher Cody.

I can recall Billy saying to me, "Steve, you know me with kids. This is my responsibility, and I plan on being there for him financially."

I looked at him and told him, "Bo, it's something for a man to stand up and do the right thing. Financially, I'm glad you're able to, but ya know what, you do it no matter what."

We looked at each other and just smiled without saying another word. We knew; we knew.

That night, while Billy was meeting with Kristin and their son, Christopher Cody, I received a call from Al about a situation for tonight's show. Apparently, a letter had been sent to the McFadden office from the boyfriend of Kristin Luckey, stating that he was going to take matters into his own hands. Because of his army training in explosives, the promoter and Jack had serious concerns about the safety of the venue. The arena and outside areas were inspected by the local police, and the security team did a complete sweep inside the facility, and no explosion of any sort was found. So the day ended well. Billy saw the woman that he had an affair with, met his out-of-wedlock son, and put on a fantastic sold-out performance—the day in the life of Billy Ray Cyrus.

Another time stood out when a *gun* was involved. It was a complete sold-out show. From his first song, the crowd was on their feet shouting, "We love you, Billy Ray!" and you could see how many cameras and cell phones were being held up for their photo opportunities. For every show, I would always position myself on either side of the wings of the stage, enabling me to have full access to my artist and the immediate ten rows directly in front of the stage.

Prior to an outfit change when Cyrus leaves the stage, I had noticed a couple in row three that stood out. The girl was wild as she screamed and constantly waved her arms at Billy Ray. Yet the guy with her stood firm with a face that expressed pure madness. As she would gyrate and look at Cyrus, he would grab her by the arm to pull her back down. Words were exchanged, but that was impossible for me to hear over the sound of the show. Billy noticed her as well, which then meant he would give her that little extra attention. A smile or a wink was all it took, as every woman would melt. This woman was truly beautiful and had a body that was close to perfect.

Billy hit his last note and was making his way off the stage to change outfits. As I cleared him off the stage, I saw from my purifiable view that same guy pushed his girl out of the way and reached down his leg, presuming he was going into his boot. He did. As he began to stand erect and raise his arm back up, I noticed the handle of a gun.

I yelled out, "Gun!" as I pushed Cyrus away from the sight and shouted to Al, "Get him back in his dressing room!"

All this was done as I ran to the edge of the stage and jumped into the crowd, hoping that my aim was right on top of the man with a gun. Perfect aim. As I wrestled him to the ground, I was able to get my hand around the gun to control its direction. Within seconds, there were two uniformed police officers already grabbing for his arms. The outcome was that he had a room at the state penitentiary for a number of years. This was a part of my daily responsibilities. I was hired for my expertise and training, and this is what personal protection is about: the safety of your client always comes first.

Around this time, cash float for the tour was being controlled by the road manager. Billy and I had our own separate float, but when it came to production costs, I had to go to the road manager for the cash. I knew something was not making sense based on the receipts and accounting sheets. My next move was to notify Jack McFadden since I knew he had been asking.

"Jack," I said. "There's something going on with the cash float out here. There are way more receipts than what has been spent."

I questioned the accuracy of the road manager and his wife BOTH handling the float and accounting. So Jack and I decided to dig deeper. When I was told to get something from our coach, I was able to open the safe and take out a few hundred dollars in $100 bills; this I and Jack agreed to do. One day before the float accounting sheet had to be sent in, it was amazing that the account sheet balanced out correctly. Really? How could that be? It should have been $300 off. It balanced exactly. Now Jack and I knew someone was taking cash from the float and blindsiding it with bogus receipts. Once again, I passed this information on as directed, and from that point, it was not my concern unless I was directed to get involved. I was not. Jack said that he would handle it his way. Later, it was obvious. Jack never did. The redirection of command began. It was visible that Al was smothering Cyrus with his bullshit of promises and commitments, something that ended up hurting Billy Ray Cyrus later in his career.

By the time we were in our third year, Billy's attitude was again changing. From the onset of every tour, I would say to Cyrus privately, "Bo, don't let all the fame, power, and money change you. Remember where you came from, a bar band singer from Flatwoods, Kentucky."

He would always look and listen to me and give me that stare, but further down the road, eye contact became less, as he himself had changed.

Playing any hotel/casino all had the same level of attitude and security. They took both quite seriously. New Year's for three years was always fun. It would be at Bally's Hotel/Casino. We thoroughly enjoyed these gigs because everything was perfect and high styling. Our accommodation was excellent, the food was outstanding, and the security was something taken extremely seriously. Combined, we were a strong unit. That was until Billy Ray Cyrus came to town.

For high-performance artists, almost every venue has a security fence, usually ten feet out from the stage. This area is secured for security personnel, photographers, and emergency exit if needed. No matter whether at an inside or outside venue, you will always find fencing for all festival-type concerts. Trump's Hotel/Casino was one of them. Their security team was one of the best I had the pleasure of working with. As with any venue, we would always advance the venue for all security personnel and positions. Production had been set, sound check completed, and dinner was on the way in the green room. Band and crew always enjoyed their meals together. Billy did, too, but most times, he would not eat prior to a show. Afterward, it was as if he hadn't eaten in weeks.

Our final show in our two-day concerts went off without incident. The sound was perfect, and the sold-out crowd stayed on their feet most of the evening. Toward the last few songs, many fans were caught running down the aisles to get a closer look at their favorite country music artist. Their attempts were unsuccessful because we had the venue's security detail. They would quickly stop the crowds, and without incident, it worked. For the last couple of songs, the crowds have now formed in the aisles leading to the stage. From the tenth row back, the security officers in uniform and the plain clothes detail were doing their best to hold these screaming and adoring fans back. Then suddenly, as if the clouds above separated, under the glow of a red light, a voice came screaming throughout the venue, "Don't you hold those people back! You let them through! Come, my people! Come down front! Get outa the way!"

I felt sorry for these people who were only doing their job in trying to keep the area free, clear and safe. As order was finally in place, there were some fans who were stomped on, knocked down, and one lady suffered a broken arm. Here came the lawsuits. Some suits were settled out of court while others went to court with a jury. One case (in particular) was with the lady who broke her arm. My deposition went on for hours. I recall having to fly to Philadelphia for my deposition. Bottom line, I told the truth, and my understanding of the matter was settled, and the payoff was huge. This was the start of a sleuth of times Cyrus would get the crowds fired up and tell them to rush down front, knowing that someone could possibly get injured. Every show was an adrenaline rush for Cyrus. It was as if the screaming crowds were his addiction. In many shows, Billy Ray would remain on the stage, sometimes for over twenty-five minutes. The venues would be clearing out as Cyrus would sit on the drum riser, waving to the last holding-out fans who would always stay pressed up to the stage as they spoke directly to Billy Ray. He rarely would come to the edge of the stage to sit with the few remaining unless there was an attractive girl there. He always had a weakness for many of the gorgeous women

THIS LIFE OF MINE

that attended his shows. Let me tell you right here and now: Cyrus knew exactly what he was doing, whether it was staying on the stage or hospital visits. There were numerous times I would have to sit and talk with him about some of these issues. My job was for his safety as well as his responsibilities.

On days off, I would sometimes go out to Billy Ray's home either for some business or just to hang out. The early days of my time with Cyrus, we would enjoy four-wheeling or even riding horses, something Billy loved to do and proud to show off his horses. Did I like riding? Hell no, but if it made sense to do it, then I did it. Billy learned quickly that me on a horse, galloping through the fields on his estate, was not high up on my scale of activities. The horse's name was Roam, a beautiful horse that we first saw in Lima, Ohio, on the day of another sold-out concert.

Patrolling the areas backstage were mounted police officers riding high in the saddles of some magnificently groomed horses, all dressed in clean leather reins and saddles that fit like gloves. Billy immediately took a liking to these horses, and once again, as timing had it, one of the police officers mentioned that there was a horse for sale. We followed the officer's outstretched arm to view a magnificent horse by the name of Rome. Just like that, I arranged the ground transport, and within five days, Rome was delivered to the Cyrus estate.

But this one day of riding, Billy took it upon himself to saddle both horses. I knew he had done this many times before, so I had my trust in him to make sure my horse was properly prepared. When I pulled myself up onto the saddle, I could not help but feel that my saddle was not tightly secured.

"Hey, Billy!" I shouted out. "This strap seems a bit loose, don't ya think?"

As Billy climbed off his horse to double-check my straps, I could not help but wonder to myself, does he really know what he's doin'? I had no choice. Life was in the hands now of a horse named Roam and Billy Ray Cyrus.

The ride through acres and acres of Billy's property was truly inspiring. The paths we rode were single paths, surrounded by all types of foliage. As we approached open fields, of course, this enjoyable pace turned into full gallops, with Cyrus always way out front. I kept looking down the side of Roam to make sure my straps were doing their job, holding my saddle erect. All seemed to be going fine until the next open-field gallop. Cyrus takes off, which then causes my horse to follow suit. Halfway through this field, there it goes!

I am now riding in a true side saddle style, yelling out to Cyrus, "Yo, Bo! Stop this horse!"

What seemed like minutes were merely a few seconds until Billy came back and was able to get Roam to stop. You would have to picture this; here stands a magnificent sixteen-hand horse with its saddle laying perfectly even on the side of the horse and me, a six-foot-four-inch grown man holding on for dear life. I knew that if the saddle kept sliding, my head would have been inches from the ground.

We then rode up a steep hill to an area that Billy had already visited and made his own. There were logs for sitting, and there was even a small stone-outlined firepit. It was a nice place to stop and sit for a spell.

"Ya know, Steve, I've had some interesting times up here," Billy said as he would look up into the clear blue sky. "I've had others talk to me here, Steve," Billy remarked this one time. "In fact, this was another place Elvis came when he spoke to me." I could not help but tune further into Cyrus's eyes now. You see, I do believe that Billy Ray Cyrus had a sense that could allow others to communicate with them. Most of us have that ability; whether actual or not, it does not really matter. I immediately thought of my nanny. I saw her a few times, so yes, I believe that we do have this ability. Maybe not everyone, but it looks as though Billy Ray and I share this. I never brought up my nanny, though. I felt it was not the time nor the place.

What matters is that you yourself stand true to its belief. This was the first of three encounters with Elvis I would hear about. Billy would insist that Elvis was there to tell him not to worry about what others would say about him. Billy would look at me as if the word truth was spelled out on his face. His sincerity was as deep as what he believed that Elvis told him.

"Steve, I know you think I'm crazy, but I'm tellin' you, Elvis came and spoke to me," Cyrus would say.

I just stood there, not saying anything. How could I? I had had the same encounters but with a relative. Does this happen to others? Apparently so.

The tour returned to Nashville for a one-week break. The only scheduled event was this ABC Special, Memphis, Tennessee. ABC had done three or four ABC Television Specials on Billy Ray Cyrus, so there was a strong relationship there. They knew of his quirks. I unfortunately came home with the flu, which kept me in bed for the next five days. On the second day home, my cell phone rings, and I could see it was Jack McFadden, Cyrus's manager.

"Steve, you better talk to him!" Jack was screaming into the phone. "I'm tellin' you, if he doesn't do this special, it will cost him serious problems! Now get on the fuckin' phone and talk some sense into him."

"Jack, I said in a calm but sore throat voice, "I'll call him right now."

As I hung up from Jack and searched for Cyrus's speed dial, I could not help but wonder was this something with Elvis since he was doing this special show with Priscilla, I thought. As the phone rang, it was answered, and all I heard was Billy's voice saying, "I'm not gonna do this show, Steve, not happening! You hear me! You" (meaning me) "call Jack back and tell him no, and then call ABC and tell them no!"

As I just listened, I waited until the end, and then I calmly said, "Billy, what's going on? You gotta fill me in."

Immediately, Cyrus begins to tell me that he received not only a call in the sky from Elvis but that Elvis came and knocked on his front door at home to warn him not to do the show.

"What do you mean he knocked on your door?" I said back to him. Thinking my nanny only comes to me through a cloud.

Right away, Cyrus says, "Steve, I'm tellin' ya, Elvis knocked on my front door, and when I opened it, there he stood in front of me."

"Well, did you at least invite him in?" I said back. What else was I supposed to say at that moment? I had to say something. This continued into having three separate calls with Cyrus and two with McFadden. It seems clear that excuses had to be made to ABC and Priscilla. There was no way we could tell them this story about Elvis visiting Billy and telling him not to do the show. What was the reasoning behind this 180-degree turn? There must be a reason. I know Cyrus too well. Something serious has set him off. Something had to be so impactful to cause him to refuse a live ABC show, tributing the King, Elvis Presley.

On the final phone conversation Billy and I had before this live television show, which was starting in six hours, I kept pressuring him to tell me what the reason was. It was then that Billy said, "I must do the long version of my song. I am not going to cut it down. It stays the long version else I'm not doing the show." With a short pause, Cyrus then said simply, "I can't."

"Billy, just give me a reason, any reason as to why," I said. "You know I'll back you up. I always have."

I, too, became silent on the phone.

What felt like an hour was a mere minute of silence. I said, "Hey, Bo, let me call Jack and ABC and discuss this with them."

I hung up and immediately called ABC. I did not call Al because I knew his involvement would delay and cause more bullshit. ABC welcomed my call, and after coming up with a solution, they said, "Steve, it depends on how the time is running. If there is extra time, we will pass onto Billy Ray."

Awesome news. I then called Jack and told him what ABC said. "No time to waste here, Jack! I called out over the phone," as I lay in my bed, shivering with a temperature and snot running from my already-red and bruised nose.

Even after I explained what ABC said, Cyrus would not alter his decision for the next thirty minutes. Time was getting very short before ABC just scratched Cyrus from the lineup and host. Bo called me back within thirty minutes and said, "Get the jet ready. I'll go, and I will sing what I'm supposed to."

You see, this was a live television show, and every second was accounted for. There could be no changes or alterations.

I sure wish I was able to join him on this special, but I was too sick to go, and I did not want to jeopardize getting Billy, or anyone for that matter, sick. Billy takes the stage for the grand finale and sings his heart out. The only problem was that he went way past the time allocated and caused ABC a huge penalty fee for not ending as instructed. So maybe Billy and Elvis had a pack. They do it their way no matter what, and they did.

When it was time to hit the road once again, the crew and band departed Nashville in their custom coaches, where Billy and I waited until it was time to jump aboard and jet off to the next gig. The shows were still coming strong, and our schedule had become hectic, not only for us but especially for the band and crew. We did not complain, though, for we were all working full-time and enjoying the fruits of paydays. It was during this segment of the tour that I decided to pack things in. Not only was I tired, but having to work with an anti-Semite like Al Schultz was enough to make me dream about tossing his ass in an oven to see how he liked it. But that was not my style. I had complained about it to Jack, but it went in one ear and out the other. Billy had become a pompous asshole, where he thought he was bigger than Elvis and that all of country music owed it to him to be nice because it was he who kept country music going. Okay, stop laughing. I did the same thing. So I decided it was time to retire, not just from Billy Ray but from touring. I had spent many years traveling throughout the entire United States, Canada, and parts of Europe. I wanted to take time off and see what I really wanted to do next. I was single now, and there was no better time than the present to reshuffle my priorities, and that is exactly what I did. I decided to take the rest of the year off.

I learned over time that almost everything I had accomplished up to this point in my professional life, I can relate back to my childhood. Whether they were lessons learned or times my better judgment needed a realignment, I can look back and realize that my life was built on what my parents taught me as well as the many others who touched my life in my younger years. I realize that even though there were years my father and I had our differences, I find in myself almost something daily my dad had taught me. It is the same thing with my mother. I can see what my mother gave me insofar as partnership, family, love, and forgiveness. Most importantly, it does not stop there.

The only thing that took center stage, besides this enormous tour, was my marriage. It had fallen so low. Judy and I were barely on speaking terms. We had lost our home to a fire when Nathan was just nine years old. For months prior to and after the fire, I cannot recall one time when Judy and I were an affectionate couple. It had been over two years since Judy had completely shut down sexually and romantically. Simply put, Judy became as stale as a dead fish. She would not allow me to touch her, kiss her, never mind having the sex we used to enjoy together. I tried everything to get her to seek help but to no response every time.

I felt enormous pressure, more from myself than anyone else. Nathan and I were inseparable as father and son. In fact, it meant the world to me to have Nathan out on tour with me while working for Billy Ray. Billy took an immediate liking to Nathan, to the point of giving him the responsibility to post all the signs backstage, outlining where staff, crew, artists, and bands were to go. He did a great job at it; in fact, the best part Nathan liked was when Billy Ray would pay him. It was usually $50 or $100 for each day's venue work.

"Dam, Billy," I said in a joking manner. "Heck, I'll put those signs up for an easy hundred!" Very proud that Billy trusted Nathan at such an early age.

I bring this up because when I look back at Nathan's birth and young childhood, his early life had some medical struggles. Nathan was born with a heart problem. It took the care that Vanderbilt's Children's Hospital, Nashville, Tennessee, and Nathan's pediatric did over the first few years to bring Nathan to good health. Hopefully, he still has his health. The medical problems he was faced with could have been caused by the way Judy carried him. Judy had a problem with smoking and wine, and often, I would catch her doing both during the pregnancy. I am sure there were many more times she disregarded the advice from medical experts about smoking and drinking alcohol. I could not be everywhere. I can even recall after Nathan's birth, she would breastfeed with a cigarette in her hand and a glass of wine on the table. Our arguments would become loud at times. There was nothing more important to me than my son and especially his health.

I guess you can say that in my last year (sixteen years) of marriage, I already knew there was no saving us. A divorce was adamant, and it was just a matter of time. It was at this time that I chose to seek others to satisfy my loss of intimacy. I never had to look too far. Debra Rohrer was our travel agent for Billy Ray Cyrus, and she and I had a very tight working relationship. She would handle all our travel during the tours, which made us spend a lot more time together. One thing led to another, and yes, we ended up together for a short time romantically. I think it was something like one year. One can call it what they want, but for me, I was left with no choice. I tried my best for over two years for Judy to seek the help she needed, but when that went downhill, I had to take care of myself. I would say it today as I did back then. Why should I or any other person, whether male or female, must do without intimacy caused by a partner? Let's be honest here; in sickness and in health, I fully believe in. However, anyone in their prime that stood by for more than two years without being sexually active and would still not stray is full of shit. It happens to more women than men. It is a fact, unfortunately. Well, the one thing I did hear was how Judy would lie and tell our son the evilest things about my wandering eye. She made me out to be nothing more than a cheater. I see it the other way. She caused me to go elsewhere. I had no other choice, especially after a two-year cutoff. We were finally divorced and went our separate ways.

Nathan spent time between his mother's house and my home; still the home that Nathan was raised in. Our homes were about fifteen minutes apart. Nathan spent every other week and weekend with each of us, which later turned into Nathan spending three weeks with me and one week with his mother. I cannot count the number of times I would get calls from my son pleading with me to come and get him.

"Dad, I wanna come home," Nathan would say. "Please come get me."

It would break my heart that I had to explain, "Nathan, it's your mother's turn to have you. It'll just be a couple of days."

I will never forget those calls, ever!

There were other times that stood out in my mind, unfortunately. The time my son calls me crying into the phone, "Dad, you must come get me now! Jim is screaming at Mom, and he just said if I don't shut up, he'll shut me up!"

You see, Jim was someone Judy was apparently dating. While Judy's company was setting up an event show in Reno, Nevada, and she and Jim were there working, they decided to get married. It's not marriage. Heck, I'm glad someone else will have to deal with her. Judy, Nathan's mother, did not even have the decency nor the respect to call her son and let him know what she was wanting to do. Not that she needed his approval, but out of respect for your only child.

I remember Nathan telling me he received a call from his mother from Reno, and she said, "Hi, Nathan. I just want you to know that Jim and I got married last night."

I looked directly at his face, and I could see he was holding back his tears. "She never even called me before they did it," Nathan cried out.

All I could do was console him. It was not my place to make excuses as to why his mother failed to call him. I did not want any part of her anymore.

The time went slow, or so I thought, for the next few months. Oh, there was always something I could do around the house, which I did, but still, there was that downtime, which gave me too much time to think and ponder. Ponder about what I cannot, to this day, figure it completely out. I know there was a time I thought that I should go back into touring. I had been offered a few great tours, but honestly, I was burned out. I needed the time to rejuvenate my body and mind.

By now, I had rearranged my clothes closets to be color-coordinated and seasonal. I have always been a bit guilty of being a bit OCD, so as I was doing it, I found myself more on a mission, and as a mission, I needed to defeat the challenge. I installed those closet units, cursing at each screw as I did my best to have it sturdy. Most of the time throughout, I have been able to complete these tasks.

But there were those times when I thought out loud, "Why the hell did I say I'd build this fuckin' thing?" I knew I was getting louder by the minute when my son would come into the room saying, "Dad! What the hell are you doing?"

If I smiled, then that meant I had succeeded in the challenge. If I gave him the look of a desperate man, he knew to just walk away and let my flames burn out. It is important to understand that the challenge became as if it were part of the Olympics. I was both the participant AND the spectator. I had to win to please the crowd. Next, I tackled all the pantry closets in the kitchen.

As I stared into the pantry closet, I came away thinking that no matter how great it may have looked, I had decided to be the judge and jury.

"Empty the shelves onto the counters and kitchen table," I would yell out.

You see, I was plotting just what needed to be done. And in my own mind, I was being timed on this mission. I guess that was my way of making it into something more than just a cleaning job.

So you can imagine, as much as I was enjoying myself being off the road and at home, having my wonderful labs with me, and hanging out (I thought) was cool with my son, it was obvious that I wanted more to my life right now. I knew that my daily. "Hey, let's try to find something to do," was not going to continue, especially seeing the reactions from my dogs…and son.

It was mid-April 1996. I was sitting in the house relaxing after I had tackled the game room and closet. Those were not as bad as the other closets, but still, I had my work cut out. As I continued emptying the game closet, it was obvious that I was disturbing both LuLu and Lacy, my two wonderful labs. You see, this was "their room," where a huge basket filled with their toys took up one wall. I should mention that this basket was on the left side of the closet I was working on. Their ears would perk up when I would move something as if I were disturbing them. They sat (in my way, mind you), causing me to maneuver as if I was on a track meet every time I moved from the closet. Finally, I had had enough.

"LuLu and Lacy, move your big butt! I can't finish my cleaning!"

At the same time, Nathan walked into the room to see what the noise was and found me sitting on the floor between these two one-hundred-plus-pound dogs tugging on a sock with Lacy.

"Dad! It's enough! Finish the closet and be done!" Nathan shouted out, more in an amusing tone than sounding forceful. I realized that I needed something to do.

"I know, maybe a different type of job," I said quietly out loud.

The next few weeks, I gave it a lot of thought. What do I want to do, I would say to myself, so many different jobs popped into my mind. Leaving as quick as they would come, one job kept coming back. How can I take all the knowledge and experience I gained from the music and entertainment world and mix it into something that is new and exciting? I thought long and hard. The thoughts of becoming a promotor, a booking agent, personal management and a few other things, nothing gave me any bolt of energy. *What do I love to do*? I thought to myself.

Sitting in a lounge chair, cruising to the Caribbean waters filled my mind, my heart, and my thoughts. Remember, I spent several years on cruise ships back in the seventies, so I started to tune my mind into what possibilities were there. My mind started running wide open with ideas from all genres of music—big bands, rock and roll bands, country bands, musicians, and solo acts. *How can I tie these into a cruise to the Caribbean*? I thought to myself. I spent the next few weeks working on an idea that would eventually change cruising forever.

My father taught me never to throw away contacts from a previous job. I can remember having card file cases that would allow me to store fifty to one hundred business cards I had collected over the years. I had card carriers from my time on cruise ships, including many top executives from the various cruise lines. I had way too many card cases to count during all my years on tours. Everything from personal managers, artists, musicians, road crew, promotors,

THIS LIFE OF MINE

agents, record label execs, and everything else in between, these card cases were overfilled.

What to do? I kept thinking to myself. I can recall many of these "discussions" I had with myself; I was beginning to see a bright light deep inside my thoughts. It was starting to come to me. I started to design some events that would surely be a huge hit, not only for me but for a sleuth of others. As each day went by, I created and designed some incredible shows and events. Now I just needed to complete the next step.

I contacted a friend of mine who worked for Norwegian Cruise Line, or better known as NCL. Jackie Johnson was a very attractive lady who was well-respected in a field that was primarily run by men. As the senior vice president of sales, I did my best to touch base with her. I can recall that first telephone conversation. I knew I could trust her, and I knew that anything I would say to her would be kept strictly confidential. But before any serious information was divulged, I had one major item to take care of. Without this, my idea would go to someone else. I just know I was sitting on a fantastic idea.

My attorney at the time, Norman Solomon, was married to a lady named Marjorie Solomon. Norm had a great practice in law and Margie had opened a travel agency. We had become great friends going back many years. My son and their daughter went to school together, both public school and Hebrew Sunday school, so there was a strong bond between us, even though I was already divorced from my second wife, Judy. I felt strongly that I could meet with Norman to discuss my idea and how I wanted to incorporate his wife's travel agency, Morning Star Travel, into a portion of my ideas. Norm and I met, and he gave me his positive thoughts and felt that my idea was huge. A luncheon meeting was scheduled for myself, Norman, and Margie.

As I sat across Margie, I could not help but feel as though my chest was about to explode with excitement. I said, "Margie, how would you and Morning Star Travel like to be my travel agency for my group bookings aboard an NCL ship?"

Margie glared at me with a puzzled look and said, "Sure, I would always welcome group bookings, but what are you talking about?"

As I repositioned myself in your typical light cushioned restaurant chair, I said, "I'm going to bring top artists and bands onto cruise ships where their fans can enjoy all their music while partying with them in the Caribbean!"

Without any hesitation except for those quick few seconds for it to be absorbed, Margie calls out, "What a phenomenal idea! Okay, how do you do that, and what does Morning Star Travel need to do?"

As I sat back in my chair, I took a long sip of my cocktail and said, "I need your travel agency to hire me as an outside travel agent where I can then book my groups through, at the same time selling my package to the cruise lines. I will never forget the look on both Margie and Norm's face. They were smiling from ear to ear, and they knew I had come up with a great idea. On June 16, 1996, Entertainment & Travel Alternatives Inc. (ETA) was born.

Now that I had my own company, licensed through a fully licensed travel agency, my next step was to go after a cruise line, not just any cruise line, but one where I had very strong contacts in sales. My next step was to call my contact, Jackie Johnson/NCL, and outline my entire concept. I knew that this would not go any further than Jackie and, of course, the other executives I would meet during our initial office meeting.

I found myself being introduced to a few Executives with NCL, from Adam Aron (CEO), Andrew Stuart (VP), Tasso (promotions and marketing). As I outlined my entire program to them, I could see the gleam in their eyes when I came to the profitable margins. Before I walked out from that meeting with Jackie, I felt that I had accomplished just what I set out to do. Norwegian Cruise Lines' Music Theme Cruises was established.

I made sure to include Morning Star Travel as my official travel agency. Even though I was booking the talent for NCL, I was guaranteed a strong number of cabins from each category to sell from a travel agency status. NCL saw that instead of me just blocking a group of cabins for private shows and events for just my guests, NCL was able to now have every travel agency sell individual or group bookings for these various theme cruises. The best part of the deal was that NCL was paying for all performances, travel, cabins, and transportation. I was there for my many contacts and my ability to negotiate and secure the talent. I designed the ship's daily activities sheet since not only were there performances, but I also created the basic meet and greet with the fans and passengers after each performance. Some of the first bookings I secured were for a big band music cruise, where I featured Bob Costas and the Xavier Cugat Orchestra. An orchestra consisting of over twenty-six musicians and backup singers. Because of the nostalgic theme, there was no better ship of its time than the *Norway*. Originally, the *Il de France* ship was purchased by Norwegian Cruise Line, followed by a huge interior and exterior renovation. New decks and outside areas were added, and the suites aboard the Norway were by far the biggest I have ever seen. I remember that the Sky Suite, located as far forward as any cabin could be, had the most incredible bathroom of any ship back then. Lying inside this magnificent bathtub, with your curtains opened, looking out over the bow of the ship as she shows her strength with each movement through the crashing waters. Let me not forget about those baths during calm seas, where the sea was as calm as a mountainside lake. The ship's decor still featured numerous and recognizable areas of the *Il de France*. I can clearly remember walking into the international lounge, located aft on the promenade deck, and personally seeing the history of the *Il De France* by the wall coverings, etchings, and photographs that were still proudly displayed.

I will never forget the first Music Theme Cruise I had with NCL. Not only had my block of cabins sold out, but the entire ship sold out, making the revenue department of NCL take notice. They saw the huge potential, so from that point, I had every effort to cover all genres, and I did. We had country music artists or groups, rock and roll music, oldies music, theme artist music, R&B music, Motown music cruise, and others. My reasoning for this was twofold. It gave me a reason to still be involved in live music and do what I love to do, which was cruising, being my own boss, owning my own company, and making money for myself, Morning Star Travel, the entertainers, and most importantly, Norwegian Cruise Lines.

"Never place all your eggs in one basket," was a saying that my father instilled in me. I would hear him say, "Make sure you always leave yourself with the option to do whatever it takes to protect yourself."

So I tried to make sure that everything I did where involved my company and or myself. I wanted my own options. I was able to get NCL to agree that ETA was able to negotiate and secure space aboard any cruise ship from any cruise line for their own music theme cruises. After wanting to book acts that I felt could not sell out an entire ship, I still wanted to promote and sell my own music theme cruises.

Entertainment & Travel Alternatives Inc. was just that. We offered entertainment along with an alternate way to participate and travel. When I realized that I was able to license ETA as a cruise-only travel agency, I jumped at the chance. ETA and Morning Star decided to part ways. They were a full travel agency, and I was only interested in cruises, and I felt that I could handle all areas with a good staff. Once licensed I then joined the well-respected CLIA, Cruise Lines International Association. Being a member gave you a strong status and a reputation backed by CLIA. A membership association that continues to this day as being the number one protector for everything cruises.

ETA moved home. To my residence, you see. After a few minutes of self-discussion, I came to the closing that there was no reason for me to have a store-front business. Why should I pay any huge rent for office space when all I need is a desk, telephone, internet, fax machine (they were big back then), a telephone answering machine, and a copy machine? I am not doing any walk-up business over 95 percent of the business was made up of people from all over the United States, Canada, and sometime the United Kingdom and Europe, all by phone or internet. An ETA Music Cruise became world known, as were our cruises.

It was on a Friday evening. I met a friend of mine, Thom Sgro, A&R Director, BNA Records, at Sunset, a place frequented for drinks and cuisine by many people in the music industry. He told me of a new artist that was getting ready to release his first single, and they were looking to promote its release, "Out of This World." The artist's name is Jason Sellars. Sometimes, my mind just goes off on its own path and sees things before I do. Can that actually happen? You be your own judge. I say yes, it can.

As I sat enjoying my cocktail, I looked at Thom and said without hesitation, "I have the perfect event to kick off the single and the full release."

Thom sat there staring at me as if he was waiting for me to take a breath. I sat back in my chair with that shit-eaten Wallach grin on my face and said, "You guys at the label will contact the top thirty-five to fifty country radio stations and invite them to join BNA Records and Jason Sellers on the Out of This World Space Station Cruise. There was a pause that seemed to last forever, but like everyone else in the same manner, Thom just stared back at me as if now I was waiting for him to breathe. His left eyebrow went up. His eyes were now gleaming caused of the smile that kept growing on his face.

"OMG!" Thom yells out, causing many other people sitting in proximity to stare. "This is fuckin' incredible! Unbelievable! Now what the fuck do you mean?"

As I stared back at Thom, I couldn't help but start picturing what I wanted to do for this record promotion. I had no idea what was about to come out of my mouth, but I believed in myself and said, "Oh, what the hell. Go for it."

Okay, every radio general manager or lead disk jockey will receive a custom jacketed Jason Sellars's "Out of this World" CD, along with an envelope containing hotel accommodations at the Orlando Hyatt Airport Hotel, Ground Transfers from the hotel to the Kennedy Space Center on air-conditioned coaches complete with a bathroom and video monitors throughout—a private tour of the space center, followed by your transportation cruise ship, waiting to take you out to sea for a four-night, three-day adventure. On the cruise, there will be a live performance by Jason Sellars and other BNA Record Artists. Oh, one more thing: airfare was not included. If they want to go, they can at least cover their air travel expense. And they all did. We thought there would be many "cannot attend" responses where, in fact, over 90 percent chose to join us.

The timing could not have been better. When I phoned the Kennedy Space Center, I was able to speak directly with their marketing director. One thing I am still proud of to this day is that I have a tremendous way to contact the decision-makers and usually get what I want. Remember, it is not so much winning the game as it is how to play it. As we were discussing the morning ideas, her voice became higher when she said, "OMG! You are not going to believe this? The day you want to come is the day of a launch!" It took an enormous effort to hold back my screams of joy as this will be just another part of this adventure called "Out of This World' with Jason Sellers, presented by ETA. BNA included some of their other artists and made this event truly "a cruise to remember."

It was the day of the event "liftoff." My ETA staff were all present at the entry to the Hyatt Orlando International Airport Hotel to greet the guests coming to attend BNA Records country music artist Jason Sellars in "Out of this World." Keep in mind the entire label connects guests who had no idea what was in store for them except they knew they were going on a cruise to hear Jason Sellars. They had their hotel, hotel welcome party, ground transfers, and their cruise, plus an open bar. Was there anything else? Of course, there was. Remember, this is an ETA Event, and everything ETA did was new and exciting.

After BNA/RCA Record labels hosted that evening's welcome party, we made sure that every VIP Guest found a custom-colored packet in their hotel rooms outlining the cruise event schedule. The only thing I recall I said at the party was, "It is most important that all guests meet outside in the front of the hotel to board their chartered air-conditioned private coaches at a certain time. Failure to do so means that you will have to find your own way to the port later in the day." I can say because this was my style and reputation in any work I did: do not be late. I wait for no one. Well, maybe the celebrity I was working for at the time since everything was done around their schedules.

All three chartered coaches were filled, and we started off on our adventure. The coaches were wonderful. Each had tinted windows to keep the Florida sun out, a very clean and workable bathroom, plus seating with two seats on each side and one last item. Every four rows, monitors are folded down for easy viewing by all passengers.

As we made our approach onto the freeway, in sync, every monitor came on, and the guests were welcomed by none other than Jason Sellars. I had gone to an editing facility on Music Row in Nashville, Tennessee, and produced a video outlining what Jason's guests were about to be a part of. I was extremely excited when the guests found out that they were on their way to the Kennedy Space Center for a private tour of the facility and Space Shuttle Columbia. That alone brought out the excitement in the coaches. But we were not through yet. As the video outlined our program, an executive from the Space Center came on and said, "On behalf of the Kennedy Space Center, I want to personally invite each of you to today's launch of Space Shuttle Columbia." Every guest on every private coach could be heard by my ETA staff with screams, cheers, and applause. It was truly a great day to be "out of this world."

As we began loading the buses back up, we could not help but notice how quickly the clouds were rolling in with an obvious chance for severe rain. We were still en route to the VIP observation area, which was far enough away from the launch site but still able to have a clear view to watch its entire liftoff. The area was outside but completely fenced so as not to allow anyone the ability to wander off. The time clock had been set, and the seconds and minutes were already in countdown mode. No sooner than we were comfortable, the time clock was stopped, and our escort advised us all to return to the bus as this flight was going to be postponed under the weather cleared up. Unfortunately for us, we were already on a tight schedule and had no room to extend our stay. As we all returned to our designated coach, the crowd was still impressed with what was happening. We eventually arrived at the port and boarded our cruise for a few days and nights of great entertainment and cruising experience.

I had some incredible music theme cruises. Some I'd rather forget, but most of them went great. I had one country music cruise that featured a handful of country artists, including the infamous George Jones. George had a blast, especially in the casino and at the casino bar. Always with band members, family, his close friend Peewee, and a few wannabees. I would occasionally make my rounds through the casino to make sure George was fine, and he was. When George was obviously shit-faced, he always held his composure. That was because Peewee was right there to catch him if needed.

George's show was a huge success! The band sounded great, and George was even on time. After shaking hands and having his photo taken with his admired fans, George would make his way into the casino. What we did not know, Peewee made sure that the drinks were flowing even during the meet and greet. So by the time it was casino time, George was feeling no pain. Most of the time, when George would have too many, he would have a very jovial attitude. He laughed out loud; he would wave his hands over the casino table and would just be having the time of his life. Only problem with George in the casino that week, he never won. In fact, he has a hell of a lot of money. Let us just say it was between $46,000 and $51,000.

Each night, he would ask, "Hey…is Nancy in here? Better keep a watch out for her!"

I remember Nancy coming in looking for George, and Peewee jumped into action. He made his way toward Nancy and simply guided her in another direction. It was quite amusing. I guess George knew what the mood would be if Nancy came by and noticed he was dropping thousands of dollars without having any luck at all. As I laugh now, I cannot help but look back and realize I laughed back then as well. George was a lot of fun.

Other music theme cruises did not go as well. ETA had blocked out many cabins for the Mavericks Cruise. We also tied it in with their personal manager who ended up being more trouble than was needed. I always took a disliking to power-hungry managers who thought they were their gift to the ladies and knew all the answers. A few radio disk jockeys attended, but primarily, it was a cruise celebrating the release of their new album. We did fantastically! Completely sold out. But there were a few things that stood out to me. My ship's production manager was having a hard time connecting with the Mavericks' production manager. The production equipment backline was never completed, meaning that the Mavericks would have to settle with the ship's equipment. Again, they brought most of the equipment with them, including their wireless microphones and wireless ear monitors. I guess you can figure out that I am about to go into a wireless meltdown.

The band, except for the Mavericks themselves, came to sound check. I was not as concerned with the sound as I was with their new wireless mics. They were having a hard time tuning in the mics in a room with a steal head and frequencies held by the bridge. At one point, the soundman tuned to a frequency that was interrupted by the Officer's radios. I knew there was going to be an issue.

First issue being that we could not find the band's production manager throughout the ship. He refused to answer his pager. He was not in his cabin and walking the outside decks. We were definitely in hiding. Without the production manager, the band and the house personnel decided they would have to make the best of it at showtime.

The lounge aboard *The Majesty*, the only cruise ship under Majesty Cruise Lines. The ship was at that time moderate in size and had a wonderful reputation. The lounge was packed with fans who had purchased their tickets through ETA, which gave them the advantage over non–ETA guests on the cruise of seeing these wonderful Artists in a private setting. The executives from BNA and RCA Records, over twenty-five of the top country radio stations, were also in attendance.

We were also doing something never seen on a cruise ship before. We were able to take a feed from the ship's satellite and have twenty-five country music radio stations all go live from the ship back to their station, enabling all their listeners the chance to hear interviews with Jason Sellars. I knew if I explored the communications and spoke directly with those officers on the ship, we would get a better handle on it if it were possible. I found out from the beginning, dealing with most of the shoreside personnel of a cruise line, that they had no earthly idea of the daily routines and what was available. As my father taught me, never listen to the branch personnel of any company. Always try to go directly to those that make the decisions. Here was another time: his advice was spot-on.

On the second evening of the cruise, known as the captain's Formal Night, what better night than to feature the star group, the Mavericks? As the band featuring Eddie Perez, Robert Reynolds, and others, along with lead singer Raul Malo, took the stage, the crowd was on their feet. The music started, and we were off on the right foot. Or was it the left?

As Raul Malo grabbed the wireless mic from the stand, out came this incredible voice that the Mavericks were known for. The other band members were singing backup vocals, and the first song went off perfectly. As Raul began talking to the audience, faintly in the background there was another conversation going on. Mind you, it was not a conversation among the band. For some "odd" reason, there was a completely different thing happening in the speakers. Then, as quickly as it came, it stopped. I remember looking at the soundboard and watching both the ship's production manager and the ship's sound manager grab their pagers and pick up the ship's deck phones. The band stood silent, waiting for someone to break the ice and talk. It was Raul. He was professional to make light out of it and went on to his next song.

Within the first sixteen bars of the song, the distortion in the sound began again. This time, there were voices, crackling noises, yet Raul did his best to go on; maybe for another three seconds.

"That's it!" Raul yelled out. "There is no way I can continue doing a show when the sound is this bad!"

He places the wireless mic back on the stand and walks off. His manager and I both assured him that it mattered and would be investigated immediately, but his last few words were, "This is bullshit, and I'm outa here."

As Raul and the other band members walked down the corridor to the elevators, I knew I had to do something. And I did!

"Ladies and gentlemen," I said in a loud voice (without using a mic) so as to be heard throughout the lounge. "As you can see and hear, there is a massive technical problem with the sound tonight." I went on and said, "It appears that the band's wireless mics and the satellites from the ship are interfering with each other. This could cause serious problems in the navigational bridge. Therefore, we will be delaying the show until tomorrow."

What else could I have said? It was the truth, and I believe to this day that it was my delivery of the message that kept the attitude of everyone in a good frame of mind. Many were disappointed, but I was hoping to get the band in agreement to try it another way. We did. The next evening Raul did an unplugged show with a few other band members, and that made up for what could have turned into a mutiny cruise.

Even though I retired from music touring, some things just have a way of popping up. We would call it babysitting a brat. It was another country music cruise, featuring the group Lonestar. Now mind you, when this group got together, they immediately had recognition. Probably one of the best in group and vocal groups. Having met the band earlier, it was going to be great having them on. The original band members consisted of Drew Womack (lead vocals / acoustic guitar), Michael Britt (lead guitar / background vocals), Dean Sams (keyboards / acoustic guitar), Keech Rainwater (drums), Richie McDonald (lead vocalist), and finally, John Rich (bass guitarist / vocals). Having them part of my country music cruise brought many reservations not only to ETA's bookings but more so for the cruise line. On this seven-day cruise, their only responsibility to their contract was to perform two shows and have their Lonestar fan club private party. The remainder of time was left up to each of them to choose what they wanted to do: relax and enjoy the amenities of the ship's spa and fitness room or, for some, start the partying early. Since each of the members had either their wives or their girlfriends (at the time) with them, they were sunning during the day and evenings. Well, let's just say they ran wide open.

Most of the time was spent in the casino with a few of the boys. Dean was a happy drunk when he drank a bit too much. Never out of line, he would just "attempt" to stand and smile, just smile. He was great. The others may have been a bit loud when the luck came while gambling in the casino.

I can recall hearing Keech yell out, "Hot damn! Pay the man!"

And then there was your brat. For the first couple of nights, the only concern I would ever have would be from some of the musicians. It was never physical.

It was more like me having to say, "Come on, boys. Maybe it's time to head up to the buffet for something to eat."

On occasion, you would hear that one of them had to be warned by a casino dealer to refrain from objectional words.

If it was more than one warning, the dealers could be heard telling them, "Sir, I've warned you before. Please, no foul language at the table."

Again, most times, it would be all that was needed. Let me get back to the "brat."

John Rich is a good bass player. He has a few licks that can make any song his. John knew his talent and relied on it to give him serious notice within the country music industry. One of the only problems John Rich had been was his attitude. Whether sober or drunk, John felt that HE was the best bassist, best singer, best producer, best of everything. He showed his ass a few nights in the casino and a few bars during the cruise. Again, everyone was there to have a fantastic time and isn't that what cruises are for? It was midcruise, Lonestar performed that night, and the ship was filled with happiness, fairy tales, and drunks, John Rich being one of them.

I got called to the casino because there was one of my artists making a scene. He was apparently yelling vulgarity each time he lost, or he was yelling for the server, any server, to bring him a drink. It is very rare that a bartender aboard any cruise ship will stop a passenger from ordering a drink, especially knowing if they are a guest entertainer for the ship.

So here is John Rich, sitting at a $25 blackjack table with casino chips scattered in front of him and a drink in his hand, yelling out, "This is bullshit! I can't win a fucking hand!"

At which time, I came up behind John and whispered to him, "Hey, buddy, it's time to go. Let's just do this another night."

John cocked his head to one side, and with his shit-eatin' smile, he said, "Yeah, but I gotta win my money back! I'm not goin' anywhere!"

THIS LIFE OF MINE

Between John's girlfriend at the time and myself, we were able to coax him away from the blackjack table and just kept talking to him as we moved toward the exit. All the way walking, John was still saying, "This is bullshit! Man, I want my money back!"

His cabin door opened, and he bounced his way inside. I felt sorry for his girlfriend.

As the door was closing, she whispered, "Thanks, Steve. Sorry for this."

With a nod, I looked at her and said, "Hey, it's all good. Let him sleep it off. Good night."

I thought for a minute about going back to the casino, but I chose to just head back to my cabin, marking the end, to this day, without any serious problems.

I would not have even written about John Rich and Lonestar, but what happened two nights later, you will see what made this event so memorable. I am confident that you have a picture in your mind as to who Steve Wallach is. He is a lot of fun to be around, he takes his work seriously, and he stands for what he feels is best, whether for himself or for others. Steve is also very protective—a trait he learned from his father and the family.

It was the second to the last night of this cruise. On the final formal night where, so many women were dressed in gowns or cocktail dresses, and the men were decked out in either a tuxedo or suit. Back in the nineties, dressing up for a formal night on any cruise ship was important. It was the night to show off your best. Everyone was saying their goodbyes and farewells. You could not help but notice people exchanging their cell numbers and addresses as they bid their farewells in case they did not see them the rest of the evening or the last day. All the musicians and artists were mingling with everyone on board. It was very festive. I saw John Rich and his girlfriend in the casino again but also glimpsed over to one of the casino hosts, waiting to see their eyes roll back in their heads. Good news. That never happened.

In fact, when I stopped by John's blackjack table, he looked up at me and said, "Hey, Steve. All's good!" I said I apologized, and everyone is okay."

As John was saying this, I could not help but look over to the casino host, who winked and made a gesture that all was good—great ending to another wonderful sold-out country music cruise. Time to retire the following morning for me and my staff was early.

It had to be around three o'clock in the morning. I was awakened by the sound of that high-pitched ringing of the ship's phone. It was a call from the ship's security chief asking me to come immediately to his office.

Hearing something so urgent as you were trying to regain composure since you were awakened from a deep sleep, I responded in a cloudy voice, "Okay, I will be there once I get dressed."

As I pulled up a pair of jeans, I buttoned my shirt as I was moving quickly down the hallway of my deck. Still having no idea why I was being asked to come to the security chief office in the middle of the night, I was tempted to first stop for a cup of coffee, but this time, I felt the sound of his voice. This was urgent.

Coming around the corner on deck 2, crew deck, I was about to knock on the security chief's office door, but to my surprise, it was wide open, waiting for my arrival. As I walked into the room, I noticed his deputy of security sitting there, looking straight ahead with a serious nonemotional expression on his face.

"What's up? I asked as I walked into the room.

"Steve, I'm afraid we have a serious problem," said the chief. "It seems that one of your artists got into an argument with their wife, and things got out of control in the cabin. The wife and all her belongings were physically thrown out into the hallway outside their cabin. The wife contacted our security and asked us to come here."

As this was being explained to me, the chief had already stood up and walked over to the detention cell's solid door. As the door opened slowly, I was like a kid at Christmas. I was trying my best to get a quicker look at what was behind the door by stretching my neck, thinking I could look around the door quicker. When the door fully opened, I recall my face just freezing with my mouth open. The person who was sitting directly in front of me with his head in his hands as his arms rested on his legs was none other than John Rich.

All I could say was, "What the fuck!" as I watched the chief close the door.

Well, this is going to be a long night, I thought to myself.

"Steve, it seems that this person"—pointing to the closed detention door—"had a fight with his wife." The chief went on to say, "She complained to one of my officers who arrived on the scene that John slapped her a few times and threw all her belongings and herself into the hallway. Apparently, she went to the ship's phone and called us." As I sat there listening to this, the chief again said, "Steve, this is a serious situation. This will have to be reported to the authorities upon our arrival."

Trying to think quickly on my feet, I asked the chief, "Have you received a written statement from his girlfriend?" (I advised the chief that they were not married.)

"Not yet," the chief said to me. "She said she wanted to freshen up before meeting with us."

That was my cue. There was no way I was going to allow one of my artists to get locked up on one of my ETA Cruises. I had my work cut out for me.

I first called the girlfriend and asked if it would be okay for me to come to the cabin to speak with her and make sure she was alright. I may have had my allegiance to John Rich as my artist, but there was no way I would sit idle if I saw for myself that he went way over the line. When I knocked on the cabin door, she opened it with tearful eyes and her mascara running down her cheeks. Immediately, I could see she was in no condition to talk logically with me. You see, she, too, had had a bit too much to drink as well, so rather than subject me to having to make any sense from someone who was already not making sense, I would wait until morning.

"I have a great idea," I said to her. "How about I phone you around 8:00 a.m. for breakfast, and we can go over all of this then."

She turned that frown into a small smile and said, "That would be fine."

As I stepped away and closed her cabin door, my mind was already plotting out what needed to be done to either make this go away or what the best solution would be. After entering my cabin, my last job for the night was to call the security chief and let him know she was too tired and needed a fresh mind to speak with anyone so she would be available tomorrow morning.

Morning came quicker than expected. I got dressed and phoned John's girlfriend to see if she was ready to meet over breakfast. It was agreed, and we both met up with one another in the dining room, where it would be quieter for us to speak privately. Her appearance was fine. If you did not know any better, you would never have thought anything took place the night before. So I began to explain to her where John was, and the ship's security was waiting to take her statement and see where you stood insofar as pressing charges or the ship's security against him.

"So"—with a long pause—"you have to decide what you want to do," I said. "I don't think it would be best for anyone's interest if he has to stay locked up until we arrive back in Miami."

"Oh no!" she said to me. "I'm not pressing any charges. I just want to get off this boat! The quicker I can be gone, the better!"

As I watched her mannerisms, she was very alert and attentive to every word I said.

"The only thing I want is that I get my own room for the last night," she asked of me. "I wouldn't think that would be a problem, but first, I have to escort you down to the security chief's office," I spoke.

"Let's get your story down," I told her. "It's really important that you say exactly what you want to say and not let them think and decide for you."

She agreed, and I phoned the chief to let him know she was ready to meet with them.

Arriving in his office, we were met by the chief and the staff captain, second-in-command of any ship. Introductions were made, and I opened with, "Gentlemen, last night's event was bad, very bad. I never would have expected anything like this to happen because ETA has never been involved with something like this. I know that John's girlfriend has something to say."

The meeting and discussions went on for about fifteen minutes while John Rich was still locked in the detention room just on the other side of the door. Bottom line, they agreed to have the ship supply her with her own cabin for the last night. She was instructed not to speak nor go near John for the remainder of the cruise. She thanked me, and I knew that I would see her throughout the day and again in the morning when we would be disembarking the ship. As everyone exchanged their appreciation through handshakes, we still had the matter of what was to be of John Rich.

I always had a very strong and respectable reputation among the officers of every ship I was on for a long period of time. I worked hard to establish that reputation how, simply, my father once again.

"Son," my father said to me, "always remember, it takes years to build up a strong and respected reputation, but it takes only a few seconds to destroy it all. For those who had the pleasure of knowing my father, his composure was amazing. My father could walk into a crowded room, and almost everyone in there would look, gaze, and watch my dad's every movement. He had this air about him. He always walked with confidence and a determined look on his face. Not that of being serious, more of a look that had a bit of a smile. His eyes would always study the room, so he knew exactly what he wanted to know. It was amazing to watch. We would sit on the side and watch with such pride. These are the things I wanted in myself, and I am proud to say I had them with me.

It took me some time to convince the staff captain and security chief that this was truly an isolated incident, all brought on by consuming too much alcohol. I was pulling out all the stops to allow me the task of being responsible for him until he got off the ship. Crimes at sea automatically call in the FBI because of international waters. Once the FBI comes in, depending on the crime, it is usually handed over to the local authorities once the ship docks.

Luckily for John, our next stop was Miami, Florida. "Steve, you know we would not do this for just anybody," the staff captain said. "We don't want this going shoreside either if we can prevent it." I was nodding in agreement during his entire talk. In my mind, I started thinking, *Okay...it's sounding like I might be able to keep this on the ship.* My mind was already searching for the "out" explanation. I was ready.

"Hey, staff," I said to him.

(Calling a staff captain just staff is a sign of friendship between both of us.) A few pleads and a few pride swallows, the officers decided to keep the matter shipside. No report since his girlfriend chose not to press any charges and to forget the matter. This was pretty much kept quiet for the duration of the cruise. Here yet another matter was handled professionally and with respect (along with a few private agreements). Finally, another cruise is complete. The night will go quick, and tomorrow's disembarkation should go like all others, smooth…real smooth.

It is six o'clock the following morning, and the ETA staff has escorted all the country music artists, musicians, production crew, and lighting crew to the private lounge solely secured for us. Within a few short minutes, the ship's coordinator arrived to escort us to the gangway for disembarkation. I am first in line to handle the escort, with everyone mixed behind me. As we begin to walk down the final gangway to enter the terminal, you can clearly see a gentleman standing there with a dog, not just any dog. This was a trained canine used for sniffing contraband such as marijuana, cocaine, explosives, etc. I am a complete dog lover. I have always been.

As we began to move slowly toward the terminal, someone behind me called out in a whisper but loud enough to reach me, "Steve! Shit! I got some weed on me! What should I do?"

Panic, yet a calm came over my face. I thought I was back on the road again with a group that loved smoking pot. When our tour bus would get pulled over, they would all turn to me 'cause, hell, I guess they counted on me covering their asses in times like this.

With just roughly ten feet to the entrance of the terminal, I was handed a clear sandwich baggie with what appeared to be marijuana. I quickly took the bag and stuffed it down the front of my pants, thinking foolishly that my pants were made of steel and nothing could penetrate them, especially the dog that was now in reach of me. As I walked in front of the cutest beagle I had ever seen, my right foot touched down for a quick second I thought I got this! I am almost past the dog with the nose. No sooner than I thought this, I could hear the dog bark and sit. The next thing I heard, and still hear it to this day, was a customs officer saying, "It's gonna be a long day."

Needless to say, I was not arrested as I only had to pay a five hundred dollar fine on the spot, and that would be the end of it. My credentials were handed back to me, and I walked away with my receipt for $500. Was I nervous, hell yes. This was something I did not want, but I had to protect my entourage. And I did, and that's what made my name respected while on tours.

Back in Nashville, many people in the music industry had their favorite places to dine and drink. One place that was loved by all was Sunset Grill, Hillsboro Village, Nashville, Tennessee. The Sunset had a fantastic bar that was usually elbow room only, and it had a few rooms strictly for tablecloth dining. One night, while I was there, I remember Dean Caine was there, country artist Billy Dean, and a handful of record executives. Walking into the bar was the one and only John Rich. I remember this like it was yesterday.

John walked over to me and said, "Man, I know you're gonna hear soon, but I just got fired from Lonestar."

At first, I just looked at him with this blank look on my face. I said, "What? You just got fired from Lonestar? Bullshit." I called out over the voices of many.

John nodded and said, "Yeah, man, I fucked up. My drinking and shit got me in trouble again, and Richie and the Boys told me they were done with it."

As he looked up at me, I could see in his eyes he was serious. "Man, this sucks. But it is what it is, and I'll be okay."

As my eyes were still focused on his face, he said to me, "Hey, Steve, you saved my ass on that ship. I will never forget what you did for me."

As he shook my hand and looked right into my eyes, I truly felt he was truthful and really appreciated what I did for me. Real simple. I stopped his ass from going to jail for federal assault and battery.

"Man, Steve," John said to me, still holding and shaking my hand. "When I make it as a solo artist, I will remember you. I promise you, man, I will show you how much I appreciated all that you did for me that night."

As I write this portion of the book, I cannot help but smile and laugh, knowing that John Rich's words to me were as useless as a water drop on a duck's ass. I have seen John over the years and have admired him for what he has accomplished within the country music world, as well as in his political stance. But I will never forgive him for being so full of bullshit and blowing me off when I had asked him to please headline a cruise with his successful duo Big & Rich. There probably would not be any Big & Rich, nor would John have had the tremendous success he has now. I wish him no ill feelings, but I do not have a spot in my heart for those who find the need to lie to get through. I should have allowed the authorities to lock his ass up.

By 2000, I and Entertainment & Travel Alternatives Inc. had a spotless reputation among most of the cruise lines. The ETA Music Theme Cruises for NCL were doing fine, and most of the ETA Music Theme Cruises were selling strong. I was the first to bring Bluegrass Music Cruises to the public. Granted, there was another person who had done two or three small cruises with bluegrass music but not to the size of attendance I was looking for. The ETA Bluegrass Music Cruises ran for thirteen glorious years. ETA was the only company offering bluegrass cruises filled with daily events and entertainment from some of the biggest names in Bluegrass. In our eleventh year, other bluegrass cruises started to pop up. It was not that I was upset because I was always a firm believer that competition is good for business. I was appalled that some of the Bluegrass Artists that I had on my roster annually chose to break away and try themselves.

Herb Sandker, manager and husband of Bluegrass artist Rhonda Vincent, asked to meet me one morning during the cruise.

"Sure," I said. "Anything of importance."

"Nah, not really," Herb said back. "Just want to pick your brain a bit."

Not thinking anything was out of the ordinary, I said, "Sure, let's meet at nine at the coffee shop."

The following morning, Herb and I sat down and informally talked about my bluegrass cruises. As the discussion continued, I noticed that Herb's questions were more of being a promoter for such a cruise, and his continuing took me by surprise. When I finally blew him off and went about my business, I completely forgot about it. That night was the final settlement with all the artists/bands that appeared.

I always made it a habit to have the following year's contracts with me for those artists I am looking to bring back the following year. Herb came in for settlement, but when I handed him the contract for the following year (as I have done with him for the past five years), Herb surprised me and said that Rhonda would not be back.

"She has decided that she wants to do her own cruise," Sandker said with a smirk on his face.

At first, I was a bit surprised. "Really?" I said to him. "What caused this, Herb?"

"We want to do our own bluegrass cruise." As Herb turned and started to walk away, this poor excuse of a redneck just smiled and said, "Thanks for the info!"

So Rhonda Vincent, along with her husband/manager Herb, ran their bluegrass cruises for three years, duplicating my schedules, events, and lessons. But it was obvious that the fans of bluegrass came back to ETA. Their cruises each year got smaller and smaller until they had to close due to poor attendance. ETA retired their bluegrass cruises after thirteen very successful years. Always leave on a high note, my father always taught me. And I did. What I did learn was that you never divulge your hand to anyone whether you know them or not. If they are not your business partners, keep it all close to the chest. Wise words from a very wise man.

Some of the greatest in bluegrass music performed on one or many of the ETA cruises—names like Jesse McReynolds, Phil Leadbetter, IIIrd Tyme Out, Grasstowne, Mark Newton, and a special group to me, the Cherryholmes Family. Cherryholmes was a true family band. From Commander Jere Cherryholmes; his wife, Sandy; daughters, Cia and Molly; and sons, B. J. and Skip, this family was probably the best as a Bluegrass Group. Having won numerous awards over the years, I knew that they were going to be incredible from the minute I heard them.

Walking through the hotel lobby area during any Bluegrass Music Convention, you could not help but listen to a huge stream of bluegrass. Musicians were huddled in various spots throughout the area, playing their best of bluegrass. It truly is a strong representation of just how good these bluegrass musicians are. As I turned the corner, I came across a group consisting of six. Their sound was impeccable. The harmonies were perfect blends of six different harmonizing notes. As I stood to listen, I couldn't help but notice how everyone passing would slow down or even stop in their tracks to listen to this well-tuned group of musicians and singers. I had to have them on my next Bluegrass Music Cruise. And that I did. In fact, the Cherryholmes Family was ETA's headliners for the next eight or nine annual ETA Bluegrass Music Cruises. Having won almost every award for Bluegrass Music, the children who were young adults and now most married with their own children left the family group and went out on their own, continuing with their award-winning songs and carrying out the traditions of not only bluegrass music but other genres as well.

I remember one time when I had Kenny Chesney on my roster for one of the ETA Country Music Cruises. Kenny was fairly new to country music and country music fans, so I saw in him great ticket sales for ETA. Young, good-looking, fantastic songs and style, I knew it would be a hit. And it was. When the ship arrived in Jamaica, I offered to escort Kenny and his entourage to the Sandals Resort in Ocho Rios. This was Kenny's first time on a cruise and first time in the Caribbean. He fell in love with the water and the beach. His bandmates and crew were having the time of their lives as well. It seems that none of them had ever been outside the United States, so when they explored every port of call, they truly appreciated it.

I had set up about four lounge chairs and umbrellas for Kenny and some of his staff. I, of course, included my lounge chair there as well. But I recall Kenny getting up from his chaise and walking to the edge of the water as the calm ripples would further sink his feet into the sand. I could not help but notice how he would stare out into the ocean. I knew inside that his mind had to be running wide open with fantasies of having the money to really break out into the Caribbean islands. David Farmer, Kenny's tour manager, and I walked over to Kenny as he continued staring out over the waters.

"Boy, I could get real use to this," Kenny said. "Man, this is just beautiful here, Steve. Thanks for bringing us here."

I could not help but notice the huge grin on Kenny's face. His smile was saying it all.

"I'm tellin' ya right now," Kenny said to David and myself, "I'm gonna buy me a house on a Caribbean Island and write some of the best hit songs ever."

I guess Kenny Chesney knew at that time that he was going to be a huge success. You could see it in his eyes. Fast-forward to today, Kenny Chesney has become a household name, and his fame and success have given him numerous Caribbean homes, beside his homes in Nashville and Knoxville, Tennessee. Keep writing the hits, Kenny.

It was now the magical year that everyone was afraid of: 2000. Computers did not crash as the high-tech giants had thought. The stock market never crashed as the top brokers had thought. In fact, there really was not any serious interruption of any sort. Bank accounts were untouched, as were credit cards, and of course, no debts were washed away as many of us wished for.

One of my most memorable cruise events was ETA's Munchkin of Oz Cruise, featuring the remaining munchkins from *The Wizard of Oz*. Not only was the movie one of my favorites (and still is), but having the title as "Representative for the Original Munchkins of the *Wizard of Oz*" felt wonderful. In fact, it felt incredible. Here I am, an adult, who has worked with some of the biggest names in entertainment, have worked on some of the highest revenue music tours worldwide, running a very successful even company, and I am now hanging out with the most sensational "little people" known as the Munchkins of Oz. I have watched *The Wizard of Oz* every year for as long as I can remember. Every year around, Thanksgiving, *The Wizard of Oz* would be on the television, and every year growing up, I would sit with my family in our living room, and we would watch this legendary movie. I even played the Tin Man character in my fifth-grade class play. But to be able to not only see the Munchkins live but to represent them for bookings was so cool to me.

I recall one Thanksgiving, the Munchkins were booked for a book signing at a major mall in my hometown of Nashville, Tennessee. While they were there, I wanted to do something special for them. I actually had a Thanksgiving dinner at my home for Margaret Pellegrini (sleepyhead, flower pot girl); Clarence Swensen (first trumpet) and his wife, Myrna; Mickey Carroll (munchkin); Karl Slover (soldier); Meinhardt Raabe (Coroner); and of course Jerry Maren (Lollipop Guild Leader) and his wife Ruth. Along with them were the munchkins photographer Carla Sellers. The timing was perfect. Coming on the television that same early evening was *The Wizard of Oz*. I was ecstatic with joy. Here we all are, sitting in my den, at my home, with the remaining Munchkins from *The Wizard of Oz*, watching *The Wizard of Oz* on television. It was unbelievable. To this day, that was still one of the best days of my life. Why? Simply said, the Munchkins from *The Wizard of Oz* were in my home.

The following day, I met with the Munchkins at Opryland and enjoyed a day of sightseeing at the property of Gaylord Hotel. That evening, I had arranged a special evening for them as guests to the Grand Ole Opry, not only guests but VIP guests, where I was able to have them backstage at the Opry, meeting many of the Opry Entertainers, including one very special man. You see, Margaret and Ruth Swensen both had crushes on Little Jimmie Dickens, who was on the roster for the evening shows. As we gathered in the Green Room with other VIPs, they were welcomed with open arms from so many. People were taking photos with them; they were signing their names on anything they could hand them. Cocktail napkins were being put in front of them as quickly as they were signing. And then it happened. As if the crowd in the Green Room was the ocean's water, and Moses came in. Standing as tall as he could at the entrance to the Green Room was their idol, Little Jimmie Dickens. At the far end of the room stood Margaret, Clarence, and Ruth and Gerry and Ruth Maren. The crowd all moved back as if it were in slow motion, and Little Jimmie made his way to these wonderful people known as the Munchkins of Oz.

"Hello," Little Jimmie called out as he extended his arm to shake hands with Margaret.

"Well, hello to you, Mr. Dickens!" shouted Margaret with excitement.

"Oh, you can call me Jimmie. It's okay," Jimmie said back.

They exchanged a few words before Jimmie said, "I must go get ready to walk out on stage. Do you mind if I call you out and introduce you all to our Grand Ole Opry Guests?"

THIS LIFE OF MINE

I have never seen such smiles come from so many at one time.

"Of course, you can," Margaret called out.

And so it was, five minutes after Little Jimmie Dickens took the stage, he said to the audience, "I have a few friends of mine I'd like to introduce you fine folks to. Ladies and gentlemen, please put your hands together for my friends, the Original Munchkins from the *Wizard of Oz*!"

I can remember standing on the side of the stage as Margaret, Clarence, and the others walked out on the stage of the Grand Ole Opry, invited out by Little Jimmie Dickens. As the standing ovation and applause settled down, Jimmie grabbed the microphone and said, "Boy! I'm finally not the shortest one out here anymore!"

The roar of laughter came from the crowd, and they all said their hellos and thanked Jimmie for the introduction. It was a night to remember for us all.

The relationship we all made with each other was strong. These fine people were not just clients of mine. They became great friends as well. I believed in them so strongly and knew that their fan base covered four generations. I designed one of the best cruise events for ETA. Ladies and gentlemen, boys, and girls of all ages, welcome aboard the Munchkins of Oz Cruise! And so the first of three Munchkins Cruises was started. When choosing a cruise line and ship that could relate to the choice theme, I always chose based on how they would relate to each other. There was (and still is) one specific cruise line that seemed to have been built to satisfy our Munchkins of Oz Cruise. What stood out over everything when one would think of the *Wizard of Oz*? What is that one saying that so many still say? Are you ready? Here it comes!

"Follow the Yellow Brick Road! Follow the Yellow Brick Road! We're off to see the Wizard, the wonderful Wizard of Oz...."

The pool and sundecks aboard one cruise line had what we were looking for. In fact, we could not have asked for anything better. Costa Cruises had on the outside pool decks; gorgeous teak wood outlined with what else but a full yellow colored walkway. It was as if Costa Cruises painted their open pool decks for our group cruise event, the Munchkins of Oz Cruise. And that was one of the strong features all my guests loved about the cruises with these wonderful people. When the music would blare the theme song of "Follow the Yellow Brick Road," everyone, whether part of my group or not, would stand, cheer, and sing every word. During their autograph and storytelling events, the lounge would be packed with people just wanting to hear actual stories of the making of the *Wizard of Oz*, including stories of Judy Garland (Dorothy), Jack Haley (the Tin Man), Ray Bolger (scarecrow), Bert Lahr (Cowardly Lion), and of course Toto (real name was Terry). A remarkably interesting man also joined our cruises for *The Wizard of Oz*; author and great-grandson of creator L. Frank Baum was Robert A. Baum Jr. He was a true historian of his great-grandfather's *Wizard of Oz*, and all his stories were truly interesting to hear.

It was the second day of the Munchkin Cruise, and everyone was looking forward to the evening's events since it was known as a formal night. It was the night all the ladies and young ladies would dress in their formal attire of sequined gowns and long dresses, and the young men and older men would have on their tuxedos or suits. The champagne would be flowing in all the lounges, and the casino would be in full gear. Carla Sellers took on a few separate roles besides the Munchkin's photographer. Carla always made sure she was not too far away from them while in public. If any munchkin wandered off, we always had a crew officer with them.

As I walked into the casino to check out the action on the tables and the slot machines, all I could hear was, "Stevie! Stevie! I'm over here!" happy shout-outs from Margaret Pellegrini. Margaret's personality was huge! She was always the life of the party and never turned her back on any adult or child who wanted to say hello to her.

But this one night while in the casino, I made my way over to her and said, "Hey, gorgeous! What ya doin' in this here casino!" Margaret, with her contagious smile, looked up at me and said, "I'm trying to sit at this blackjack table!"

Without insult, it was a bit humorous to watch this petite lady grab hold of this tall bar seat and climb her way up.

"Okay, I'm ready to play!" she shouts out.

I stayed and watched her for a few minutes. She had her scotch and chips, and she was all set, hopefully, to win big. I had a special place in my heart for Margret Pellegrini. She became great friends with my own mother and spoke volumes for me.

"Okay, Margaret, I said to her with a grin on my face. You're in good hands here. Win a lot of money, and don't give 'em all of yours!"

As I leaned over to give her a kiss on the cheek, she leaned over and said to me (loud enough for most at the table to hear), "Boy, Steve, you handsome man, you can leave your shoes under my bed anytime!"

As all of us began to laugh, I felt my face get bright red as I turned and said, "Oh, Margaret, you say that to all your men."

We said our good nights, and down the yellow brick road, I went off to find my cabin. Imagine, who else today can say they were hit on by Margaret Pellegrini, a lead Munchkin of the *Wizard of Oz* (chuckle)?

ETA Munchkins of Oz Cruise, Steve Wallach and Robert Baum
(grandson of writer L. Frank Baum The Wizard of Oz)
Below: Carl Swenson (soldier) Jerry Maren (Lolipop Guild)

The ETA Munchkins of Oz Cruises was successful. Having block out enough cabins for my group, each year was marked as a complete sellout. We sold close to three hundred cabins, most being double occupancy. By the time of the third cruise, it was becoming difficult for all the munchkins to continue traveling, especially out of the United States. There was always a lot of walking and time slots filled with back-to-back events, and it was taking a toll on some of them. I was always taught that it is best to remember the fun times of an event. I would not want anyone to think for one minute any negative comments because of their fitness to attend these types of events, so after our third sold-out cruise, we all agreed to mark it as their farewell Munchkins Cruise, leaving so many with such great stories and signed memorabilia by the Original Munchkins from the *Wizard of Oz*.

I was never one to sit idle and wait for ideas to come to me. I always pushed myself to think creatively, especially when it came to designing private group events for my cruise business. I would sit for hours in front of my computer and look at all types of land events. There were music events, autograph events, oldies music events, singles cruises, knitting cruising, and more. But I wanted to come up with a huge event, and it had to be different, completely different from anything else.

I recall sitting in front of my laptop, thinking and staring at the screen as if something was going to appear and make this easy. Well, hour after hour, day after day, came and went, and I was beginning to feel frustrated. More at myself because I was always able to produce ideas, so to now be unable to, I knew I had to just walk away, and it would eventually come to me. Three days later, it did.

Have you ever sat in front of your computer screen and began surfing mostly the quick thoughts that your mind was touching on? Well, I did and what I found ended up being a brilliant idea. Watch my screen flash many stale ideas. On one particular screenshot was a photo of a private yacht and this gorgeous female model dressed (or should I say scantily dressed), in what appeared to be a very sensuous bikini covered with a colorful scarf dancing in the wind. It was as if I was suddenly stopped at the edge of a six-hundred-foot drop.

As if it were yesterday, I sat back in my chair and just grinned as I said in a soft voice, "Man, do I have a great idea for a theme!"

It was loud enough that I found myself answering back.

Mind you, I did not want to do a model cruise similar to that of a pageant, but I needed to come up with an idea that would be a first in the cruise industry and generate incredible revenue. As I began to surf the web for something that I knew would not only sell but enable me to bring on sponsors, it could possibly be a huge hit. But the question was, What kind of model's cruise would attract more than just one group of people? My father always told me that when you're planning something, no matter what it may be, you want to be able to build off of your main attraction. He would do that in his real estate ventures. Always making sure that his anchor store(s) were well-known and strong in revenue and that the secondary stores played off the anchor in keeping the center active.

It was exactly how Donald Trump explained it to me years ago, "You must surround yourself with the best, so you will always look the better."

And so that is what I did. I reviewed probably fifty various events that had to do with modeling—modeling of all types: swimwear, clothes, beachwear, etc. Then I realized exactly what I wanted to design for the event. What started simply as a model's cruise, I designed an event that would feature top exotic models from all over the world, well-known photographers specifically in that business, and shore excursions where people can participate in a complete photo shoot on one of our visiting islands. My ideas began to pour as though I had turned my mind on like a faucet. One idea after another idea fell into place in my mind. Now to go and find the resources to begin my negotiations to secure the models and photographers.

There are so many websites listing models—everything from clothed models to sexy models in lingerie to "adult" models. I wanted something that stood out on its own and had a strong reputation for being completely professional. I began searching for model conventions to see *if* I could gather ideas from them. I was amazed at the number of conventions there are for models. And like most things, either the lingerie or the adult models had the strongest attendance. I recall it took me several weeks to surf through all the websites to find the top five possibilities. Always keeping in mind that it had to be a cruise event not seen before.

I am one of these sticklers when it comes to ideas that I want to work with. I guess it had to do with how I have always tried to work at full speed. I know I got that from my father; you know, it was always designing the plan, approving the plan, selling the plan, and reaping its rewards. So over time, I finally came down to the one company I felt would be well-received and a grand home run.

I came across this one website that had some of the most exquisite women I had ever seen cover the pages of their annual magazine. It was not so much (at first) that some of the photographs were of a nude model, but more so were the backgrounds and clothing (more or less) that created a photo that said more than your typical nude lady's magazine. I spent hours researching their website and reviewing the numerous books, magazines, calendars, and articles that I found and immediately knew that this would be the company I wanted to approach with this new and exciting cruise event.

Mystique Magazine was a company based out of Texas that had a very strong reputation among many of the top-producing model feature magazines and modeling exotic agencies. Known for their worldwide models and worldwide exotic locales, the lead photographer at the time for *Mystique Magazine*, Mark D. I first had to make my initial introduction to the editor(s) or owner(s) of the magazine to have access to Mr. Daughn. So the gamble was to sell this directly to the final decision-makers and bypass their photographer. Why? At that moment in my business, I felt extremely positive and knew my ideas for this would be greatly received. Within seventy-two hours, I was on a conference call with the publisher/owner, production assistant, AND Mark D.

My idea was quite simple. I wanted to offer both my client, *Mystique Magazine*, and the consumer a unique and working cruise. This would be the first *Mystique Magazine* model and photography exotic cruise. What would be one of the farthest places to travel that included some of the most breathtaking scenic views, I thought. Having researched numerous cruise lines, I came across the only one

I felt would be a great match: Renaissance Cruise Lines. They already had a strong reputation throughout some of the most exotic places such as Tahiti and the Fiji Islands.

I remember starting my conversation strongly and quite detailed. Those on the other end of this telephone conversation had to have thought I had prepared this idea, and in front of me, I had to have had designs, diagrams, itineraries, island towns, and more because they would keep asking me to look at my paperwork and see what this was or that was. Honestly, I had a brochure of Renaissance Cruise Lines and a notepad. My design was being thought of as I spoke. It was so creative that I, too, was impressed with coming up with a scheduled idea. Mind you, this was known as an overview or treatment in the video/filming business. The CEO asked me to hold on so that he and the others can discuss a few matters. I immediately said yes, but at the same time, I could not help but think, *Hmmm, why didn't they just call me back? Was it something that easy?*

I could hear the telephone click as they each came back on the line, saying hello once again.

"Steve, you really have made us sit up and think about this," said the chief editor. "In order for us to do this as a worldwide event," he said, "we need to go and do a full sight inspection."

I sat listening to each of them offer their thoughts and suggestions, which, in turn, I wrote down as fast as I could write. I wanted to be able to incorporate possibly some of their ideas into what I was designing…in my mind. I will never forget how detailed my imaginations were, especially knowing that they were going to be fantastic and memorable.

Ending our telephone conversation with a cordial goodbye and thanks, I immediately got out of my chair with a bundle of satisfaction and yelled out, "I did it! I really did it! I cannot believe I, me, solely by myself, created an idea without any real comparison."

All I knew was that I now have to turn this idea into a great reality. I was able to achieve what I set out to do, but now I needed to bring this idea to fruition with a cruise line. I already had a cruise line in mind. It was time for me to do my magic and see if I would be able to convince them to be a part of this cruise event.

Renaissance Cruises was an upper scale cruise line and consisted of four beautifully appointed cruise ships. Their world itineraries were some of the best, offering their guests wonderful ports where the ships would stay for a few days. Having overnight stays involving a cruise can be somewhat short on selections, especially if you want to incorporate an island excursion. With this in mind, I elected Renaissance Cruises to be my first contact. They offered numerous port stops with a few overnight stays, allowing me to have as much time as possible on each island visit. I made sure to have a few selected itinerary choices, offering some of the most breathtaking views. There was one special itinerary that would be a great blend with *Mystique Magazine*. My choice was the magnificent islands of Tahiti. Some of the best island beauty can be found on Papeete, Moorea, Bora Bora, and Raiatea; therefore, my approach to the cruise line would include these islands.

My plan was to offer ideas in my promotion but at the same time allow the cruise line's director of sales to think it was their idea. I was going to take an average model's photo shoot and turn it into a cruise event open to all consumers. Now I have created a group cruise where it would be advertised and sold to those who either just wanted to be there with a dozen gorgeous models from all over the world, photographers wanting to polish their craft through our onboard and site photo shoots, or to those who just want to get away and cruise with the Models of Mystique Magazine.

It was difficult for me to wait until I spoke to the cruise line to begin the process of building a group cruise. It made zero sense for me to establish island contacts without first having a secured cruise ship in place. So the quicker I was able to get Renaissance Cruises to offer me group space, the faster I could go to the next step.

My conference call with Renaissance Cruises took place on a Monday morning. On the line were the vice president of sales, vice president of groups, marketing director, and myself speaking on behalf of my company, Entertainment & Travel Alternatives Inc./LLC. I started the conversation with, "Have I got a group for you!" I then laid out my concept and plan. I recall it took me approximately twenty minutes of nonstop talking, outlining my group sales and marketing plan, island excursions and photo shoots, and shipboard activities where the cruise line would benefit financially. Remember, it was important to make the cruise line think that they had another means for onboard revenue from my group. And I did, which allowed me to receive a confirmation from the cruise line.

"In order for this to happen, I will need the following from you," I said to the Renaissance executives. "Would you please extend complimentary cabins for us to do a full site inspection and discounted airfare through your own air/sea program?"

Prepared to defend my requests, I was somewhat shocked to have received a yes response. So it became the ETA present, the *Mystique* Models Cruise of Tahiti.

Now that the cruise line has been confirmed, I need to reply to the Renaissance Cruises Shoreside excursion director to supply the names and contact details for each of the islands we would visit. I was not going to use the ship's island excursions, but I wanted to begin talks and negotiations for the contacts on the islands that could be our private excursions. With contact information in hand, I was ready to begin my negotiations. Within the following days, I made contacts and agreements with each of the island's tour excursions and confirmed our site inspection within the next few weeks. Dates had to be cleared especially by *Mystique* photographer Mark, his assistant, and a few others who would be making the trip with me.

I arrived in Los Angeles one day prior to our long-awaited flight to Tahiti. Arriving at the hotel, the *Mystique* team met me. I felt immediately comfortable with them. Mark was a quiet-spoken man who came across as quite professional. The others were as excited by the way they carried themselves. It looked as though this was going to be a great site inspection. The following morning, we arrived at Los Angeles International Airport about two hours prior to our fight for check-in. We boarded the plane in coach but were able to secure the first middle-row bulkhead seats, allowing us to stretch our legs out.

Upon our arrival in Papeete, Tahiti, we were met by the representative of Renaissance cruises and taken by transport to our cruise ship, R4. Renaissance had named their four ships R1, R2, R3, and R4. All four of the ships were the same build. The only differences were some of the carpets and furnishings in the public lounges. But the layout and design of the ships were identical. Once onboard, I was directed to my stateroom, which consisted of a well-appointed cabin and my own private balcony. I will say that the Renaissance went out of their way to take great care of us. It was already late in the day, and our dinner reservations were for the first seating, 6:30 p.m.

The dinner conversation gave us the time to go over the schedule I had planned for each island visit. The meal itself was fantastic. From the service to our dessert, everything was superb. After dinner, I had the opportunity to go shoreside and stroll through this area that was filled with an array of food vendors and shops. It was an amazing scene because this area is completely vacant during the day, and once evening comes, it is made up of many vendors offering incredible smells that fill the air. Having just had dinner aboard, I enjoy the time just walking among the hundreds of others doing the same thing. After about one hour, I made my way back to the R4 and spent the next hour sitting out on my balcony, hearing the festive sounds of music and chatter. My evening ended in a pleasant way, and I was looking forward to the following morning when my plans would finally take effect.

Meeting in the dining room for breakfast, we were all excited, knowing that our adventure would be starting here in Papeete with our escorted ride to some of the most exotic places here, deep in the bowels of the island. I will never forget just how beautiful this area was. We were taken deep into the mountains. Every turn into the foliage was better than the last. Driving deep into the areas was done on dirt roads that were most likely made years ago, as the lines for the tires surrounded tall grass. As we were approaching another turn, one could not help but hear a roaring sound. This sound became stronger and stronger as we approached what appeared to be a sharp turn in the roadbed. As our open-top jeep made the next turn, standing directly in front of us, one of the largest waterfalls I have ever seen anywhere. The sounds of the water when it landed in the water below were so powerful, as if the sounds of a rumble were thunder after thunder after thunder. The force of the water was evident by the

THIS LIFE OF MINE

sight of all the white caps and white foam fuming from the water as it began its overflow to the bottom.

"This was an area we would definitely take advantage of!" shouted photographer Mark. "This area would be perfect for a number of different photo shoots."

As I stood watching the facial expressions of my clients, I knew I had thus far hit a home run. They were thrilled. We spent the next few hours onsite inspections and went away knowing that this wonderful island would welcome us to take incredible photographs of some of the *Mystique* models of the world.

When we made our way back, our guide stopped at a local outside eatery. Well, I do not know if I would call it an "eatery" as it was made up of only a small table with a colorful umbrella open. On the table were a bowl of fresh limes and a few island spices. This was lunch. I thought to myself. Where is the kitchen, the stove, or the refrigerator? On the chalkboard leaning against the tree was their menu consisting of two types of fish meals along with premade sandwiches of cheese and butter or ham and cheese. I was more impressed and curious about how they cook and prepare their fish dishes. I remember our escort driver telling us to try the fresh fish dish. Not being much of a fish lover, I passed on the fish and chose the ham and cheese sandwich along with a soft drink.

So here we have the "chef" standing on the other side of the table, reaching below into what appeared to be a cooler. Taking out what were small pieces of fish that were already fileted, he prepared a stone bowl filled with slices of limes. As we all watched with anticipation, the pieces of fish were placed on top of the limes in this stone bowl. I guess the look on my face was noticed by the chef.

"I'm cookin' da fish," he said to us. "You see, the fish will cook from the limes in the bowl."

We stood there looking puzzled because there was no flame or hot plate to cook this fish. The only object on the table was this stone bowl now with lime and fish.

"Ah, you look confused," the chef said to us with a slight chuckle in his voice. "The citric acid of the limes will cook this fish right here in this bowl."

Cook this fish, I thought to myself. *Where is the flame?* The chef explained to us that lime is used to "cook" this fish slightly, enough to taste the flavor of the fish. I decided to pass on this fish dish. I am not a favorite sushi, and therefore, there was no way I was about to taste this. However, my clients were waiting patiently to taste this prepared local fish dish, cooked on a bed of lime in an old stone bowl. Photographer Mark was first in line.

As he picked up a piece of this "lime fish" and placed it in his mouth, he said, "Oh my god, these tastes fantastic!"

The others followed suit. They each tried this for the first time and walked away fully satisfied. Me, I said, "Hey, anyone want a bite of my ham and cheese sandwich?"

You can only imagine. The answer was no, thank you. We finished our meal and made our way back onto the tender, which was being used to transport all guests and crew from the pier to the ship. Our day was complete, and I know my clients really enjoyed it because they kept offering praises of thanks and excitement—another end to a fantastic day. As the ship pulled her lines and I watched as the R4 moved away from the dock, I looked up to the sky and said, "Thank you. Thank you for making this day go so well." Next stop is Moorea.

It was approximately eight thirty the following morning. I had ordered room service and was looking forward to starting the day. My breakfast came, which consisted of scrambled eggs, extra crisp bacon, hash browns, and buttered white toast. Coffee was without saying. We were already anchored just outside of the port area. Moorea really had no full pier to speak of. There was no room for any size dock; therefore, when cruise ships arrived, they would anchor out and offer tender service every fifteen minutes. This was a beautiful way to get ashore, the mountains in the distance and the foliage for as far as the eyes could see. I was looking forward to this stop because it would involve inspecting what is known as Motuo, an island not fully established. There are no necessities such as running fresh water, no electricity, no housing or businesses. They are strictly uninhabited small islands. The interesting note is that anyone can claim a Motuo if there are no others on it claiming squatter's rights. This is exactly what *Mystique Magazine* was looking for. His photo shoots can be done as far as his imagination will take it. We would, of course, bring the required and necessary equipment, but the truth of every photograph of these beautiful women will be accented just by the scenery of the shoot.

As we arrived at the pier, we made our way over to where our guide told me he would meet us.

And yes, right on time, introductions were made, and he said to us, "Please, follow me, and I will bring you to your chartered boat."

As we made our way to another pier, we were met by a young man who we were told would be our boat escort and driver. Small introductions were made by all of us, and we all began to board our chartered boat. The boat itself was known as a Boston Whaler—nineteen feet in length with two outboard motors. The boat had a sleek bottom hull, which would allow the boat to cut through the waters, causing the least amount of movement and sway. As I observed each one of my clients make their way into the boat, I could not help but get a feeling that came over me as if I were being warned of something. I could not pinpoint the feeling but knew deep down in the pit of my stomach something was just not sitting well with me. Even with the temperature already in the high eighties this early morning, there was just this feeling of "Hmmm, should I be worried and what was I so concerned with that?" I paused for that slight few seconds. Did it have to do with this boat and its captain, I would ask myself. Whatever it was, I brushed it off as if it could have been just the excitement of heading out into open waters in search of a Motou. All Boston Whaler designs of this size are basically the same. The steering and controls are under a tarp canopy, which is in the center of the boat. This design enables those onboard to move about more freely from bow to stern or stern to bow. Photographer Mark and two others chose to take their seats aft and Mark's assistant, our tour guide, and I took advantage of the bow with enough room to move about.

The waters surrounding most of the islands in Tahiti are calm, with very small waves. The crystal aqua-blue waters were so enticing. I was looking forward to the chance to swim. Most of the islands are surrounded by these incredible rock formations. The difference in the waters from inside and outside of these jetties is night and day.

Where the waters are calm and relaxing, the ocean's water is mighty, as these enormous waves build out at sea and crash with mighty force onto the rocks, only to calm their force. To see these enormous waves and the power of the sea to calm within seconds calm, was amazing to me. Granted, there are numerous locations where the mighty ocean comes all the way to the shoreside. These areas are where one could find many of the world's champion surfers. With huge waves, these areas are a surfer's paradise.

As our whaler made its way, there was a change in the ocean. A Boston Whaler is known for being one of the best boats for riding the waves and whitecaps done properly. Our escort spoke well in English. However, our "captain" spoke very little English. Therefore, our escort was our tour guide. As we would pass some Motuo's, we noticed that there were people on some of them.

"I thought you said that Motuo's are uninhabited," I asked our guide.

"Well, it has been a way of life here forever, our guide told us. Since these small little islands cannot be built on with all the necessities such as running water and electricity, they stay abandoned."

He went on to tell us that it was the law of the land as far back as he could go. Most of the Motuo's we saw, some had what appeared to be families enjoying a day out in the sun and beach as their children were in the ocean or on the sand's edge, playing and building sandcastles.

Our guide went on to explain as he was pointing to one specific Motou, "Here you can see that those people on this island have built themselves a little hut. Look at how their hut was built. Made up of bamboo and limbs with a cover of branches and leaves for their roof."

I could not help but think that if you really need to live, you can do so with your own imagination.

Our ride thus far has really been fine. Our speed was on cue and the captain seemed to be enjoying hearing all of us expressing how much we are enjoying this. As we were approaching what appeared to be a Motuo without any people on it, the boat came to a stop. Our guide picked up the anchor and dropped it overboard.

"Okay, people," he said. "This is as far to the shoreline we go,"

We looked at each other, and I remember Mark's assistant shouting out, "Let's go! I'm in!"

And with that, she and the others jumped out of the boat into this crystal-clear ocean. I followed next and can remember just how wonderful the water felt on my body as I laid on my back and took in every moment of this.

I could not help but think to myself, *Damn, Steve, you're gonna pull this event off! Things are going great!*

Our plan was that while our boat was anchored just offshore, our guide told us that this Motuo would be a great location. It was not a small island nor was it a size that we could not completely walk around in less than ten minutes. My guests were all in agreement that this Motuo would be the one they were interested in. After approximately some forty-five minutes later, we made our way back into the ocean and swam back to meet our boat. This was another huge grand slam. So far, we were batting one hundred percent, and I could not have been any happier. I was thrilled for my client but at the same time, I remember how my adrenaline was flowing at maximum speed. Everyone was busy talking about how they would take advantage of this Motuo. Our guide confirmed that he would secure this Motuo for a specific date. We were set.

"Rather than go back the same way," our guide spoke out. "He told the captain to take us completely around the island of Moorea back to the dock."

Everyone agreed, and we each took the same seats as though our names were on them. As our captain set a course to continue around the island, some of us realized that the boat was going at a faster pace. Some of us spoke out, and I remember Mark's assistant calling out, "Hey! Let's slow this thing down a bit!"

The swells were getting stronger and larger. Any Boston Whaler can cut through waters safely so long as the operator knows how to ride over the white caps and waves. It was not ten minutes later that my life would change so drastically.

I could hear my escort yelling to the captain, "Slow the boat down!"

For some reason, the captain started to take on the waves with a more drastic approach. Every boat operator knows that if you approach and ride a wave, it is best to do so using an angled approach, especially with a whaler. No sooner than the guide said this, the whaler was going directly into a huge swell. As the boat crashed on the ocean's top, both I and the guide were tossed up and out of the boat. It came so fast. Neither one of us was able to secure ourselves. I remember going airborne and just missing the bow's rail. The guide was fortunate because he was able to grab the edge railing and not go out of the boat. Every professional boat operator knows how to handle their boat in all types of conditions. Rather than follow the procedure by pulling back on the throttle and angling the boat's direction, the boat's captain chose to do the opposite and gave full throttle.

One would assume that the captain of a chartered boat would know how to maneuver a Boston Whaler through swells and waves. When that next swell had taken the boat's bow and had it now projecting upward, I knew that was not good. I found myself thrown out from within the bow, then looking down and seeing the boat below me. The captain, not following proper maneuvers, changed my entire life. Falling back down, because of the full throttle, the boat became a rocket and shot directly out of the water, causing the point of the bow to strike me at the lower portion of my spine. The first bounce immediately shot pain from my back immediately down to my toes.

"Oh, my fuckin' back!" I screamed out as I tried to sit up on the seat. What was later told to me was that I had fallen forward, forcing the left side of my face and neck to slam against the boat's siding. I can remember hearing the others telling the guide to call for an ambulance, and they were also deciding where it should meet us. We needed a dock, and they were not easily found. I remember slipping back into unconsciousness. I do not know if it was from the pain or because I hit my head. All I knew was that I could not feel my legs.

The boat finally pulled into a private dock. It seemed we sat there for hours waiting on the ambulance, but in fact, it was less than a few minutes. I was still lying in the bow of the boat when the ambulance arrived. It was through the conversations I heard them saying I may have broken my back. Not that I can fully remember everything that was happening, but I do recall the medics coming into the boat and speaking to me. It was decided that they would attempt to remove me from the boat using a wooden backboard. They explained that they did not want to cause further damage. They were having the hardest time getting the backboard under me completely. From what I do remember, I was secured on the board waist up. They had to use their own manpower with assistance from some of my clients to pull the board up, with me attached. By doing so, they would be able to get the entire board under me for the lift into the ambulance. The pain was excruciating. I could not feel my legs, and I felt myself going into shock.

Not being able to speak with the medics, it was as if I remembered the medics sliding me into the back of an "ambulance." Note that this was not your everyday ambulance. This was more like a station wagon. There were no clips to secure the stretcher while in motion. They relied on their own strength to keep it from sliding around. Mark's assistant rode with me to make sure that I was not left alone on a strange island far from the United States. I was extremely blessed to have had her with me. They said the ride only took about thirty minutes to get us back to the pier. It felt as though it were hours. At first, they wanted to take me to their local hospital which my client profusely said no to. It was odd. All of us were talking about islands and third-world hospitals not more than four days ago. I have traveled the world and know better than to be taken to any local hospital, especially in a third-world environment. Her decision was for them to take me back to the pier, where we would hopefully be met by the ship's doctor, medical staff, and security.

I heard sounds and voices speaking, yet I could not open my eyes. It was as though I was in a trance and could not react. There were bright colors with no real design. The colors were as if someone had just thrown wads of paint onto an exceptionally large canvas. For some reason, I do not believe I saw the color red. As the colors stood out with such brightness, I would remember if such a brilliant color as red would not be there. Yes, there were other shades involving mixes but there was no trace of anything, just red.

As I lay there in shock and severe pain, I gazed up into the sky to concentrate on anything that was taking place. To my amazement, I recalled seeing this formation of a cloud separated from the others in the sky. It was as if this cloud was a perfect circle. Not really recalling anything having to do with clouds or skies, I heard in the distance a voice, not just any voice, but the voice of someone I knew. As I remember looking deep into this cloud, there directly in front of me, was my nanny. Was I really seeing this, or was this just an imagination for which I was hoping? I was completely lost. I recall lying very still for the next few minutes.

There were no other voices I heard around me, just this ever so softly spoken voice that said to me, "Steve, I am here. You are going to be all right. Please do not worry. I will not let you die. I love you, my grandson. I love you very much."

As quick as I saw this image of my nanny, it was gone. The cloud faded back into the other clouds, and she was no more. What just happened to me? Was it that I was in shock, and this never happened? Absolutely not. I was able to see her entire face with her pearl necklace on and matching earrings. Her dress was a medium shade of blue, with white trim along the collar as if it were a doily, crocheted with these small circles and lines. I know what I saw, and I know it was real. But how, I will never understand.

At this point, what I do remember was that photographer Mark's assistant made sure she stayed with me even when I arrived back at the pier. Anything would be better than putting my life in the hands of a third-world hospital, so the choice to return to the ship was fine. It is hard to explain, but I was able to recall almost every portion of what was taking place while I lay there in and out of consciousness and in extreme pain. I remember calling out and saying that I felt extremely nauseous, so I was given an injection into my stomach that was supposed to take the nausea away.

Next thing I knew, the ship's medical staff and ship's doctor decided I needed to be placed into a cocoon pouch so I would not move. Well, I can tell you this: I was not in favor of any pouch, and from my recollection and what was told to me, I was not in favor of being placed in one. It was later told to me. I started screaming my daughter's name. "Rachel! Rachel!" supposedly, I called out. I have tried for years to understand why. Rachel had passed in 1991, yet it was her name I longed for. Was she sending me a sign? Was I about to meet her? What was the message that she was trying to tell me? These are the thoughts even to this day I continue thinking about. I recalled hearing those around me confirming a tender boat was on its way. What I missed was that I never got to thank those from the island who assisted in getting me back to the ship's pier. But I want them all to know my appreciation is as great as my life became.

Once in the ship's hospital, the doctor decided he wanted to take x-rays of my back to ascertain whether there was a spinal cord injury. I was somewhat shocked yet pleased when he reported back that he could not see any breaks, but he felt sure that there was "heavy bruising," and he wanted me to be taken to a land hospital the following morning for better x-rays and an MRI. Since he felt certain there were no breaks, they had me sit in a wheelchair and be taken back to my stateroom, a ride to this day I do not recall, but I was told how I would call out in pain. I do, however, remember my room stewardess. She was a tall blonde and had a great European voice. I believe she was from Slovenia. I know that a steward was sent from the medical facility to assist me in showering since I had not washed off the salt water from our previous swim before the accident. I only hope that I was proper and all went well because I do not remember a damn thing about it. Again, events were told to me later. The shower is something I have no recollection of. Someone made sure I was put into my bed, lying completely flat.

I later found out that I awoke around ten o'clock. You see, I had only been asleep for less than two hours. My head was pounding, and the pain in the left side of my neck was getting worse. It was like a 'thump'. I pressed my stewardess call button, and within minutes, my stewardess was knocking on my cabin door. I received an email from her but did not read it until my healing was close to complete. Truly a beautiful message of prayer. The ship's doctor stopped by my cabin to check on me and was concerned about my head and neck.

He had the ship's guest services already make the necessary arrangements to transport me to the hospital.

I did not have a good night. The pain was getting worse, and my head started to pound as if there were ten men jackhammering at the same time. Finally, I had to call the ship's hospital and see if there was anything they could do for me. The doctor and a nurse came to my cabin within a few minutes to speak with me. It seems that even though the X-rays showed nothing, they felt that I needed direct care, and they had contacted the hospital in Papeete to advise them of my condition. Since the ship was not due to arrive back in Papeete for another two days, it was decided that I would be taken to the small airfield in Moorea and be flown back to Papeete. For some reason, I was under the belief that I would be able to return to the ship; therefore, I left all my belongings in my stateroom, and my stewardess was kind enough to make sure I had documentation of who I was and my passport. I was taken off the ship and wheeled in a wheelchair, not a stretcher, to another medical vehicle where I had to ride in a seated position. The pain was unbelievable. I could not sit still as I felt a crunching sound from my spine. But remember, the X-rays taken aboard the ship R4 showed no breaks.

If anyone looking at me needed to make a quick observation of me, it looked as though I just stepped out of a shower with my clothes on. I was dripping wet. My pain level was off the charts, and I desperately needed water. The driver was also the agent for the ship that met me on the dock. As I said my goodbyes to those crew members who wheeled me onto the pier, I could not help that my clients would not want to complete the full site inspections. As Mark's assistant said goodbye, she told me that they would complete the inspection and had contacted my island contacts. At least I knew that my clients were being taken care of and they would still be able to finish what we had set out to accomplish. Me, I found out then that my next stop was at the airport, and I was to be flown back to Papeete since the hospital there was more prepared to handle serious medical emergencies than Moorea. I asked the driver if the plane was a medical plane and if I would be able to lie down.

"Si, si," the driver said. "You be good there. Si, no problem. Plane already waiting."

I remember Renaissance Cruises gave each passenger a nice wallet where their important documents could be kept. No other clothes or toiletry were packed for me. Everything remained in my stateroom as if I was returning. I do not remember much about the ride to the hospital. I would find myself remembering many times of either falling asleep or losing consciousness due to the severe pain I was feeling.

"You won't need to check in at the counter," the driver said to me. "I drive you to the plane."

Who was I to argue with? As we cleared the airport gate, he was correct; I was taken directly to the plane. It was as if I had chartered this plane solely for myself. The car stopped in front of the steps leading up to the plane's entry. I came to find out the reason was because there was no wheelchair available at this "airport," and they did not want me to have to walk any great distance. As my car door was open, the driver offered me his hand to assist me in getting out of his car. My pain level was off the charts, and my head started to pound with what I felt was the worst headache I had ever experienced. This was not a medical aircraft. This was not an island commercial airline, nor was this a jet. This was a four-prop aircraft with one plus two seats making up the ten rows. I had no choice. I had to get myself to a hospital, and if this was the only way to do it, then that is what I did. As I began my climb up the wide steps to the aircraft, every step brought tears to my eyes. I knew I had to do this and do it well. It was obvious that the ship never had an officer escort me during this ordeal. It was as if once I closed the car door, they were finished. "You're on your own," I thought out loud.

I made my way with the help of the one flight attendant who was kind enough to assist me as I had the hardest time moving my legs. I made it onto the plane and was fortunate that my seat was only one row from the entry/exit door. Again, I kept reassuring myself that my back was not broken. The pain I was feeling was from a bruise. I kept saying this over and over as if I needed to convince myself. I carried myself over toward the seats, enabling me to make myself as comfortable as possible. The taxiing down the runway was unbearable. We must have hit every bump and every hole. The plane's vibration alone frightened me about its safety for flying. Once we were up, the flight attendant did everything she could to make my journey easy. Unfortunately, no matter what position I tried to find, every movement was felt with pain and dizziness. As I looked over toward the window, I could see that we were airborne, and I was finally on my way. As I looked out over the clouds trying my hardest to stay awake, I could still hear the ship's doctor repeating to me over and repeatedly that he did not see any breaks in my X-ray. Yet I knew my body and what I was feeling was not merely a bruise.

I slept through most of the ride even though the flight itself was only forty minutes. Things started to get hazy for me. I have tried desperately to remember actual events, but I had to rely on notes that were kept on my behalf. I imagined the landing was smooth. I opened my eyes when the flight attendant nudged me. "Wake up. Wake up," she said to me. "We've landed here in Papeete."

I tried to focus on what she was saying; however, I personally had no idea what was happening.

I was told later that the gentleman who met the plane on my behalf was the emergency director for all non-Tahitians needing emergency medical assistance. He refused to allow me to just walk off the aircraft, so he demanded that the airport medical staff come with a stretcher to carry me off so as not to cause any further damage to my spine. He was screaming in shock that the ship's doctor sent me alone in this condition.

He had placed one of his business cards in my shirt pocket with a message on the back that read, "If you have any problems, ask someone to call MD911." It was not the traditional 911 call most of the world knows about. This was not calling requesting police, first aid, or even fire. This code was specifically meant for all Americans to gain immediate medical assistance in any hospital in Tahiti.

What I have been able to piece together, I was taken to the hospital in a van-type vehicle. They were able to slide the stretcher into the van from the rear, enabling me to stay flat if there was someone to hold the stretcher in place. I recall opening my eyes at the hospital and recall that I was met by someone in a hospital scrub and a stretcher. Finally, I thought I was in good hands.

"Oh, I'm glad to see you're awake," said the emergency director. "I must go now, but remember, if you are not being treated once inside, call out MD911. Remember, that's the emergency code Americans are to use in case of serious medical emergencies. I must have dozed off again as I do not recall ever saying thank you and goodbye to him.

I awoke in a hallway. It appeared to be inside the hospital corridor because I remember seeing many people all crammed into a small room, waiting to either see a doctor or someone to walk out. Upon opening my eyes and adjusting to the ceiling lights, I noticed that while I was asleep, someone had started an IV in my left arm. Was I truly asleep when this was done or is it that I just could not recall? As I glanced down at my watch, my focus seemed to be getting worse as I was having a hard time focusing in on something…anything. I was able to determine that I had been lying on this stretcher for well over four hours. The hallway was lined with stretchers and patients. It was obvious that there were more sick people here than the hospital could handle. As I tried to get one of the nurses or doctors to stop and speak with me, it was almost impossible.

I recall calling out to them as they passed me by, "Hello. Can you help me, please? Hello?"

No one would stop. The doctors who did stop would pick up my chart to glance at it. None of them spoke with me. Once the chart was looked at, not one of them would answer my questions. I'm sure I was not making much sense since I was going in and out of consciousness. It was now almost five hours, and I was still in the same hallway with the same IV dripping in my arm. I thought back to what the emergency director told me.

I took a deep breath and started calling out, "Call MD911! Call MD911!

Within just a few minutes of my shouts, a doctor came by and introduced himself to me. "Hello, Steven. I am Doctor, and I have been assigned as your caregiver." I tried to find his name but to no avail. He continued with, "I'm going to get you moved shortly into a room. I will meet you there to discuss your condition." This was good news for me. Finally, someone is showing some care here. The doctor also said, "On the way to your room, I'm going to have some X-rays and an MRI taken so I can see what is going on."

"Thank you, Doc," I mumbled, knowing that my words were slurring. I also gave it some thought about this MD911. It seemed to work for me and that was the most important step to take thus far.

Unfortunately, I do not recall the X-rays nor the MRI being done. I do, however, remember being rolled into a room where there was another patient occupying the other hospital bed. The nurses did their best to slide me off the gurney and onto the hospital bed, which I was thrilled to see. At least this bed had somewhat of a true mattress and blankets. The bed was not electric. If I wished to have my head or feet adjusted, I would need to have someone crank the bed.

"Hello, Steven. My name is Donna, and I will be your nurse," she spoke with a beautiful accent as if she were singing every word.

Since I was completely unable to make full sentences, nor could I fully understand what was being said to me, I just lay there, looking up at the ceiling.

"Would you like something to eat?" the nurse had asked me.

As cloudy as my mind was, I was still able to comprehend that something was drastically wrong with me. The pounding of my head and the continuous pain I was feeling took its toll on me. But being so vain, I thought that if I ate anything here, eventually, I would have to move my bowels. However, that was out of the question since I was confined to this hospital bed. There was no way consciously I would succumb to using a bedpan to move my bowels. A bed urinal was no issue, but using a bedpan was not going to happen while I was awake.

"No thanks," I said to her. "I'm not hungry."

As she smiled back, she said in her soft voice, "How about I bring you some fruit and if you wish, you can eat that?"

I simply nodded to her and dozed off to sleep once again.

It was a deep sleep, so I thought. But it was that night that I had some incredible sightings as I lay there, not able to move. As I lay in a hospital bed somewhere in Papeete, my eyes focused on the top of the walls surrounding my room. The walls were painted white, the floors were tiled, and the roof consisted of plywood and tin. The only problem was that the cinderblock used to make the walls did not meet the roof. Therefore, there was a gap on one side. Now I know this sounds far-fetched, but please understand there was no one I reached out to from Papeete that would either confirm or deny this. The worst thing was, there were pigeons, yes, pigeons that perched themselves on top of the cinderblock and used the edge of the rook as their weather protector. Throughout the days and evenings, I swear I could hear the chirping of the pigeons, whether I was conscience or not.

The following morning, two doctors and two nurses awakened me, all standing at the edge of the bed.

"Good morning, Steven," one of the doctors called out with a heavy accent. "Can you hear me?" he said.

My head was still hurting when I woke up, and I could not move my legs freely. I, at once, called out, "What's wrong with my legs? What's wrong with my legs?"

This jolted me so badly that I passed out for a brief period of time. And when I came to, I could overhear the doctors talking among themselves. I was able to understand some of the words I heard, such as back surgery. When they realized I was awake, I assumed it was the lead doctor who began to speak.

"Hello, Steven," the doctor said in a nonmelodic tone.

I am sure he introduced himself and the others to me, but I honestly have no recollection. The only thing I focused on was when I heard him say that I had a severe broken back in a few places and surgery was needed to hopefully repair it. The doctor also told me that I had a severe bump on my head, yet no concussion and possible damage to my jugular vein. As I lay there, helpless, in a hospital bed in some godforsaken country, he said that they planned on taking me into surgery later that day to operate on my spine. I again remembered MD911.

"Call MD911!" I shouted. "Call MD911!"

Once these doctors heard my cries, they did let me know that an American doctor would see me shortly. I lay there for the next few minutes thinking and saying aloud, "What the fuck is going on here? Was I to accept what this doctor said to me and allow them to operate on my spinal cord? No fuckin way," I said aloud.

I again started calling out, "MD911! Call MD911!"

I again found myself going into unconsciousness. I remember being able to hear voices near me, but I could not see them. It was the strangest thing I had ever witnessed. My head was pounding so hard it was as if I was continuously banging a hard-covered book on the side of my head. Not only could I not see them, but I could not even call out. What was wrong with me? Why couldn't I speak to these people standing in front of me, yet I could hear them but could not react? The only thing I do remember at this point was that my head gave off a steady, low tone that was continuous. That was all I was able to relate to.

That evening, another doctor came into my hospital room. Trying to focus for the next few minutes, I heard him say hello, and I opened my eyes.

"Hi, Steven. I'm the MD911 doctor on call here in Papeete. Can you understand me?" I looked at his eyes and blinked my eyes so that I fully understood what he had said. "Don't worry, Steven," he said to me. "I am not going to allow anyone to operate on you here. There has been severe damage done to the lower portion of the spinal cord, as well as a small crack to a vertebra closer to the top of your neck. Because of the severity of your injuries, I feel it is most important to get you back to the States and into a hospital there." As I tried to understand what was being said to me, it was extremely difficult for me to not only understand but simply to understand it all. "Don't worry, Steven," the doctor said to me. "I will arrange everything, but I do need some contact names and telephone numbers."

Once again, from the teachings of my father, I had in my wallet a card listing all important contacts of mine in case of a serious accident, and I was unable to verbally give this information out. Thank goodness, I still had my papers and wallet in my pants pocket with the help of photographer Mark's assistant.

I came to find out that Debra, sorry…my third wife, had received a call directly from the ship on the day I was taken off and sent to a hospital. She had asked the ship for the details of the accident and where I was. The worst of all messages ever heard, but this officer just said, "Your husband was hit by a boat in Moorea, and he was flown to a hospital in Papeete."

No other information was said. The ship's officer never gave her any further instructions or contact information. Debra did say that the ship would be calling her back with further details. That was the end of phone calls from Renaissance's R4 to my wife.

The smartest thing Debra could have done was to contact my father and mother. Thank goodness, she had the sense to do that. At the same time, the American doctor, now in charge of my case, had contacted Debra back in Nashville, Tennessee. The doctor was explaining that I would need to be medivac from Tahiti back to the United States. My condition was severe, and my consciousness was in question.

"He must be transported strapped in a gurney so there would be no major movement of his body, along with IVs to keep him stable. A nurse would also have to escort him on the aircraft to control his vitals during the fight."

A lot needed to be arranged before I could ever leave this hospital. To make the next couple of days bearable, the American doctor prescribed medications that I continued to take as I lay there.

Later that very day, the American doctor came to see me and explained that he personally had been conversing with my father and not with Debra. Seems that Debra told the doctor to speak with my father since he would be the one making the arrangements to get me home. Strange, I thought afterward. Here was my "wife" pushing her responsibilities on someone else. Therefore, all remaining communication was going to be overseen by my father. I felt much more secure knowing that my parents were now involved. I was to be leaving the following morning via medivac. It was explained to me that I would be flying on Air Tahiti Airline. Because of the enormous size of the plane, they would remove a section of seats in the rear of the plane for a stretcher to be used and secured in place, as well as an area for the traveling nurse. I could only say okay since my entire life was in this doctor's hands. I had to place my trust in him. As he was leaving my hospital room, he turned to me and said, "Try and get some sleep, Steven. I will see you in the morning."

Again, that evening, I was awoken by the sounds of the pigeons. Please, I'm sure some of you are now laughing, but I am being as honest as I can. I know I saw and heard pigeons from my hospital bed. In fact, tonight there was a heavy rain falling in Papeete so almost the entire wall had pigeons from one end to the other. When a nurse came in to check on me, I know I asked her about these pigeons, and from what I recall, she confirmed that they like to sit under shade and out of the rainy times.

I was going on my third day without solid food. I was kept only on liquids because, even in my state of mind, I was not going to use a bedpan under any circumstances. If I was somewhat coherent, I would still make final decisions for myself. So I thought.

That evening, as I lay in my bed, I could not help but look up and notice an odd design where the ceiling and walls would normally meet. I cannot confirm, nor was there anyone I was able to contact to inquire about what I still believe was the hospital room I was in. I clearly heard noises as if there were birds in my room. Not just any bird; it was the distinct sound of pigeons. Not one mind you, many pigeons perched on top of the painted cinderblock walls. As I gazed up to the tops of the walls, it was visible that the roof of the building was pitched to extend out past the walls, allowing rain to run off and collect in rain barrels located outside the walls of this hospital. Most buildings I came to find had the same design. However, I found myself still worrying about why my legs were still numb. I was now able to slightly move my legs in this bed that has become more than just a hospital bed to me. I felt secure as I lay there with the side rails up to protect me from sliding off. Hell, I did not have the strength to even try such as fete. As I sit writing this book, I am still puzzled about the pigeons. Later, on my final evening, I was told by a nurse that arrangements were almost complete, and they were hoping for a departure in the morning.

Early the following morning, I apparently had a major setback. I was told a few hours later that there was something seriously wrong with my jugular vein. If my neck was in a certain position, my jugular vein would stop the blood flow and cause me to have these episodes of unconsciousness. It was as if the vein was being pinched. Because of this new concern, my departure was delayed by at least one day. I remember asking someone if I could call my wife and parents. It was time they heard my voice and for me to hear theirs.

The doctor replied, "Yes, that would actually be something good for you."

I called Debra first. I do not recall much of our conversation. I seemed to have been on the phone for a long period of time, but in the truth of things, my time with her ended as she told me to call my father since he was handling the details of getting me back to the States. I thought that made sense…at the time.

I watched as the doctor called my parents' phone number. When it began to ring, he quickly brought the phone up to my ear just in time for me to hear my mother's voice say, "Hello."

"Mom," I said softly, as if it was taking all my breath. "Mom, it's me, Mom."

One thing that I could hear my mother say over anything else being said was, "Oooo! It's Stevie! Stevie's on the phone!"

I do not know if it was her pitch or just her voice, but no matter what my mother would say to me, I knew I had her attention.

"Bernie! Bernie!" I could hear her yelling out. "Quick! Stevie's on the phone!"

In a deep and concerning tone, I can hear my father say to me on the phone, "Son, are you alright? Steve, talk to me."

I knew my voice was going to crack, followed by the flow of my tears as I gained enough strength to say, "Pop, please get me outa here. I wanna go home."

Unfortunately, that was the last time I spoke to either my mother or father from the hospital. As I felt my eyelids start to close, there was a feeling that came over me that I had not felt before. I felt as if I was now inside a tunnel, floating midair with nothing holding me up. I felt a calm come over me, and that was the last time I had any recollection of that hospital. That is, not counting on those hospital pigeons, right?

I felt as though this free-fall had colors, too. There were shades of beige, moods of blues, bright reds, and then a mix of pale blues and greens. I had no control of anything. In fact, if this is what it is like when one is about to crossover, I was in it.

I do not really remember anything that happened that day. I know there were doctors in to see me. I felt them. I felt their presence in the room. I heard their voices talk back and forth but I could not make out what any of them were saying. It sounded like gibberish. When I tried to make any movement in the bed, I felt as though there was nothing to move. I felt nothing when I thought of my legs moving. It was nothing. No signal. I tried to move my arms down toward my legs so my hands could rub them. Nothing. Nothing at all. I felt myself just lying there, knowing what I wanted to do but could not. What was happening to me? But it became relevant within those few seconds that I was not feeling all the pain I had been feeling for the last few nights. I was breathing with no problems. Shallow, but breathing. I then focused on the fact of that emergency director who was now standing over me, calling out my name.

"Steve! Hey Steve! Can you hear me?" I felt him there and heard his words, but I could not answer him.

As much as I tried, I could not utter a word. I remember trying to tap my fingers to get his attention, but nothing. Not a damn thing was I able to do. Finally, I could hear him speak to the other doctor that was in the room. Their conversation was something I was not able to remember. I don't even know if I was even a part of it.

I then felt my bed start to move and heard someone say, "You can bring the gurney in. He's unplugged."

I then felt my body being raised by a sheet and slid over onto a gurney. As I stared directly upwards, I felt IVs again being hooked to the existing ports that the hospital left in. It was the oddest feeling that I just cannot understand even to this day. I felt myself being wheeled through the corridors of the hospital and then loaded into an ambulance. I knew everything that was going on, but I could not respond to anything. This is as vivid to me today as it was back then. I fully recall being taken out of the ambulance on the gurney and being placed inside what I would say was some type of lift. I felt standing right next to me was the nurse and another gentleman who I later found out was assigned to making sure I made it through the flight and safely back into the United States.

I was in a very strange time. I wish I could offer some insight as to the feelings and the experiences I had during this time, but it is far more difficult now for me to find any closure to this. All I can say is that it had me in a different zone—a zone like no other. There was nothing that I could pinpoint, nor did I have a good sense about it.

I can recall being lifted onto a plane by use of a luggage cart, able to lift a gurney in length, and for some reason, I heard voices around me discussing the method of attaching the gurney once I was in place. The sun was extremely bright that morning. I felt it through my skin.

A voice called out, "The patient has tears running down his face! He's feeling an emotion!"

I found it very strange how I can remember certain events during this ordeal, yet I offered no response. The doctor's report showed that the patient (I) had an episode prior to being loaded into the plane where my muscles throughout my body tensed up. My fingers, they said, were contorted as well. It only lasted a few short minutes, but during that time, I cannot describe it without this sounding odd, but my eyes were now wide open, and I could see up in the sky, a cloud—not just any cloud but like the cloud I had seen several years ago. It was my nanny.

Her vision, her voice, calmly said to me, "It's okay, Steven. I'm right here with you, and it's not the time yet for us to meet. I love you, my grandson. Now go. Your parents are anxious to see you."

Within seconds, she was gone, and my muscles all relaxed as did my fingers.

I wish I was able to remember the return flight. The initial flight from Los Angeles to Tahiti took a little over eight hours so I knew that this flight was to be long. There were times during the flight when I was able to hear what was around me, but again, I could not respond in either movement or voice. I could feel myself tensing up as I tried so desperately to make a sound…any sound. There was one time I remember when I apparently awoke and screamed out in extreme pain. As quick as my episode appeared is as quick as it went away. I know that the nurse was standing over me, injecting something into one of the IV lines. Within seconds, I assumed I fell into that deep, mysterious zone where I thought I was sleeping once again, pain-free. I felt myself releasing the tension that had built up in that short amount of time.

I awoke to find myself being wheeled across the tarmac of an airport. I could not pick my head up because they had a soft brace that went around my neck, keeping it positioned straight. I did see my traveling nurse walking next to me. The sky was filled with the sounds of other aircraft engines. As I lay there, I felt the movement of the gurney across the pavement as it was not the smoothest of surfaces, but less, I was being taken somewhere. I had no idea where I was. I recall someone saying we were at Los Angeles International Airport, and I was being transferred to another medic jet.

"Mr. Steve," I heard my traveling nurse say. "It's my time to leave you. You are in good hands now. My prayers are with you and stay blessed."

I felt her hand in mine. She squeezed my hand in hers, and I did my best to move my fingers. The gentleman who traveled with us also said his goodbye as new faces appeared next to me.

"Hi, Steve!" one of the men said to me. "If you can hear me, please say something or squeeze my finger." I felt it immediately. "Steve, we're here to take you home, back to Nashville, Tennessee," the man said to me. "We have our medivac jet ready for you. I felt tears running down my face. I was back on American soil, and I was being taken care of by an American medic.

This medic then introduced the other pilot and nurse to me. Again, I could hear them but just could not respond. Loading me first onto another med-vac's gurney, I was then lifted inside. Once inside, it was obvious I was in a true medical aircraft, equipped with all the required and necessary equipment in case of most medical emergencies. I recall taking off as the jet's engines propelled us upward into the sky. Within the next few minutes, I could start feeling the pain meds begin to do their due diligence via the IV, and it was no time until I dozed off.

It was sometime during the flight that apparently something was going on, and alerts began to sound off. There was nothing I could do for myself. At this point, I have no recollection of the remaining flight. Those alarms became faint sounds, and eventually, they went away, or did I? My experiences were just about to take a turn. In what direction, I had no idea.

I overheard the men talking in the jet but could not make out what was being said. I knew and felt that I was in that state-of-mind like I was in during my hospital stay in Tahiti and the transport from hospital to aircraft. I could hear things around me, but I could not answer or make any movement. I just lay there, trying everything to get them to hear me.

Nothing! I was able to hear the nurse call out, "Steve! Can you hear me? Steve, blink your eyes or move your finger! Steve! Steve!"

As hard as I tried, I could make a sound. I could not even move a finger. I just lay there, staring up at the ceiling. I then overheard the pilot speaking with someone over the radio. He kept calling back to the nurse, "Touchdown is in ten minutes. Please secure the patient for landing." I felt myself calling out.

"I can hear you! Can you hear me?" I repeated this twice both times, having the same response.

Nothing. I could not sound back to them. It was pointless. The next thing I knew, the jet had landed, and I was being transferred to a helicopter that medivac me to a Nashville Hospital.

Once we landed, I was then placed on a hospital gurney and wheeled toward the emergency doors. The only voice I was able to hear was that of my mother. Everything else was garbled, but my mother's voice stood out.

"Here comes Stevie!" I was able to hear her say.

As the emergency doors swung open, I felt myself being wheeled in, but that was all. I do not remember anything else.

It was now weeks since I arrived in the hospital. I opened my eyes to find Debra, my son Nathan, and my mother all in the room surrounding my bed.

As I tried to focus, I called out in a very soft-spoken voice, "Hi, guys. Mom, Deb, Nathan, can you hear me?"

I remember them each looking at me with tears in their eyes. My mother grabbed my hand and brought it to her face for one of those motherly kisses. Debra had my other hand. My son made his way to my side and leaned over and gave me a kiss on my forehead. I was too weak to have any sort of a conversation, but I knew that I was finally home, back in my city of Nashville. I came to find out that the family visit was cut short because I was no longer able to stay because I kept going into unconsciousness.

Days have gone by, and I was seen by numerous doctors and specialists. It was obvious that something was wrong. My legs were still extremely numb, and my pain was extremely high. I was on a morphine drip now, which I was able to control every thirty minutes.

I was still having setbacks. I did find out that I had sustained serious breaks in my lower vertebrae as well as cracked vertebrae close to my neck. My spine had been damaged. They felt that I would heal from the large bump on my head, but it would take many months for the healing process to be effective. I also sustained damage to my jugular vein. Damage enough to tell me that caution is now serious, and I must always be alert to the causes that could affect me throughout life. They felt that my condition would not allow for surgery because additional damage may occur, leaving no one wanting to take on that responsibility.

"Doc, I still cannot move my legs freely," I said during his consultation that day. "Please, there must be something that can be done. What's the problem?"

Once again, I could not stay awake. My questions were never answered. I again fell into this sleep zone where I could hear but not respond. What was causing this? I asked myself time after time after time.

It was days later, and I was still listed in serious but stable condition, and yes, I still could not freely move my legs. Without remembering, I was now in a half-body cast. I still find it hard that I do not remember when this was done to me. Was I that drugged? Did I speak at all during this? I had a sleuth of questions but would never push the issue with anyone. The next few days, I recall being taken for an assortment of tests, X-rays, and procedures. I really was not feeling well overall. My alertness was as if I were on a weekend drinking binge. The pain was still severe both in my back and neck. That headache was still giving me problems, and that may have been why I was not able to really focus on anything. All I knew was I controlled the pain meds. My thumb had become professional. I was able to click my button quickly. The problem was once I clicked it, I could not do it again until thirty minutes.

My father had flown to Nashville from Florida within the last few days, and I had seen him, but I just do not remember it. Hours ran together as did days. I had little recollection of who came to see me and when. As the days went on, I was able to answer questions that were being asked of me. Maybe not in great length, but at least I stayed awake for more than a few minutes.

I believe it was that evening when I heard someone call out, "Knock, knock!" Since I was not able to turn my head toward the door, I had to wait for them to walk in and come next to my bed. To my surprise, a dear friend for many years was standing next to the bed.

"Damn, Steve," he called out. "What the fuck happened to you, brother?"

A friend for many years and still considered one of my best friends as of this writing, Mike Lawrence, was standing next to me. It was kept a secret what happened to me so seeing someone not related to me was a complete surprise. I felt a smile come over my face for the first time in weeks.

"Holy shit, Mike! Look what I did." I spoke.

Mike was moving to the other side of the bed where he could set his things on. It was easier for me to move my eyes to the left than right, so I was fine with the move.

We spoke for a few short moments. I remember Mike pulling out a box of saltine crackers from the small duffel bag he had.

As Mike was bringing the box closer to me to see it, he said, "Enjoy the crackers. Open the bottom container first."

I looked at him and thought to myself, *Does he want me to eat them now?*

"Awe, hell, Steve," Mike said. "I'll have a cracker with ya!"

As I was really in no condition to try to open something, Mike chose to do the honors. As he pulled out the package, I could not help but notice something else at the bottom of the package. I gave a weak chuckle to remember it to this day. My buddy brought me a nicely rolled joint and a lighter.

"Here ya go, Steve. Here's something that will take any pain away. Let's enjoy it now!"

So right there, as I lay in a hospital bed, my best friend lit the joint. He took the first hit with a deep inhale and brought the joint to my lips. I did my best to inhale.

"Ahhhh," my response was.

I think we were able to each take one more inhale before he put it out and sprayed the hospital room with a canned fragrant. No more than three minutes, a nurse came into the room and immediately asked questions.

"What is that smell?" she said sternly. "What was burning in here?" I could not do anything except look up at the ceiling. I started clicking my morphine button as if I was in a race. "I believe it's time to say good night to your visitor," she said sternly.

After she walked out of my room, Mike and I both gave a quiet chuckle. "Man, brother, thanks for coming to see me," I said. "It meant the world to me."

No sooner than Mike left, than I drifted off to sleep.

Why is it that hospital nurses and staff think we, as patients, enjoy being woken at five in the early morning to have our temperature taken? Do they think that taking a pill at 5:00 a.m. is any different from taking it at eight? I have never been able to understand that, and back then, I had no idea when it was daytime or nighttime. Later that morning, Debra came to the hospital. I thought to have a pleasant visit, but instead, I remember her being extremely upset. Just by the way she came into my room, it was obvious that this was not going to be an easy visit. She did not prove me wrong.

"I can't keep up with some bills," Debra said in a nasty tone. "I need you to take care of this."

So unless I was mistaken, I was lying in a hospital with a severe broken back, a head injury, and concern with my jugular vein. There was no good morning. There was no "How did you sleep?" It was a complete disrespect to me as I lay there completely helpless. The next thing I knew, this lunatic of a wife stood next to my bed, ranting and waving papers at me yelling, "You better take care of these!"

At that moment, a nurse rounded the corner and was standing in my doorway, witnessing what was about to happen. At this point, Debra was standing next to me bedside. Debra smacked me on top of my head (since she was not able to get my face due to the halo). I recall the nurse coming to my aid, and I knew that my wife would be denied entry to the hospital from that point on. Here I am, lying in a bed, completely helpless. It turned out this was apparently the start of the downward spiral of our marriage.

The doctors and surgeons came into my room later that day when my parents were there. Apparently, by this time, I had taken another turn for the worse. Was it due to my wife's behavior or cause or something else? What was eventually told to me by my parents had to do with the decisions that were being made at the time for my welfare and prognosis. Months later was when this part of my rehabilitation was told to me. To this day, I am so grateful that it was my parents who took over my welfare, and my former wife was no longer handling anything pertaining to my wellness.

My parents were told that the condition of my spine was not good. Apparently, the angles of the breaks and their severity left me with two options. The first being full surgery on my spine, followed by a full body cast for a period of twelve months. No guarantees. The second option was a small incision in my back to realign the damaged vertebrae and fit me with a plastic and removable torso shell, which I would wear for the next four to six months, all depending on how quickly I healed. The only good thing I saw in this plastic torso was that it reminded me of a gladiator. I was wearing my "suit of armor." It was important to note that as my father and mother were told these two options, they completely ruled out option one. Knowing the severity of that type of surgery with no guarantees made the choice easy. But there was one final part for option two. As I listened with bated breath, my father told me that I would have to be put into a self-induced coma, which would stop me from moving.

My spine had to stay in one position and one position only: perfectly still. Just listening to this even after the fact, brings back everything, well, sort of. I can literally picture the boating accident and many of the incidents that followed. I may not have been coherent during some of the times, but my mind took into almost every aspect up until my Nashville hospital stay. I also recalled the time that I knew I saw and spoke with my Nanny. I can actually tell you what the conditions were at those times and what she was wearing. I have always been concerned talking about these episodes because (as most would) I tend to think I was merely dreaming all of this. But again, I can tell you that they were real times, not dreams or wishes. I knew she was with me, holding my hand tightly so that I would not be alone.

They kept me in the hospital for another week as they wanted to make sure that I was leveling out. They had started a few IV drips, with one being used to take me to another level. I felt higher than the clouds. At the end of the week, my parents were then given another choice.

"There's nothing else we can do for Steve here," the doctor told my parents.

The choices for his rehabilitation are transporting Steve to a medical facility where he would stay there in his state of mind, or he could be transported home as long as there was one room in the house that could be redesigned as a sterile location and a nurse to over-see his daily progress.

So now my parents were once again making what they felt was the best decision for my rehabilitation.

"Steve," my father said to me during our lengthy discussion, "there was no way I was going to allow them to put you in this rehab hospital. I would have been afraid that when you woke up and looked at your surroundings, you would completely have lost it. I did not want that to happen to you."

My father explained to me that the second option was doable if the room in my home was basically converted to look like a hospital room, completely sterile. The most important task was I would have a registered nurse and aide to watch over my vitals day and night. The required machines would be ordered including a hospital bed.

So my parents had the room painted white, and couches were moved so that the bed and machines would have ample space. In fact, the couch was moved in front of the closed-off fireplace so that the evening nurse would have a place to lie down next to me. I was thankful that this room was large enough. The chairs remaining were all covered with white sheets so that the room was as germ-free as possible.

The day I was being transported by ambulance to my home is still a blur to me. I do not remember leaving the hospital or the actual ride.

The only thing I recall was hearing my mother's voice calling out, "Stevie's home! Stevie's home!"

I recall the ambulance door opening and the voices of the medics as they maneuvered the gurney along my backyard patio. Even though I was not fully awake, I was still able to see that the French doors to my den were open, and I was carried up the two steps, bringing the gurney alongside the house hospital bed. I could not react, but I was able to hear and see. They said there were times, many times, that my eyes were never closed shut. They said my eyelids would partially open so I would assume those were the times I was able to comprehend events around me, but I could not respond in voice or movement of my arms and hands.

I felt being lifted onto my hospital bed and felt the hands of others on me, strapping down IV lines, placing the tube on my nostrils giving me the oxygen that I apparently needed. I recall seeing my father's face as I was brought in. Just thinking about the anxious expression he had on his face brings tears to my eyes even today. I was filled with tears of happiness, and I am sure with emotions. Being home, no matter what state of mind I was in, I felt it. I felt the protection I now had.

Starring up at the ceiling, I made every effort to move my eyes in the direction I would hear a voice. I knew that my parents were there. I heard Debra's voice and that of someone I thought to be my (sister), Toni. I knew that the medics were still present as they were explaining the details of every machine. It was amazing to me because I felt my presence but could not respond. It was as if I was trapped inside. I later found out that there was an intern also there to explain my medications to my family members but, more importantly, to the nurse who was going to be there for the first twelve-hour shift.

I was very lucky to have a day nurse that was more than just a nurse to me. She was the mother of Lynn Dunn, operations manager for my company at the time.

My mother had asked Lynn, "Would your mother would be interested in helping out?"

I was very much blessed because Myra was more than just a registered nurse. She helped in my rehabilitation and was my sound board later down the road. Myra gathered with the others as they listened to what the medic was saying. Again, as hard as I tried, I could not make a sound. I know I was in a sleeping state of mind, but I could not understand why I was able to hear but could not respond. This was the start of the next level of rehab for me.

Once I had settled in and the ambulance staff and medic had left, I remember hearing my mother's voice. I felt a warm rush come over my face, and I remember catching a tear as it came over my upper lip and touched my tongue. I knew I was crying, and I felt that it was due to the emotional day of finally coming home and knowing that I was still alive. As my mother wiped away the tears from my face, that day was the start of healing, and I was not going to let anything stop this. A warmth came over me then. I knew I was now being automatically fed the morphine through my drip. Even to this day, I can recall that specific feeling. It was a never-ending fall. A fall that can only be described as a calm, relaxed feeling where your pulse becomes much slower but still strong. Your heartbeat becomes slower and holds to that pace. That is the best way I can describe this slow fall. I was not able to have twenty-twenty vision but the best way I can describe it was that I could focus on things close to me. If you were standing on the side of the bed and partially leaning over me, I would be able to see your face. If you were standing directly in front of me, I could not vividly see your entire body or anything near you. It was as if there was a lens, and the only clear picture was the person speaking. I do recall going from face to face if there were others next to my bed. Yet as hard as I tried to whisper one word, I just could not bring myself to do it. Again, the same unanswered question would appear, and again, I would have no answer. Was this how one feels when in a coma, or was this something that nothing could be related to its cause? Was I ever so deep in unconsciousness that I had no full control over my mind and body? It made me question for years as to what would allow me to be in the form of unconsciousness. I was simply floating. My space had no bottom, and I could virtually see upwards for as far as my sight would allow. Floating endlessly as I tried desperately to be heard.

Yet another episode with reference to my then-wife, Debra, my mother brought to my attention months later that they were collectively given instructions on my care. One of the most important was to massage my legs and feet so that the blood circulation would flow without causing damage. A simple task, one would think. Granted, I was wearing those pulsating socks that would continuously create movement in my ankles and feet; however, getting Debra to help with my circulation seemed out of the question. I remember how I felt during these hand massages. It was as if I could feel the blood flowing in my veins. It is important to remember that during this, I was not alert for any amount of time. I was in this state where my medication would have me down every twelve hours. At which time, I would be able to orally take some of my medication and somewhat speak even though it was for a very short amount of time. It was still difficult for me to do this for any long period. The pills would be taken, and the drip would continue, and off I would go, deeper each time.

The machines that I had in my homemade care room consisted of some type of breathing machine, oxygen tanks, IVs, and a machine that was able to record all my vitals. One thing that was installed was a video camera that was connected somehow to someone's cellphone at the hospital so that they were able to view not only me but the vitals on that one machine.

It was now sometime in early September. After being here for weeks, my father chose to return to his home in Florida. My mother, on the other hand, chose to stay, finding out months later she stayed because she just did not trust Debra. And rightfully so.

Again, relying on firsthand knowledge, my mother, a few years later, told me a story that happened during my comatose state involving Debra. I had a difficult time falling back into my sleep zone this one early morning. I had been woken up by the nurse as they had started a therapy program by having me move my feet. This was to keep the blood circulating after they removed those two sleeves that vibrate so your blood is constantly flowing.

Months later, "Steve," I heard my mother say to me as she began the story. "It's important for you to know everything that took place in your house once you came home." I just looked at her with a puzzled expression. I never had to say a word to her. She already knew that I was completely focused on her, and no matter what was going to be said by her, it was okay. It truly was okay.

One early morning, I was awakened hearing my mother's voice.

"What are you doing?" she said in a stern tone.

She was firmly speaking to Debra, who was standing on the side of my hospital bed, closest to my head. My head was finally cleared of any devices and bandages. Oh, I forgot to mention, that Debra was holding in both of her hands a pillow. Not the size of a sofa pillow, but it was a bedroom-size bed pillow.

My mother again asked her, still in a stern voice, "What are you doing with that pillow?"

My mother then looked over to me still flat on my back with nowhere to go. "Oh, I was just fixing his pillow," Debra told her.

Since I was relying solely on my mother's memory, I never once believed she was not telling the truth. My mother and I had a special bond, and I knew what she was saying was true to the facts. Now I am not saying she was about to place the pillow over my face, but there was no reason for her to make any adjustments to my pillow. I was sleeping. It was becoming more obvious to my nurse, parents, and others that she was already furious that I had been in a horrible boating accident on the other side of the world! Debra was heard saying that she was too young to be "strapped" down right after being married. She felt it was unfair to her. Nothing about me.

Interesting story: I was told that on September 8, Debra had told my mother and the nurse that she had to go to New York on business. Debra was employed as one of the licensing agents for Broadcast Music Incorporated (BMI), a job that I got for her through my contacts with executives at BMI.

So my mother told me that the following morning, Debra flew from Nashville to New York. It is important to note that my condition, as severe as it still was, Debra would not have canceled her business trip. It was obvious which was more important to her.

The prescription for putting me in and out of the "ozones" usually kept me in an induced coma now for almost twenty hours a day. Others would tell me I would slowly come off the medication, usually at six o'clock each morning. My short time awake, I remember that I could not really focus my eyes or my mind. It was enough for me to just have my eyes open and say a few words. Everyone told me when I was researching for this book, my three favorite words were, "What da fuck!" not directing them to anyone or anything specific; it was just my daily quote. It still sometimes comes across my mind because I still say the same quote to this day. Funny how certain things stay with you.

The most horrific day in American history took place as I lay in a hospital bed, hoping that my spine was healing properly. Once again, I fall into this specific space in my mind, where it repeats itself. I have no movement at all. My breathing is steady, my heart is quietly beating, and my breathing is even. Once again, my eyes were ever so opened slightly, and I felt that I was back to the initial time in the hospital where I could hear people speaking, whether physically in the room or on the television, but I could not reply either in words or movement. The frustration of this I cannot imagine since I am not able to recall everything.

I believe it was a morning news show that the nurse had on the television. Months later, I was told by my day nurse, Myra, that she had *The Today Show* on the television. Flashing across the screen, she said the words, "WE INTERRUPT THIS PROGRAM WITH A SPECIAL NEWS ANNOUNCEMENT." Already sleeping now for over two hours, I was already deep back in my comatose state of mind. There was to be no movement from me for the next twenty-two hours. Remember, when I explained this previously, nothing changed. When I was drugged and motionless, I could still hear people around me; however, there was no response from me.

I do not remember anything about World Trade Center Tower One or its collapse. I did hear Myra yell out, "Oh my god! The World Trade Centers are collapsing!" I can still see to this day the second plane crashed into Tower Two. I know it is hard to understand how I would be able to see anything, let alone this horrific event. I still can see the plane approaching and striking the tower followed by huge flames and smoke. Myra told me later that my entire body began to shake uncontrollably to the point where she had to come over to me and give me another injection just to calm me down and put me further to sleep. I had no recollection of this incident until mid-December.

Going from the accounts of others, my mother had received a call from Debra. My mother said all she was able to understand was that there was a plane crash, and she was two blocks away from ground zero in a hotel.

"All flights have been canceled, and I can't get out of here!" she was screaming into the telephone. My mother made a few suggestions to her.

One being, "Debra, first, calm down. You're safe. We can figure something out. Just stay in your hotel because the streets are not safe right now."

My mother suggested renting a car and driving home. "Start calling all of the rental companies."

A couple of months later, I was told that Debra met some others in the BMI New York office who had company cars and that she could share a ride with one of them. So she came home from New York. One would think she would be happy to finally be home. That was not the case.

"Steve, all she did when she got home was blame you for what she just went through," my mother said to me. "It was your fault that she went through such turmoil."

"Why wasn't he up and taking care of me?" Debra shouted to my mother. "He should have made sure I was okay!"

"So what did you say to her?" I asked my mother.

"What else could I say to her, Steve? She's a selfish bitch!"

She refused to allow Debra to continue with her attacks. Even Myra was shocked at how Debra was acting.

Like I said, I really do not remember much of what happened to the towers until December, when I had some thoughts of mind. I lost people I knew. Some work at Cantor Fitzgerald. One of my closest friends who worked with me on the cruise ships was a man named Richard Cudina. Ritchie was a funny guy. A true comedian at heart, Ritchie was my assistant cruise director aboard Home Lines' *Doric*. I think of Richie often. We were never close after he left the ships, but we would talk to each other on the phone every few months.

September passed, and it was now October. I was able to watch the weather outside from the large bay window on the side of my hospital bed. The trees were starting to change their colors, and they said the evenings were cooling down from the summer's heat. I was becoming more alert as time went on. I was now receiving physical therapy every other day. Some days were better than others. When the therapists would push me to my limits, I let them know under no circumstances that I was not enjoying my workouts. I can remember a young therapist who came by that I released a wrath of words and comments that would make a sailor stand up. I will never forget her response after I finished my rant.

"Are you finished, Steve?" she said to me in her soft tone. "Is there anything else you want to say, Steve?"

She had me every time. I would just have to look at her young smile and chiseled body, and I would slowly sink back into my bed.

"You know I don't mean anything I say, right?" I said to her with this innocent smile on my face.

She would just smile back and say, "Okay, lift that leg."

At the end, she was one of the best therapists I ever had.

I recall when my older brother Chuck came to 'visit' me while I was still heavily sedated. With the very short hours, I was able to visit with family and friends. My brother stayed (not at my home) at a nearby hotel. I thought that was strange after the fact since my home had extra bedrooms. Needless to say, he spent a couple of hours at my home, which I guess I should be thankful for that he showed some form of sympathy for me. I know he only came to Nashville for two days, and on the second day, I recall he and our mother talking secretively not more than four feet from my bed. The whispers were obvious, but at the time, I had more important things on my mind.

My wonderful mother decided it was time for her to go back home to Florida to be with her husband. I, too, thought the same thing since she had been with me for so many months it was time for her life to go back to normal. "You take care of my boy," she said to Myra as she was getting ready to leave. "I'll come back for any reason. Just call me," she said as her voice began to choke up. We were both upset about her departure but knew it was time. Like it was yesterday, I can still hear my mother say, "If she" (referring to Debra) "acts up, you just call me, and I'll be on the next flight."

With that, we kissed and said our goodbyes. Remember, my mother and I had a fantastic relationship. We would and never have let each other down.

It was midweek, and I was not feeling like I had the last week. I was sleeping more than I had been. Maybe it was because I was now having therapy to teach me to walk again. My legs were like rubber, and I needed help when I first stood and tried to walk with a walker. I could not believe that the accident caused such a negative reaction to me. Going to the bathroom became a twenty-to-thirty-minute ordeal. And that was just getting me from the bed down the hallway and into the guest bathroom. My legs could hardly walk. It was as if I was taking baby steps and learning how from the beginning. But at least I was now able to get to the bathroom. To answer your question now, during my time in my own home, I felt more comfortable using a bedpan and had no choice. But I felt it was on my terms.

I now only had a day nurse since I no longer needed around-the-clock care. Myra would finish up at five o'clock, and with Debra coming home after work, I would only be alone for a short time. My son, Nathan, was sixteen at the time of my accident, and he had his permit to drive. He had been staying here at my home during these past months. His mother lived only a few miles away, so it was great having my son here when needed, whether it was to help me with my therapy, just sitting and keeping me company, or taking me to my doctor's appointments. I was able to count on him.

Nathan and I had a very strong bond between us from when he was a baby. When we returned home from touring, we were inseparable. The chores of taking care of a baby came easy to me. Much more than Nathan's mother. These times, whether it was diaper changing, new foods, or new ventures, are the things that make up one's memory. That was why I never made any negative comments about having Nathan with me. I loved every minute of them. No matter if it was to the store or to join me on part of Billy Ray Cyrus's tour, my son was right there with me.

As Nathan got older, I could see that he was growing into a mature young man. Unfortunately, there were your typical teenage speeding tickets and just your juvenile nonsense that kept coming up, but overall, I felt that he would outgrow it. There was also a serious theft charge that I had to use my influence to get him out of. It worked, and hopefully, that was the last of his sticky fingers. I believe it was. There are many more stories regarding Nathan throughout the reading. In time, you will see the outcome of what was to be or not to be. That became the question and the answer.

It was a Friday afternoon, and Myra was getting ready to leave. "I think I'll wait until Debra gets home," Myra said. "I just want to make sure she's here."

I looked over to her and said, "Myra, it's all good. It's Friday. Go ahead and leave. She'll be here soon."

After being a bit hesitant, I convinced her to leave and said I would see her the following morning. As she was leaving, Nathan came over for a short visit. He had said that he was on his way over to his friend Brian Lavender's house for the weekend but wanted to check on me. We had a quick visit, and he was on his way. I knew I would not be home alone too much longer, so I felt good not making him stay until Debra got here.

As I lay in my hospital bed, it was now going on at almost seven o'clock. I was starting to get worried and upset that I hadn't heard from Debra at all. Not even a call saying she was going to be late. No text either. My concern grew when the time turned to eight o'clock and then ten o'clock. Still no Debra and no phone call. I had my cell phone next to me but noticed that the house phone was put back on its cradle, and that was too far for me to reach. Thank goodness, I had a portable urinal container next to my bed. Since I was not able to roll myself into a seated position, I could not get myself up to go to the bathroom.

Evening came, and I was still left alone. My cell phone had lost power, and I was now here with no communication to anyone. I was feeling my temper grow with disgust. Here I was, stuck and confined to a bed. I could not take myself to the bathroom. I had not eaten since one o'clock that afternoon. Where was my wife? I still have not heard from her. When the house phone rang, that was when I realized something was not right. The more I thought of it, the more I was making myself more upset to the point. I just went to sleep out of disgust.

I woke up around six o'clock the following morning. I called out, "Deb…hey, Deb, are you here?"

There was nothing but silence. I remember shouting out her name a few times only to hear the silence of the house. What was I going to do? Where was my nurse? It was morning, and she was due here at seven in the morning. I tried to call out on my cell only to remember that the battery died last night. I would prefer to tell you the overall picture of how my next two days went. Even writing, I am too embarrassed to say how bad it really got.

Just picture this. I had not been given any food for over twenty-four hours. The only liquid I had to drink was the water that I had on the stand next to my bed, which ran out the night before. I recall a half box of cookies that I devoured in a short time. I started getting desperate when I had to go to the bathroom. That was not going to happen! I did not even have the bedpan with me, so I was in a serious spot. The morning came and went, as did the afternoon. I had to have fallen asleep at some point during the day, but I also had a huge accident in my sleep, and there was not a damn thing I could do. Where the hell was my wife? Why and how could I be left here without any attention? I never received my daily medication because it was always prepared by someone in the house. How could I be left here like this, by anyone, never mind by the person who was my wife? Where was the "in sickness and in health" part of the wedding pledge? It was not a good situation, especially for me. Even my dog could not hold it any longer as the scent of dog poop floated into my room. So between everything, the house had a very distinctive odor, as did I. There was nothing I could do about it. I could not move on my own to get out of the hospital bed. The bed controls were off since they had to keep the bed in the position so as not to hinder my back.

That evening also came and went. No sign of anyone. Nothing except the house phone was ringing throughout the time and there was nothing I could do about it. I found myself screaming into the air.

"Help!" I would scream out, hoping that someone outside would hear my cries. "Help! Anyone! Can anyone hear me?"

Realizing that my home is situated high up on the street, there was no chance anyone would hear me.

It was around nine o'clock Sunday morning. There was a knock on the door leading from the den where I had been for so many months onto the backyard patio. Thank goodness the door was not locked.

"Come in!" I screamed. "Come in, please! Can you hear me?"

As the den door opened, I saw the faces of friends Gary C and his fiancée, Lisa. Gary was a Metro Police officer, and Lisa was a fantastic piano player/singer.

"Help!" I remember calling out in a hysterical voice! Please, Gary, help me!"

From the look on their faces, I knew what they were looking at was not good. As they covered their noses, Gary said, "What the fuck is going on in here? Where the hell is Debbie?" He called out. "How long have you been like this?"

He and Lisa were so upset. Just the look on their faces said it all.

"Guys, I've been lying like this since Friday," I said. "She left for work and never came home. My nurse was supposed to come on Saturday morning, but she never did."

They must have stayed with me for the next few hours. They were kind enough to get me up and into the bathroom. Not knowing if I was able to take a full shower, I still had Lisa turn the water on, and I did my best with the help of Gary, cleaning myself up while Lisa changed all the sheets and got my room back into a clean and sanitary condition.

When I came to find out, Debra decided to phone Myra on Friday evening and told her she was not needed over the weekend. I can still remember Myra telling me, "Debra said she was going to be home the entire weekend, so she would take care of you."

I was shocked to hear that. Debra lied to her and to me. She planned to be away for the entire weekend, and she still told my nurse not to come in. I was so thankful to both Gary and Lisa. They also went and picked up food for me. I was so appreciative. From that moment on, I learned what it was like to be bed-stricken. When my son found out what happened, he was furious, but there was nothing he could do but voice his feelings toward her, and he did.

A few weeks later, the leaves were in full color, and many trees had already started to lose their leaves. It was an afternoon, and from my back den door, there were a few knocks on the door.

"Come in," I called out. "The door's open."

As the door slowly opened, in walked a deputy from the Davidson Country Sheriff's Department. As I glanced up at his face, I saw that it was a friend of mine who's been with the sheriff's office for many years.

"Well, this is a surprise," I called out to him. "William," I said. What's going on?"

I could see that this was more than a social visit. He had papers in his hand, and from being a former police officer, I was able to see that it was some type of a summons.

"Man, brother," he said to me as his head shook from side to side. "I wanted to be the one to bring this to you since we go back years as friends. I can't believe you're lying in a hospital bed! What the hell happened to you?" As I told him of my Tahiti story, I could see on his face that he truly felt my pain. "Bro, I'm sorry to have to do this, but I have to serve you with a summons filed by your wife, Debra."

As he stretched out his arm to hand me these court papers, I could see on his face that he was not happy doing this, especially to me under these circumstances.

A summons? I thought. *What was this for?* It never dawned on me what it could be. "So, Bill, what's this all about?" I asked.

"Well, your wife has filed for divorce and this summons covers the charge for it. I wish I didn't have to do this, but I felt that it should come from a friend, not a stranger."

As he handed me the summons, all I could do was look over to my nurse Myra and say, "Ain't this some shit."

Bill turned to me and said, "Steve, her claim is that she doesn't want to be married to a gimp."

"A gimp!" I shouted out. *What a load of shit*, I thought. Here I am, in a fucking hospital bed, and my wife of just a few months is filing for a divorce because she doesn't want to be married to a "gimp." Welcome to my world.

As time went on and my recuperation was going extremely well, I had already hired a divorce lawyer, Nathaniel K., who was a very prominent divorce lawyer here in Nashville who was well-respected by his peers and the judges that sat in Davidson County. I was ready to protect my interests and all that went with it. Because of my prenup that was signed by both of us, I believed that I and my personals were protected. I was ready for my day in court.

Between the time of the initial summons and court date, Debra was allowed to stay in my home but had to move into one of the spare bedrooms. As I was beginning to go back to work part-time, my home became a very toxic environment. With my son now residing in my home, he was subject to having to put up with Debra's nonsense. To touch on this lightly, it appeared that Debra was now sharing herself with another female. When my son phoned me to tell me that he caught Debra and another girl in her bed embracing and kissing, I had to do what any father would do.

I immediately phoned my attorney. "Nate!" I called out into the phone. "Nate, this fuckin' bitch is now bringing some broad into my home and sharing her bed." Nathan has gone past her room numerous times only to find her and a female cuddling and kissing on the bed. "I want this bitch out of my house now!" I knew that Nathaniel was upset by his tone. An emergency hearing was brought in front of Judge Muriel Robinson, the toughest known divorce judge who also had a reputation for not siding with men. The judge had been married five or six times, and her position for men was far less pleasant than it was for women in divorce hearings. However, the judge was on my side for this. Debra was now only allowed to be in my home alone. She was not permitted to have anyone join her if I and/or my son were present. Her game-playing was so obvious for her remaining time in my home. She would sit in the den while I was in the kitchen, and there would be a war of the television volumes between two sets. She would raise the sound so as to be heard over the TV in the kitchen. If I increased my TV volume, she would follow suit. I allowed this for about five minutes more and then I put a stop to it. My house, my rules. What a horrible way to exist. Thank goodness, the divorce was granted, and everything that was in the prenup stayed.

The best thing was the morning she was finally leaving with her six large garbage bags filled with her clothes and other items. I remember saying to my son, "You see, Nathan, after two years, this is all that she has, a stack of garbage bags. No suitcases, just garbage bags."

As she was loading her car, Nathan turned to me and said, "Hey, Dad, watch this."

"Oh, please, Nate," I said. "Let's just get her outa here."

Nathan had this huge grin on his face and all he said was, "Dad, watch this."

As she loaded her last bag and made her way around to her driver's door, I watched as Nathan clicked his car fob. All four windows in his car rolled down, and the music started blaring that famous song, "Hit the road jack and don't cha come back no more no more no more no more."

As we stood there laughing, we watched her car drive down my winding driveway and head off to whatever greener path's ready for her. That was the last time I ever saw Debra Corso. I only wish I would not have listened to the hundreds of calls I received over the years and even today from Collection Agencies and Banks searching for her.

But being the Good Samaritan that I am, I would say to every agency, "Debra Corso doesn't live here anymore. We are divorced, but here is the last address where she moved to."

It felt great letting others have a go with her. I was finally freed.

I realized that, once again, I am reminded that only you can take care of yourself as long as you are of sound mind. Having daily routines back on track was a welcoming emotion; one I still refer to as a bad situation became a positive driving force within myself. I was now prepared for what was in front of me, both professionally and emotionally. Lights on…camera…action!

There were many trips I took to Florida to visit my parents. They were getting up in age, I just wanted to spend more time with them. It was too much of a drive for me to take, with my back being as bad as it was, so I flew constantly.

I decided after numerous conversations with myself, I decided that I wanted to take some time off—time to do what I wanted to do or not do. I had no planned schedule, nor did I even want one. It was nice not having to worry about meetings or travel—nothing but letting time go by. I enjoyed entertaining myself with my music and the little odds and ends I had put off at earlier times. I was really looking forward to receiving a medical clearance from my doctor to allow me to go on a cruise. I kept telling my doctor that I was fit and able to take care of myself. I had my plastic gladiator torso on, and wheelchairs we available on the ship. It was time to hear those words, "Watch your step, and welcome aboard."

For the next few months, I found myself running out of things to do around the house. Mind you, not that there was always something to do, but I had to make certain it did not involve any heavy lifting or pushing. Even though I was now back on my feet (with a cane), I still had to make sure I did not overexert myself. The office had still been running. Lynne and even Rusty continued handling the daily phone calls and reservations. If they had a question or if they needed something approved, it was an easy, no-traffic walk from the office upstairs down to where I was.

It was early afternoon. I was able to sit and find tranquility as the birds sang up into the sky. I would come outside my times just to be able to clear my head with things that may be bothering me.

It was one afternoon when I was outside with the dogs, enjoying the day, when my son came outside and said, "Hey, Dad, we need to have a talk."

There have been many times when Nathan and I would sit down and have great talks. He would come to me for any reason. Whether it had to do with money, ideas, and even girl problems, Nathan knew he had a friend in me besides just father and son, so I was completely open to hear what was on his mind.

"What do you mean we need to talk?" I asked. "What's on your mind?"

Nathan pulled over one of the outside patio chairs and said, "Dad, I have an ultimatum for you."

"For me?" I said. "What do you mean you have an ultimatum for me?" As I readjusted myself in the chair, I could not help but wonder what Nathan had on his mind that would warrant him to offer me an "ultimatum."

Nathan, too, had adjusted himself in his chair, facing me only by a few feet, and said, "Dad, you really need to find something to do."

I looked at him for a second with a dumbfounded look on my face and said, "Well, son, that's not really an ultimatum."

Nathan quickly came back and said, "Oh yes, it is, Dad. Ya see, if you don't find something to do, the dogs and I, we're gonna kill ya! You're driving us crazy!"

We both broke out in laughter for the next few minutes. Even the dogs were prancing around and barking with excitement.

"Why would you say that to me, Nate?" I asked him with a puzzled look on my face. "What, don't you feel that everything is great?"

Without skipping a beat, Nathan looked over to me and said, "Dad, everything is great, but"—as his voice changed, sounding more like a soft-spoken child—"you have to find something to do! You're driving the dogs and I crazy!"

We were now both laughing and really made light of it. We both agreed that I would do my best and find something to do with my time.

The same evening, I enjoyed a relaxing dinner at home with my son and dogs. We both enjoyed grilling outside, so that night, I made my famous grilled New York strip steaks, French fries, and salad. Growing up, Nathan had horrible eating habits. He was extremely picky about what food(s) he would put in his mouth. I guess both his mother and I were to blame for that. Nathan did not like having anything to do with vegetables. I can remember offering him a $100 bill if he would just eat one kernel of corn. I had a better chance of getting the pope to come over and eat it than getting Nathan to. I will say that it was nice seeing my son eventually expand his horizons when it comes to eating habits. Like most things, it comes with maturity. I listened to what Nathan had said to me earlier that day and went to bed that evening with it on my mind.

I awoke the following morning like any other morning would be for me. As I was having my first cup of coffee, I could not help, but I found myself reliving the dream I had just had. I sat erect now, concentrating on this magical dream I was hoping to remember. It involved my passion for cruise ships as well as the Caribbean islands with its aqua-blue and deep-blue waters. That was not the complete dream. There was one more item that filled this entire dream image. It appeared in almost every scene that I remember as if everything I was envisioning was in 3D. The depth of the ocean, the ship's interiors were so clear to see, and the one thing that changed my life.

Picture this. Directly in front of you, more toward the left side, is a passenger ship's gangway—not the gangway used for passengers, but the gangway located almost even with the dock, the crew gangway. This is one of the busiest gangways of any passenger ship. Alright, back to my dream. As I approached the crew gangway, I heard one of the most recognizable sounds. A sound like no other. The roar of its mufflers and the crackling of its pipes, which was the sound of a Harley-Davidson motorcycle. There are no two different motorcycle brands that sound like Harley. As I glanced at the gangway, I saw myself riding my motorcycle up the gangway and onto the ship. Directly inside the ship, I rode. I was followed by other Harley bike owners and a few Hondas and BMWs,

My dream became very visual. I was remembering the ship's arrival on the islands and seeing each motorcycle, one by one, ride down the gangway and onto the port. Even as I write this, I am feeling as if I was the proud father, watching my son take his first step. The dream became more vivid as I sat quietly with my coffee, doing my best to recollect this incredible story.

The people in "my dream" were, for the most part, unrecognizable. They all were as real as a dream would allow, but few had their own identity, nor could I give any of them names. There was, of course, the captain of the ship and other ship's officers, all dressed in the same white uniforms, but some had more gold strips on their lapels than others. I recall seeing the true sailors at the gangway as each motorcycle rode up into the ship's hull. I can say that every portion of this dream was so vivid. The clarity of being on a cruise ship, the workings and daily activities of guests and crew was very clear to me as if it were taking place in real life. But not only did I see in the dream what I have already remarked here about, even on the islands with their beaches and beach bars and swaying palm trees, I was able to see what this was becoming. *Could this really become reality for me?* I thought to myself.

I spent the next few weeks doing extensive research, covering the local government island laws of each Caribbean Island, and their traffic and motorcycle laws were included. Because of my past experience working with so many cruise lines and their ships, I knew I had to read up on the ship's safety and protocols as well as SOLAS (Safety of Lives at Sea). There was not any format I could rely on for anything like this. This had never been done before by any passenger cruise ship anywhere in the world. Of course, there are many ferry boats and ships that were built to export and import motorcycles and cars and trucks, but no such passenger ship has ever been used for the purpose of allowing guests to board with their motorcycles.

The detailed work that I was faced with consisted of so much that I was, at first, overwhelmed with it all. Nowhere is it written that a passenger ship can be used for the purpose of carrying motorized bikes or vehicles. This may be somewhat impossible to pull off. I pushed back from the table and put my brain into overdrive. Who did I know was an executive with a cruise line and rode a motorcycle? I called an acquaintance that I met while loading band equipment onto a ship for one of my music cruises. He and his wife both worked for Royal Caribbean International and had their offices directly in one of Royal's dockside warehouses in Port of Miami. I made it a point to call them, and so the story begins by making something that was never done before into one of the best-kept secrets in the world of group cruising.

I made sure to arrive at the port on a day when there were cruise ships in port doing a turnaround. A turnaround means the disembarking AND embarking of passengers from a cruise ship on the same day, hours apart. I was met with their smiles and a fresh cup of espresso. I felt as if I was already far from being in a Royal Caribbean warehouse located in the Port of Miami. It was always wonderful to see both Pedro and Marlene Camacho. Pedro was the supervisor for Royal Caribbean, and Marlene was the one you went to in order to get anything done that was not on the list of things to do. Marlene was like the godmother of the dockside.

Later that day, when things got quiet and the ships were preparing to depart, we were able to sit and relax. As the conversation was made and again, I cannot say enough how much these two people meant to me. They were my true contacts in getting anything dined dockside that I would need to make things run smoothly.

"Not to worry, Steve," Pedro would tell me. "I have your back if this gets approved."

The same can be said about Marlene. As things would progress, it was Marlene who made sure I had the proper contacts to get things done.

That afternoon, I noticed an Anniversary Harley-Davidson motorcycle parked inside the warehouse.

"Whose bike?" I called out to Pedro.

"Oh, that's Captain Newhoff," Pedro said back to me. "Hey, he's the one you need to talk to about what you want to do. He's the head captain over them all! And look, he rides a Harley!"

My head was already in motion.

"Hi, Captain Newhoff," I said to the gentleman walking toward me. "Got a minute?"

As he extended his arm and gripped my hand to shake, I felt a feeling come over me like I've never felt before. No sooner did I welcome his handshake, then I heard Marlene say, "Hey, Captain, wait until you hear what Steve has come up with! You're gonna love it!"

You ever get that feeling when there are thousands of eyes staring at you, waiting to hear what you have to say?

I will never forget that first introduction. What I remember most was that here stood a very powerful and respected man within the cruising and shipping industry, not just for Port of Miami—rather the world. If there was a port and a visiting cruise ship belonging to the Royal Caribbean International brand, you can be certain that Captain Howard Newhoff has visited them. When he was introduced to me, he looked directly at me as I to him. I was told by my father that when another man looks into your eyes, that means that he cares about what you have to say. It shows true respect from man to man.

"Captain Newhoff, I came up with a fantastic idea for a group to cruise," I said to him with a tone that expressed excitement. I worked my words to my advantage but left it open as if he was the one who thought of some of my ideas. It is a great marketing tool that I have used throughout my adulthood and career. You lay out your idea without giving away the key element. You just without giving notice to it, you get the person you are speaking to say what you wanted to say. Alas, making it appear that it was their idea, bringing it to tap into your idea, making the complete idea stupendous.

"Captain, what would you say to having a group of bikers ride their motorcycles up into the hull of the ship?" I asked.

THIS LIFE OF MINE

With a blank stare, it was as if Captain Newhoff was looking right through me. "You want to do what?" he said in a questionable demeanor.

"You heard me, sir. I'd like to see if we can get permission to bring motorcycles owned by guests onto the ship to visit and tour the various islands the ship stops at," I said proudly but with a little emphasis on shyness. By now, we were standing next to his Harley as I was waiting for him to start telling me one of the many stories his bike has.

"Steve," he said to me, "I wish it was that easy. There is no way that could ever happen. In fact, it's never been done before anywhere in the world," he said. "You can't put a motorcycle on a cruise ship." He chuckled for a moment, not really realizing that I was, in fact, quite serious about this.

"But, Captain, what if it were possible? Would you permit me to do it?" I quickly responded back with.

"Steve, there is no way you would get all of the governmental clearances," Newhoff said in a direct voice. "I just do not see it ever being cleared. Not only that," but he also said, "where would we store them on the ships?"

Here's where my comedic aspiration came into play. "Oh, Captain, I thought we would just keep them in our cabins!"

Laughter broke out among us all, which then gave me an immediate open door for my next move.

"There's still one of your ships in port," I said. "Can we take a quick tour of it and see if it would at least be possible?"

I had already done my homework and knew that the ship in port would be a perfect match. There were two areas in the hull that would be perfect for us to store the motorcycles while in transit. They were filled with luggage trollies, and I felt they would be able to be repositioned somewhere on the ship. Next thing I realized: I was on my way aboard the Explorer of the Seas for a site inspection.

I wanted Captain Newhoff to see my vision and I was prepared to sell like nothing else I ever had to sell before. I have been told that I could sell someone a bucket of steam before they realized there was no such thing. We continued our walk down the main artery of the crew area until we came into this enormous area that was completely emptied. You see, the luggage was still be brought on board, and all of the ship's trolleys were being used for this purpose, leaving this area wide open for inspection.

I immediately started to walk off measurements and just how (I thought) would be the best layout for stowing the bikes. But again, I wanted Captain Newhoff to come up with an idea; therefore, as I walked off the measurements, I was hoping to hear him say (which he did), "I think the bikes would have to be placed in this direction. Marking off spots for each bike which would then allow us the most available spots.

"Captain," I said, "is there anywhere else the trolleys can be stored during the cruise so that we would be able to use this space?"

As he began to think, one of the other officers in the immediate area suggested that the trolleys could be stored in two of the four conference rooms located one deck up. Who was this officer that came to my assistance? I could not have asked anyone better. It was the chief housekeeper who oversaw all of the trolleys.

"Let's seal the deal right now," I said as we made our way to the crew gangway.

As the captain and I walked back over to the warehouse, I again kept pressing him with giving me an open road with my idea and let us see if this could possibly be done. An immediate no was not on the table for me. I wanted this challenge in the worst way.

I kept saying repeatedly, "What if? What if I can get all the other governments from each of the Caribbean islands, US Customs, insurances, registrations, and much more on the table? Will you then at least consider it?"

The pause that followed seemed to have lasted ten minutes, but it was only a minute when I heard those wonderful words come from the mouth of Captain Howard Newhoff, "Okay, I'll make you a deal. You bring me all the signed agreements needed to make this happen, and I will approve a test run."

I must have shaken his hand enough times that would make anyone else's arm fall off. I was so thrilled, I just remember saying,

THIS LIFE OF MINE

"Captain, I won't let you down. I will make sure this happens, and I will have every bit of the policy signed for your review."

As I watched the captain ride off on his Harley, I could not help but notice the smiles on both Pedro and Marlene's faces. It was as if this was completely planned out. A good day's ending, I felt as I drove over the bridge and watched as the ship made her way out into the ocean's waters.

The next few months involved a tremendous amount of phone calls, emails, document filings, and more. I was not only dealing with the required paperwork from the United States Customs and Border Protection but also required documentation of motorcycle ownership, registrations, and insurance for every motorcycle on each island ride. I also had to contend with each island's policies and requirements and much more. I was able to tell that this was not going to be a quick process. The more of a challenge I saw the more I wanted this to be approved of. There was so much riding on this to be the start of a very successful and lucrative goal. My connections on many of the islands played an important role in the process. I am proud to say that my reputation among so many islanders gave me a wonderful feeling. Seeing how I was respected by so many only once again proved my father's words true.

"Respect is earned, not given out freely."

I was now going into my second year of preparation for what I was hoping to accomplish: getting the clearances required. The one thing I realized quickly is that there is no "quickly" on any of the islands when it comes to communications, especially within the government agencies. The next thing I realized is that there are no shortcuts for any of the important documentation required. You must get it in the order that it is expected. *What does that mean*? I thought to myself. I learned quickly. If you make any effort to get documents ahead of the actual steps needed, you must go back to the beginning of that process and start all over. I can say that only happened to me one time. A lesson well taught.

Almost two years to the date, I phoned someone I was waiting patiently to call. As the phone rang, I could feel the anticipation building from within me.

Then I hear a voice say, "Hello. This is Captain Newhoff. Can I help you?"

Taking that final swallow, I can still hear me say, "Hi, Captain Newhoff. Steve Wallach here. Hope this call finds you doing well."

It was nice and rewarding to hear the captain say, "Hi, Steve. Nice hearing from you. What can I do for you today?"

Without hesitation, I replied, "Captain, I'm gonna be in Miami next Wednesday, and I was hoping to meet with you if you had some time."

An immediate response usually means it is very welcoming as the captain said, "Sure, how about eleven Wednesday morning?"

"Any time would have been perfect for me." I told him that I was looking forward to our meeting, and we ended our telephone conversation on a high note.

When I arrived at Royal Caribbean International Headquarters, I walked in confidently, knowing that I was able to obtain every clearance and permit needed for what was about to change my life once again. Walking into Captain Newhoff's office felt huge to me. I was about to sell my idea for approval to a multibillion-dollar corporation. On the left side of his office, there was a table just waiting for me. As I said hello and shook Captain's hand, I stepped over to the table and proceeded to dump out a sleuth of papers from my briefcase. He stood there watching as I spread the papers out in a fanning motion. I was so excited.

"Captain," I said, "I have here before you every agreement and contract signed by each island government official, US Customs and Border Protection, numerous island insurances for all the motorcycles, permits, licenses, and full approvals from all."

I could not hold back my enthusiasm. I was about to burst at the seams. As the captain stood, gazing over some of the papers, I could see on his face this huge smile coming out. His expression was like mine; we were excited that something like this may very well take place. The first time, passenger cruise ships carrying personal motorcycles were on board and headed to the Caribbean. Life was good.

ETA Motorcycle Cruises Logo

ETA Motorcycle Cruises President/Owner
Steve Wallach, Port of St Maarten

In 2002, we started with three cruises for the first Caribbean season. By 2019, we were spending, on average, twenty-six weeks on various ships within the Royal Caribbean Group Brand each

Caribbean season—approximately twelve years with Royal Caribbean International and eight years with Celebrity Cruises. We have had over ten thousand satisfied guests who brought their motorcycles with them. We were the top-selling travel company in Tennessee for both Royal Caribbean and Celebrity. I must give credit where credit is due. Royal Caribbean was not the first cruise line to do our motorcycle cruise program. We had the pleasure of putting motorcycles on board the *Costa Atlantica* for our initial cruise. Unfortunately, with itinerary changes, *Costa* ships were no longer here in the US ports year-round, and their choice of itineraries did not allow us to take full advantage of island rides. Therefore, only offering a very small window of cruise dates, we made the change to Royal Caribbean International.

ETA Motorcycle Cruises riding St Kitts

THIS LIFE OF MINE

Steve and Traci of ETA Motorcycle Cruises, Bonaire

    When dealing with people from all walks of life, occasionally, you will come across someone who either made a great impression on you or failed terribly and left a sour taste. Now imagine dealing with bikers, all types of bikers. Men and women, straight and bi, gay, adventurous, middle class or upper class, mostly educated, but again, you always get that one or few who stand out. We have had pipe fitters, lawyers, doctors, police officers, firemen, postal workers, mechanics, surgeons, teachers, CEOs, FBI agents, construction workers, household wives, veterans, active-duty service men and women, and the list goes on and on. The reason I am saying this is that there was no set styler of people that came on an ETA Motorcycle Cruise. What they all had in common was they loved riding motorcycles. They loved sharing stories and helping one another when it came to assistance of any type. Be it a medical fundraiser for a child or for a widow who just lost their husband in a horrific motorcycle accident, no matter the reason, the comradery of these people is awesome. Sure, there are stories or the bad-ass motorcycle gangs that do nothing more than rob, steal, or murder. Don't we also have that in some of our top professions? The have been doctors, lawyers, judges, police officers, and yes, politicians who have done some of the worst crimes known, yet for some reason, the stigma of bikers stayed for many years. It is so far from the truth. Motorcycle clubs continue to be the top organization that donates money, clothing, homes and so much more to families from all paths throughout the year.

Traveling the world on numerous music tours enabled me to see and meet people from all walks of life. As great as it was to be part of huge world music tours, the meeting of so many different people is what I am thankful and blessed for. It amazes me every day when I come across someone who is different from the next person. Isn't that what makes our world so interesting? It is meeting and working and living with others from all over the world. Learning their stories can make one realize just how lucky they are and what they have, or maybe it has to do with the love of another. People are people no matter where you travel to. We all have a heart that is built on our own feelings. Some better than others, but isn't that what the world is made up of? Go ahead.... Answer it.

I had a chapter of Hell's Angles on one of our bike cruises that left from Cape Liberty, Bayonne, New Jersey. As we do with all our groups, a general meeting is held with the bike operators just to go over the island's procedures and protocols. I treated this group just like I would treat any other biker club: respect and attitude. I set the goals from the beginning and most of the time, it is followed. One must understand that bikers are ALL A-type people. If you fail to take control of the group from the beginning, you lose them for the remainder of the cruise. It was that simple. I let the rules be known and by doing so, everyone knows from the onset what is expected. I had what I considered some wonderful and professional road captains and I have to say that for my twenty years of bike cruises, this Hell's Angel's chapter was one of the best group of people I ever had on. They had a blast, which in turn made everyone dealing with them feel the same way. It was a grand slam. The one thing that separated this group from the others was just a small feat. Years ago, all the photographs taken by the ship's photographers were done using negative prints. The only request I had from the HA captain was that they needed to be given all the negatives from the sleuth of photographs taken of them as a group or single shots. And believe me, they had so many photos taken of them throughout the cruise. They were having the time of their lives. As I brought the captain and his sergeant-of-arms to meet with the photography manager, all was taken care of, and the negatives were handed over without any cause. That would never happen in today's market. All photos taken aboard any ship are now digital, and no negative prints are even thought of anymore.

We had one incident that involved a couple. Of course, it is on a cruise, so alcohol must be involved, right? My staff and I are given deck phones once we arrive on board. This is so that we are available to the ship's staff and crew in case of any occurrences. I received a call from the ship's security chief that a couple from my group got into a verbal argument that escalated into a slight roar. Doing what any good babysitter had to do, I met the security chief outside the couple's cabin, and we both had a discussion with them, advising that if they could not act reasonably, they would be separated and would have to leave the ship at the next port of call. Usually, that works. No one really wants to lose out on their cruise, especially when they were here to ride their motorcycles on the islands of the Caribbean. Thinking that our words would be adhered to, we left them and wished for the best.

It was not thirty minutes later that I now received a call from the staff captain asking me to meet him immediately in his office, which I did promptly. As I walked into his office, I could tell by the look on his face he was not in a great mood.

"What's up, staff?" I said in an easy, welcoming voice. "Steve," he said to me, "we seem to have a problem and it concerns one of your guests. Two of your guests." As his voice became more direct and stern, he said, "The ship received a distress call from the United States Coast Guard located in New York City saying that they received a call from a female passenger on the ship saying she was being held captive in her stateroom, and at one point, the male companion she was traveling with held her upside down over the side of their balcony by her ankles, threatening to drop her if she continued acting the way she was. There was complete silence in the room. Nothing was being said by either of us."

As I let this sink in, I asked him, "Are you sure it was one of my guests?"

Without hesitation, the security chief said, "Steve, it is the same two people that we put in their cabin."

Well, on that note, we all got up and made our way to the cabin where (hopefully) both of them were inside.

Upon arriving at the cabin, we found the female inside, but her companion was nowhere in sight.

"What is going on?" asked the staff captain. "Do you know anything about a call to the US Coast Guard?"

Without hesitation, the woman screamed, "Yeah, I made the call to my brother, who is stationed at the New York Port. I was scared and wanted to go home."

The security chief immediately checked her ankles to ass if there were any marks on them. Unfortunately, there were. It was obvious that her boyfriend caused physical harm to her ankles. Could he have held her over the side of the ship by her ankles? The thought of it was becoming more obvious.

The outcome was simple. Security was sent throughout the ship until the boyfriend was located and detained. Even though the ship had no real proof that she was held over the side of the ship from her balcony, the only thing they would do was separate the couple until we reached the first port of call in thirty-two hours. She continued to stay in her cabin, and her companion got to stay in what was referred to as the Hilton Hotel Holding Room. Upon arrival, neither one of them wanted to bring charges against the other; therefore, it was the decision of the staff captain to allow them to remain on the cruise if there would be no problems. They completed the cruise without incident.

There was another time was had a group of seven couples that booked the bike cruise within another group we had also booked for that time frame. The only request this group had was that while on board the ship, they wanted to be able to enjoy the specialty restaurants on their own. A simple task that took no energy to approve.

The first night of any of our ETA Motorcycle Cruises, we start off the evening with a private open bar cocktail reception where everyone can meet and say hello to their group bikers and learn valuable information on our island bike rides. From the time we left our cocktail reception to the dining room, I watched as the group came in to be seated. Immediately, I noticed that all fourteen people in the group of seven were now seated with different people. Every couple was seated with someone else. I thought it was a bit strange, but I went along with it. Maybe they just enjoyed dining and having different conversations. The night ended with everyone dancing the night away in the ship's disco lounge. Fun times had by all.

    Breakfast for me on a ship was like clockwork. I went up to the buffet for breakfast always at the same time. Same table, same seat, and the staff knew exactly where anyone could find me if they needed to. After so many cruises, it was by habit that I had a full morning schedule on sea days. As I sat and enjoyed breakfast, I started to see some of my guests appear. Their appearance left the impression that whatever they did the night before, they really enjoyed it. I will leave it just like that for now. I was dating a girl named Tami at the time and had her join me on some of my cruises. This is one of them. Tami was a tall attractive blond that I met onboard another ship. She was working with the music duo, the Nelson Brothers, the two twin sons of legendary Rickie Nelson. We met and hit it off and so that chapter began. I am sure you can see that I had many chapters in my life. No matter good or bad, they each played an important role in my life. Everyone made their typical morning talks as we could hear them planning out their day at sea.

    "Remember, tonight is formal night," I called out to them. "If we don't see you throughout the day, we will see you tonight at dinner."

    Remember, we have special dining tonight in one of the ship's alternate dining experiences. I chose Chops for this evening's dinner plans. It is one of the finest restaurants on any ship. I had made the reservations when I first got onboard and wanted to make sure that I had a special table large enough to seat that entire group of seven couples. I must give credit to the dining staff even though there was no actual table designed to seat fourteen people, the dining staff were able to combine two tables so that all fourteen could be seated comfortably.

As with all my groups, I would always have my staff greet our guests as they came into the dining area. It was this hands-on service that ETA was known for. Once everyone was seated, I would go to each table as the "official greeter" for tonight's dinner extravaganza. It was nice seeing most of my guests enjoying this: the first formal night of the cruise. As I came over to my seven-couple's group, I immediately noticed that none of them were sitting with their spouse. Again, they have all changed so that they were all with a different person yet matched up like a couple. I looked at Tami with this puzzled look on my face as if I did not notice. They were seated at a huge round table with extended sides to accommodate this large group of fourteen.

Walking over to the table to greet them, I could not help but notice there were numerous wrapped gifts, all scattered out on the table.

"Someone's birthday," I called out as I made my table rounds. I guess my question was funny because they each chuckled as they watched me.

"No, Steve. It's no one's birthday. In fact, this is the first time most of us have met each other," said one of the guests.

Even though I was smiling, I could feel my mind filling up with many scenarios. I could not help but feel that there was more to this group than I was told by my office. Each guest had striking features. Some had shown obvious signs of cosmetic surgery, whereas others just had natural beauty. Nonetheless, this group now intrigued me. The door was open in conversation so now was the best time to ask questions.

"So I gotta ask…since most of you had never met previous to this cruise, how did you end up with me?"

There was an immediate response from them. Getting through the laughter, one of the ladies said, "We belong to a special motorcycle group. Maybe you've heard of it."

As she kept her eyes on mine, I had to ask with an inquisitive look on my face, "Is it within the Harley family?"

She responded with, "Well, kinda. The club is called the Harley-Davidson Swinger's Club."

As they each were now looking at me with enormous smiles on their faces, I could not help but say, "Hot damn! This is gonna be a hell of a cruise!"

We all raised a glass to toast. All I could think of was imagining their evening ahead with a smile on my face.

Having just gone to each table to see if they were enjoying the food and service, I noticed that our "swingers" table started opening the gifts that were on their table. As each gift was opened, their laughter became louder. It was time I made my way over to their table. Of course, I was curious to know what the gifts were, especially since I now know what type of group this is. Slowly glancing at the table and guests, I noticed there was one seat vacant.

"Where did our little lady go?" I asked aloud.

Only a few seconds went by when out pops her head from under the table. Let me repeat myself. Out popped her head from under the table and at the opposite side of where she was seated. Enough said.

There were pink handcuffs and little black leather whips that were in some of the unwrapped packages. Let me not forget the mention of lotions and potions, prophylactics, and more. It seemed that the handcuffs were the winners because there were three sets of them offered as gifts. I wished everyone a pleasant evening and bid my farewells to the entire group of guests.

Our port of call was St. Maarten. One of my favorite islands in the Caribbean, St. Maarten, is an island split in two. One side being Dutch and known as St. Maarten, and the other being French and known as Sint Martin. One of our favorite venues we stop at in St. Maarten is on the French side of the island. It had one of the best recommendations for its clean beaches, crystal blue waters, fantastic cuisine, a few incredible bars and, most importantly, the employees.

Waikiki Beach Bar was owned and operated by a dear friend named Albert. Albert hailed from France and had been on the island of St. Maarten for many years. The reputation of this venue was exactly what we were looking for when we first made our commitments to each island. Imagine making a left turn and coming face-to-face with a view of nothing but white sand and crystal blue waters. Every so often, you can see a water glider moving in the direction of the wind. One of the most memorable parts of coming to Waikiki was that Albert had included in his new build-out a section where the motorcycles would ride directly into the venue, past a few clothiers and one of the two bars, and would be staged on solid wood flooring with the ocean as our backdrop. Every arrival was filled with pure excitement, not only from my guests but from all the other people who enjoy the beach and Waikiki.

Waikiki was also known for the best Sunday Buffet Magnifique. Probably the best buffet I have ever seen anywhere. From different salads to start you off to various French breads and butter, this buffet was nothing short of enormous with flavors from great European locales. There was an area offering smoked salmon, herrings, capers, smoked white fish, fresh-cooked shrimp cocktails, and scallops. That was not all. There were always five different vegetables offered in various preparations, three styled potatoes, three completely different rice dishes to filet minion, slices of New York strip steaks, veal dishes, pork strips followed by three different dishes of shrimp; prepared scampi, breaded, or grilled. Further down this enormous line of eateries, you could find your typical American dishes like hamburgers, hot dogs, and French fries. Wait, there is more! For dessert, you had your choice of freshly baked pastries, fresh fruit, chocolate cake, and of course, espresso. In all the years of bringing my guests to Waikiki, I have never been able to eat everything offered. Albert and his staff were amazing. Our guests always complimented the staff and especially the food like no other. Unfortunately, Waikiki could not hold up against the power of Hurricane Maria, which plummeted the entire island of St. Maarten/Sint Martin in 2017. This most memorable place was completely wiped off any map. I say that because there was nothing left standing of what was the best place to visit. I was fortunate to be cleared to fly into St. Maarten, hoping to get some idea of when the ships would return to this, the friendliest island in the Caribbean, and was able to drive over to the French side to see for myself, the devastation throughout this wonderful island.

Walking to the beach where Waikiki once stood, I saw something shining and reflecting a bright lite off the sky. I walked over and bent down to pick up what was making this bright reflection. As if this was a staged scene, my hand reached into the sand to retrieve this partially visible item, only to find that this was a bent fork from the silverware of Waikiki Beach Bar. There was nothing else visible. I stood for a moment in complete silence as I stared out into the ocean, clutching this bent piece of silverware and said a prayer for Albert and all those who worked at Waikiki. Truly a wonderful place that I will remember for years to come. It was my understanding that Albert decided to take his family and return to France, as did some of his other staff. Most, I am sure, found employment somewhere else on the island, and I always hope to run into it once again. Today, the sight is run by another eatery and bar.

There was destruction throughout the island of St. Maarten/Sint Martin. The only Harley-Davidson dealer's buildings were destroyed as were most of the motorcycles inside. The entire metal roof collapsed, and the brick-and-mortar walls were crushed as if they were made from paper. There was also severe damage done to the clubhouse of the Caribbean Eagles of St Maarten. I was just devastated seeing all the destruction throughout this beautiful island. I knew I had to do something, so I started a GoFundMe page for Caribbean Eagles of St. Maarten. I was proud to see that this benefit fundraising page raised thousands of dollars which helped in the rebuilding of the clubhouse and its outside stage that lost its entire roof. Money raised was from many of my ETA Motorcycle clients. As I always said, when it comes to clubs that offer charities and benefits, you cannot find any club better than a motorcycle club and its members. They give their time and effort, never looking for anything in return. That is how it should be among us. Maybe someday in our time, we will once again see the generosity of who we are and represent.

ETA Motorcycle Cruises gained huge respect and admiration from so many people on all the islands we visited throughout the years. "It means more than anyone will ever know," I would say during the many interviews I was doing throughout the years. "You need to remember this has never been done before by any passenger cruise ship or cruise line. Nowhere throughout this incredible world has this been done. Whoever heard of bringing motorcycles on a cruise ship? You know, my father again comes into my light. His advice was always given, sometimes not listened to or followed, but mostly, I am proud to say I followed and learned from it." It still pleases me to this day to look at my shelves and walls and see the many crystal plaques with my name chiseled on welcoming ETA Motorcycle Cruises to their wonderful Caribbean Island, marking our visit and ride as the first in history to have such an international event. Meeting with Prime Ministers of some of these incredible and colorful islands meant that I, Steve Wallach, did something no other person has ever done before. Those were memorable times.

One of the proudest moments was when ETA Motorcycle Cruises was featured in the *New York Times* Sunday edition in 2005—a front-page coverage and the entire center two pages. Imagine, the entire center pages were about my company and what I have accomplished. What an awesome feeling. We also had a media promotion running on one of the jumbo screens in Times Square, New York City.

The amount of time I had to put into this to get the clearances and approvals needed was mind-boggling. Each time I would feel overwhelmed, I would stop and say aloud, "Steve, remember, this has never been done before. You are making history!" It worked for me. I did make history with all the involved companies, agencies and individuals that became a part of this incredible event. No one could negotiate a deal better than my father. Hands down. I have heard about and have personally witnessed how he works with some of his negotiations. It was like a play performing before my own eyes. As to this writing, I cannot help but smile at the memories of him.

"It is so important that you focus on what you're trying to succeed at," I can still hear my father say to me. "Focus, mark your mark, and follow through," were the words of my father.

Now I did not agree with him on everything. There were times when we bumped heads (not literally of course), both of us set in our own idea to ever think about a change. There were times when we each apologized to each other, and that was what made our talks exciting. Again, I truly believe I was taught by my father (and of course, my mother as well), and I have made some very good decisions. Of course, as with anyone, you are faced with situations that could very well affect your business, so as with any ole owner of a business, you will do just about anything to protect it.

I can recall having to contact Roseau, Dominica, and asking for their approval to allow motorcycles and guests on an escorted ride on the day we are scheduled to arrive. Most times, there would be a long pause, and you would then hear, "What? You want to bring motorcycles and do what with them while you're here? What?"

I knew I had to win over the person I was speaking with, so my plan was simple: just tell him the overview of what you are wanting to do on their island, along with mentioning that you would be returning to the ship and reloading the bikes back on board and cruising to the next island stop. What I did was always make it sound as if they came up with this idea for their island. *Hey, that was fine with me*, I thought to myself. If it helps in securing a confirmation, they can believe whatever they want.

Most of the islands welcomed my new and exciting idea. Why shouldn't they? I was taking tourists to their island to leave behind their hard-earned money and hopefully want to come back and stay a few days. We had devised a goal that we worked with each island on. Because of my best years coming to these islands as a cruise director or musician, it enabled me to have my one foot in the door. Remember, many years have passed since I worked aboard the ships, so I was fortunate that most of my connections were still somehow involved with the agencies I needed to be cleared by. This made the initial connections go somewhat smoother, but one has to realize that we were dealing in "island time," which meant everything goes r-e-a-l s-l-o-w.

Because this was new to the islands, I wanted to make sure that my company was protected and that we would hold the exclusive rights and agreements. It was their pleasure to allow this, especially since my name has the respect that it does throughout many islands in the Caribbean. Again, representing myself as a travel company that promises to bring tourists and American dollars to their island was something they were extremely thankful for. I made a promise and commitment and followed through with my promises. That, I will applaud my father for teaching me the internal divisions of my own work attitude. The process that followed on every island was similar in most points. However, without quick thinking on my part, there would have been sections I never would have thought of. I wanted to make sure that I covered all the bases for each island so that any questions are directives I received could be addressed immediately. That, they found to be positive on my part, as did I for its accomplishments.

Like any business where you are relying on the assistance of another, there are some that always fall into that "entitlement" mode. You know, it's when a representative feels the need to try and squeeze more money from you based on the services being offered. One thing is for sure: this is a requirement if you live on an island in the Caribbean. Let me first say that this is not true with everyone. I have some of my dearest friends living on the islands who were also our representatives for years. But when you have those who think the picture is much greener on the other side, they will try and test the water by wanting to renegotiate in the middle of any season or even days before the season starts.

The ETA Representative I had in St. Maarten was best known on the island as Big Daddy. Here was a man, quite a large man, who rode a BOSS HOSS motorcycle, a bike that needs a large man on top of it because underneath, he was sitting on a corvette engine. Anyway, the runs on the island are going great. Big Daddy was going into his second year with us as our island representative. Three days prior to our arrival, I received an email from Big Daddy outlining what he was now demanding for his services. Rather than email, I chose to call him direct. He answered on the second ring.

"Big Daddy," I said to him. "This is Steve with ETA. What is this all about?"

I could hear a chuckle in his voice as he said, "You got my email, it sounds like." There was silence on the phone for a few seconds until I heard him say, "Let's discuss it when you get here."

"No, that's not gonna work for me," I said back. "I want to know why all of a sudden, you're demanding more money?"

Added money after all funds had been collected from my guests. This went back and forth.

"Let me put it this way, Steve. Either I get what I asked for else I will stop the bikes from coming onto the port off the ship."

At first, I was taken aback by his threat, but then I thought to myself, *I seriously doubt you have that much pull here on this island.* I came to find out, he does not. The only pull he has is when he's jacking himself off with his false and fake powers, I thought to myself.

I said to him, "I guess we'll discuss it when I get there. There is no way you can expect me to go back and recharge my guests in the middle of this cruise."

He agreed, and I recall just hanging up from my end without saying another word. I thought for a minute and then knew what had to be done.

Max Phillipe was a very distinguished man who was the director of security for the Port of St. Maarten. Max was also a renowned artist whose art has been seen worldwide. A position that held tremendous responsibilities and overseeing the movement of every cargo ship, yacht, and passenger cruise ship that docked on the island. Not to mention the huge amount of shipping containers that pass through, I was introduced to Max by a dear friend of mine whom I have known for over thirty years. When I was a cruise director, I dealt with this man on every arrival and departure. This was the Port Agent and my friend, Frank Bruny.

Frank was loved by all who he dealt with. Truly a man who always had a smile on his face and was willing to help you out at any notice. Frank's position as Port Agent controlled the movement of every cruise ship and all movements while in port. When I received the call from Big Daddy trying to squeeze more money from me, I immediately thought of calling Frank and explaining what had transpired. My question was, Did he have any power here on the port, and does he have any power to stop us from enjoying our tours here? Not only were the answers NO, but Frank also called Max and had us on a conference call where he gave Max the rundown of what was going on. There was no hesitation at the end of that conversation.

"Steve," Max said to me, "I want you to come to my office in the port upon your arrival, and I will contact Big Daddy and tell him to be here as well."

I agreed without hesitation, and before I could even say thank you, Max said to me, "And I will assure you that Bid Daddy has no power within the port, nor does he have any power to control the roads. I will set the record straight tomorrow morning."

I quickly said, "Thanks, Max. I just didn't know who else to turn to, and that's why I called Frank. I will see you once the ship has been cleared."

We each said good night and ended the call.

After I hung up, I took the next few minutes to think about how this had started. All of greed. No other purpose. The route was not changing. We were going to his bar as well and spending money there. I could not figure out any other reason except to be greedy.

"Oh well," I thought aloud. I know Max and Frank had my back.

Without letting anyone, even my staff, know what transpired the night before, I just explained that I had to meet the port security director and that I would be back. There was no point in having this be the talk of the morning as we were on the dock with our motorcycles waiting for full clearance.

I arrived at Max's office before Big Daddy did. I wanted to make sure that I had covered the ground and knew the layout of Max's office and how the chairs were positioned. Again, being taught by my father on what are the best room layouts when holding a meeting. I knew that Max would be behind his desk, but I wanted to know how any other chairs were positioned.

"You always take the seat directly across from the main desk," I could still hear my father say that to me. "Make sure to always position yourself directly across from the main person in the room," he would say.

This way, you have his full attention, and he does not need to turn his head to listen and speak with you. It was perfect. There was only one chair across from the desk, and the other was up against the side wall next to the filing cabinet.

There was a knock on the door followed by its opening and there stood Big Daddy, with a smile on his face as if he swallowed the parakeet. As I was preparing myself to speak, Max chose to begin the meeting simply by saying, "Julian Chance, it has been brought to my attention that you're attempting to throw your weight around and demanding more compensation on something that you already signed off on. Is this true?"

You could have heard a pin drop. Silence for a few seconds, and then Big Daddy decided to enlighten us with, "Well, ya know, Max, it was I who originally cleared this, and I believe that ETA is getting paid a lot of money for their tours. All my hard work, I should be able to reap its benefits, too!" he said as he shifted his enormous weight from one side to the other.

Preparing myself to jump in, I was stopped by Max, who clearly said, "You, Mr. Chance, have no business with this port and definitely have no say, who comes and goes here! Do I make myself clear?" All I could do was sit there and watch this over-weight man turn into jelly as he was berated for his failed attempt to extort more money from me. His response was simple. He said, "Very well. I understand."

Since I knew from the day before that things could not go as I hoped for, I contacted another friend who lived in St Maarten and asked if he would be interested in being the ETA representative for St. Maarten. I knew he had the time and was thought of by the others as a good choice. As we walked out of Max's office, before I would let Big Daddy utter one pathetic word, I turned and said, "Ya see, Big Daddy." I said proudly, "You don't mean shit on your own island! Thought you were going to have me thrown off and deported?"

I was going to continue, but I chose just to tell him he was no longer needed for my tours and I would prefer he not ride with us any longer. I watched as he took his fat ass on his Boss Hog and rode off into the sunset. Well, okay. It was not dark outside yet, but I always loved that saying. I arrived back to the pier where everyone was just being cleared by St Maarten Customs, and there stood my new representative, Peter Gunn (no relation to the gun fighter). Introductions were made, and off we rode with the fantastic Caribbean Eagles/St Maarten as our Traffic Team.

I appreciated Peter for taking the helm for our St. Maarten Tours. He was well respected on the island, and his knowledge was appreciated. Peter's time with us was for two seasons; as his real estate properties were taking a strong amount of his time, I needed to begin my search for our next St. Maarten ETA representative. Time was of the essence, but I knew that if I just focused and kept positive, someone would hold the position.

That final ride with Peter and the Caribbean Eagles SXM road team, a person, whom I have the utmost respect for was standing before me. Just like my sister, I held this wonderful lady (and still do) in my heart. Jane Netto-Therond has been the president of the Caribbean Eagles for several years. Loved by not only the club members but also when you travel throughout this wonderful island on both the French and Dutch sides. Everywhere we went, people would call out to Jane with waves and heartfelt hand gestures. Truly a lady with so much. Jane hails from the sister island, Aruba, but has lived on St. Maarten for most of her adult life. Along with her husband, Bruno Therond, they live on the edge of one of the tallest mountains on the Dutch side, with million-dollar views of the entire Port of St. Maarten and the magnificent French Street Boardwalk in Phillipsburg, the ocean and sunset views that are so incredible.

ETA Steve Wallach with Caribbean Eagles of
St Maarten, Jane Therrond-Neta

Jane was our ETA representative for over sixteen years. Up until the COVID-19 pandemic closed all US Ports and completely shut down the cruising industry for over two years, the relationship I had with both Jane and Bruno has stayed strong to this writing. In fact, Bruno was one of my ETA road captains. It was an impressive feeling having Bruno with us. French speaking with a thick French accent, the ladies adored him, and the men respected him. Most appreciated for the times Bruno was with us. I noticed from my office that we had a large group of bikers coming from Montreal, Canada; most of the group spoke French with just a few able to speak broken English. This was another perfect time to bring Bruno out as Road Captain. It was truly what made the success of this group run smoothly. This, too, I give thanks to my St. Maarten brother, Bruno Therond.

Jane and I speak almost weekly, and we continue to build each other up when our emotions run out. What I did learn from Jane throughout those years was patience and understanding…to a degree. To know me, I have patience until someone shows me their ignorance. From that point, my attitude changed. It was Jane who taught me to respect what I gain and my accomplishments. I always looked forward to our rides in St. Maarten because being with sister Jane meant so much to me.

ETA Motorcycle Cruises lead Road Captain Steve Sollenne

There are numerous stories of many during my bike cruises. Most memorable, some would wish you could forget and others that were funny. No matter what, we had no two cruises the same. The people made up our bike cruises, and they came from all walks of life. The rider who has saved for this bike cruise for the past three or five years to the executive who made sure to book one of the top suites. Some people stood out more than others.

We were leaving out of Miami, aboard a Royal Caribbean ship; cruising for seven nights and visiting the Eastern Caribbean islands. On the first night of any of our bike cruises, you could tell just how excited our guests were. From meeting initially at the hotel before riding over to the port to our first ETA Welcome Aboard Party, many had been drinking all afternoon and were already primed for the night. Primed for what, only I could assume they knew. There was always that one person in every group that just had to show their ass on the first night. Whether it was for being loud and obnoxiously drunk to acting funny and a happy drunk would be. Nonetheless, they were there to party, and ETA made sure to fulfill their wishes. Well, again, most of them.

We were aboard Royal Caribbean's Explorer of the Seas, departing from Cape Liberty, Bayonne, New Jersey, cruising for ten glorious days to the Eastern Caribbean. The cruise was fantastic; our guests did nothing but talk about every island ride and what memories they were taking home for a lifetime. This was a great ETA Staff run. I had hired Ted Walker (Tanya Tucker days) as one of my Rd Captains and had the pleasure of having my son out with me. It was always a pleasure when Nathan was with us. Made me proud.

I had already decided to head back to my stateroom for the evening.

"Hey, guys," I said to both Ted and Nathan. "Come by in about thirty minutes, and let's go over disembarkation procedures."

We still had two days at sea remaining, but I wanted the process to run smoothly. I picked out a good movie to watch, changed into my bathrobe, and poured myself a glass of merlot, St. Francis.

Nathan and Ted arrived, and we went through the process and covered every possibility to make certain for a smooth disembarkation. I stood up to say good night, and all I remember was falling forward—forward directly into the glass table that was made of wood and glass.

When I came to, or did I, I saw myself below me. By now, I must have been taken out into the hallway (for some unknown reason), and there was a ship's officer performing CPR on me and another officer assisting. I looked around and found that I was inside some type of cloud or was it a mist? Maybe a fog, but no matter what it was, I was floating in it. Now understand and picture this: there was a bright light beam shining directly on me from above. There were no walls, hallways, or ceilings. It was as if everything above me had no ending. It was as if it was a cloudy, sky-filled day.

"We have no pulse! We have no pulse!" shouted the second officer who was taking my vital signs. As I am looking down at myself, I can see the officer giving my mouth-to-mouth was the security chief, John Tartaglia. Then suddenly, he starts beating on my chest, calling out, "Steve! Steve! Come on, Steve. Don't you die on me!" I completely recall the events that followed.

I felt myself floating above my body. Sometimes, I would float higher, and other times, I would float back down.

"Please don't let my father die!" I could see Nathan calling out.

He was crying, sitting on the edge of my bed, repeating those words repeatedly. I tried to reach out to his arm, but it was as if he never felt me touch him. I would try repeatedly to no avail. As I would get closer to him, another voice would fill my space. "It's okay, Daddy. It's okay now. Daddy, Daddy, I am here. Please come and join me."

I would find myself turning as though I was now facing my… my daughter Rachel. Rachel passed away in 1991 from a horrific medical disease, as I explained earlier.

So here I am, floating in the air. I think it was air. How else would I be able to continue this? Is this what happens when you pass on? Was I now being met by my loved ones? Yet I felt at peace. As Rachel would extend her arm and hand to me, I do not think I ever reached out to her.

The more she would call out, "Daddy, please join me," my son would still be crying his eyes out, begging G-d not to take me away from him. I watched as the ship's medical team arrived. I could literally see these men and women work feverishly to save my life.

"Clear! Clear!" were the words that the medic yelled out, followed by "Stand back!" To see and watch yourself being hit with thousands of volts through a defibrillator was amazing. I felt helpless as I watched my body gyrate on both hits. Yes, there were two attempts to bring me back, and the second one was my saver.

As my daughter and son's voice became faint, I heard another voice clearly saying, "Steve, it's not time yet. We have no time, but you still have time." The voice was that of my Nanny, once again. Now I know you may be thinking he hears from his grandmother often. Actually, that is not the case. I have only heard of and or seen my grandmother when my life was on the balance of living or not. I wish I had been able to speak to this incredible woman throughout the years. If it was her voice and presence that surrounded me to be unafraid and believe, then I really do not think this book would have ever been written.

What happens to you when you experience death? Do we each see things differently from each other? Is there a bright light? Is there an end to "a" tunnel? Does your life really flash before your eyes? I cannot write about another's experience, but I can write about my own. And yes, I saw a wide, bright light extend from above down to my body. It covered my body from head to toe. The light touched no other area, not even the other people working over me or the hallway carpeting. Only I did the light touch. As I said before, there are no ceilings, walls or any interference between this light and the heavens above. I do not recall any type of tunnel as I felt myself just floating freely. It still amazes me that these people saved my life, especially Security Chief John. If it weren't for his quick response and action, I honestly do not think I would be here writing this book.

After that final defib jolt, I saw myself floating closer to my body. As I turned, I was able to see Rachel as she faded into the air. My son was becoming more visible to me, as was Ted and the other medics and security staff. My eyes opened, and I felt as though I had been asleep for days. I remember looking at John and hearing him say, "Bloody hell, Steve! You scared the shit out of me!"

I saw my son stand along next to me as he rubbed away his tears of sadness, which were replaced by tears of joy. As I was wheeled to the ship's hospital, I was monitored for the next twenty-eight hours before I was wheeled back to my stateroom for the duration of the cruise, alive and happy.

Having been flown at once back to Nashville, Tennessee, I was taken to Centennial Heart Hospital, where I underwent immediate surgery. I am now the proud owner of my very own pacemaker and defibrillator. They said I had flatlined on the ship for seventy-two seconds. Granted, that does not sound like much, but that was a long time to be dead.

Well, over ten thousand people enjoyed the ETA Motorcycle Cruises. In the twenty years of operations, we fulfilled many bucket-lists for those who already knew their fate. My eyes would fill every time someone would come to me during the cruise and say thank you. Literally, I had one couple on a ten-night cruise to the Southern Caribbean, and during our welcome reception, the wife came over to me and said, "Thank you, Steve."

As I looked at her, I could see that her eyes were beginning to swell with tears. As I reached out and gently took her hand, I said, "Well, I'm glad and thank you for booking with us."

She just smiled at me and said in her soft voice, "No, Steve, you don't understand. This is my husband's bucket list, and he wanted to make sure he could do it. Ya see, he has stage four cancer, and he won't be with us too much longer."

What do you say when someone, a perfect stranger, comes over to you and says thank you and gives you the reason why? It is a very powerful way to receive any message from another. Yet we are each programmed to learn and accept the negative as much as we accept the positive. I kept in touch with this couple for the next year. Every few weeks, I would give him a call and see how he was doing. The last time I called, the phone just rang and rang and rang. Seemed that the voice message would ask for the message. This time, when I was just about to hang up, a voice answered the phone and said, "Hello, Steve."

Before I could even ask how she knew it was me, she reminded me about caller id. As she began to speak to me, I could tell just by her tone that she was upset over something. Trying to bring focus to my thinking, she softly said, "Jeff's gone. He passed away in the middle of the night. He's gone, Steve."

What was I to say except extend my condolences? "I'm truly sorry to hear this," I said. I'm so happy I was able to meet him before he past.

Before hanging up and ending this emotional conversation, she said to me, "Ya see, Steve, he knew it. He knew when, and he wanted to make sure he did one of your bike cruises before it was too late."

In a way, I felt honored that here was a perfect stranger who wanted to experience one of my bike events before he died. And he did. It truly touched my heart.

I found myself getting inspired by many of my guests. Not that all of them were positive inspirations, but many brought with them yet another opinion to weigh on. Granted, there were some that were completely off the grid. It made you wonder if they really were like this at home. One couple that felt the need to join our happy group was a man who arrived at the post-cruise host hotel along with his lady. If it were not for the motorcycle, one would have thought Zorro (a bit overweight). His name was Al Black. Dressed as if he were going to a formal masquerade or an incredible Halloween party, from his three-point black "pirate" hat, his black scarf neatly tied around his fat neck, to his long sleeve black silk-type shirt only buttoned halfway so he was able to how off his many "gold" chains, to his black pants being held up by a black belt and silver buckle. Oh, and let me leave out his black sneakers and black socks. Trust me, I cannot make this up. Now the lady with him was thin, maybe in her thirties, dressed in jeans and a top. Nothing unique about her dress. She just seemed to go with the flow with whatever her man told her to do. I am not one to tell someone how to dress but…

I want to bring Al Black up because out of the thousands of bikers, spouses, and friends that joined an ETA Motorcycle Cruise, he was the only man who acted and performed like a complete disgust. Body odor that could stop a train at full speed. It seemed by the second night, he had not changed his clothes either. During the day in the hot sun, you were able to see him walking around with sweat running down his face. I just cannot imagine what their cabin's odor was. Now I cannot guarantee his under garments, and personally, that was fine with me.

That night at dinner, my ETA Road Captains and I welcomed our guests into our area of the dining room, asking each if they had a great day. Seeing the smiles and sharp colored red from their sunburnt bodies, it was nice to see all enjoy their sea day. On the first sea day of every bike cruise, the ETA Staff would set up an area in one of the "not being used" lounges and pick an area off on the side to sell our lunch packages and, of course, our commemorative T-shirts. I was very proud to say that the monies made off the sale of the t-shirts, minus costs, went directly to our top fundraisers, St. Jude's Children's Hospital, American Cancer Society, and Leukemia Foundation. Very proud to say that we always reached our goals for each foundation.

So as I was telling you, here comes Mr. Black and Guest. Even by the second night, other guests at the same table were asking me if they could be switched. "Absolutely!" I said. "I will speak with our head waiter about it."

Right now, I was able to convince the two other couples to sit there this evening and would be moved by morning. A message would be sent to their cabin later that evening with their new table assignment.

Dinner seemed to be going well for my guests. You could hear the laughter among the tables and many different conversations taking place. The next three nights would be filled with daily bike rides on some of our favorite islands. One could only imagine how excited each guest was getting as the time ticked away.

I noticed that Mr. Black's table was just now getting their main courses. If they were getting what some of my other guests were having, then it should be just fine. Everyone thought the dinner tonight was fabulous. All but....

"I'm not eating this crap! I wouldn't even feed it to my dogs!"

"Oh shit!" I called out. I knew exactly where it came from and who said it. One of my road captains and I immediately approached Mr. Black's table, and I said, "What seems to be the problem here? Why would you cause such a scene here in the dining room?!"

"This food sucks!" yelled those words from Al Black. You see, this poor excuse for a person chose to take his full plate of food and turn it upside down as he slammed the plate onto the table. I stood with amazement and could not believe this just happened.

As I could see many of the head waiters walking toward us, I said, "Let's go, Black! You are out of this dining room. Get up and walk the fuck out!"

Lo and behold, this pure scum then looked over to us and called out, "Fuck you too!"

Security had been called, and they took it from there. All I know was that he was given his final warning for behavior and was banned from eating in the main dining room for the remainder of the cruise. Th final straw was his anti-Semitic remarks when he found out that I was Jewish and owner. By this point, his removal from the dining room and island rides satisfied me and I refused to lower myself to his white-trash habits.

There were other instances involving Mr. Black, but the last was, again, it fit well with who he was. The rides went great, people dressed in comfortable attire, and many had some sunburns from the rides. That was part of the adventure. Mr. Black did not attend our farewell party on the last evening. It is here that we go over all disembarkation information and answer any last-minute questions about disembarking the motorcycles. One of my road captains received a call from Mr. Black asking if someone could bring some luggage tags to their cabin. So we did not have to. We asked our ship's group coordinator to please have some sent. The entire ETA Group had special luggage tags enabling us to disembark first as a group. This way, there would be no stalling in getting the bikes cleared with US Customs.

Fits the part. Thirty minutes went by and just before I was handing my ship's deck phone back to the security division, it rang.

"Steve, I can hear the director of housekeeping say to me, can you please come down and meet me on deck one by the bikes."

Immediately, I said, "Sure, I'm on my way now."

As I made my way down to deck one, I could not think of any reason he would want to see me except if it had to do with luggage tags. As I made my turn around the partition, there stood the director of housekeeping between what appeared to be two paper sacks. You know, the paper sacks you can still get at the grocery stores. Both arms were stretched out, pointing toward each bag as he said, "Can you please explain this to me, Steve?"

These bags came from Mr. Al Black's stateroom with your special ETA luggage tags attached. I stood there starring up and down a few times and quietly said, "Are you shittin' me? This is what they're saying is their luggage? Two paper bags?"

I was dumbfounded. What could I do but laugh?

"I guess put 'em through on the belt as luggage," I said. "Let CBP deal with them if needed."

Again, I tried to hand over my deck phone, but again, it rang. "Hello," I said, "this is Steve ETA can I help you?" Here, once again, is the howling of Al Black. "I left our fuckin' passports in our bags! You gotta get 'em for us."

There was no hello, no good morning, no hi Steve. Just his disgusting way of speaking. "Well, it looks like you got yourself in a bind," I said. "The only thing you can do is when you get down to US Customs, let the agent know that you left your passports in your luggage. They will be able to help you."

I immediately left the ship with my road captains and our guests and escorted them to pick up their luggage and move to customs clearance.

I think the appearance of Al Black and Guest, after a seven-night cruise, looked a bit disheveled. Their clothes looked as if they never took them off. Come to find out, they only packed a swimsuit each and spare T-shirt along with a few bathroom necessities. They were both taken into secondary inspection by the Customs Boarder Protection agents. Next was his motorcycle. I normally stay available if my services are needed by ETA. Always wanting to be there for my clients and to assist CBP. But for this couple, I could care less about any further dealing with them.

I can go on forever with the stories from the high seas. Many very similar, especially the ones where alcohol was involved. But as each of the true-to-heart stories unfolded, they each touched me deeper than any other situation. *Why?* I thought to myself. What is causing my mind and heart to feel an emotion that touches me so deep? It is as if I have this sense that sends out special vibes or a stimulus that attracts their emotions and heart where it somehow connects. This is the only way I can describe it. It is not something I learned from books or through teachings. Even as I sit here writing, I can physically feel an emotion come over me, as if there was a very thin but strong wall circling me. Not to defend myself from the outside but rather to secure and keep all of me inside. Does that make any sense? Picture it and see for yourself if you can relate to it.

I had come to the hospital for my daily visit with my dad that day. My father was to have a major test performed regarding his kidneys, so we were concerned as to the results. Upon my arrival, we were met by my father's main doctor, who did not have good news for us. The overall conversation was that my father's organs would start shutting down shortly, and he had just a few weeks left to live. The hardest news I have ever been told next to me was having bone cancer. As we were trying to collect our thoughts, another doctor came in and asked us to go with her to the meeting room down the hall.

As we sit in a circle, she introduces herself to us as one of my father's urologists. She began by explaining a procedure they wanted to perform on my father and that within three weeks, we should see an improvement in him. There was complete silence in the room. All we could do was look at each other. Eyes went back and forth between my mother, brother, and myself.

Finally, I looked over to this doctor and asked her, "Have you read the overview report from my father's doctor?"

"Well, no," she replied. As puzzled as we all were, I could not help myself, but I looked directly into her eyes and said abruptly, "You have no earthly idea as to what the fuck is going on. You want to do some procedure on my father in three weeks?" I toned up and said, "He's gonna be dead in less than three weeks! What is wrong with you, Doctors? Don't you read each other's reports to see medically what should be done?"

I was shocked at her reply, "No, Steve, we each concern ourselves with what our specialty is and focus just on that."

"What the hell does that mean?" I said back in a stern and questionable tone. "You mean to tell me that you, Doctors, don't cover each other's notes?"

Her reply was, "No."

I helped my mother up and brought her back into my father's hospital room. As we were approaching the door entry, I looked at my mother and brother and said, "We are not telling Dad any of this. Do we understand each other?"

Nods came from them both.

Standing on the side of the bed, I started to explain to my father that they have and want to run all these tests, not knowing if they will determine anything. My father's eyes were locked onto mine, and we both gave each other a strong sigh of emotion and trust.

"Pop, tell me what you want to do," I said as I picked up his frail hand and placed it in mine.

As he stared back into my eyes, I could clearly hear him say, "Son, I want to go home. Please, take me home."

I paused for a moment and glanced over to my mother and brother before I turned to my dad and said, "Okay, Pop. Let me go to the nurses' desk and tell them what your wishes are."

As I stood and made my way to the door, I turned when I heard my father say, "Steve, take me home."

The nurses' station was a few doors away. I met with the head nurse on duty and said, "My dad has decided he wants to go home."

Her response was, "Okay, we will meet with his doctors and would let you know something tomorrow."

"No, that's not gonna work," I said. "My father wants to check himself out and leave today as soon as possible."

I could see on her face that she fully understood what I was asking for on behalf of my father. When she turned to me and said, "Steve, if it were my father, I would do the same thing," I knew I was doing right.

Within fifteen minutes, we had met with the social worker who would set up hospice to come to the house for my father's final care, and an ambulance was ordered for the transport. The social worker came in and said that the medical supply company would be bringing a hospital bed and the necessities within the hour.

I walked back into my father's room and said to him, "Okay, Pop! Let's go home."

He looked at me for a second to understand what I had said, and as if it was like past times, that Wallach grin appeared on his face, and his eyes even sparkled. My dad was going to where he belonged, home.

During the time my father was in the hospital (weeks), I would fly down to Florida from Nashville and stay four days. Then I would return to Nashville for two days and repeat the same itinerary. I did this for many weeks. It never concerned me about the flight costs. I was taught that when it comes to family, you must be there. I did this on my own. I was never told that I had to be there with him, but it made him feel better as it did myself.

I was at the airport getting ready to board my flight for my return to my parents when my cell phone rang. Without even thinking anything negative, I answered and said, "Hey, Mom! I'm just about to board the plane. What's up?"

My father passed away fourteen days after we brought him home from the hospital at six-nineteen in the morning. Fighting back my tears, I said to my mother, "Please don't let them take him away until I get there. Promise me that."

"Steve, don't worry. Daddy will be here waiting for you." To see the man you did not get along with in your early years growing up become your mentor, best friend, and loving father lay in front of you, motionless and now cold really took its toll on me. I am proud to say that even at this writing, I am sitting here with tears rolling down my face. This is what I am proud to say happens to me even to this day when I talk about my dad. A brilliant man, Bernard Wallach, who I am so grateful that we mended our differences and became so close like I always wanted it to be.

I arrived at my parents' condo to hear voices coming from the right-side area, closer to the den, but my focus was going into the living room where my father was. Cold to the touch, unfortunately, rigor mortis had set in. I leaned over him and cried my eyes out. I found myself talking to him and saying prayers in Hebrew, prayers I never recalled knowing. My mother came out of the other room, and I recall she and I standing over the man who brought us all a wonderful life, even filled with some not-so-wonderful times, and both of us sharing words of strength.

I remember something out on their balcony getting my attention. To this writing, I cannot think of what it was, but it got me to the point of going out to see what it was. As I could not help but look over the magnificent golf course, I noticed some of the clouds moving in a circular pattern. Immediately, I thought of the clouds I had witnessed through the power of death and thoughts. As I looked up into the circle of the clouds, there before me stood my father. I felt as though I was in a trance of some kind. As the image became a bit clearer, there stood in front of me in the sky, my dad wearing shorts and one of his golf shirts. His smile stood out as I heard his voice call out.

"Hi, Steven," he spoke to me. "Please do not worry. I am right here. It's now up to you to take care of your mother. My trust is in you."

I recall finding myself in a tunnel, shocked and stunned. I know what I saw, and I know what I am hearing. As my eyes filled with tears once again, I found myself having a conversation with my father, who just passed not more than five hours ago.

"Please, Pop! Please come back!" I said softly. "I can't do this right now. It's not your time."

Tears streaming down my face, I was now standing on a balcony waiting to hear that this, too, was only a dream. But it was not. My father lay inside the living room, still and silent.

"It's time, Steven," I heard a voice say.

There was a faint shadow of my nanny reaching out to take my father's hand. Again, if I did not hear and see this for myself, I would not believe it. But this is not the first, second, or even third time I have been faced with this. When there is a tragedy in my life, I have always been comforted by my nanny. Was I making this up in my own mind? Impossible. As signs would be left that were visible to whoever was with me at the time.

As quickly as the circle clouds appeared, they were gone. I turned to walk back into the living room and again stood next to my dad with my mother. "I heard you talking to someone when you were on the balcony," my mother said softly.

"What do you mean?" I said as I kept my eyes directly on the father. "I heard you say Nanny. Were you talking to Nanny? My mother or dad's?" she asked me.

All I could say was, "Yeah, Mom, I was asking her to please watch over him."

We held each other's hands tightly as the doorbell rang. "They're here from the funeral home," someone called out.

I watched carefully as they moved my father's stiff body onto the gurney. I rode the elevator down with my dad and "made sure" he was carefully placed into the vehicle for his last ride from the great place he called home. Bernard Wallach, may you always rest in peace. Amen.

Time went by and my mom and I were as strong as possible. We shared more than just mother and son. I was trusted—as was she. I was honest—as was she, and most importantly, she knew I would never let anything happen to her. A lot of our time was spent reminiscing about the past and what plans need to be done for the future, her future.

"So, Mom, I said to her one afternoon. I gotta ask ya a question. Why is it that when Chuck's kids come down to Florida to visit their other grandparents, they never come up to see you? Heck, they're only in Boca, less than twenty minutes away."

After much delay filled with other questions and easy talk, I was able to convince my mom to open up to me. "My son," as she starts conversations that are troublesome to her, "you see," as she continues to fumble with what words she wants to use, "we didn't pay for their flights or hotel stays this trip. Barbara's parent did, so they won't bring the grandkids up to see us. In fact, they never did except for one time when your father raised hell!"

I just stared at my mom at first. I saw her smile turn to sadness, and her demeanor even changed as her arms just dropped to her sides. That's when it dawned on me. All those trips for Chuck and Barbara and then when their kids came along had a price tag.

I could only sit there so long without making some kind of a comment. "Mom," I said with a concerned tone, "did you and Dad pay for all their flights AND hotel stays when they came here to see you and dad?" It became so silent you could hear a pin drop. "Mom, please," I said in a softer tone. "Seriously…was that the only way they would come down? You guys had to cover their flights and hotels?"

Mom just looked straight ahead and said yes. I was shocked, to say the least, but then again, my brother only spent money first on himself and then his family. I never even received a birthday card or Chanukah card from my brother after fifteen years old—nothing. Whether I continued giving him gifts on those holidays for the next number of years, that was not by brother Chuck. So it makes sense that he would hold his children over my parents' heads for visits. Understand, my brother was making six figures annually, and his wife, Barbara, a hygienist for a very well-known dentist, had the money. To this day, Traci and I both find it troublesome, and this is what was happening to my wonderful parents. Even their meals were paid for by my parents. Never once did my brother ever offer to pay for any meal at any restaurant.

It was during this time that my mother and I discussed her personal information.

"My Stevie," she would say to me, "I need to go over some things with you about my will and what your father had built up. There is a lot of information I must share with you…and only you."

I thought for a minute that this was the time when parents sat down with their children and go over everything, including the burial information.

I said to my mother in a soft voice, "Why are you going over this with me and not Chuck? He's the oldest."

I could see my mom was hesitant in her reply as she was thinking about what to say to me. "Stevie, your father had made a few changes to his will, and I want to discuss this with you." It was an hour later when my mom concluded the conversation with, "I love you, son."

I understood, accepted the responsibilities, and respected our conversation and my promise to her was that I would never divulge it to anyone. Well, except for portions read to my brother only after our mother passes.

During our twenty years of business, we had so many clients asking us about the possibility of getting married during the cruise.

At first, I would refer them to the cruise line for their wedding package, but then I realized this was another incredible avenue to bring in more revenue, not for ETA Motorcycle Cruises but for me personally. After researching what I needed to do to become ordained and legally able to marry people, I am honored to say that I have married over fifty couples through my cruises. Every wedding ceremony is different, I believe. Even though we would always perform the wedding ceremony stateside while still tied up in the home port, there were some islands that allowed me to legally perform weddings. Of course, Puerto Rico and St. Thomas were US territories and there were a few that allowed for it. Needless to say, we would still perform their ceremony sometimes on the water's edge on Magen's Bay, St. Thomas, US Virgin Islands, or standing on the edge of a cliff with the Grand Pitons, St. Lucia, in the backdrop. Couples loved holding their beach ceremony in Aruba. The atmosphere was awesome, and everyone had a terrific time.

Well, my father has been gone for almost three years now. My wonderful mother, still living on her own in their condo in West Palm Beach, Florida, began to have medical issues that had to be attended to with many hospital stays.

One day, I said to Traci, "I think I want to move my mom up to Nashville. She's alone except for her wonderful aide, Jean" (who took care of my father for the last nine years of his life).

Traci immediately started naming a few adult living centers. I could not help but chuckle when she said, "I have just the place, but we will look at a few."

I need to interject here with the answer to the question, Who is Traci? As I wrote this book, the most difficult part to write about was Traci. Where do you begin when it comes to writing about the most important person in your life right now? As my father always said, "Son, you might as well start from the beginning."

My father had been gone only two months when this woman walked into my life. I was not one of these bar men, going out every night and hitting a few great bars where your chances of meeting someone a sure thing is usually. At least it was for me. Those days were far gone, and I became more of a home body.

I agreed that I would try this for a few days. "If nothing happens, I'm off of this," I said to Nathan. The agreement was made, and let the dating began. I sat and searched through options, and lo and behold, there were a few I knew and others that, through friends, I knew.

From her profile, she was a very attractive woman. A busty blond who had a wonderful and inviting smile. Did I mention she had an incredible smile and bust? So we texted back and forth a few times and mutually decided to meet the following evening for cocktails.

"How 'bout five thirty?" I asked.

She replied, "That's fine. I will see you then. I work across the street, so the meeting place is perfect. I look forward to tomorrow."

There have been many who have complained that the person they end up meeting is not the same person they saw a photograph of. I was hoping that was not the case. Well, it was the case. The woman who walked through the door at O'Charley's was far more beautiful than the photo I saw.

I said to myself as I turned to eye her up and down, "Damn, I hope this is her."

We looked at each other and that is all it took. We did an arm motion at each other as she walked closer to the bar. "Hi, are you Traci?" I said with a grin from ear to ear.

"Yes, I am. You must be Steve," said a cute Southern voice.

That lady who walked in just for cocktails has never left my side going on twelve years. That lady is Traci Eells, who is "my better half," "my partner," the love of my life. If the name Eells sounds familiar to those from the Southern states, especially Arkansas, her father, Paul Eells, started as a television sports announcer for WSMV, Channel 4, Nashville, Tennessee, then moving over to call the games for the Vanderbilt Football Team, Paul ended up being the famous voice of the Arkansas Razorbacks. Every game you heard from their stadium was the voice of Paul Eells. Off track just a bit, sorry.

THIS LIFE OF MINE

Steve and Traci, Welcome Reception ETA Motorcycle Cruises

Traci and Steve, ETA Motorcycle Cruises, MSC Divina

Months turned into a few years for Traci and me. A serious medical matter came up with Traci, which has since been taken care of. Without going into any part of this, I remember hanging up the cell from Traci as my body went into an intense shake with tears beginning to stream down my face. As I stood in the kitchen, I saw through the window a bright light shining directly in my face. As I brought my arm up to block the brightness of the sun, I looked up into the sky only to see a circle of clouds (on a sky-blue day). As I focused my eyes through the brightness, there before me was a man. A man with a golf hat on and a golf shirt with the logo of the Arkansas Razorbacks looked down on me with this gentle and calming face. He had silver hair and shiny teeth. His smile was contagious. I realized that before me was someone who looked familiar, but I just could not think who it could be. As I went directly outside and looked up into the sky, he was right there in front of me, as if I could just reach out and shake his hand. Can you imagine if people like me were able to physically touch a spirit?

As I stood in complete silence, I heard a voice say to me, "Hi, Steve. I'm Paul Eells, Traci's father."

My tears were gone, my face was puzzled yet I was calm. I have only seen my family and a very few deceased close friends. Here is a man I have only met once while working in Tennessee in 1978. He spoke about Traci, and he wanted me to know that she would be alright. We should not worry and that she was in great hands. He pointed at me and said, "She's in your hands."

I just stood there. I could not move. My eyes were glued to this image, and I knew what I heard. Once again, it is like tunnel vision. There are no other images I can see on either side, above, or below. I am completely focused on this image.

What felt like an hour was only a few seconds. He wanted me to know again that he was Paul Eells.

He said to me, "Please, Steve, ask Traci what I used to call her."

As the image began to fade, Paul's last words to me were, "My little monkey is gonna be alright."

Paul Eells
Sportscaster & Voice of the Arkansas Razorbacks Football Team

As quick as it appeared, that was how quick the circle of clouds vanished. Sounds a bit strange doesn't it, but it has been like this every time. I stood in my backyard until Traci pulled up the driveway. I met her with hugs and kisses and decided not to say anything now. Traci had enough on her mind right now.

It has been years later, and in passing, I said to her, "Hey, my little monkey!"

She turned to me and said, "My dad would call me that!" I just smiled back and left it at that. It would be years later that I made mention of my conversation back then.

We laughed about our first evening to this day and with our friends. After a few good cocktails, I turned to her and said, "Traci, I have two voice-overs I must get done tonight. Would you care to follow me to my house?"

There was a pause, and then she replied, "Sure sounds like fun."

As she followed me in her car back through along the winding lit street, I was already thinking like any man would.

"Hell ya!" I called out in the car.

No one was there to hear me anyway. I had to mention this because that first date/night, we spent together made us realize that we lived less than five minutes apart for many years, yet we never ran into each other yet frequented the same eateries and lounges.

I must give credit where credit is due. It was my son, Nathan, who suggested that I turn to social media.

"Come on, Dad," I could hear him say. "Go on something like Match.com and see what happens."

Just the look on my face told him (in so many words), "Not a chance in hell."

A deal was made, and I would try this thing called Match.com. Look what happened. I am still amazed by it, but we both continue to build on our incredible relationship.

I could write for hours about our relationship and the things we have encountered together. Traci and her sister, Jennifer, chose to close their store and concentrate on other ventures. I recall saying to Traci, "Why don't you come and work for me at ETA?"

Her marketing and customer service, combined with her outgoing personality, would be the perfect mix. And it was.

I recall my mother telling her after we were together a few months, "My Bernie brought you to my Steve."

I believe it. Why not? There was an incredible relationship between my father and mother. There were times when my mother would look up in the sky and say, "Puny" (a nickname she gave my dad) "give me a sign you can still hear me."

Before my father passed away, he told my mother that when she needed him, he would respond with a raindrop. If I had not witnessed this myself, I would never have believed it. But there, on the windshield, a raindrop would splatter. Understand, there were no clouds in the sky. I looked at my mother, and she would just smile and say, "I love you too, Puny, and miss you with all my heart." I was emotionally touched every time I witnessed this.

So it was far more important that my mother made her residence change without too much stress. This woman has lived in her magnificent condo for over thirty-three years—penthouse views of one of three golf courses at their country club. My Jewish parents from that era always have that one room where one wall is completely covered in family portraits and other family photos. It is as if this was a college course that had to be taken. Again, wanting things to be as close as her Florida furnishings and wall coverings when she arrived in Nashville, I copied the family wall exactly how she had them in Florida. Down to the very last picture placement, I knew my mom would feel "at home."

My wonderful mother had her remaining two and a half years less than three miles from Traci, myself, and the dogs. A fantastic place called Park Manor. It was a very comfortable atmosphere, where the men and women collectively had some incredible stories. We spent almost five or six days a week together. Whether it was for lunch or just to watch television, we all felt like home. When I was in town and not at sea, I would entertain these wonderful people by playing the piano for a couple of hours every Friday. I called it 'Steve's Music Livingroom." We would sing and tell stories. I was able to get some of them to open up and tell funny stories of their past.

"Oh my goodness," one lady called out. "I just peed a little in my pants from laughing so hard."

One touching lady was a famous dancer and suffered from Alzheimer's disease. She would just sit in her wheelchair or living room chair and stare. No movement or facial motions. That was until her caregiver wheeled her down to Steve's Music Livingroom to listen to me play the piano. By the third or fourth song, it was just remarkable. Her hand would start to move, as did her fingers. Her head would tilt back, and her eyes would focus as best they could, over time, on the piano. I felt her every vibe, and I know she felt mine and that of the piano. By the end of the evening's music, people would come by in amazement to see emotion coming from this sweetheart of a lady. Isn't that what music is supposed to do?

Just a small note to show just how a reputation can follow you, it was 2018. I just moved my mother to Nashville from Florida and into one of the finest senior living complexes here in Nashville. Park Manor is a property that offers seniors complete freedom to go about their business, but offers fantastic cuisine, adult exercises, and more.

What my mother found quite nice was that this property also offered assisted living, then over to a section handling dementia and beyond. The reason I am mentioning this is because, within the first week, my mother moved in, we were meeting other residents, and this one Jewish lady came over to introduce herself.

When my mother introduced me, the lady looked at me and said, "I know you from somewhere. Is it West End Synagogue?"

I replied, "No. I used to belong to the Temple, but I now belong to Congregation Micah." I said in return, "I used to own Nathan's Deli in Green Hills."

Without skipping a beat, as she turned to walk away from us, she said, "Oh yes, that Jewish deli that served ham and cheese."

Wow, some twenty years later. Some people just never forget.

What would any good son do for his mother on her eighty-fifth birthday? I hired a male stripper dressed as a cop to crash her birthday celebration with over twenty-five to thirty other ladies. The ladies that participated were each given fifty dollars in $1 bills. My mother was having a blast. One of the other ladies, Ann, jumped up and wrapped her legs around this strip and ripped his shirt off! These ladies had the times of their lives, and I will always be glad I did it for my mom…and for them.

Nelson was his name, and he came on one of our motorcycle cruises with his brother and nephew. Right away, I could see this huge personality that Nelson exhibited immediately, always with a smile on his face and the willingness to assist my ETA crew. I knew this cruise was going to be special. During the day of embarkation, ETA always had a Welcome Aboard Cocktail Reception for our guests. Open bar and eateries, our guests got to mingle and introduce themselves throughout the group. It is during this get-together, myself, and my lead ETA road captain would go over details and what is expected of our guests so that our rides were safe and memorable.

During one of the many cruises, Traci would come out and play hostess. This one ended up becoming a very spiritual cruise for many of us. It was after our initial group welcome aboard cocktail reception one of our guests, Nelson, came up to me and my ETA road captain,

Steve Sollenne to inform us that he needed to have periodic stops along the routes due to his medical condition.

"Ya see, Steve," Nelson said, "I'm stage four cancer, and I wear two bags, and sometimes, they get full quickly."

Our eyes locked in on each other, and I could feel and see our eyes filling up but holding back any droplets.

"Hey, my brother," I said to him as I was holding his hands in mine, "I fully understand, and don't you worry at all. Whenever you need to stop, just give myself or my road captains or even Traci a nod, and we will make the next pit stop for you. It's that simple. All I want you to do is enjoy these incredible rides you're about to be a part of."

From that moment on, Nelson and his family became a true part of the ETA Motorcycle Cruise family.

Nelson's brother Arthur had a very positive attitude, not only for Nelson but for life itself. He was always making jokes throughout the cruise and was very appreciative of the extra time we allowed Nelson.

"Hey, Art," I would say, "there is no extra time we're allowing. Nelson is part of our program and scheduling, and that's how it is."

I did not want Nelson nor Art and his son to feel any different. It was incredible that there were times I had to ask Nelson to stop pushing any of the bikes into their staging position.

"Awe, hell, Steve," he would say, "I gotta do something."

And I would always say back, "You are brother. You're ridin' your bike in the Caribbean!"

After the cruise, I kept in contact with both Nelson and Art. The laughs we would have on the phone were as if we were all still standing together on one of the islands. That was until my phone rang on a Sunday. As I looked at the phone to see who it was, I saw that it was from Arthur.

Answering it in a deep Southern drawl, I said, "Hello, brother! Wazzup!"

Without any hesitation, Arthur said, "He's gone bro. He's gone." The silence that fell over this phone felt as if it were hours, yet truly only seconds. "You're my first call, man," Art said in a soft whisper. "He passed about twenty minutes ago, and you needed to know."

As my eyes filled with tears, this time, I let them run down my face. I will never forget Nelson. We shared the stories of our cancers, but through it all, we always ended our conversations with, "Love ya, bro."

Rest in peace, my dear friend.

Another incident involved a senior officer and two of our guests during our scheduled ride in St. Maarten. On many of our bike cruises, I will always extend an invitation to the captain and staff captain if they would like to ride with us. I do this more out of respect to show my appreciation. I was always taught to be thankful for what I receive either personally or through business. One's appreciation can carry you a long way. There were times when I would also extend an invitation to other officers on the ship. I would always get a special discounted rental rate, so I would always pick up the cost.

Anytime an officer would join us to have their own bike for the ride, I would always make sure that they had with them their motorcycle license. Some countries would mark a person's vehicle license also as their motorcycle license. Even with those licenses that were in another language, we would expect that Officer to be truthful, right?

Staff Captain Sergey Denysov, aboard the *Explorer of the Seas*, had always been one of those Officers who believed in our program and was always on our side when it came to decisions for us. Not only was he staff captain, but he was also a friend of mine for over eight years. Every time he would be asked to join us, it always came down the wire that he had to cancel out due to unexpected matters that would require his presence. It was always disappointing, but we knew that eventually, he would be able to fulfill his dream of riding with ETA Motorcycle Cruises. That day finally came, and it was going to be on St. Maarten. I contacted Fadi Hasbani, general manager for the Harley-Davidson Dealership on the island, and he confirmed that he had a brand-new Harley waiting for the staff captain.

Once again, I asked to see the staff captain's driver's license to confirm that he was licensed to operate a motorcycle back in his country of Ukraine.

His reply, once again, was, "Of course, Steve. My vehicle license is marked on the back so that I'm able to operate a motorcycle as well. And you know, I have a bike at home."

I had to take his word for it, right? He is a captain aboard Royal Caribbean's *Explorer of the Seas*. I had to believe him; his driver's license was from Ukraine.

"I do not speak Ukrainian, staff," I said to him.

"No matter," the staff captain said. I tell you that the mark on the back of the license is good enough."

Why would I think otherwise? Why would I ever think that an officer, a senior staff captain, would deliberately lie.

We arrived at the Harley-Davidson dealership and were met by many of the local riders as well. When ETA was on the island, so many took the day off just to ride with us. Truly a wonderful feeling of camaraderie. I introduced the staff captain to Fadi and one of our island's lead riders, a man they called Cowboy. Cowboy was originally from Aruba but has been a staple here on the island for many years. As I watched Cowboy take the staff captain over to his rental bike, for a split second, I felt an uneasy feeling. I could not pinpoint what it was at the time, but shortly, I knew it was a sign about the staff captain being on that bike. Not a split second later, you could not help but hear the roaring of a Harley engine reaching high revs, followed by screams. As I looked back in the direction of these horrific sounds, I could not help but see two of my guests pinned between their trikes and the rental, still with the staff captain holding the accelerator wide open. For if it was not for Cowboy's quick action, no telling how bad the damage could have been to our guests. Not the way to start our tour here in St. Maarten. One of our guests had to be transported via ambulance to the local hospital while the other was driven back to the ship for attention by the ship's doctor.

Lawsuits were followed by just one of the injured while the other attended to his burns on both legs under his own medical team back home. I found it amazing just how unethical cruise lines (Royal Caribbean International) can be when it comes to not taking responsibility for almost every incident involving a senior officer. It was apparent that the attorney this one guest had just could not go up against this billion-dollar company. When it came down to the plaintiff going to court, they could not compete with the cruise line's legal department. The cruise line was found not responsible nor was their Staff Captain under their guidelines. The plaintiff also attempted to sue ETA Motorcycle Cruises but had filed their suit wrongly; therefore, nothing ever came of their suit. This was a prime example of an ambulance-chasing lawyer who wanted to sue everyone and hoped that something would stick. Nothing ever did. As lousy as I thought of this plaintiff and his family for attempting to come after me, they always came up to a dead end. The cruise line made sure that this Staff Captain was not on any one of their ships here stateside, causing it impossible for him to be legally served. My understanding is that it took them many months to finally serve him. With a company as large as Royal Caribbean International is, I knew that the way their suit was filed was going to be dismissed. Unfortunately, from them, it was. Once ETA Motorcycle Cruise was cleared, I immediately removed myself and my company from any further communication. The result is simple: never take the word of anyone when it comes to being properly licensed to operate anything with a motor. If you do not understand or you are not able to translate, let it go. Find someone who can translate. It was obvious that this staff captain deliberately lied to satisfy a dream that caused serious injury to others that would last someone other than himself a lifetime. I never saw this Staff Captain again throughout my years associated with the Royal Caribbean Group. A good thing because there was no guarantee that I would have acted properly. This lying staff captain caused serious problems for many, and it all could have been avoided by telling the truth.

    Having over ten thousand bikes through my twenty years with ETA Motorcycle Cruises, I have met so many wonderful people. People that have become friends even to this writing. Many of them had some of the most incredible stories having to do with their own lives. Isn't this what life is supposed to be about? Meeting new people from all walks of life and getting to be able to spend time with them. Of course, when dealing with any large group of people, you will always have that few that become known for being…well…assholes. These are the people that either lied on their legal paperwork, caused problems during the cruise, deliberately would have issues with either myself, my staff, or other guests, and of course, your every cruise drunk. We had a couple from Texas, along with his brother and wife from Florida, join us. I bring this up because this is a perfect example of stupidity.

On one of our cruises, I had a couple from the Orlando, Florida, area. This overweight, loudmouthed man named John (refusing to list his full name for any recognition) became a serious threat during the cruise. He had been having run-ins with other ETA guests, and it became an issue where guests were telling me to do something about it. They refused to dine within the reserved seating area unless he was removed. It was that bad. In fact, there were two gentlemen in my group who told me they were ready to handle it themselves unless something was done. Well, something was done. I spoke directly with our head waiter, and John, along with his wife and another couple, were banned from the dining room for the remainder of the cruise and had to either have their meals in the ship's buffet or one of the other alternative restaurants. Being loud a few times is one thing but continuously using foul language in the presence of others was not to be tolerated. At the end of the cruise, John was notified in writing that he was banned from any further ETA Motorcycle Cruises. I was hoping not to ever see him again.

It is now four years since the incident with Orlando John. I have had fantastic groups of people and bikers, and I could not ask for anything more. All was perfect.

That is until the office telephone rang, and Traci said, "Steve, this call is for you. You won't believe who it is." I thought for an instant and mentioned a couple of things, but none were correct. I had no idea.

"It's Orlando John," she said with a smile on her face. As I looked back at her, I could not help but go back in my mind to the time I banned him.

"Take a message," I sternly said. "I have nothing to talk to him about. He's banned, period." I went back into my office, thinking that would be the last time I would hear his name.

Traci came into my office and said, "So John really wants to apologize for what happened on his last cruise some three years ago."

He says that he will not step out of line and really hopes I would accept his apology. I could not help but stand there and laugh as Traci handed me the phone message.

"Are you going to call him back?" she said.

Without hesitation, I said, "No."

We went about our business, and I recall that John had again contacted my office the following week and, this time, spoke with Tami. Tami had handled his initial reservation, so John "thought" he had a better chance with her, not knowing that Traci was my better half and always had direct contact with me. On Tami's day, she had called me downstairs into their office to discuss Orlando John's new plea call. This must have been an easy and happy day for me. I had Tami call him back and told him to call me at three forty-five later that day. Cocky, I sure was, but I felt I had every right not to just agree and let him back on another ETA Motorcycle Cruise.

John called and sounded like a lost puppy. He admitted to being completely out of line on his last cruise with us and sounded apologetic. He also made sure to mention that he had six other couples who wanted to make reservations with him. I was still very weary, so I told John, "Let me think about it over the weekend and give me a call on Monday at eleven in the morning."

As I hung up, I could not help but recall what a pain in the ass he was to all my other guests and my staff, and even some of the crew. Do I believe him at his word now, or is it another one of his ways to squeeze back in? He acts like the reputation of a used car salesman. From a business standpoint, though, the revenue that could be made from his friends' bookings would be nice.

Monday morning, right at eleven, the phone rang, and I could hear Traci say, "Hold on, John. I let Steve know you're on the phone."

As both Traci and Tami made their way into my office, I felt as though I was Caesar having to make the final decision. They each had their hands out in front of them with their thumbs leveled out evenly. Do they turn upwards, or do they turn down, sending it to the grave? I could not help but smile at them both as I said, "I haven't made my decision yet. It all depends on my conversation with him." As they both took seats in my office directly across from my desk, I reached over and picked up the phone.

"Hello, John," I spoke.

My father taught me that even when you know you are about to go into a phone conversation of concern, you need to keep your voice on a positive note so that your approach is positive. So that is what I did.

"Hi, Steve. It's John," said the voice on the phone.

After a twenty-minute phone call, listening to a man do whatever it would take to get back on another ETA Motorcycle Cruise, I read him the riot act and told him straight out that I would put him off at an island if he got out of hand again. He assured me that he would be on his best behavior. I placed him on hold and told Traci and Tami to go ahead and take his reservation under the agreement that the six other couples would make their reservations within the next twenty-four hours. We only had eight bike spots remaining, so if they did not reserve in the time allowed, I know I had a sleuth of others wanting those spots. Within the next twenty-four hours, John had reserved a junior suite for himself, and wife, and the others were all set—off to a good start. So we thought. When it rains, it pours, especially when dealing with some A-type bikers or, better yet, those who think they are.

It was the day prior to the cruise. As always, we hold a pre-meeting at the hotel to introduce ourselves to our guests and go over the next day's procedures. This premeeting was always valuable to the ETA Staff. Attitudes were noticed, bike operating skills were witnessed and, most importantly, proper documents for both the bike operator and motorcycle were in order.

Here we are, going over information when one of our new guests (in Orlando John's Group) asks, "Is the shuttle from here [hotel] to the ship able to carry a scooter?"

At first, I was somewhat puzzled by the question. Never had that asked me before, so at first, I did not know what to say. One of my ETA Road Captains stepped in and said, "Yes, the shuttle has access to transport a four-wheeled electric scooter. Before I spoke directly with the man who just asked the question, I needed more answers. Sitting with him was, I assumed, his wife. I could see that she was handicapped with several medical issues. I, of course, had no issues with her as she was not a bike operator nor a rider fit to ride on many of the island bike routes we use. Just to satisfy myself, I asked him if there were others in the group not riding with us so that she would have someone staying with her while you rode.

"Oh no, she's riding with me," said her husband. I strap her into the rear seat on my trike. "That's how I do it in Florida when I ride." Before I even said anything, my mind and thoughts were buzzing, starting with his initial reservation.

I immediately phoned Tami and asked her to please look at this reservation. I explained the circumstances to her, and she immediately sternly said, "No way, Steve! There is nothing in his file that he even mentioned his wife was handicapped. By now, Traci was also standing with us outside by the other bikes. When I questioned the husband on how he made his reservation, he said he told the office (Tami) about his wife. I was not even holding my cell to my ear, and we all could hear Tami yell, "There is no way! There is no mention of it anywhere on his reservation."

From this point on, I knew we were going to have an issue. I could not help but think, Orlando John, this is one of your games."

In the back of the group, there stood John, staying away from us.

Bottom line, there was nothing written on his signed Motorcycle Agreement. In fact, when it even asked about the condition of a guest rider, there was nothing marked about his passenger being handicapped. It is important to understand that we have had numerous guests and riders who were handicapped. We even had a group of deaf bikers who were fantastic! Not one issue with them, in fact, they rode better than others in the group. This lady, unfortunately, had very little use of her legs. She had what appeared to be cerebral palsy. She had to be lifted onto and off her chair in the dining room and chairs throughout the ship. She used her scooter throughout the ship because she could not move on her own any distance. She was blind in one eye, and it appeared that her arms were also affected by her medical condition. There was no way my office had any idea of this, and I knew for a fact that my island insurance coverage would never allow this. I was not about to lie and attempt to do something that would jeopardize my coverage. We have had an excellent relationship with them, especially from being the first and only company offering such a wonderful and exciting tour.

I gave this man a choice before we left for the ship. He could either leave his trike at the hotel and just take the cruise and spend time with the group and wife as guests or he can take the gamble and see if my insurance company would approve it. He chose that latter, so we loaded his trike on the ship with the others.

Outcome was exactly what I said: your wife is not approved to ride on any island motorcycle ride. The husband threw a teenage-like tantrum when I told him the outcome. His threats and language were one thing, but to start threatening my wife and screaming out, "I'm calling Morgan," and Morgan, I had to just walk away. When his threats became physical, I felt that I needed to call the ship's security chief to report this. The security chief, Madi, hailed from Israel, but it was obvious. He was far too young and immature to oversee the ship's security and safety. He was only twenty-five or maybe twenty-six. He was so unworthy of his title; he never even made a report of this incident, especially knowing that this man threatened physical harm to me, a man with known disabilities. This was completely against maritime law. It takes all kinds, I imagine, and we have seen many of them.

Not to dwell on this group, but once again, John showed his ass to everyone in the group. John had planned this prior to even coming on board. He had set out to make sure that he and his group caused problems throughout the cruise. I was stuck with the decision: do I lock down any bike(s), knowing that it would affect twelve people, or do I bite the bullet until we get back to home port and ban every one of them from any future ETA Motorcycle Cruise?

The ETA Motorcycle Cruise had one more cruise for the month of March 2019. Not knowing immediately at the specific time, the cruising industry would be shut down by the CDC because of COVID-19. My group was on Celebrity's Edge's last run. I feel that we were blessed, for all ships that were still out at sea, guests and crew went through severe nightmares, all caused by panic from every cruise line following the worthless reports coming from the CDC. The only disappointment for our final cruise was that some of the officers, including the infamous Captain Kate, treated my staff and guests like second-class people. As on every bike cruise, we always included a private visit to the ship's Navigation Bridge. This was a great perk that my guests always appreciated. Now granted, there was a lot on the plates of these officers and captain, knowing that their ship would be locked down upon entry and docking back in Port Everglades, Fort Lauderdale, Florida. Captain Kate was standing not more than ten feet from my staff and group as they came onto the bridge. Not even to have the courtesy to greet them by saying hello, just showed once again, how two-faced, yes, two-faced people can be, even a captain. To completely ignore my guests, and especially my ETA staff, was unacceptable.

I had planned on selling the company and retiring 2021 at the end of the company's twentieth year. Knowing from my contacts at most cruise lines and the CDC, the cruise line would be shut down for at least two years. With no revenue being generated for two years or possibly longer, I made the decision to retire and close the company. I ran through emotions and frustration making that decision because the potential buyer I was already in discussions with to purchase ETA Motorcycle Cruises bowed out. I fully understood his decision as much as I really wanted to sell strongly. It was well into seven figures, something to this day still has a spot in my heart. Without having any idea *if* this industry would ever come back, it was a hard gamble no one was willing to take. Never is a long time, isn't it? I may be retired at this writing, but I will always keep a door slightly open just in case I want to "put the band back together again."

Retirement came not as a rush. The status of the cruise industry was not yet fully strong, so I felt good about my decision. My health had a lot to do with my decision as well. Not going into detail, but having beaten the most severe bone cancer, twice having kidney cancer, and a sleuth of other medical points, it was time to cut back. Am I at all bored with my time? Do I sit around and wonder whether it is the appropriate time to bring back the ETA Motorcycle Cruises, or do I just enjoy these wonderful dreams? As I did over twenty-three years ago, do I turn my dream into another reality? Only time will tell. In the meantime, I am enjoying my time between my residences. I could never give up living in Nashville, Tennessee. It became my home in 1981, and I consider myself a true Nashvillian. My roots are now there. With my parents both gone, a brother who I have not heard from since two months after our mother's death, along with a very confused son who, like my brother, I have not seen since the first-year anniversary of his grandmother's death, over four years ago. Both were only concerned with whatever financial gain they thought they were 'entitled' to. The details are not worth writing about as far as I am concerned.

I will, however, as a father, I will stress to every person out there who has children from divorced parents to be aware of their ex. As we all know of sayings that have been used by both sides, when you use your only child to brainwash, it truly shows what kind of a person, not just any person, but a vindictive person you really are. I really got tired of hearing things that she had been feeding our son for years, but I thought Nathan had the intelligence to understand the actual truth over vindictiveness. Apparently, he had not. What I do find challenging to this day is that with all the teachings Nathan was taught by me and my parents, his grandparents, they were not as strong enough to make him see where the truths lay. I guess the only thing my side of his family was good for was paying for his college tuition (one year where he never attended but told us he had), paying back tens of thousands of dollars on his student loans we knew nothing about. The loans were only brought to our attention when they had to be paid back. I find it sad that Nathan was not in a great mood when he decided to finally bring these loans to my attention. In fact, as I questioned him where these loans came from (as a parent I had every right to), his response was that his mother convinced him to take out the loans.

"Nathan, who the hell is paying them back?" I said to him with a stern look.

I was shocked when he had the audacity to say, "Mom said for me not to worry 'cause the Wallachs had money, and they'll pay them off. They won't let me default."

I sat for a short moment and reacted as any decent divorced parent would. "You've lost your fuckin' mind!" I shouted back.

This is what my only child, my son, has turned into. I could not stop there. My next discussions were with my mother since my father had already passed on. To say she was furious is not as bad as she really was. My mother and I discussed the matter over the next few days, and it was I who chose to pay off his loans from my trust fund. A fund I had no idea held what? It was never an interest to me to know anything about my parents' financial structures. So without further ado, Nathan's college fund was paid. Again, the Wallachs came to the aid of Nathan Wallach. He had just graduated with his BS degree and a master's degree, even after his tardiness in college. Do not let me forget. It took him six years to graduate, not the standard four. It seems that the four-year program has become the new six-year program.

I was hoping to avoid this portion of my life to recall as it has been nothing but time filled with emotion, hurt, challenges, love, and respect. With every parent, especially a Jewish father, having an only son is the most important accomplishment one can face. Of course, the loss of my daughter, Rachel, was devastating in itself, so having your only son meant the world to me. I do not want to hash over all the great things Nathan and I did together. But they become completely shadowed.

Nathan chose to marry his girlfriend (at the time), Jennifer. Jennifer was no stranger. She was dating and engaged to Nathan's best friend at the time. I recall Nathan driving over to my home, charging into the house, hysterically screaming, "Dad, we need to talk! Please come with me!" It was obvious that he was shaken, but from what? So I followed him outside and behind the garage.

"What's up?" I said.

"Dad, I really fucked up!" he said with a shiver in his voice and tears running down his face. "I did the most horrible thing to my best friend!"

It hit me like a ton of bricks. As I turned to him with my eyes already beaming out to his, I said, "You fucked Matt's girl, didn't you?" I know I said it twice because I already knew what his answer was going to be. "Tell me, Nathan, are you a buddy fucker?" I said calmly.

As Nathan stood there visibly shaking, he looked at me and said, "Yes."

It was not my business, nor did I have any reason to want to get involved. It was his problem. This was the lowest thing my son could ever do besides committing a serious crime. He fucked his best friend's fiancée. Nothing was worse in my eyes.

So needless to say, this started the strain between father and son. As time went on, Nathan and Jennifer got engaged. Nathan's mother immediately barged in and decided to plan the entire event, leaving me out of everything.

She even came out and said, "If your father is involved with any portion of this wedding, it'll be over my dead body!"

Now, understand, when I say everything, I mean everything. All I was to do was open my checkbook and pay for most of the wedding. Imagine feeling like a lower guest at your own son's wedding. I was not given the offer to get my tux with the other groom's party. I wasn't even allowed to participate in the groom's toast prior to their wedding ceremony. I was not to be included in any part. So when they started lining people up to walk in, they had a groomsman walking my mother in. My mother had enough.

She turned to me and said, "Steven, you walk me in. I'm not walking in with anyone else." At which point, Nathan immediately came to the other side of her and tried to walk with us. Anyway, the wedding was a joke insofar as all the Wallachs that were there felt. For many months prior to the wedding, Nathan would say to his grandmother, "Nanny, I can't wait to have that dance with you at my wedding."

My mother would grin with such happiness. It was unfortunate that this, too, was nothing more than a lie by Nathan. This (son) only came by our table (which was in the back of the room) one time and never danced with the woman who was his best friend.

The woman that took him on cruises and vacations to Alaska, not to mention the many times each year where she would bring him to Florida. This was not even counting the times when I would fly us down to visit. I remember Mom turning to me and saying, "Stevie, I wanna go home now. There's nothing here for me."

So with that, I packed up my mother's oxygen tank, got her walker and the entire Wallach family left together. Mom and her aide got in their car, and Traci, and I retrieved ours. I looked over to Traci, with tears running down my face, and said, "If he doesn't come by this car to say goodbye, we're done. I'm through. Nathan never came by the car to say thank you for even goodbye. As far as I was concerned, our relationship is gone.

I already made mention as to his attitude after my mother, and his grandmother passed. Boy, isn't it amazing how money can really cause havoc within a family? Nathan has been absent from my life for the past five years. It is at the point where I do not wish him harm, nor do I wish him good. I just do not wish for him at all. Even going through all of my cancer surgeries, I have never heard from him. Even when I found out that his mother had passed, he never even had the respect to let me know. Remember, I was half of that couple that had you. How dare you act this way toward me?

Traci and I sent Nathan a text message that read, "Sorry I had to hear this from someone not part of our family, but our condolences to you on the loss of your mother."

Never even received a response from him. No thank you, no fuck you, nothing. That I thought was the worst disrespect, but I wasn't even close. Remember, there are things said by others during times of emotions and there are those times during emotions when words come out that are meant to hurt. Rumors were running open that it was me who Nathan would have wanted to see dead, not his obsessed mother whose biggest wish was to destroy the relationship between father and son would happen. That was her warped way of saying she got even with me. How in the world could anyone wish something so disgusting about their own parent? Just goes to show you that no matter what you do for a child, there may be a time when that child turns on you. I pray others are not faced with such hatred.

Nathan was never a leader—always a follower in his personal life. He never grew a set of balls, as they say. He has always allowed the girl in his life to control him. And it is so obvious that Jennifer wears the pants in that family. Nothing wrong with it if it is over common knowledge and experience. Nathan's entire life toward me changed within months of her being part of his life. Remember, even my wonderful mother said, "I really can't stand Jennifer, but it's not up to me. Boy, was my mother ever so right. Feelings are the exact same from Traci, so who's wrong?

I never thought I would ever be faced with a child having such hatred for someone who basically gave him everything in his life up until then. As I mentioned previously, I come from a family where my father had no father. His father left the family when my dad was less than one year old. Everything my incredible father did for his family and himself came from his devotion, dedication, and love for his family, including his religious beliefs. This being taught what a true Cohane means and the respect it deserves. I tried my best to instill these beliefs in my son through his bar mitzvah at the age of thirteen and throughout the years to follow. I can remember even when Nathan moved out on his own, I continued to do what I thought was right in letting him make his own judgment. Unfortunately, after he became involved with his now wife, his attitude toward his own religion was smeared by his own warped mind.

My brother's children were adopted; therefore, they do not carry any genes from my family, nor can they be marked as Cohanes since they are not the offspring of my brother. My son was and is the only family member who can carry on the legacy of my bloodline and that of my father's bloodline, which basically means the Wallach bloodline will be destroyed if Nathan chooses not to have a family, hopefully, that of a son. It is so unfortunate for me to say in this writing that the remaining heir to our bloodline will cease to exist because of the selflessness of Nathan. Personally, I could care less about his wife and the reason I can easily say that is because his wife lied and cheated him by telling him after they were married that she did not want children. Her reasoning is pathetic as well. Remember when she was with Nathan's best friend Matt? He, too, was shocked when she also told him after the fact that she decided not to have children, so it was obvious that Nathan was also taken by surprise. Or was he? All I know is that Nathan made the choice to "kill off" our heritage and family legacy. Something no Jewish father or any father would be proud of.

I enjoy the taste of each new day as I planned out just a few things to keep me busy. There are always things to do both outside and inside the house. Since I enjoy gardening with Traci, it was always good day, especially when you plant and get to watch daily as each plant creates its own beauty as each bud turns into spectacular colors. Between my music tours and cruises, there were very few times I was able to enjoy all the blooms and colors.

They say that when one does retire, hobbies are a great way to keep your mind active and your body parts moving. After my heart surgery, I decided to build something I remember from my childhood. Model trains. Not your typical HO scale or even Lionel model trains. I wanted my trains to run outside, year-round. Needless to say, I am the proud engineer, conductor, bottle washer, and maintenance man at Wally's Central Express, where I have five separate running rails totaling twenty-seven hundred feet of brass G-scale track. It is a great adult hobby, especially since that is an expensive hobby at that. But to date, it has been a wonderful and relaxing enjoyment not only for me, but Traci and others enjoy coming by and daydreaming about a train ride.

I thoroughly enjoy all the extra time I have for Layla and Louie. I was still traveling approximately three weeks each month when we first brought them home from Maine, so being home now is extra special. If it were for our dear friends, I do not think we ever would have gotten them.

I answered a social media thread from a friend about a litter of AKC–registered black Labrador puppies. It turned out to be a friend of hers, again meeting through social media. When phone numbers were exchanged, I immediately phoned.

"Hello, Michelle," I said. "This is Steve Wallach from Nashville, Tennessee. I hear you have a female black lab for sale?"

We exchanged some small talk, and all questions were answered. I kept hearing a dog whimper in the background during our conversation. "Is that the female?" I asked.

"Oh no," she replied. "That was her brother."

Michelle proceeded to tell Traci and me the story about how this litter originally had nine puppies. Unfortunately, two were stillborn. The remaining seven were fine, but the only female, and this one male were the last two delivered and have ever left each other's side. Whether they were sleeping, eating, playing, or just relaxing, they never left each other's side.

Michelle said, "It was the strangest thing. They were happy being just the two of them."

I thought for a minute as Traci and I were looking at each other.

"I know what to do," I said to Michelle. "I'll take them both!"

And that is exactly what Traci and I did. If it were not for our dear friends, Tom and Elaine Dommell, this never would have happened.

Elaine and Tom were great clients and friends, and we shared mutual clients and friends with Dan and Cindy Berndt. Traci and I met them through one of my ETA Motorcycle Cruises. If anyone was able to help me out, it would be them.

"Hello, Tom," I said into my cell phone. "This is Steve Wallach, and Traci is with me on the speakerphone."

The hellos were given, and I paused and said, "So, Tom, I need a favor if possible." As silence filled the telephone, I started my schtick. "Traci and I have found a brother and sister lab pups that we would love to get and have them trained for my medical and support. The only problem is they're in Maine."

Now a small pause, and I can hear Tom take a breath and say, "And what can I do for you?"

Even now, I know Tom knew what I was about to ask him, but I guess it was important for me to be able to ask this favor in the proper manner.

I checked into flights from Nashville to Maine, and with all the stops and plane changes, it was going to be like a seven-hour ordeal. I concluded with, "Is there any way you would consider flying Traci and me up to Maine to pick up the pups and back to Nashville?" You see, Tom had purchased Dale Earnhardt Jr.'s jet.

Without any hesitation, Tom said, "As long as we all understand that I'm not doing this for you or Traci. I'm doing this for the pups."

We all chuckled and were so thankful. I showed our appreciation by saying, "Hey, guys, Traci and I want you both to be their Godparents."

Thus came before us, Layla and Louie.

Layla and Louie

I was fortunate enough to have the option to buy out my brother for his half of ownership of my parents' condominium. Even then, Chuck tried to make me pay over and above the even split. Even the trustee told my brother to just split it. His encouragement seemed to work; my parents' home for the last thirty-five years was now solely mine. The upkeep of the building and the grounds of the country club are still spectacular. It is amazing to me, but every time I walk into the condo, I can immediately feel as though five hundred

THIS LIFE OF MINE

pounds have been lifted off my shoulders, and I can still feel the presence of both my father and mother. Is it strange to say I can still smell them here inside when I first walk in? It is a feeling of warmth, as though I can feel their arms around me. Truly, it is a feeling of love without boundaries. That was how my father and mother were a welcoming sight if ever you needed some guidance or understanding.

It was mid-February 2021. Traci and I were enjoying the company of others at the pool in Florida. The ladies were on one side of the pool talking about, well, who knows what. And the guys, including myself, were on the other side of the pool just reminiscing of our pasts, when an older gentleman was doing his walking exercises.

A friend, Bruce, turned to me and said, "Steve, I don't know if you know this guy, but let me introduce you to him. He's been around here for years."

As I looked at his face to see if I recognized him, Bruce said softly so as not to be heard by others, "His name is Herb Scheiner."

With a confused look on my face, I said, "His name and his face I just can't place now. The name does sound familiar, but I can't place it."

As this gentleman made small ripples in the water walking toward us, Bruce said, "Hey, Herb, don't know if you know this man, but his name is Steve Wallach."

We shook hands, and this gentleman, probably in his late eighties, immediately broke off the conversation and said, "Wallach… hmmm. I used to know a Wallach." Pointing into the sky, he said, "In fact, he used to live in that building. He was my best friend for years."

As this elderly man points to the building where a Wallach still resides there, I tried to say, "Hey! That was my father!"

This man named Herb immediately looked at me and said abruptly, "Let me finish, please. I'm older than you."

A chuckle was heard from Bruce, me, and of course, Herb.

As Herb's voice became mellow, I looked into his eyes and immediately felt a lump in my throat as he said, "His name was Bernard, Bernie to his friends, Wallach. Boy, I sure miss Bernie."

I felt myself looking deep into this man's eyes and body language and I could not help but start to feel his emotions.

"We used to golf five days a week," Herb said. "He took the game very seriously, and we all had to play like that. Sure, we were able to kibitz [joke], but when it came to the play, Bernie made sure it was done right."

Still listening, Herb then said, "Every Wednesday, we use to play cards at Bernie's. His wife to have a huge spread and let us play."

As I attempted to say something, Herb pointed to me and gently said, "Wait, there's more."

So as a *mensch* (gentleman) among my elders, I stood in silence.

You could tell that others close to us in the pool could not help but start to listen to this man's story. "I remember that there was an accident involving Bernie's son. A terrible accident, I recall." I begin to think to myself, *Oh no*! This guy is talking about me. Still not speaking, my entire being was glued to every word Herb said. "I remember that Bernie and his wife, Joyce, had to go to his son. A terrible accident." As I felt myself begin to react to his every word, I knew my eyes were beginning to fill with tears.

Doing my best to hold them back for fear he would stop his story, Herb went on to say, "I know that Bernie was gone for weeks and weeks. When he came back here, he wasn't the same Bernie anymore." With an emotional sound in Herb's voice now, he went on to say, "I can't remember because it's been so long ago, but I think his son died from an accident involving a boat on some island."

I could no longer hold back my tears. Traci and a few of the ladies were all teary-eyed, even Bruce. As Herb started to shake his head as if it was an emotional moment, Herb once again said, "My best friend was never the same after that. He was sad but would not let others know his emotions. But me, we were best friends."

As I was bursting at the seams, I called out, "Herb! It's me! I'm the son you're talking about! Herb, look! I'm not dead! The look on his face was a stunned man that just received wonderful news. He expressed it when he grabbed my arm and shook my hand with such strength. "I'm so glad to see you, Steve. I haven't spoken about Bernie in years. There's hardly anyone left here."

Herb Scheiner and Steve Wallach

I looked at him and said, "But, Herb, you're still here, and that alone is truly wonderful. Herb and his wonderful and very funny wife, Helen, have been married for over seventy-seven years. To date, it is always a pleasure to see them together. They still come down to the pool with their aide and Herb, carrying his radio in hand to softly listen to his classical music.

As we both stood there for a few minutes, I could not help but feel now at peace. It is hard to explain, but it is as if I went full circle to this point in my life. I felt complete if that makes any sense. As I made my way out of the pool, Traci already knew what I wanted to do. Our towels and drinks were bagged, and we said our goodbyes to everyone, especially the man who made me now feel complete, Herb Scheiner.

I understand the circumstances a little better now. Things do happen for a reason. Whether good or bad, we are each given a door to open and walk through. The decision is always left up to us, isn't it? I have led a very exciting life, and there were many incidents that people will either believe or not. The best part of each is that we are all individuals, and decisions and thoughts are left up to us to believe what we want to. Me, I felt the desire to share most of my life's memories. True there are portions that were left out because of one thing. Promise. In today's time, there are so many people that use the promise as a free passage. When I make a promise to someone, I will never break that promise, even after they're gone.

I feel better inside. My emotional track, my medical roller coaster, and my peace of mind have now enabled me to enjoy my life. One thing I did learn is that prayer does play a large part. Please know that I do not want to preach, but it is important for me to share with you what I learned during my serious medical times.

I feel gifted when I am able to see, hear, and speak with the deceased. Not just anyone but the people who have been the closest to me throughout my life. I have learned over time that these encounters happen only at the most severe and emotional times in my life. I always knew that my Nanny (mother's side) was the most powerful and loved woman I ever knew. When she left this world, her power was given to my mother, her adopted daughter. You see, it is not always blood that binds us together. The love between my mother and my Nanny was instilled in me for many years after she was gone. My mother kept her alive through stories and facts. Maybe that is why she was my initial contact during every encounter. I believe it was she who brought forth my daughter Rachel to me, my father, my mother and, most importantly, herself. I am as sane as any sane individual, maybe with the exception of my wit and personality. What I have seen and what I have been part of, I will always believe that I am left here for a purpose. What that purpose is, I have no idea. A few thoughts but no solid leads. You know it is said that we all are here on this earth for a purpose. All I know is that I am very blessed and thankful that I can still walk this earth and enjoy the fruits of what I worked so very hard for.

I have been blessed to have a wonderful lady by my side. Traci keeps me leveled. It is funny when I see her starting to wave those arms toward me, saying with a smile and soft laughter, "Hey, babe, it's ok. Now bring it back down."

Then like magic, the calm sets in. So my days are spent enjoying the pleasures of retirement. No schedules, no meetings, no bullshit; just easy days filled with daily chores around the house and basically doing as little as possible. As distant walks have been cut to shorter walks due to my legs having other ideas, Louie, Layla, and I get into our favorite Grand Cherokee, and off we go. Driving with the windows open, the breeze against our faces is priceless. Neighborhood drives are calm and enjoyable as you can easily see new home construction, neighbors walking their dogs, and neighbors visiting neighbors. Most of this area is very neighborhood-protected. My friends Mike, Wayne, and I get together every month for lunch, beer, and whatever comes up. My phone would ring, and I heard Mike on the other end say, "Hey it's that time!" That is all I have to hear. "Name the date, place, and time," I would shout back. "I'll be there!"

We are fortunate enough to be able to travel to Florida and spend quality time at my family condo, which I bought my brothers half. With a slight chuckle, I could not have helped but notice that here, too, he tried to make a profit off me. Quite often. It still feels as though my parents are there. They are. There is a calmness that comes over you once you step in and close the door behind you. I can faintly hear my mother say, "Bernie…Stevie's here."

Prayer is good through any religion. As far as I am concerned, there is but one G-d. Now you may immediately question why I would not spell G-d's name out? I am of Jewish descent, and we have been taught through scriptures, Hebrew school, and our parents that one never writes G-d's name completely out on anything that would eventually be trashed, thrown away, and destroyed. That would be the biggest insult; therefore, out of love and respect, we honor G-d by following these rules. Does every Jew follow this? I would say no. But I do not care about the thoughts of others on this subject. Me, I can close my eyes every night knowing that, as G-d is my witness, I have this day shown nothing but respect to G-d Almighty and myself.

I would be lying if I said I do not feel a great sense of proudness when I run into one of my past ETA Motorcycle Cruise guests in so many places worldwide, to hear them say how they loved their bike cruise, always pointing out the ship they were on and the islands we visited. "Oh my *gosh*! It's Steve from ETA!" they would call out. It always made me feel good inside. As I said, so many of my clients became friends. We have stayed in touch throughout the years. Many times, my phone would ring, and I could hear those infamous words of ETA: "If you're on time, you're late!"

I will keep my memories as long as I am able to. As we all have the ability to go back in our own time, keep my words close to you. For they have done such greatness for myself and others. Good night.

"Positive thoughts bring positive reactions" (Steve Wallach 2010).

Caribbean sunset

Bernard Wallach, Joyce Wallach, Steve Wallach

THIS LIFE OF MINE

Bernard Wallach

Double rainbow, St Thomas, STVI

STEVEN M. WALLACH

Traci and Steve Wallach

About the Author

Steve Wallach has always been known as a man of his word. Steve has taken many years of thought, advice, and determination to make him who he is today. Even through the numerous health issues, and the loss of his daughter, it gave Steve the reason to fight and maintain a position in life to see things through. Steve is a man of compassion, which is noticeable to others. Having to face serious medical challenges, Steve has fought the fight, and yes, he absolutely believes that his prayers got me through the turmoil of facing death not once but three times.

Steve built a most respected name over the many years he spent in entertainment, travel, and producing many well-known events throughout the world. His ability to craft what he saw in his mind came from his passion for always doing the best. The stories told by Steve through his own words will enlighten the readers to appreciate and understand who Steve Wallach is. During his lifetime thus far, Steve has met and spoken with the deceased for over forty years. Not just once but many times throughout his life. These have been documented throughout this manuscript, and it is important to understand what gave him this sense of the afterlife.

Steve opened up his entire life. His family, his failures, and his achievements have become an open book. "I cannot expect anyone to say they know me until they read this manuscript. I want everyone to know that you can achieve whatever you put your mind and heart to. This book took me over two years to write, and I am thankful that I can now enlighten others to see what I have seen and accomplished. Thank you."